Travels with My Amp

Travels with My Amp

Greg Godovitz

Abbeyfield Publishers
Toronto, Canada

Copyright (c) 2001 Greg Godovitz. All rights reserved.

The use of any part of this publication reproduced, transmitted in any form or by any means electronic, mechanical, photocopying, recording, or otherwise or stored in a retrieval system, without the prior written consent of the publisher, or, in case of photocopying or other reprographic copying, a license from the Canadian Copyright Licensing Agency – is an infringement of the copyright law.

All lyrics reprinted with kind permission of Loose Lizard Music/Pondwater Music except where otherwise noted.

Published in 2001 for Bullseye Records of Canada by Abbeyfield Publishers,
a division of The Abbeyfield Companies Ltd.,
33 Springbank Avenue, Toronto, Ontario, Canada   M1N 1G2

Ordering information:
Distributed in Canada by Hushion House Distributors Ltd.
36 Northline Road, Toronto, Ontario, Canada   M4B 3E2
Phone (416) 285-6100 Fax (416) 285-1777

Canadian Cataloguing in Publication Data
Godovitz, Gregory G., 1951 -
    Travels with my amp : sex, drugs and rock and roll

ISBN 1-894584-06-6

1. Godovitz, Greg. 2. Goddo (Musical group). 3. Rock musicians – Canada – Biography. I. Title.

ML420.G596A3 2001   782.42166'092   C00-933017-8

First Printing October 2000
Second Printing February 2001

Editing by Greg Godovitz and Sharon Vernon
Cover and book design by Karen Petherick
Front cover photo: The Godovitz archives
Back cover design: Jaimie Vernon
Printing by TTP Tradeworx Ltd.

For more information contact:
Bullseye Records Of Canada at: http://www.bullseyecanada.com or email:
president@bullseyecanada.com so that future editions of this book can be corrected.

In memory of my dear friends
Christine Webb and Brian Pilling.

The Program

Foreword by Ronnie Hawkins vii
Forward by Mike Myers ix
A Few Words Before The Trip Begins xi
From The "Arthur" xiv
Tuning Up xvii
Overture xviii
Set 1 – The Pretty Ones 1
Set 2 – The Backdoor Blues Band 25
Set 3 – The Pyggs 35
Set 4 – The Mushroom Castle 45
Set 5 – Sherman and Peabody 55
Set 6 – Fludd 75

Intermission 165

Set 7 – Goddo 1975 166
              1976 193
              1977 208
              1978 224
              1979 253
              1980 269
              1981 292
              1982 316
              1983 362
Encore 370
Acknowledgments 371
Discography 377

RONNIE HAWKINS PROMOTIONS

HELLO SIR GREGORY !!

About that foreword to your book, I'm not much of a reader myself, but if you really want me to write it, I'll say something nice that'll make it look like I read it. Let me know what you think.

'Bout time you're done with all that writin', now we can get back to ROCKIN'!

The Workin' Girls' Favorite,
The Housewives' Companion,
The First and Last of the Teenage Idols,
The Magnificent Silver-Tongued Orator,

Ronnie Hawkins

Two Mental Giants! Photo: Bob Reid

MIKE MYERS

October 26, 1999

Greg Godovitz
███████████
Toronto M1B 4T1
Canada

Greg,

Thank you so much for thinking of me to write the forward to your memoirs, "Travel With My Amp." Sadly though, I'm currently writing forwards to three other books. To write another forward might be diminishing my value as a forwarder. And who, I ask, wants to be labeled a forward whore?

So it is with deep regret that I must kindly pass on your offer. Nevertheless, please know how proud I am that you're Canadian, keep up the good work and best of luck with "Daytrippers."

Yours,

[signature]

A few words before the trip begins...

Greg Godovitz. The name itself conjures up a series of unforgettable images for me:

Holding court in the upstairs dressing room of The Rondun, a diseased rock bar in a rundown hotel in a seedy part of Toronto's Parkdale. A full floor above a room packed with rabid Goddo fans, half of who want to be him, half of whom (for some still unexplainable reason), want to sleep with him.

Working 15,000 screaming fans into a beer-fueled Frenzy at the now sadly missed Forum at Ontario Place. His manager and a shit-for-brains record executive from the USA failing to notice his effect on the record buying public for the umpteenth time and waddling, addled by their own self importance, off to dinner, oblivious to one of the best rock shows I have seen in 40 years of rock shows.

A vision of loveliness in plaid and make up, careening around the hallways of CFCF Television in Montreal, for an appearance on Like Young, a Dick Clarkian teen show, with the oddly named and odder spelt, Fludd.

Greg Godovitz. Ask anybody in the Canadian Music Industry, (stop laughing, there really is one), and they will unfurl a Greg story or nine. They come in two categories. The, "...and then, he actually..." "...couldn't fucking believe..." "...never laughed so hard in my..." stories, and "The, ...stupid son of a..." "...shot himself in the foot again..." "...own worst enemy..." "...never work in this town again..." stories.

Greg, like Bill Clinton, would bounce back from every bad career move, every stupid mistake, and every little-boy temper tantrum he ever threw. Why?

Because the boy is talented.

Greg is an original. Not just a Canadian Original, but a full-blown Rock And Roll Original of the first water. He is a consummate performer, sweating away enough weight at any given Goddo gig, to form an entire Gary Coleman. He is a fiercely loyal man, who would rather hurt himself in the process of being loyal before he'll abandon an idea, a project, or a friend.

He is a mind numbingly stubborn purist, constantly trying to re-invent his beloved music, and show the world that they can still be entertained, still blown away, by the power of a handful of well chosen chords, and a lyric that reflects their lives...or their dreams.

He is also, as you will discover when you finish this sordid tome you're drooling on, one hell of an entertaining writer.

It took G a long time to write this damn thing. I know this because the little weasel would call me at 3 in the morning, half in the bag, and demand to read me his latest scrawl, only to break me up so badly, my Mrs., pissed off at being woken up, thought I was doing drugs or having a stroke.

Not only did the calls continue for well over a year, it has taken no small amount of time for Greg to find a publisher, and, dear reader, it has probably taken a few ticks of the clock to reach you.

The beauty of this book, fortunately, is that it is timeless. It will be as funny and as spot on in a hundred years as it is now.

One of the reasons it took a while to reach you, is the fact that, outside a small group of us Canucks, a sprinkling of Aussies, a spoonful of Brits, and a smattering of Krauts, not a whole lot of people know who the fuck Greg is.

Doesn't matter.

Doesn't matter one, tiny, bleeding, bit.

If you have ever been in a band. If you have ever been a fan of rock. If you have ever had the dream...this book will touch you as surely as if you yourself had lived it.

You might not know who Greg Godovitz is right now, but a few hundred pages to the right, you will not only know him, you'll be waiting for him to write the sequel, and tracking down every recording the little brat ever made.

This book isn't just about Greg. It is about all of us that cherish The Rock And Roll Circus. It is about a young boy that grew up to be a young boy. It is the story of the uncontrollable passion of youth, written by a man that never out-grew it.

Bob and Greg backstage 1979

You, my rabid little friends, are not only in for a great read, you are about to meet one of the REAL deals. Greg Godovitz is just sitting down to hold court with a new circle of friends. You might be a little slow to warm to this cocksure, hell, arrogant little hiccup, but believe me, your going to be telling these stories and waking up your Mrs. or Mr. with laughter, for a long time to come.

Bob Segarini
Toronto, Ontario, Canada

1964...

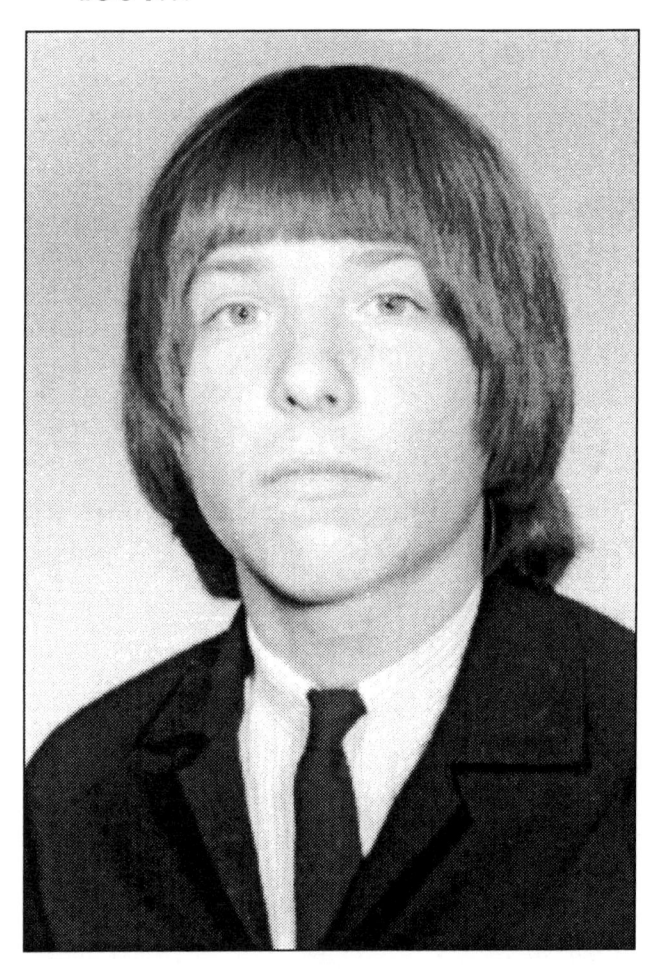

The "Arthur"

From the "Arthur"...

I was sitting at my computer banging out another sordid tale of drug abuse, sex addicted debauchery, and general lunacy on the road, when it suddenly occurred to me that there may be a lot of people who read this that won't get the joke.

At the ripe old age of forty eight, and with most, but not all of my personal demons now in check, I can sit back and marvel that I lived this amazingly strange lifestyle that should've seen me dead countless times, but somehow managed to survive where many friends did not.

My story is the story of every dreamer who ever picked up a guitar, smashed a cymbal, or impressed his buddies with his microphone twirling technique.

The language is sometimes strong because that's how musicians speak, the never ending parade of willing sexual partners there not as gloating statistics, but because they were there. The booze and drugs fuelled the childish pranks, numbing the pain, and helped relieve the often-accompanying boredom of too many hours with nothing to do.

Someone said to me after reading an early draft of this book, "Would you let your mother and family read this?" to which I replied that although there are things written about here that I'm not overly proud of, there are more things written about here that I am extremely proud of.

The life was lived, you can't go back, and it makes no sense to lament the mistakes. Creating music and performing in front of who knows how many hundreds of thousands of people over the years has been the greatest source of comfort for me when the "what if's?" and "any regrets?" rear their ugly heads.

Sitting in an old trailer with Ronnie Hawkins one day, bottle of rum and handgun on the table between us, we talked about just this thing.

"You know son," he began, "I spent ninety percent of what I made on whiskey, women, cars, and dope...and I guess I just wasted the other ten percent."

The cup is half full, the other half was delicious.

Guido Poppe and The Tennants ...er Torquays?
Guido Poppe, second from left and Brian Schut, third from left.
Photo: Brian Schut

Tuning Up

The gymnasium at Regent Heights Public School was packed to the rafters with the graduating class of 1964. Because of my extremely poor eyesight I was pressed up to the very lip of the stage watching Guido Poppe and The Tennants run through their repertoire of rhythm and blues standards. Guido was a dead ringer for a youngish Woody Allen and the other Tennants were not exactly matinee idols themselves, with the possible exception of drummer Brian Schut.

Mean, moody, and magnificent was how ex-Beatle drummer Pete Best has been described and Brian had those same qualities. At least that's what I gathered from the female types around me who, oblivious to my own magnificence, were swooning over him.

I couldn't really see any of them anyway as I didn't even own a pair of glasses at the time, but he couldn't have been more than sixteen or seventeen and in his shiny blue stage suit he looked more like a grownup to a thirteen year old kid anyway.

In my collarless black Beatles jacket and matching pants, skinny tie on white button down shirt and shiny new Cuban heeled Beatle Boots I was the real star of this night's show, except nobody else was aware of it.

After their set I made my way backstage, the scene of my own triumph in public speaking the year before, and sought out Brian Schut where I complimented him on the band and his playing and told him that I would like to drum in my own group someday.

"Do you play?" he asked.

"Uh, not really just yet," I nervously replied.

"You wanna have a bash?" he offered.

"SURE!!" and I jumped behind the kit and began bashing away.

So caught up in the moment was I that I didn't even notice the stage curtains parting. The packed room exploded in applause of surprise and recognition at my first public efforts as a musician. Most people would have skulked off in total embarrassment but the audience's response only fuelled my performance. I finished my flail to a thunderous ovation and with a goofy grin handed the sticks back to the bemused drummer.

"Not bad at all," he said and I went off to join my friends at the local restaurant for chips and a coke.

I was hooked.

Overture

Danny Cooper had a wagon. It was more than just a wagon however; it was the solution to a problem. How do I get my very heavy amp to practice? The transportation of one of the few working bass amplifiers in my neighbourhood, perhaps the only bass amp in the entire suburb of Scarborough, maybe the whole city of Toronto for all I knew, was a serious problem!

Fact! It was the only amplifier The Wanderers had. The Wanderers were my first group...that is... after we learned how to play. This is why we had to rehearse and this is why I had to borrow the wagon from Danny.

With the 30-watt Magnatone amp and 3/4 scale Supro Bass Guitar now firmly strapped to this rather juvenile conveyance I stood back to admire my efforts and how professional it looked. I was thinking this very thought as I made my way north on Westbourne Avenue, past my buddy Phil Joyce's house, up past the Old School where I was colouring with broken crayons just a few years earlier and finally across the field to lead Wanderer and keyboard player Brian Fraser's house.

Typically, the old Joanna, marginally tuneless but with all 88's intact resided in the Fraser's living room, and seeing as no one was home, this would be our rehearsal pad.

Jim Stockley was the stickman with Donny Janke on guitar. Donny "played" a homemade copy of a Fender Telecaster if memory serves, but with a neck as thick as the working end of a baseball bat. No problem, Donny had big hands, much like his younger brother Jimmy, who used to beat me up after school.

Things had changed, the sixties now had a direction, I had re-invented myself, and Jimmy had to search out other victims while his older brother and I became pop stars...

It was far too early to be up. On a normal day I would probably be just falling into bed, or at least near it.

As the stretch limo pulled down the ramp at the CNE Exhibition Stadium someone pointed out, "Hey, The Argos!!"

The mighty Toronto Argonauts Football Team looked like a gladiatorial honour guard as the limo made its way down into the bowels of the stadium en route to our dressing room. A loud rap on the tinted window and a heavy sounding voice screaming, "Is Greg Godovitz in there?" caught my attention and rolling down the window I looked through very tinted sunglasses at a not so familiar face.

"Paul Bennett man, we went to Porter together!"

This was sort of a fallacy as Paul was a bit younger than me, and had we indeed gone to W.A. Porter Collegiate at the same time he probably wouldn't have wanted to know me anyway. But here we were, him a Toronto Argo, good as it gets, and me a Goddo, about to climb on the stage in front of 50,000 maniacs just getting up and waiting for Moxy, The Ramones, Johnny Winter, Nazareth, Aerosmith and THE NUGE!!!, Ted Nugent, Mr. Wango Tango Hisself!!!

So Paul and I exchange phone numbers, celebrities do that sort of thing, and off we go in search of our individual destinies...

I absolutely loved The Beatles! I still do. Their name will probably come up a lot in this story. I wanted to be in a group to play songs that THEY wrote and THEY performed. This made me really want to learn my instrument, practice vocal harmonizing with my band mates, and to always keep my Beatle hair cut shiny and helmet-like.

Right now, however, The Wanderers had to run through 'Little Honda' by The Hondells. I sort of liked surf music as a kid but now that I was thirteen I didn't really care about "goin" down to the Honda shop anymore. I wanted to hold somebody's hand, to twist and shout, or to please please me as I hadn't any experience with girls just yet.

I could sing falsetto harmonies almost by instinct, having learned how by accompanying the hits of the day whenever the radio was on in my Dad's ancient Studebaker.

Brian Wilson, with his soulful soprano, was my favourite Beach Boy, and Paul McCartney, with his glorious vocal range, was my fave Beatle, so my job in The Wanderers was trying to find those tricky 5th harmonies.

I could sing, but I wasn't very good at playing bass...

The limo deposited us at our dressing room, a cold grey metallic concrete bunker that smelled of defeat and other bodily functions...er...sweat. Our "Big Time" dressing room consisted of bare cement walls, a couple of rough wooden benches, and a garbage can of Heineken beer, or "Goddo pop" as the fans called it. As an added plus there was also a deli tray of cold cuts and cheeses that nobody in their right mind would eat at this time of day. Drummer Doug Inglis was busy with a triple salami on rye as I settled into an interview with Mr. Local FM-DJ Guy about the upcoming performance.

"I'm here with Greg Godovitz of Goddo and how are you guys feeling about today?"

What nobody had told me was that these interviews were being broadcast live and very loudly through the gigantic concert PA to the assembled hordes in the stadium just a short limo ride away.

Drawing on years of eloquent public speaking I snarled, "We're going to kill that fucking audience when we get out there!!"

Through the walls of the fortress I heard a roar unlike any other I'd ever heard before. Our road manager shot through the door and said, "You guys are on in two minutes!"

The 30 watt Magnatone amp was useful. Danny Cooper's wagon had been useful. My helmet-like hairdo was useful. My bass playing however, was useless. I was the Stuart Sutcliffe of Scarborough.

Truth be told, I was only in the Wanderers because of the amp. Bass players were in great demand but short supply in 1964. What I did have however was the right equipment and the right haircut, so we plugged the homemade Telecaster and two mics for Fraser and his piano into the Magnatone.

My bass guitar, its cord plugged pathetically into the jack input, was sadly denied access to the amp...

There are so many things right about what I'm seeing here. There's Mr. T. in his limo, no real reason for him being here but there he is, all gold chains, wraparound shades and holding court from the comfort of the back seat.

The original cast of Beatlemania stopping by backstage as I had invited them down to the show after their amazing hospitality to me at their O'Keefe Centre show.

Gino's old lady, dubbed Gypsy Eyes in honour of Jimi, is adjusting leather thongs on her tan suede outfit, her monstrous magnets literally bursting in their cowhide restraints, aching to be free in an orgasmic explosion of firm nubile flesh. Gino, no stranger to a mirror himself, is lightly flexing his pecs and admiring the results, a pint-sized Hercules in brown leather.

Kids are leaning over the end zone sections to scream profanity-laden words of encouragement. The sight of 50,000 drunks in the sweltering sun, before noon, and from the amazing vantage point of on stage is something everyone should experience at least once in their lives.

Our old pals Moxy, (big in Texas!) open the Canadian World Music Festival and do well but I was too busy backstage to see them perform. We plow through our set on pure adrenaline. 'So Walk On', 'Tough Times', 'Cock On', and 'Oh Carole' scream by at twice their normal tempo. The crowd is digging us, and we in turn are digging them, but what really bothers me is that all I can see, through all this mutual admiration, about ten rows deep there is one guy giving me the finger! The Finger! Fuck You Greg Godovitz Up There In Your Purple Iridescent Suit Of Lights!

This guy really hated me! I wanted to dive into the masses and throttle him! I could not take my eyes off that huuuuuge billboard of a finger. I played exclusively to this guy. He knew that I was playing exclusively to him and really started to pump that finger in my direction. All of a sudden my bass amp quits...

My first gig was at Cedarbrae Community Centre and it was arranged by some mid forties guy who used to take an interest in my interests but whose name escapes me and for that I'm sorry. He was just a nice guy and not the hidden agenda type that you expected you sicko. Anyway, he got us the gig and The Wanderers were now set up on a six-inch riser at one end of the hall.

My Beatles haircut, well polished, was flying about in very stylish sixties fashion. I was resplendent in black jeans; black turtleneck and I had The Boots!

Even though I didn't have a microphone of my own, I sang note perfect harmonies almost loud enough to be heard above the swinging beat music that was The Wanderers. My bass, which was still not plugged in, was an extension of my body, of my very soul if you will indulge me. I could not play a lick, but I was doing it in front of an actual audience.

'Little Honda' went down great. 'Bits and Pieces' smoked, what with Fraser's white pants and black jacket giving him that DC5 mod thing. Jim Stockley beat his drums and smashed his cymbals in a ritual that would continue for the next thirty-five years and eventually pound my left eardrum into a serious case of tinnitus. Donny's faux Tele, marginally in tune, squealed as the ham-fisted guitarist ventured too close to the over burdened amp.

As we slammed into 'Twist and Shout', our last song, and I sang the McCartney parts in answer to the lead vocal I noticed my older gig-arranging friend listening at the side of our makeshift stage. It took me quite by surprise then to see him suddenly lurch across the stage, grab the mic and stand from our leader in mid yelp and place it directly in front of me. I didn't miss a beat.

"YOU KNOW YOU TWISTA LITTLE GIRL!" I screamed in full

throated John Lennon style. Nobody was singing the backgrounds. The Wanderers were in shock. I was in heaven. "YOU KNOW YOU LOOK SO FINE!!!!"

The set ended to a smattering of applause, more relief that it was over as opposed to genuine appreciation and the group fumbled offstage.

After the show a young guy approached me and told me he thought my playing was awesome. I didn't know what to do. I couldn't play and this smartass probably knew that I couldn't play. I blushed out a "Thanks man," and beat it backstage.

"Great show eh?" I announced breathlessly in the dressing room but something was wrong.

Stony silence.

"What's the idea man? I'm the singer in The Wanderers!" said Fraser.

Now I was totally confused and attempted to explain that I had nothing to do with the pilfered mic incident. I couldn't quite find the right words to express myself so I just stood there while I was told that as I couldn't really play anyway my services in The Wanderers were no longer required. I packed up my bass and the 30-watt Magnatone amp and as my older friend drove me back home he told me that I was the only one on that stage with any talent...

I don't know if you've ever played on a stadium-sized stage with a monitor system designed to destroy small cities but no sooner had my custom-made $10,000.00 bass rig died than Uncle Mike, the bands monitor mixer had punched in a sound through the massive side wash that was not unlike GOD giving you the answer. The answer it turns out is to play bass guitar at excessive volume for a field full of loonies and one guy flipping you the bird!

"FEEL IT, I KNOW IT, THE TIME IS RIGHT! FEEL IT, I KNOW IT, THE TIME IS RIGHT!" I screamed and then Rock Star Move #746, "LET ME HEAR YOUUUUU!!!!!"

The band cuts out but only about 10,000 people join in.

"I CAN'T FUCKING HEAR YOUUUUU!!!!!"

Eleven thousand give or take a few.

The guy with the finger now has both arms pumping furiously!

"THAT STINKS!" I scream now waving my finger at the crowd like a grade school teacher admonishing his class. "THAT FUCKING STINKS!" and there is a sudden stirring in the crowd but not what I want at all.

I want them ALL to do it.

TRAVELS WITH MY AMP

All right, I'm thinking, if they don't want to join in on the fun but prefer to act like they're sleeping then that's exactly what I will do. Gino and Doug don't miss a lick as I lay down on the stage and pretend to catch forty winks. I lay motionless on my back for what seemed like an eternity but the next sound that I hear is the roar of the beast. That moment when performer and audience connect. I sit up. I rise to my knees. I smile. This audience is mine!

"THERE'S FIFTY THOUSAND FUCKING PEOPLE OUT THERE AND IF YOU ALL DO IT THEY'LL HEAR YOU IN ETOBICOKE!" and laugh as I rant.

In leafy Etobicoke the sound of suburban lawnmowers is momentarily interrupted.

"FEEL IT! I KNOW IT! THE TIME IS RIGHT!" the mob shouts as one.

As we leave the stage the roar intensifies, it crescendos into a sound unlike anything I have heard before. Bathed in sweat I stumble offstage with Gino and Doug, past promoter Michael Cohl.

"Thanks for the opportunity man," I say as we make our way down the ramp.
The roar grows louder with every step.
Has some roadie brought out Johnny Winters trademark Firebird guitar?
Has some chick leaped onstage to pull out her massive tits?
I glance back and see Cohl nodding in my direction and waving us back.
Fifty thousand people are calling for an encore.

Canadian World Music Festival, CNE Stadium, Toronto. 50,000 people behold the spectacle that is GODDO. Photo: Pat Harbron

— *set one* —

The Pretty Ones

"Hey Beatles! sing 'im a little tune."

It was too hot a summer day for grave digging. These two sweat-soaked ruffians were filling in the hole as Brian Pilling and I made our way up Birchmount Avenue en route to rehearsal. 1964 was a great year to be 13 years old. We didn't know how old the individual in the freshly dug hole was but for some reason we felt that we owed this person a little musical tribute.

Brian, tab collar under corduroy jacket buttoned right up despite the heat was as usual quick to size up the situation. His red Harmony Rocket guitar, slung casually across his back, was brought into playing position with the most modest of effort. I could see him eyeing the hole from beneath his brown fringe.

"Ferry 'Cross the Mersey?"

I nodded affirmative.

My bass, still unplugged but in the last couple of months a little more user friendly gave off the faintest essence of bottom as we sang, "Life goes on day after day, hearts torn in every way..."

The gravediggers, who had initially hailed us in a piss take, were genuinely impressed and applauded our efforts when we'd finished.

To this day I have no idea what the party in the hole thought.

High school presented an unusual challenge. I wasn't really ready to be in high school, as I was only thirteen, having skipped grade 5 in public school and I was already carrying some serious emotional baggage around.

At Regent Heights Public School friends and enemies alike had affectionately dubbed me "Pimplehead." Girls I dreamed about called me this.

When tickets for The Beatles September 7 show at Maple Leaf Gardens went on sale I, Pimplehead, was deemed responsible enough to act as ticket emissary for the entire school. It was safe enough in those days to sleep out of doors and my parents, who I believe regarded me as a rather solid thinking individual did not object to me camping out in front of the venerable hockey shrine in order to fulfil my appointed task.

I can't remember where the huge wad of bills was stored but for the sake of romance let's say that it was stored along with other precious jewels in the front of my briefs.

It was cold out there but everyone had their sleeping blankets for warmth and people shared their hot chocolate as well as their enthusiasm for the adventure at hand. Aside from the constant cacophony of a dozen portable AM radios blasting Beatles hits on CHUM, the only real excitement was supplied by a native Indian lad with a full healthy head of extremely long black hair who managed to set the young girls bonkers merely by walking down the south side of College Street. He did this every ten minutes it seemed. A sound not unlike a jet engine would break the silence as a dozen or more teenage banshees raced off in pursuit of this phantom Ringo. I'm sure that not one of them had the faintest idea what to do with him if they had caught him but it was great to just sit there and wish your hair would grow out faster.

As dawn broke on the icy pavement I had the most awful feeling that I was being trampled by a herd of wild beasts. In actual fact, thousands of smarter Beatles fans, who had enjoyed the previous evening in the comfort of their suburban homes were now jostling for position and using the campers as feet warmers. The police, out in full force to ensure safety for one and all were in no ways prepared for a gaggle of highly emotional fans who had endured a night on the streets and not about to be butted out of their rightful place in line. I believe that our weathered little group became the first wristband policy ticket buyers. We were escorted to the other side of the main doors to snooze in peace until the priceless ducats went on sale!

At ten a.m. we were none the worse for wear and standing at the ticket counter. The big moment had arrived at last. I was only a few kids back from the head of the line. Those other suckers were in a line that snaked along College Street west and north up Yonge Street to Richmond Hill for all I knew. I could see me and all my little school chums sitting in the first couple of rows before our heroes.

I, Pimplehead, would now be a hero.

"How many kid?" asked the under whelmed ticket guy.

"One hundred and sixty two tickets sir!" I blurbled out.

"Sorry kid, two to a customer," he droned.

"B..b..b..But I've been sent by my school to get tickets for everyone!!!"

"Sorry kid, you'll hafta get back in line," he said pointing to the doors.

With that I paid him for my two tickets, grabbed up my meagre belongings and went out the front door.

The scene outside was pure bedlam! Thousands of mostly teenage girls crying, pushing, and screaming, and this just to get near that old ticket guy.

After a little quick math I realized that there was no way that I would line up again eighty times and at least I had a great pair of tickets for all that I'd endured.

Now let's see here, two Gold front row seats right in the middle?

NOOOOOO!!!!! Blues!

I had slept on cement all night for this! I raced back in but couldn't get near the counter in the ensuing melee. In desperation I went up to one of the ancient guards and showed him my tickets.

"Sixth row kid," he croaked

"SIXTH ROW!! WOW!" I yelped.

"Behind the stage."

There were little tears welling up in my eyes all the way home.

The Beatles were great.

I didn't really notice Brian Pilling, even though we shared homeroom, until Twerp Day.

Twerp Day was a hazing ritual for first year high school students where you would dress up in some Halloweenish costume and then be humiliated by any other grade-ten-and-up students who felt the sadistic urge to vent their spleen in your direction. Brian, whose hair had been slicked back up to this point in time, had washed the grease out and combed it over his forehead into a very smart do indeed. With the addition of pencilled-on sidies he was the very approximation of a fourteen-year-old John Lennon.

"You dig The Beatles?" I asked the obvious.

"Yeah, they're Fab," Brian replied with a noticeable trace of English accent and I liked him immediately.

At lunch, instead of being tortured by the so-called adults of the school, we played this game where we would run as fast as we could, eluding hordes of imaginary screaming fans bent on tearing us to pieces. Exhausted, we collapsed in a pile on the playing field.

"My brother Ed's a drummer and he's coming back from England soon. You want to join our group?" Brian breathlessly inquired.

"I play bass and I can sing!" was my excited response, and in fact I was getting quite good at both.

A bond was cemented right there that would carry us through many years of musical adventures.

Ed Pilling

The three teenage girls were making a big fuss over Ed, Brian and myself at Shoppers World Mall one evening in the fall of 1964. Actually they were making a big fuss over Ed. In his double-breasted pea jacket, complete with epaulets and matching brass buttons, he was a vision of pop finery next to Brian and I who merely looked like we were just tagging along.

"Hey, check out the fairies." Three leather-jacketed and much older greaseballs were taking umbrage at our sense of style and were probably just a little pissed that these girls, rightfully theirs you must understand, were paying us, and in particular Ed so much attention.

I was petrified. Looking away from the ladies Ed looked directly into the eyes of his aggressor and said, "What did you say, hardknock?" I truly believe that at that precise moment the greaseball knew that he had made a very bad error in judgement.

I was still petrified.

Amongst duellists throughout history there is a natural order in which these events are played out, a certain etiquette involving manly pursuits and matters of honour. The scene was set. Trying his best to compose himself, in light of the fact that this soft spoken guy with a girl's hairdo had dared to even answer back, let alone with an obscure colloquialism far removed from anything he had ever heard before, the greaseball offered up a far-from-heartfelt, "Maybe we should step outside."

"I don't go in for formalities," were the last words the greaseball heard as Ed's massive ham-like fist smashed into the guy's face. The girls shrieked and backed off, Brian taking his place alongside his brother, while the two shocked friends of the greaseball, who was now blissfully asleep on the floor, rushed to lift their pal off of the concrete. As they lifted him up, one on either side, his eyes momentarily flashed on and off, which of course was the cue for Ed to put the heel of his Beatle boot into the middle of the guy's nose. The sound of his head hitting the floor was one which I'd never heard before nor wish to ever hear again.

Sitting outside on a small retaining wall Ed was busy studying his slightly damaged knuckles with the three girls now cooing and fawning over him. The greaseballs had dragged their unconscious pal off somewhere to heal, and a change of venue had seemed like a good idea, what with the prospects of someone calling the cops who wouldn't like us any more than the thugs had.

Glancing to my right I was somewhat alarmed to see about thirty guys spill out of the local pool hall and turn in our direction. "Oh Ed, I think we should be leaving now," I said and I really meant it.

"I'm not going anywhere!" said Ed.

The mob was now in a semi circle, facing us and not very pleased. The guy who Ed had recently pummelled came towards him and I was stunned to see him extend his hand in friendship and say, "You're okay man."

A reprieve!

I wouldn't be needing a change of underwear after all.

And then this very dark, throaty and thoroughly ominous voice, way in the back of the crowd said, "You may be okay with him, but you ain't okay with me."

Now let's see here, my Mom puts my fresh undies in the second drawer, correct?

The mob parted, not unlike Moses at the Red Sea, but greasier, and this absolute monster strode to the front.

Ron Cameron!

This guy, no, this man, was feared by everyone in the east end and without further ado he jumped on Ed who unfortunately had his hands tucked into the pockets of his jacket. I watched in horror as Ron twisted his knuckle into Ed's eye socket.

Brian, who was standing on the wall beside me, now dove directly onto Cameron's back and wrapped his arm around his throat, freeing Ed's hands. Another greaser started pounding Brian as Ed and Ron battled on the ground. I realized that although I was about to get killed I jumped off the wall but was instantly caught by the scruff of the neck by another gang member who looked at me with true pity and said, "Look kid, your friends are being done and you're too small to hit so you just stand here and learn."

I could have kissed him.

Many punches and curses later it was over and the greaseballs went off to celebrate leaving Brian and Ed in rumpled disarray on the ground. Brian was okay but Ed's right eye was full of blood and would stay like that for weeks to come. Ed had known all along that he was going to get his but he would not leave. Ladies and gentlemen, meet Ed Pilling.

I was very nervous when I first met Brian's big brother Ed. First off, he was six feet plus with a perfect blond Brian Jones hairdo, he spoke with a decidedly English accent and at the ripe old age of seventeen he was already an adult. I got the feeling right off that he would tolerate me for Brian's sake until I could prove myself worthy of his friendship.

Having freshly arrived back from a recent trip home to Birmingham, Ed said that it was time to get our act together. He had run into British R&B group The Pretty Things on a ferryboat in England and was so suitably impressed with this brush with greatness that with a bit of creative thinking we now had a name, The Pretty Ones. A good name for the times and very accurate in that we were quite cute at this point.

Brian had enlisted the services of fellow classmate Don Harbor for lead guitar duties. In those carefree days the lead guitar player didn't solo freely as much as play the song's melody instrumentally. Don became known as "The Harbor Roak" for his endearing pronunciation of the word "rock" which was rendered in Chuck Berry's classic Stones cover Around and Around as, "I said the joint was roakin'." We all found this quite amusing and Don earned himself a nickname which he probably still cringes over to this day.

Armed with Ed's Ringo Starr Ludwig drums and matching Hagstrom guitars we spent every available moment rehearsing at whoever's house was momentarily without parental supervision. For kids we were quite good and soon Ed, Brian and I were singing three part harmonies with a blend very much like our British heroes. We did not sound like kids when we sang and I remember a rehearsal in a church basement where the vicar enthused that he thought it was the record of 'Twist and Shout' playing as he entered his sacred domain. We were scheduled to play our first show at this very church and the vicar was kind enough to let us defile the sanctity of our surroundings with the demon rock and roll in preparation of the upcoming event. For weeks before the gig Brian and I would race to whichever class we were marking time in and scrawl "COMING SOON- THE PRETTY ONES-CHURCH OF THE EPIPHANY" in huge letters on the chalkboard.

Even our teachers got sort of caught up in the event and you could see the look of genuine pride on their faces as they had us erase the dusty marquees upon their arrival in class. We were young, we were in a group and in Carole Burke we even had a genuine girl from Liverpool in our homeroom class. I'll let her tell you about it.

Carole Burke

Greg, Brian and I were in the same grade nine class. I had known Brian the previous year in elementary school when he had moved to Canada from England. Everybody, both kids and teachers, loved Greg and Brian. Even as the year wore on and they became more committed to their music and much less to school, they endeared themselves even more to our teachers. I think the teachers were able to appreciate the fact that despite their having become virtually unproductive academically, Greg and Brian were still the life of our class. They were so smart and witty and, of course, always respectful beyond reproach!

Long before we even heard them actually play, we were all big fans of The Pretty Ones. The girls were fans because we all had a huge crush on Greg- he was everything a girl could want ie. long blonde hair, very charming, a cute face, and totally cool clothes. I remember when I heard them perform for the first time; I was taken aback at how good they actually were! The more often they played; their fan base grew, until they had become our very own local celebrities!

You know readers, had I known how cute I was back then I might not have had to wank as often as I did. I really like the line "virtually unproductive academically."
Perfect!

Gigs were a different animal in those days. For starters, you didn't have to be very good at all on either your instrument or in your vocal ability to draw a capacity audience to whatever venue you would be performing at. Church basement, community centre, high school gymnasium or your buddy's wreck room was instantly turned into a seething mass of kids starving for the mania sweeping the country. Image was the thing. As long as your hair was right, your pants were tight, and your boots had two inch Cuban heals you could literally do no wrong.

Most parents at this time, steeped in Eisenhower era morals and Ward and June Cleaver dress sense would not tolerate their little Johnny growing his hair into that silly style. Having long hair in 1964 was a constant running of the gauntlet in school and on the street that could see you held down while Bif and Marf shaved your head, (which never happened to me), to being punched out in the cafeteria by someone five years older than yourself simply for gazing in their direction, (which did happen).

I clearly remember sneaking from class to class not only avoiding the less informed jock types who viewed me as no more than a fox in a hunt but teachers and the vice principal who would drag me down to the office and phone my home at every opportunity to complain about the offensive follicles. My mother would always say that, "His hair is clean and I don't really see that it's any of your business," which was great and I loved her for it but it only made them seem to want to make my life an even greater hell for all of her support. Still, I had bigger fish to fry so the bullshit was well worth it.

As we got further and further into the music my school work began to suffer to the extent that I went from straight A's to straight E's. My Dad knew what the trouble was right off and he dragged me into the car by my hair and drove me up to the barbershop where he casually informed this cigar-breathed, ex-army-type to "Give this animal a human being haircut." My eyesight has always been worse than my breath, but as I squinted into that mirror, at that perfect shiny bowl cut, my ticket to the ball, it was all too painfully clear.

I had to get the hell out of there. I sprang from that barber shop chair with an Olympian's agility and with a hearty "Fuck You!" went tearing out of that plaza with the bib still around my neck. That reminds me of the time my Godfather, Jimmy Leone, an important man in my life and the owner of Leone's Beauty Salon, shaved just half of my head right down the middle and then proceeded to tell me that he was finished. I looked in horror at the fifty-fifty bar that was my head but he wasn't laughing so I knew that he was serious. I ran back to my Dad's Smoke Shop holding both of my hands over my head and crying like an eight year old, which I happened to be at the time. My Dad explained that it was Uncle Jimmy's idea of a joke and then took me back to have the job finished. I loved my Godfather but I never trusted barbers after that.

Anyway, after I fled the barber shop I ran like hell to a safe haven, Dave Miller's basement, where I called my Mom who advised me to lie low for a few days until my Dad cooled off.

The curtains parted at the first Pretty Ones gig to reveal an undulating throng of teenage boys and girls, who just yesterday were mere classmates, but had now become screaming fans because the school of Ed Sullivan had taught them that this is what you do! Bo Diddleys 'Mona' gave way to 'I Feel Fine' which became The Kinks 'C'mon Now' and then my solo turn singing 'I'm Free' but with no bass on as it made my Mick Jagger turn all the more realistic. Nobody noticed the absence of bottom end. They were at a pop concert! The Sykes column speakers were "custom made" and could easily handle the tricky vocal load. Our tiny amps were turned up to the point of distortion, but we never quite crossed that line as that was the sound of a time yet to come. Ed would half smile at the girls swooning in the front row as he shook his hair in time to his drumbeat. "I SAID THE JOINT WAS ROAKIN'," sang 'The Harbor Roak' and it surely was. 'Ferry Cross The Mersey' went down a bomb, no stiffs at this gig man! Sweat soaked frilly shirts under green corduroy jackets, the perfect sculpture of your hair spoiled with perspiration matting the fringe and stinging your eyes with the salt. Brian, legs apart, head tilted back in proud tribute snarled the words to the anthem that would bring an end to the show and the evening. "WELL SHAKE IT UP BABY." he wailed while Ed and Don and I sang the response in perfect harmony. The show ended with our bow in unison as the vicar drew the curtains back in place. The kids made their way backstage to congratulate the group or raced to the parking lot where their parents picked them up. I don't know if anyone else there that night could even remember this as an accurate description of that first real gig but this is how I remember it and I'm standing by it. I can't recall if we even got paid for that performance but it matters even less now than it would have then.

A ritual had been played out.
Trial by fire.
A rite of passage that left us wanting more.

During the summer we arranged our own show at The Old School. Before they built Regent Heights this building served as the local public school, but it was now a community centre and soon became the place to be as The Pretty Ones were scheduled to perform.

I believe it was only one measly dollar to get in but as we performed we noticed a commotion at the side door. Shit, it was Jolbin and his gang of toughs! Ed casually left his drums and strode towards the door.

"Can I help you?" he asked politely.

"We're comin' in for free!" sneered Jolbin.

"You'll pay at the door like everyone else, it's only a buck," said Ed.

"I don't care how much it is, we're not payin'," sneered Jolbin who checks his goons to see that they're still behind him. They were.

"Then you're not coming in," offered Ed who then added, "even if you do pay."

"And you're going to stop me fairy?" sneered Jolbin.

The last sound Jolbin heard was the sound of the wind around Ed's ham-like fist as it smashed into his nose, knocking him over the railing for a good six foot drop where he lay peacefully until his buddies dragged him off. Ed nonchalantly reclaimed his place behind his kit and counted in the next song. I noticed drops of blood on his frilly shirt, but certainly not his.

The Friars Tavern

During this time my mother, whose name is Vera, worked as a coat check girl along with my Aunt Eileen at The Friars Tavern on Yonge Street. The Friars is now a Hard Rock Cafe, which is perfect irony as some amazing musicians passed through its doors when a live venue. Before the British Invasion mostly jazz greats such as Lionel Hampton, Oscar Peterson and Ramsey Lewis played there but the times were changin' and in order to step up business a rock and rhythm and blues policy was initiated. Levon and The Hawks were the first group booked and opened a floodgate of classic entertainers including David Clayton Thomas, Robbie Lane and The Disciples, Dion, and The Female Beatles.

I loved the Female Beatles and in particular Marilyn, nicknamed "Boots," who was the bass player. She was cute, totally old enough to be pure fantasy to a budding Lothario like yours truly, and her group played Beatles songs in mini skirts and white go-go boots.

The Friars manager was a fellow named Gord Josie who was a very nice man but an imposing enough figure who commanded respect from solid citizens and the wide variety of "rounders" alike who frequented the joint. Mr. Josie allowed youngsters to attend Saturday afternoon matinees, which is what I would look forward to each weekend. Those days can be totally relived in The Bands 'Moondog Matinee' LP, which they recorded in honour of their Levon and The Hawks days. A budding musician could drink coke after coke and eat fries with gravy while grooving to the sounds of these soon-to-be legends who worked off Friday night hangovers entertaining Saturday afternoon shoppers breaking from their rounds at Eatons and Simpsons, just outside the door.

It was great that both my Mom and aunt worked there as they were well liked by the bands and quite often I would find myself chatting with Rick Danko of The Hawks about bass tips or getting a small piece of advice from "The Teenage Idol Of Yonge Street" as Mr. Ronnie Hawkins jokingly referred to himself. Heady stuff for a thirteen year old.

It wasn't long before my Mom convinced Mr. Josie to let us sit in and there we were one Saturday afternoon, playing in between sets for The Female Beatles. We went down great and were invited back to do the same with The Hawks. My Mom recalls Levon Helm giving Ed a drum stool as a gift and my first bass amplifier was purchased from Rick Danko. A Traynor Combo Bass Amp with the serial number 003. What I wouldn't give to have that back. Miss Boots thought we would do a great version of Len Barrys big hit '1-2-3' and she then proceeded to tell that to anyone within earshot while I vacuously nodded agreement while trying for a closer look up that mini dress.

Someone spotted us doing our thing one matinee and offered us a paying engagement at the Rocket A Go Go which was located a few doors south of The Friars. The only problem with this idea was that it was an after hours club which meant that we started at one in the morning and played until three. We somehow managed to convince our parents that this was a great idea and soon found our fresh little faces on our own Yonge Street stage before an audience of rounders, drunks, hookers, drunken rounders and other n'ere-do-wells of Toronto nightlife.

We had taken to turning our speaker cabinets to face the wall. We did this because Robbie Robertson of the Hawks did this. I'm certain that he had a good reason; we just did it because He was fast becoming a local god.

The hookers took quite a shine to us and one extremely buxom brunette had no qualms at all about little boys stuffing their "treat" money into her ample cleavage while she made kissy faces at them. God bless that girl. This gig didn't last long as our school work was really beginning to suffer and somebody was probably beginning to question the wisdom of youngsters staying out until sun-up.

About this time we were forced to find a new lead guitarist as Don Harbor had sufficiently "roaked" his last joint and, with a part time job to look forward to, he made the fatal leap into relative obscurity. Enter a fig newton...

George Kelly

As I mentioned earlier, proper lead guitar players, at least at entry level, were virtually non-existent in those days. Don Harbor could pick out solos based strictly on the song's melody but the fretwork of a George Harrison or a Keith Richards was what was really needed but sorely lacking. I believe Ed found George Kelly through an ad posted on a bulletin board at Kalua Music.

A great guy named Fred Beresford, who was an old school player who did not turn his nose up at new trends, ran Kalua Music. Fred was exactly what a middle aged musician should be, mildly eccentric, rumpled and above all willing to impart musical tales of wisdom on any and all who would listen. He was the slightly strange uncle most of us would eventually become ourselves with a totally endearing habit of calling you "boy" as in "Now look here boy, when I was gigging at the Palais Royale in 19...." I know that that doesn't exactly read as warm as I would like it to but Fred gave off a kindly glow that was alright with us kids. Kalua was also situated on Danforth Avenue near Broadview, which was in the heart of Greek Land.

Enter a fig souvlaki...Yorgo Kalaitzis or George Kelly. When I first laid eyes on George I thought to myself that Brian and Ed must be kidding. George was ever so greasy with a pompadour of brilliantine'd hair, a gold lame jacket, white shirt with collar stuck up ala Elvis and wraparound shades. Brian could see that I was shocked by George's appearance but gave me a look that said that I should just play along. All doubts about George quickly faded as he plugged in his solid body Harmony guitar and let forth a flurry of British Invasion riffs so perfect in tone and execution that Keith and George themselves would have smiled down upon this little Greek boy. The Pretty Ones had the best lead guitar player in town!

Something had to be done about the image, though. Ours! George would not budge an inch. So the band went on stage with three of us in lace and corduroy and one lone figure in early greaseball. But could that guy play guitar. Soon people were coming to our shows to hear George not only replicate Beatles and Stones solos but he insisted on doing an instrumental of 'Memphis' which brought the house down by virtue of his amazing technique. The neatest thing to me, though, was that when we performed 'Boys', Ed could say "Alright George" just before the solo; just like Ringo did on the real version.

Things started to get very strange soon after when we would call George's house, only to be told, "Yorgi gon prateek," by his Mom.

"Prateek??..er, practice?? We have a show tonight at Doug Lauder's party!"

It turns out that another group, a Rhythm and Blues outfit was wooing our George away with promises of better paying gigs, better looking girls, and most importantly, they would buy him a new Fender Telecaster. With George busy rehearsing Sam and Dave songs we somehow managed to deputize a guitarist from The Myna Birds, a Yorkville group that would eventually spawn Rick James and Neil Young. This guy was much older, much cooler and as it turns out much more otherworldly. We take you now into the furnace room of Doug Lauder's house.

"You guys wanna smoke some reefer?" asks the dark stranger.

"What's that?" we say.

"Reefer man...Boo...Marijuana."

"MARIJUANA??"

The Pretty Ones huddle with our host, Doug Lauder, behind the furnace of his parent's house.

Do we call the cops?

Do we kick this drug addict's ass back downtown?

IN GOD'S NAME WHAT DO WE DO?

Why not just ask him to leave.

He splits.

We are relieved.

Scarborough is pure once more.

Things would change.

December's Children

December's Children were another Scarborough beat group that specialized in Stones songs.

One blustery winter night they asked me to join them at a high school dance because their regular bass player couldn't make it. They would supply me with an amp so I agreed, and packing up my new Eko violin shaped bass made off for the rendezvous. Imagine my surprise when their real bass player came along, bass in hand and saws me sitting in his spot in the car. Not pleased. I can still picture him to this day, shoulders hunched, muttering curses under his breathe and casting evil looks in my direction as he dejectedly walked away.

Arriving at the school I'm pleased to see that we're playing in the gymnasium. Perfect amount of echo to make up for the occasional musical faux paux. I'm also extremely pleased to see the biggest Magnatone amplifier ever and make a beeline for it.

"Wow, the bass will sound great through this!" and begin to unpack my bass and a chord.

"Excuse me, but this amp is mine; that amp over there is yours," says the rhythm guitarist.

It didn't take me long to find the amp that I'd be using.

It was a 30-Watt Magnatone, back to haunt me.

The tone was so farty that you felt compelled to excuse yourself every time you plucked a string.

Soon the gym was packed and December's Children were rocking. Things were fairly uneventful for most of the set until I began to smell smoke. I immediately ran back to the little amp but it wasn't electrical smoke that I was smelling, it was the other kind. As we slammed into 'Satisfaction' the stage left curtains burst forth into a glorious light show as flames began to devour the fabric. Maybe the group's blue and red Christmas spotlights were just a tad too close to the curtains after all.

The band, oblivious to the lethal aspects of the situation, played on. The audience, eyes riveted to their gym being torched now began to panic. The fire alarms were now employed, adding a delightful element of danger. Teachers ran helter skelter through the gym, yelling orders for evacuation over the group's din and were now joined by the screams of young girls. I personally thought that the screaming was a lovely little touch, it made you feel wanted. Someone was finally smart enough to cut the stage power and the gig was basically history. The fire department raced in and dealt a severe blow to what was left of the once fashionable draperies. The group, ever conscious of public safety was now pissed off that it was over so soon. I packed up my bass and went home.

My Mom asked me how it went.

"Nothin' special," I replied and went downstairs to bed.

It was time for The Pretty Ones to hit the road. With Ed behind the wheel of a very English Bedford step van we were soon hurtling down the 401, en route to Windsor. With our modest equipment crammed in Brian rode shotgun and George straddled an amp in the back, while I sat on the passenger side stairwell, door open and facing backwards with my left foot bouncing off the death dealing pavement racing by. We were on tour, heading in a new direction, pop pioneers in search of adventure.

One minor problem, though. We had no place to play once we got there. We also had no place to stay once we get there. Did this matter? Not at all! We were on the road! That mattered.

The Kitten Club was a former funeral parlour located on Wyandotte Street in the heart of downtown Windsor. A dark and forbidding environment, owing far more to its recent past than its glorious future. George and I were told to wait in the van while Brian and Ed went in and negotiated a deal with the club owner. We could play Friday and Saturday night for $5.00 per man and we could sleep in the club.

Big Time!

Even without advertising we attracted a small crowd of curiosity seekers and regulars. We played our sets in this absolutely morbid hole to a handful of people but we had pulled off the impossible, a paying gig far from home. Things would've been much worse if we hadn't stumbled on to this place. Turns out we didn't even have enough gas money to get home. Now we did!

There was even a guy in attendance that had recently won a trip to England courtesy of CKLW radio to meet The Beatles! George Harrison gave him a pair of his own beautiful suede Beatle Boots, which we spent many hours talking about and admiring.

"Can I try them on? Can I?" I begged.

"No way man, I never take them off!" John Bradack replied. John Bradack was the guy's name.

Bradack, who had extremely long hair for the time, got laid just for wearing those bloody boots!

With the final notes of 'Hey Little Girl' by The Syndicate Of Sound drifting off into the cosmos we settled down for the night. Three girls from Michigan exchanged numbers with us and headed back across the border. I ended up with Brian, and I swear this is true; Brian and I spent the night sleeping in two discarded coffins in the basement of the club. Creepy? Very. Scary? Nah.

Next we had a trip to Kingston, but this time it was a paying engagement where we played a pub night at Queens University. Two things happened that somewhat ruined the event. First, Ed and Brian got into an actual punch up en route to the show. Perhaps Brian had stolen a girl from Ed? Money? Nothing as simple as that. These two bruisers were doing battle over who would wear the band's only John Lennon cap during our performance.

Sitting in my basement today, surrounded with tons of Beatles memorabilia and with the benefit of hindsight I can see now that this was the proper course of action.

Their faces were bloody with the effort and they fought with such emotion that there was no clear winner. I can't remember if it was myself or George who got to don the cherished icon that night, but I'd like to think that it was George as he would have looked the silliest wearing it. I do know that Brian and Ed started drinking a great quantity of beer to ease the tension. Both of them were vastly underage and not very experienced drinkers. It was quite late by the time we'd finished our show and packed our gear into the back of Ed's boss's station wagon. As usual Ed drove, Brian climbed into the passenger seat beside his brother, and George and I shared the back of the car along with the equipment. It's sort of funny now to think that at one time you could actually fit four guys, drums, amplifiers, a PA system, two guitars, a bass and one John Lennon cap in one vehicle but we did it.

Brian and George had passed out leaving me to amuse Ed as the dawn broke on another day. I was discussing something of no fixed importance with Ed when I glanced over his shoulder and noticed that the car directly in front of us was coming up, and very fast. I don't know when it dawned on me that my conversation had put Ed to sleep but there he was; sound asleep, behind the wheel. I managed to yell loudly enough to awaken him as we slammed into the back of the guy in front of us. George, who had been dozing peacefully beside me, decided that he had had enough of this and leaped from the out-of-control car, landing in a heap on the side of the road. The PA column speaker smashed into the back of my head, bending me over double as it made its way into the front seat. Both Brian and Ed were alright.

Needless to say, the guy whose car we hit was none too pleased to have his morning interrupted in such a fashion, especially by a bunch of sissies and he told us to stay put while he went to call the cops. The Cops! Holy shit! Ed decided that it was in our best interests to get the hell out of there and off we went. About three hundred yards from the accident Ed's boss's station wagon let out a sigh, a fountain of steam and with a mighty death rattle, gave up the ghost. We were going nowhere. The farmer who we had back-ended arrived shortly thereafter along with one of the Ontario Provincial Police's finest and we were now in big trouble. The cop looked in at Ed and asked, in the friendliest of tones, "You boys weren't tryin'to get away now were you?"

"No sir, I just wanted to see if my boss's car still worked," was Ed's shaky reply. Mr. Pilling came to fetch us and Ed's now ex-boss came to fetch his ex-station wagon. All of the parents agreed that perhaps this was a little bit much and they decided to disband our little group in our own best interests. It wouldn't be long before we were back at it.

Like A Rolling Stone
– a Brian Jones story

The King Edward Hotel was the place where all pop stars stayed when playing Toronto. When I finally made an honest woman out of my long-suffering girlfriend Renata, we too stayed in a suite to mark our wedding night. Our daughter Jazzmin, then two years old and not quite free of her mother's womb, stayed there as well. I requested the suite that The Beatles had stayed in but no one working there could even remember what floor they had stayed on. It was alright with me just to be in the same opulent surroundings and fantasize about what it must have been like for THEM. With Jazzmin sharing the honeymoon boudoir fantasies concerning the Fabs were all I would be having at any rate.

Ringo Starrs All Star Band had played in Toronto this very evening and it certainly crossed my mind that I just might run into him as he placed his room service tray outside his door. Not to be as he was suitably uptown by this time in his career.

When The Beatles stayed here in February of 1964 the hotel was literally under siege from teenage girls and guys alike. My old neighbourhood pal, Phil Joyce, and I managed to convince a guard that we posed no threat to the group and he whispered to us that they would be coming out the back entrance in a police paddy wagon in ten minutes for their first show at the Gardens. We raced around the corner, found the escape portal, and waited for what seemed like ten minutes impatiently for our heroes to come out. All of a sudden the corrugated metal door flew up revealing a police paddy wagon, which proceeded to gun its engine and race into the street.

Phil and I looked at each other and in a split second we knew what had to be done. Jump on the back of that paddy wagon and scream stuff at The Beatles!!

Which we did.

I can't remember if I was yelling for any particular Beatle or just to the group as a whole but I became painfully aware of a rather large blue suited policeman's arm around my waist and him none-to-gently tearing me off the back of the paddy wagon as it picked up speed with Phil still attached to its back door.

Phil, who was one of my best friends ever, and who died on me many years ago of cancer, was also amazingly adept at the finer points of yarn spinning. In other words, he was usually full of shit. When we connected later on he told me how The Beatles had invited him into the paddy wagon and had offered him great hospitality all the way to the show. I didn't believe him but played along as it was a great story, but in saying that I also didn't believe him when he told me about his cancer either, so you never know. Where was I? Oh yeah...

TRAVELS WITH MY AMP   19

1964 ...

Greg with Ed Pilling (back)
Photo: Vera Godovitz

Greg and George Kelly
Photo: Vera Godovitz

Greg Sings "I'm Free" sans bass with
Ed Pilling. Photo: Vera Godovitz

Ed Pilling, drums and George Kelly,
guitar.

1966 ...

1968 ...

Ed Pilling and the "Bedford Van"
Photo: Barb Pilling

Brian Pilling
Photo: Barb Pilling

Like A Rolling Stone
— a Brian Jones story

Brian Jones, for anyone who was a fan of English rock groups, was definitely the coolest of all rock stars. He was The Rolling Stones back then. He had the coolest hair, a perfect blond mop top that looked like a golden feather duster, beautiful baggy eyes that hinted of too many late nights, and he dressed as no other rock star before or since. After their 1965 show at the Gardens, Brian Pilling and I made our way down to The King Eddie as that was the place to be and hung out waiting for a glimpse of an actual Rolling Stone. The hotel, as usual, was under siege but for some strange reason the only two fans at the front door were Brian and myself.

All of a sudden a stretch Cadillac Limousine eased up to the curb and from out of the corner of my eye I saw..No way man.. Brian Bloody Jones Hisself walking out of the bloody front doors and right at us as we are standing in his way to enter the car. He was immaculate in white shoes, pants, with a black turtleneck sweater under a pink and white striped jacket. I was speechless. All at once, out of nowhere, this rather large girl fan flew out of the shadows, placing a strangle hold around Mr. Jones neck.

"Would someone get this bird off my bleedin' back?" the pop star said nonchalantly while waving his cigarette like a conductor's baton.

Did he really say that?

He did!!

Too cool for words.

A number of burly Toronto's Finest then surrounded our little group and proceeded to tear the offending damsel off of Brian Jones. As Brian P. and I were no immediate threat we were not removed but were instead allowed to witness the hysteria up close and personal as dozens of arms were now clawing through the protective cordon in the general direction of the pop star and ear piercing screams of undying love shattered the night air. Brian Pilling, in a moment of divine inspiration, opened the limo door and the Stone leaped in. As the door was closed behind him my Brian Pilling called out, "Hey man, why did you get your haircut?"

The rock star simply looked at us, smiled and winked. The limo now tore off with a horde of screamies in hot pursuit. Brian Pilling and I, still in total shock hardly noticed as Bill Wyman, in the company of two beehive'd, peroxide-headed hookers jumped into a cab and raced off to the Place Pigall in search of a little Toronto R&B. My Dad worked there as a waiter.

When Toronto's The Ugly Ducklings opened for The Stones at Maple Leaf Gardens in '65 it is legend that Stones manager Andrew Loog Oldham, spotting Duckling guitarist and Brian Jones look-alike Glynn Bell backstage, grabbed him and said "Wot the fuck you doin' here then? You're on in five min...er, fuckin'ell, come with me!" and proceeded to drag the clone backstage.

"Here Brian!... Look at this!" Oldham said, proudly displaying his catch to Brian Jones in The Stones dressing room.

Glancing back at his mirror image Brian Jones casually shrugged off the intrusion with a quiet "Get him the fuck out of here."

That would be too cool if it's a true story!

Yorkville

We began hanging out and occasionally performing in Yorkville Village in 1965. The Village, as it was known, was the former haunt of beatniks, poets and other artsy fartsy types but was now a Mecca for suburban kids eager to experience the growing music scene. Grand Victorian homes along Avenue Road, Cumberland Street and Yorkville Avenue now housed coffee bars that featured live music every night of the week. The Ugly Ducklings and The Wee Beasties at Charlie Browns, The Paupers at The Flick, Luke and The Apostles at The Purple Onion, The Stitch In Tyme at El Patio, The Myna Birds at The Myna Bird and a virtual who's who of future international stars such as Neil Young, Gordon Lightfoot, and Joni Mitchell at The Riverboat.

In this safe haven kids with long hair and dandified clothing could gather without fear to hear these great bands and socialize. Cover charges were minimal, one club boasting "ONE SMALL COVER, TWO GREAT GROUPS!" And for the price of a coffee or soda you could sit for hours thrilling to The Ducks playing their hit record 'Nothin' or The Wee Beasties covering 'Lies' by The Knickerbockers, note perfect.

Our own Village debut was somewhat marred by the total collapse of our PA at Charlie Browns. The band was set up in a very small area that would have normally been the front bay window. There was seating for maybe fifty people and another twenty-five or so crammed around the back and sides. At the back of the room an espresso machine worked overtime, further hyping the kids with a solid caffeine rush. The place was dark, smoke filled, and hot; the perfect combination for a frantic evening of rock and roll. Within twenty minutes of our PA problem we were saved by The Ducklings, who loaned us some extra gear. We played our set of British Invasion covers and something new, original compositions by Pilling and Pilling.

"I lost my love yesterday, I just don't know what to do, she packed her bags and went away, I'll think of her again some day, and I know that I can't go on this way," we sang and everyone there knew exactly what we meant. I can't recall if our trip downtown was considered a tremendous success but it was great to be a part of that wonderful time in that wonderful place.

First Recording Session

On a return trip to Windsor our new "manager" Jim Sawyer, accompanied us. Jim's musical background was none, but as he had convinced the good folks at Pearson's Men's Wear to supply us with paisley shirts and Madras pants and that, coupled with the fact that he owned a flashy new convertible made him an obvious choice for management. I clearly remember sleeping in the well where the ragtop was stored when it was down while we cruised the 401 at 100 m.p.h. This was the genesis of my infatuation with dangerous car routines that would get worse as my career developed.

Our second trip to Windsor was notable in that we committed to tape our first musical offerings. The Kinks' 'Lover Not A Fighter', 'I Feel Fine' by The Beatles, The Stones version of Bobby Womack's immortal 'It's All Over Now', and two Pilling and Pilling originals, 'Hey Baby' and 'Lost Love.' The modestly equipped studio was in a suburban basement with absolutely no separation between drums and amplified guitars, so that all of the instruments "bled" into each other's microphones. To further compound the situation the vocals were sung live with the instrumentation but already the tightness of our little group was evident and as we listened to the tape playback we were convinced that the "Big Time" was just around the corner.

The End Of Innocence

George Kelly finally caved in and left The Pretty Ones early in 1966, the obvious attraction of a free Telecaster proved too irresistible a temptation. Brian had been long gone from my everyday life when the Pillings had moved and he changed high schools. I began to discover new friends in the Village. The Pilling brothers decided that the only thing to do was to move to England. Move to England? I was only fifteen years old and even if my folks had agreed to such a crazy scheme, I wasn't legally allowed to leave the country. Brian and Ed were hell-bent on going, however, and if I couldn't make it, then so be it. Seeing them off at Union Station was one of the darkest days of my life. I cried as they boarded that train, en route to Montreal where they would pick up their flight to London. My friends were gone and my first real band was finished.

I was about to get the blues.

Bo Diddley, Bo Diddley Have You Heard
– a Bo Diddley story

I push out of the front door of my downtown Montreal hotel and into the hustle of Crescent Street. All of a sudden I make out the unmistakable black Stetson hat of one Ellas McDaniel. He's walking, no, he's grooving towards me.

The silver Conchos on the hat's headband flash in the noonday sun.
I scream out "HEY!... BO DIDDLEY!"
The gunslinger smiles as he walks past me.

...another Bo Diddley story featuring Ronnie Wood...

The scene backstage is somewhat chaotic. Your actual god-on-earth Rolling Stone is accompanying his legendary blues mentor in an all too rare club performance. It is deemed necessary for my presence to be felt in the rather less than spacious dressing room as I have graciously loaned said rock legends some of my gear for this evening's performance.

People are clamouring to be admitted to this smoky sardine can while I melt somewhat uncomfortably into a rear wall and nurse a double Bacardi and coke. The gunslinger is looking rather uncomfortable himself; sitting on a cheap velour couch and studiously ignoring two finely endowed groupies bent on seeking his favour. Ronnie Hawkins claims that "Anyone who believes that all men are created equal hasn't seen Bo Diddley in the shower!"

Bo is also ignoring myself, perhaps not realizing the historical importance of our Montreal experience a few years previous.

Ronnie Wood, triple something or other in hand, instantly sizes up the situation and stumbles over to my area. With his wonderful beak of a nose mere centimetres from my own, he shakes his rooster coiffed head, tries to focus his eyes on mine and hiccups, "Bo Diddley is a very strange individual," before stumbling off in search of another distraction.

For some reason this all made perfect sense at the time.

— *set two* —

The Backdoor Blues Band

Even at my then tender age I had a pretty good idea about the blues. From Guido Poppe and The Tennants, Richie Knight and The Midnights and on to Levon and The Hawks, I'd listened firsthand to many blues classics like 'Who Do You Love', 'Bo Diddley' and 'Hoochie Coochie Man', but it took The Rolling Stones to bring the idea home to me.

I remember my Mom calling me in one day to see something on The Mike Douglas morning show. The Stones playing Willie Dixon's 'Little Red Rooster' was a virtual epiphany. This was not the light pop music the invasion had brought forth. This was something else entirely, something mildly sinister, sexual.

In those days the camps were divided, Beatles fans or Stones fans. No middle ground. I instantly knew that I could love both groups with even zeal. My Mom would laugh out loud while my Dad sat grim faced as I did the perfect one leg twitching in air Mick Jagger impression. The Bissell carpet sweeper my mic stand, two large table spoons my maracas.

"I'm gon' tell ya how it's gon' be..." I sang, my body jerking spasmodically in time to the Stones jungle beat. Lord knows what my Dad thought. Just make sure to shut the drapes so the neighbours can't check out the family weirdo. Looking back, I can't say as I blame him.

With the Pillings now in England I was in a temporary state of flux. I needed a change and one Mark Smith supplied that change. Mark was a senior at my high school and a budding vocalist and harmonica player. We met through the network of musicians now cropping up all over the school. Mark needed a bass player and I was a bass player. Soon he had me listening to The Paul Butterfield Chicago Blues Band, Muddy Waters, Willie Dixon, and my personal favourite, Junior Wells. Mark had a good friend, a fat black guy who played drums. Perfect. We talked the blues, we walked the blues, and we played the blues. We never got further than the odd rehearsal but the seed had been planted. Mark moved away and eventually found fame as an engineer on Bachman Turner Overdive albums while I continued learning the subtle nuances of playing the blues.

It was at about this time that my formal musical education came to an end. I'd sort of taken guitar lessons from a guy named George Armstrong (not the Leafs captain) years earlier as I fancied myself a natural successor to Ricky Nelson. I would never practice at all but instead would stand in front of the bathroom mirror with my cheap acoustic guitar on and approximate Ricky's sneer. It was a great sneer, all curled up lip and punk cool. After ten weeks Mr. Armstrong calmly told my Dad, "You're wasting your money, Mr. Godovitz, this kid will never play a musical instrument." At the time this was quite true but all was not totally wasted; at least I now had a killer sneer.

I began playing tenor saxophone in music class. My older brother Gary had been a wicked sax player who could belt out 'Tequila' with the best of them. The only problem was that, as I didn't wear glasses, I couldn't see the sheet music so my sight-reading was terrible. Also, Mr. Simard, who had been my brother's teacher and was quite pleased that another Godovitz would soon be playing 'Tequila' for him, was replaced by a guy who shall remain nameless. I'll call him Mr. X.
  "Godovitz, can you stay after class for a minute?" said Mr. X.
  Godovitz stays after class.
  "I want that hair of yours cut before you return to my class," said Mr. X.
  "Beethoven had long hair!" I said and I really felt that I had him.
  "That's another thing, you have a smartass attitude Godovitz. Don't return to my class even if you do get your hair cut," said Mr. X and with that my chances of ever properly reading music were finished.
  This is funny, as years later, when Goddo was at their peak in popularity, we played a concert at my old school and this guy, who had

been telling his students that he had taught me music, now asked me to sign an album for him.

I did it but I really enjoyed watching him squirm.

Browsing through the want ads of the old *Toronto Telegram* one day I see an ad stating: "WANTED – bass player and vocalist for blues band-call John at...."

Hey! I'm a bass player and I sing and I'm also now into the blues.

And with that I called the number.

John (BJ) Bjarnason

The voice on the other end of the phone had the alarming quality of adulthood. After a few perfunctory blues based questions I was asked, "How old are you anyway?"

"Sixteen," I lied.

And with that being a correct answer I was on my way to meet the other guys in John's blues band. Now John, who is still my good friend, best man at my wedding, and underwater chiropractor par excellence was a different guy from those that I'd previously known. First of all, he came from a very upper middle class background; his father was a successful lawyer and, his very tolerant mother the typical matriarch of a well-healed family. John spoke proper English, not the bastardised version we poor folk in Scarborough used, and carried himself like a straight ahead preppy type guy with a certain haughtiness that was at once both endearing and annoying as hell. He had already found his life mate in his girlfriend, Robin, a knockout blond who also had that air of upper class drifting about her and strictly off limits to a still wet-behind-the-ears kid like me.

What really set John apart was that he could play the harmonica, or "harp," as he called it, like an old black blues man. The phrasing and tone of his playing was a symphony of lost love and down-and-out despair. This straight looking guy was an absolute killer musician!

Now it was time to meet the other guys. Dave Wood was a greaseball type from the east end who played Telecaster in deft homage to Domenic "Donny" Troiano. Troiano was the current Toronto rock guitar god, in the Robbie Robertson mould. He played for Mandala, which also featured the amazing vocal and dance abilities of the legendary George Olliver. Dave was tall, liked to eat and would eventually wash the grease out of his hair to become another Brian Jones clone. He could be silly on occasion, invented his own gobbledy gook language, and had an absurd sense of humour that could render you hurting with laughter. He was a great guitarist.

His buddy Wayne Wilson was the first real Zen hippie I'd ever met. He could play a shuffle beat like no one I've worked with since and was a guy whose buttons were hardest to push. Lord knows I tried. Wayne espoused peace, love, and harmony long before it was fashionable and had the longest hair I'd ever seen. Should you chance upon the right button he also wouldn't hesitate to pull a kitchen knife from the drawer and try to butter your spleen, which he did to Wood on one memorable occasion.

The last piece of this particular puzzle was keyboardist Dieter Billinger. He was the exact twin of bass playing brother Ralph and a pair of odd socks you should only meet. The other guys could sense my confusion; Dieter was old enough to be our dad.

"He has a station wagon," said Wayne in Zen-like tones and all was clear.

I was now the bass playing "16"-year-old vocalist for The Backdoor Blues Band.

Our level of musicianship was now greater and our circle of friends likewise equally accomplished. Players like guitarist Joey (Miquelon) Roberts and bass phenomenon Prakash John, who would eventually work for Bob Seger and Lou Reed respectively, were now part of our musical orbit.

Great R&B wailers like Valentine Kelly, Johnny Wright, Brian Maxim, and Bobby Dupont were busy fine-tuning their chops on classic Sam Cooke and Wilson Pickett songs.

Jams, organized in any basement or hall accommodating enough to allow the din, turned into cutting sessions of musical virtuosity the likes of which were not experienced since the golden age of jazz.

The Saturday afternoon matinee thrived, and as my Mom still worked at The Friars, it was only a matter of time before we played there.

"Good afternoon, ladies and gentlemen, we're The Backdoor and we play Chicago Blues," I nervously said before launching into a set that included 'Born In Chicago', 'Good Morning Little Schoolgirl', 'Mojo', 'You Don't Love Me Baby' and other classics of the genre.

"What we gon' do now is get down," I said in my best Junior Wells affected voice. "Down in de alley. And when we get down in de alley we like to play da blues about da little girls. Young, tender..."

"Don't forget ugly!" hollers drummer Wayne, off mic, and it gets a good laugh.

"Dem girls," I finish as we slide into 'Early In the Mornin'.

"Now when a girl reaches the age of sixteen, she begin to think she's grown, but that's the type of girl that you can't never find at home..." I wailed and the band was tight.

We closed our set with Billy Boy Arnold's 'I Wish You Would' and my Mom was beaming as we descended from the bandstand to a tremendous ovation.

Not all of our gigs ended quite that way, however. This was still an era when your appearance could get you beaten up, run off the road, or worse yet, no service in greasy restaurants.

It would be early in the morning, travelling a deserted stretch of highway, and the band is totally whacked out from five sets in some shit hole of a club. Everyone is hungry. The boys spill out of the station wagon at some truck stop and stumble through the door, a tangle of matted hair, perspiration, and blue jeans. The conversation stops as you grab that last booth in the back, trying to be as inconspicuous as possible. You talk softly, your nervous chatter now lost in a chorus of drunken asides, snide comments, and horsy laughter from the drunks and truckers who frequent the place. Where is that waitress you saw coming in? You see her smoking a cigarette and drinking coffee with the locals over at the counter. You do not exist. Ten minutes become twenty. Tension mounts. Finally Dave, the hungriest always, would stride purposely over to her and asks for menus.

"We don't serve your kind in here," she'd say, almost like she wants to spit after saying it, and she goes back to her drink. With a look that suggests death Wood looks her up and down and returns to our table.

"We're not eating here tonight, let's go," and we'd leave hungrier than when we came in.

Glamour!

Showbiz!

Wasn't that what this was supposed to be all about?

A police escort out of Sutton because the locals hadn't liked the way we looked.

Things had started on the wrong foot as the first question to greet us upon our arrival was "Where's your suits?"

This promoter was dead serious.

Suits?

"All the groups who play here wear matching suits," he said while eyeballing us suspiciously.

"We all have matching jeans," said Wayne but this guy was in no mood for hippie logic.

The dance smacked of fifties sock hop, boys on one side, girls on the other. The locals, up until this moment had been spoon-fed a steady diet of rhythm and blues. Well, that's okay because blues is a part of rhythm and blues isn't it?

It's not?

At least not to these assholes. Our music, as foreign to them as fine dining, was sensual all the same and soon some of the girls were dancing and creeping closer to the bandstand. Eye contact was made, sly smiles exchanged. The local toughs, just looking for an opening, now have one. The band huddled backstage while the scene out front, fuelled with stolen whiskey and beer, became louder and uglier. A beer bottle smashed off a cymbal, showering the stage and our gear in broken glass. The promoter simply pulled the plug and called for the law. The scene outside was tense as our car was surrounded. We packed up our gear quickly, now under the watchful eye of the OPP. The cops liked us less than their son's did.

The cherry top glowed bright red as we were lead through the mob and deposited at the town line.

If memory serves, I don't think we got paid either.

For dazzling excitement and sheer terror try lifting a five hundred pound Hammond B3 Organ up a flight of ice-covered stairs in February.

"Oh no man, I was on the bottom last time we tried these fuckin' stairs, put BJ on it."

"He's parkin' the car man, put your shoulder into it."

"He's always parkin' the fuckin' car when we have to lift this bloody thing!"

And up you would go, knowing full well that one missed step and the world's heaviest toboggan would be riding your sorry ass downhill.

For the most part, it was carting Dieter's bloody organ up and down stairs that gave me a life long hatred of keyboard players. It's funny in a way, because now there's a rack-mountable module called Vintage Keys which weighs about ten pounds and perfectly approximates the sound of Vox Continental, Farfisa, Moog and the dreaded but much loved Hammond B3.

It kinda makes you hate keyboard players even harder doesn't it?

Somehow we got booked into The Downstairs Club in Hamilton. This joint turned out to be a black's only blues and R&B club, but for some reason they liked us. By this time we had included in our repertoire Bobby Hebb's 'Sunny' which was a current radio hit and it went down great. The jukebox in this place was loaded with classic black music but all night one couldn't help but notice the repeat performance of Alfred E. Newman's fartbuster, 'It's A Gas.'

The club was not licensed but the smell of whiskey was everywhere and the washrooms were teeming with discarded bottles by night's end. All of the guys carried clubs and going up and down the stairs gave one the sense of running the gauntlet. I don't really think we had anything to fear as we were a sort of novelty to these guys. After all, our attention to detail in recreating these blues standards was impressive enough; it had nothing to do with our youth or whiteness.

We played on a small riser, two six-foot column speakers on each side of the band for our PA. BJ would place his harps neatly on one of the columns, arranged alphabetically so that he could easily access the proper-keyed harp for whatever tune we were performing. At one point a guy so tall that he could put his elbows on top of our column speakers was doing just that on BJ's side of the stage. Besides making himself comfy he was also lifting and pocketing the neatly arranged harps. What could be done? Grin and bear it. And pick songs in the keys left to us that hadn't been borrowed. Soon after BJ began wearing a custom-made leather harp belt.

My eldest brother Ted drove me to our gig at the Balm Beach Club one summer night. Ted had been a Roy Orbison and Elvis fan but I think he sort of enjoyed watching his kid brother on a stage. The Balm was one of those pre World War Two wooden dance halls that our parents had danced in to the sounds of big band giants like Tommy Dorsey and Glenn Miller. Now the place was crawling with summertime cottage types, weekend thrill seekers and bikers out to create their own fun.

I'll make this short. The Backdoor played the blues, which bikers and other ruffians liked, so we went over well. A girl with great taste and loose morals made advances on sweet little innocent me. As my brother Ted was there I felt kind of goofy, but he took me aside and said, "If you want a little lesson in life little brother I would take that girl for a walk along the beach."

My little lesson in life turned out to be that if you have sex on a deserted beach, you will find that sand makes a lousy lubricant. In the morning my brother was asleep in his car while drunken bikers were smashing the shit out of our equipment.

The gig in London had been okay by our standards. We got paid and nobody was bleeding as we all piled into BJ's car and started for home. It was the middle of winter, the kind of night where you wouldn't dare breathe in with your mouth open for fear of instantly freezing your tonsils.

The drive from London to Toronto in those days was two and a half hours under perfect conditions but could take as much as two days with the weather not permitting. This was the snow belt but the night sky was cloudless. Tonight was just cold. Real cold.

About twenty minutes into the trip, with us laughin' and scratchin' over the evening's highs and lows the rear passenger side window blew completely out for no apparent reason and exploded into a billion shiny shards of glass on the eastbound 401. There was no point in even stopping. Instantly the temperature dropped to below freezing and idle chatter gave way to screaming. The people in the front seat were sort of okay, as they had the heater on full blast, but not a lick of that warmth found its way to the back. The wind howled through the opening, forcing the back seat occupants to cower beneath the window line. Jockeying for position, you would place your hands or whatever part of your body was most likely to get frostbite first under your neighbour's leg or arm, in an effort to survive the ordeal.

I lost both of my hands as a result of that evening and tears from that painful memory are welling up in my eyes even now as I type this story with my nose.

Just wanted to see if you're paying attention.

There was little any of us could do about the horrible situation were in so we spent the remainder of the trip home screaming and laughing and then screaming a bit more.

HEY! THIS JUST IN...

Jim (JAMES YOUNGER GANG) O'Leary just called (10:20 pm- November 23, 1998), to tell me that he's off to Sault Ste. Marie tomorrow. Then Lively (an actual place), then Sudbury for a date at The Coulson. His brother is a drummer named Matt O'Leary and they played gigs with me as GODO! Don't ask.

We have no snow in Toronto on this day and it is so warm here that you can walk around in just a sweatshirt. I have one on now. Where James and his lucky band mates are heading tomorrow there are signs reading DANGER! MOOSE CROSSING! every mile or so and the locals have two-skidoo garages.

He sounds like he's preparing for this trip by drinking lots of brew and smoking tons of cigarettes.

He sounds like I do but I'm just going downtown tomorrow.

What's that old adage about everything changing really just staying the same?

I'm standing here in yuppie heaven with a glass of vintage wine, the soft glow from the hearth dancing across the dark oak hardwood and this maniac is going up north on tour at the worst possible time of year. I don't know whether to laugh or cry.

I casually let slip that I'm working on a book.

I hear a sound not unlike a coin dropping.

"Remember that time we put that naked guy on the elevator at The President in Sudbury?" Jim blarps and instantly makes the book.

"Nooooo...," I say, drawing a blank but definitely interested.

"Yeah, we stuck a joint in his mouth...or was it his hand? and sent him down to the lobby naked!"

I can't remember any of this but play along.

"In the book we'll say that we stuck the joint in his ass so that it read's better!" I enthuse.

"Yeah, in his ass," snerfs Jim thoughtfully. "Remember they had those old biddies working at the front desk?" he gerfs but I'm still drawing a blank.

We both enjoy a little chuckle though at the thought of the naked drunk's arrival at the old biddie's post.

"Hey man, are we on a speaker phone?" blorbs James in a brief moment of thought.

"No man, it's just a shitty cordless," I hartle.

I'm now beginning to understand. Jim is being delicate in case Renata or the kids are listening.

James continues, "Yeah man, that guy brought his girlfriend up to blow you, and then he started drinking all the rider booze, and then he fell down, and then we ALL wanted her to blow US too, and then they had a fight, and then he passed out, and then you suggested that we rip off his clothes and send him down to the lobby naked with a joint stickin' out of his ass!"

Oh, that guy?

Now I remember.

— *set three* —

The Pyggs

And in a vision a man appeared on a flaming Cadillac and said unto us: "From this day forward you will be Pyggs with a Y...er... and two G's!"

Henry Taylor, of Henry Taylor and Associates, was slick. A Ramsey Lewis look-alike in very sharp mohair suits and in possession of one very fine smile. Henry saw us one Saturday afternoon at The Friars A Go Go as it was now called, sitting in with Glenn Smith and The Four Fables. By this time Dieter was gone and his Hammond B3 would not be missed. Dieter had been fired and The Backdoor Blues Band was now a quartet.

After our set Mr. Henry Taylor requested an audience with the group and offered his services as our manager.

A manager!

We could hardly wait to be taken advantage of.

Henry's associate Terry Fillion would handle the bookings and Henry would organize certain creative issues that needed addressing. Like the name of the group, for instance.

"Let's see here...hmmm...how about The Pigs?" says smiling Henry.

"THE PIGS?!" we cried in disbelief. "No way, man!"

"Yeah man, The Pigs, but we will spell it P-Y-G-G-S," said Henry in full creative mode.

Now that was different!

Why hadn't we thought of that? So The Backdoor Blues Band became The Pyggs.

Armed with our snazzy new name, we now needed a snappy new image. It was off to the tailor's for these boys. We were about to be suited up. The assistant tailor kneeled before me with a look of absolute disgust on his face. I had never been in a place like this before and he knew it.

"What side do you dress on?" he asked.

"Hmmm...Let's see," I thought hard for a second or two, "My bed is on the west wall facing north so..."

"What leg of your pants do you tuck your balls into?" the assistant asked in a tone much like pity.

I still had to think about it but managed to blurt out "Left side sir!" like I'd just answered a skill testing question.

The rest of the Pyggs, now armed with the proper response as a result of my recent humiliation, rattled off their dressing arrangements in confidence.

"Left," "Right," "Left," and so on.

It almost made you want to salute.

The material for these new suits, chosen by our manager for our classy new image, had to be seen to be believed. The suits were black but covered in vertical and horizontal stripes of red, green, blue, yellow and on and on, creating hybrid colours as they weaved their way east and west, north and south along the contours of our bodies.

In a word, silly.

Henry, sensing our rising displeasure, offered us a big friendly smile and said "Man, when you cats top off these suits with some fine yellow shirts and purple suede shoes you-will-be-bad!!"

That's what we were afraid of.

Henry's next idea was that The Pyggs needed some publicity photos to send out to club owners.

Location, location...always a problem, thought Henry, and, as I began to smell wood burning it was decided that the best choice for our photo shoot would have to be no other place than...The Slaughterhouse!!

It was a very hot day. The slaughterhouse, the one we were in, stunk.

Dressed in our fine suits of many colours, guitars in hand, we tip toed delicately around the gore underfoot and soon found ourselves in a rather large holding pen. BJ had a white Tele, Wood likewise with the word "AX" carved into the pick guard. Wood had decided that the E augmented 9th chord would photograph best so that was the fingering used by both BJ and Wood. I cradled my Gibson EB0 bass lovingly in my arms as Wayne, walking cane in hand, ushered in our models for this afternoons shoot.

The real pigs were glorious in their frantic rush to immortality. The photographer, now lying on his stomach in the disease-ridden pen, positioned himself between their legs and furiously began firing off rolls of film. The other Pyggs, serious blues afficionados to a man, lost it. The band was virtually doubled over in fits of hysterics. We could not control ourselves. The pigs squealed and ran amok. The photographer, now in peril of being crushed to death but professional to the bitter end, implored us to stop laughing so he could get a decent shot. We ended up at High Park where we posed around a fountain, still stinking of pig shit, for the amusement of passers-by.

I was now sixteen years old, the exact same age that I'd been a year and a half earlier when I first joined the group. I had a manager, a nifty suit and most important of all, I could now join The Toronto Musicians Association. The Union. In those days the TMA was a very powerful organization that protected its members and collected their dues. Mostly they collected dues. You must keep your union card with you at all times, as Vic Bridgewater could arbitrarily show up at your gig and fine you for not carrying it.

I was afraid of Vic. We were all afraid of Vic.

I believed in the union and only left when many years later I was scheduled to attend a meeting where I would receive my twenty-year membership pin and use of the secretarial pool washroom. Testimonial pins are important to the Godovitz clan.

I waited and waited while the trombone players aired their grievances about some silly issue or other, and having a radio interview to do I finally got up and walked out of that meeting pin less. I never went back.

Anyways, being in The Union in those days meant that you could now play the "A" rooms and our managers were about to make that an unreality.

Our first union gig was at The Broom and Stone, a cavernous curling rink, where we opened the show for Shawn and Jay Jackson and The Majestics. Shawn Jackson was and is a Toronto legend famous for her amazing vocal ability, good looks and the most brilliant smile to ever light up a stage. The Pyggs, now nattily attired in their suits of many colours, died the death.

The greaseballs didn't want to know and heckled us mercilessly throughout our set.

It didn't matter, as I was now a Union man bombing in an "A" room.

After that gig, we bombed in all the places Henry put us into. The Club 888, with its revolving stage depositing us in front of a very hostile audience; The Gogue Inn at the Luttrell Loop, where purple shirted toughs in 30" bell bottoms laughed at our test patterned finery! On and on the humiliation went. We were no longer a serious blues band. We were a bloody novelty act!

Drummer Wayne Wilson had had enough of the suits and the lousy gigs and skipped off to Montreal with his buddy Charlie Smith to live on a commune. Charlie was a drug-addled hippie of no fixed mentality who once pushed me off a subway platform at Yorkville station and wouldn't let me get back up. I only survived by remembering which direction the train would be coming from and then gingerly running like hell to the opposite end of the platform where enjoyment boy Charlie couldn't stop me from getting up. Someone had called the cops so we ran up to the exit only to be met by one of Metro's Finest and instantly collared for public mischief. Fortunately for me the cop was a great friend of the Pillings and he let us go with a stern warning. I never went near the subway with Charlie again.

Around this time Henry Taylor began promoting shows at Club 888. Occasionally I would be asked to act as a runner during these shows. The Ike and Tina Turner Revue were this evening's feature attraction and I was told to be at the club early, in case any running was required. The dressing room area at Club 888 was the only access point to the stage itself. Henry, spotting me out front, said, "Go up on that stage and see if everything is alright." Even though Henry could easily just walk over the five feet necessary to accomplish this task himself from the front of house, I took my orders and dashed off, opening the dressing room door to fulfil my appointed mission. Keep in mind that I still didn't wear glasses at this time so my world looks not unlike a photographic filter with Vaseline on the lens. I'm not blind enough however to notice that The Ike-Ettes are in various stages of undress, and Ike is sitting in a chair with a barber's bib around his neck, having his "process" attended to. Everything was fine on stage and I dashed back down the stairs, through the dressing room and out into the hall.

"Everything's fine on stage Henry."

"That's good man," says Henry, "but see if there's enough water up there for the band, will you?"

I darted off on this important mission and was sure to avert my eyes as I bowled through the dressing room once more. There was indeed enough water on the stage to save the evening's performance.

Henry sent me up at least two more times on likewise fruitless quests and it was only then that I noticed the clickety-clack of stiletto heels racing after me. Tina Turner spun me around and began screaming in my face, "What's the matter with you, white boy? You some kinda pervert or somethin', racin' through our room like that without knockin'?" I manage to stammer out that, as I don't wear glasses, I can't see too much anyway and that the promoter, one Henry Taylor, kept sending me up that way.

"Show me this man!" she screamed and I wasted no time fingering Henry.

Tina Turner tore a strip and a half off poor old Henry and I made myself invisible until show time where I would be treated to the sound of legend.

Ike's greasy "Process" looked wonderful.

Despite how this may read I always liked Henry Taylor. He never ripped us off, and if anything, he was only guilty of managing the wrong act. The best thing he did for us proved to be the last thing he did for us. The Pyggs were scheduled to open for Mandala at the Milton Arena.

We had to find Wilson! Our drummer had run off to join a hippie commune in Montreal.

I never knew about this back then, as I was too young to be let in on band politics, but BJ told me about it a couple of days ago. They were quite right in suppressing the information as I would've freaked had I known.

BJ and Wood hitchhiked to Quebec and actually found him. Seemingly impossible tasks were quite easy to accomplish in the Sixties. It was just like that back then but finding him was one thing, they still had to convince Wilson that this was The Big Gig.

"Wilson, man, The Pyggs are opening for THE FUUUCKIN' MANDALA, MAN!!!"

"Yeah man, I'll do it," says Wilson thoughtfully.

A squirrel breaks wind.

"Donny!" says Wood with a goofy grin.

(All three in solemn unison) "Donny."

Donny Troiano would be on that stage over there in the cool shade of Milton Arena about ten this evening. We didn't have to be told to be early for this one. Tonight we play our first arena gig and we get to do it with the Mandala. Our gear, fresh out of the back of the wagon is off to the side until the headliner's equipment is set up.

"You don't want your stuff in the way when Roly and Carmello arrive guys," we'd been forewarned. Randy "Dandy" Markowitz, their manager and a former children's television character was checking out the venue.

"Concrete floor...shit acoustics...smells bad...small-town hockey rink."

Just then a huge truck roars up to the back loading bays and finds its brakes just shy of the door. The doors open and Toronto's most renowned road crew scramble out of the cab.

Roly Paquin and Mellow Carmello Pallumbo.

Without skipping a beat the back door of the cube is ripped open and both roadies are up on the truck. The sight of the beautiful Traynor Custom Special cabinets, their silver mesh shimmering in the midday sun, had us gasping in awe from our vantage point beside the stage.

The Custom Special was the biggest amp on the scene. They even had cooling fans in the side so the tubes wouldn't overheat. We realized that we've been inching forward towards the truck.

"Back off or you'll get hurt," one of them said with not a trace of emotion in his voice.

With that said he pushed the speaker cabinets off the tailgate, the six-foot high tailgate of the truck! The cabs hit the floor with an awful crack.

Hmmm..Where have I heard that sound before?

Next come the glass-tube amplifier heads. Giving the lads their proper due I must say that these delicate items were not kicked off the truck but just sort of dropped roughly. Now, with the drums and guitars, DONNY'S TELE amongst the pile, lying in a heap, it was time to get to work.

"You guys in the opening act? C'mon in," says Carmello, ushering us into the stars dressing room. I guess we had kinda followed Donny's Ax into the backstage area.

"What's the name of your group?" he asks.

"The Pyggs," we mutter, embarrassed.

"Yeah...right," says Carmello and stifles a little grin. "You guys wanna see Troiano's guitar?"

Someone passes gas.

The sacred icon is removed from the case.

"You the guitar player?" says Carmello offering BJ the guitar.

"No man, Harp," BJ says, "Him" and points at Wood.

Wood is passed the holy ax.

Someone passes gas. I suspect it's Wood.

"Donny" Wood peels off a few nice licks and ends with a good chord, E augmented 9th, our old friend from the slaughterhouse story. I glance down and swear he's poppin' a bone.

"How does Donny get that tone man?" Wood asks like he's sitting with Jesus.

"We don't usually tell people that but you guys seem okay so I'll show you," and with that he motioned for us to close the dressing room door.

Placing the hallowed instrument of God gently down on the bench we were first bewildered and then totally freaked out to see him extract a bottle of lighter fluid from a tool box and then proceed to light the guitar on fire.

Wood almost passes out.

"And if you want a creamy tone cover the neck of your ax in butter and leave it overnight on top of a hot water rad," Carmello snickers as we exit.

We didn't wear the suits that night and Wilson left for good soon after to be a communal hippie.

*Left to right:
Actual pig,
Wayne Wilson,
Dave Wood,
Greg Godovitz,
John Bjarnason*

*At London Gardens
Left to right:
John Bjarnason,
Greg Godovitz,
Wayne Wilson,
Dave Wood,*

Photo: Robin Bjarnason

Imagine No Possessions
– a Cat Stevens story

When the Pilling's had left for England they somehow ended up in Cat Stevens backing group.

They played mostly package shows with Cat that featured The Walker Brothers, Englebert Humperdink and a new guitar sensation named Jimi Hendrix. They even performed at the Paris Olympia and at the prestigious Saville Theatre in London, which was then owned by Mr. Brian Epstein. I'm glad I never found out about all of this until after they returned to Canada because all I was doing was wearing the silly Pyggs suit and bombing in R&B venues. I would have been green with envy.

Anyway, I was chosen to accompany Skip Prokop's wife Marsha to see Cat perform at Massey Hall during his Tea for The Tillerman era. By this time I was in Fludd and we did many shows with Lighthouse, and as they were gigging, I got to take Skip's wife to the concert. I told Brian and Ed that I was going, never questioning them as to why they were not, and they told me to say hello to good old Steve, which was Cat's real name.

I wrote out a little note about how I was currently working with the Pillings and how, if I had only been sixteen when they went to England that I too would have been in his group and so forth and so on. I sent the little note backstage. His show was tremendous and afterwards we were invited back to the star's dressing room!

The postage stamp sized room was filled to capacity with the usual assortment of record company types, fans, and groupies but there he was, my new pal, good old Cat and I immediately went over and introduced myself.

As I stood there with my hand extended in friendship Cat sized me up and then offered to the room at large, "Are you the guy that sent me that fucking note backstage? Look mate, the fucking Pillings ripped me off, right? They took equipment of mine that didn't belong to them, right!"

It got very quiet in that room.

The centre of attention had shifted from HIM to me.

I still had my hand out, my foolish grin now frozen in place.

"The Pillings are NOT MY FRIENDS!!" he wailed.

My skin colour up to this point was like a ripe pomegranate, but as I became somewhat conditioned to my humiliation I began to thaw out and lamely offered, "I never ripped you off, man."

With that, Marsha Prokop, who I'm sure was absolutely thrilled to be there with me, grabbed my elbow and backed us out of the room.

Now all was clear. This is why the Pillings were not in attendance. I had been had!

Looking back on it now, so many years later, sitting here in my striped boxer shorts and pecking this out with one finger, something just came to me. Shortly after this episode Cat Stevens changed his name to something in the order of Yucachew Bogadin and became a disciple of mystical mayhem.

He gave away everything!

All of his stuff!

Perhaps I, Salmon Rushfan, had shown him the error of his ways.

And so I say, before jumping back in time a few years, and continuing my story: "Accuse not thy neighbour of pilfering the Selmer column speakers and beer encrusted microphones. Forsake your worldly possessions and wear a clean turban at all times."

So let it be written, so let it be done...

— *set four* —

The Mushroom Castle

I couldn't help but overhear
The wind was whispering in my ear
Had I known or realized
The place I loved was oh so near
Sapphire world is hanging by a string
Now it's gone, yes it's gone
Won't you come and live with me inside my Mushroom Castle?
Crystal air and flowing hair of white horse silver mane
Won't you come and live with me inside my Mushroom Castle?
Crystal air and flowing hair of white horse silver mane

A little theme song written for The Mushroom Castle by Brian and Ed Pilling.

Now dust off those caftans, light that joss stick, turn on that lava lamp and read on...

Left to right: Kerry Crawford, Eddie Schwartz, Peter Flaherty, Lyndon Henthorne, Greg Godovitz.

Lyndon Henthorne ran The Head Shop on Scollard Street in the Village. He was a drummer who looked a bit like Pete Townsend and because of this, Lyndon was a mod. He was a dedicated follower of fashion.

The Head Shop sold psychedelic posters, incense, lava lamps, rolling papers and little flasher adaptors that would make the lights in your room blink on and off. Blinking lights were essential in those chemically imbalanced times.

One night Lyndon had to leave on an errand and as I was just standing there, watching the blinking lights, he deputized me into minding the store. It wasn't long before one very stoned hippie came in, looking for one of those flasher thingies.

"There's none left man," I said, looking around and under the counter like I knew what I was doing.

The hippie called my bluff.

"How 'bout the one that's working right there," the hippie said and pointed over my shoulder to the blinking lamp in the corner.

"I guess I can sell you that one," I said as I made my way over to the blinking lamp.

I unscrewed the red light bulb that was blinking on and off and stuck my finger into the socket to dig out the flasher. It's a funny thing but there is just enough moisture on your fingertips to insure one hell of a shock when you attempt this.

The lamp crashed against the wall as I crashed into the counter.

The flasher rolled on the floor and was retrieved by the hippie.

"That'll be a buck man," I said, readjusting my cool and with that the transaction was complete.

As the hippie left Lyndon returned.

"Anything happen?" he queried.

"Nah, I just sold the last flasher from that lamp over there for a buck," I told him.

"I hope you unplugged it first," he chuckled, lighting up a thin joint.

The first time I ever smoked a joint was at Lyndon's parent's house. I believe they were out at the time. Lyndon's very cool guitar player Kerry Crawford was over and they had just dropped acid. They smoked me up and put me in Lyndon's bedroom to amuse myself while they tripped. I amused myself by nearly burning his parent's home to the ground after I found a Mexican metal lampshade that had cut out stars and crescent moons on it and decided that it would look great on one of the candles that were burning in the bedroom. The images flickering on the walls and ceiling were very nice to look at.

They were sort of...funny. In fact they were hilarious and soon I was doubled over in fits of sidesplitting laughter. It was the funniest thing I had ever seen. Remember when pot could do that to you?

It took about two minutes for the flame from the candle to ignite the metal lampshade and soon there was a very comfortable blaze going in Mr. and Mrs. Henthorne's suburban house.

I was laughing and laughing.

Smelling smoke the two cosmic travellers burst into the room and with a hearty "WHAT THE FUCK ARE YOU DOING MAN!" set about extinguishing the fire and getting me under control.

Imagine what I could have accomplished had I dropped the acid.

Now Lyndon and Kerry had a group that included Eddie (Hit Me With Your Best Shot) Schwartz on 12 string Rickenbacker and Ed's long time pal Peter Flaherty on electric piano. The later two were originally in a duo called The Beauts and later The Chosen Few which of course would be perfect for the mostly Jewish Mr. Schwartz but not necessarily so for the extremely Irish keyboardist. Their new group was called The Mushroom Castle, which was a just and true name for the times. Eddie, who would go on to become one of this planet's great song writers was already showing a great talent in that area and the group would feature his earliest folky psychedelic offerings. Even though I had met Lyndon in the Village, he was after all a Scarborough boy and as my developing musical reputation had preceded me I was soon asked to replace their departing bass player.

We set about rehearsing in a local YMCA and things were quickly sounding great until we noticed Kerry's predilection for never playing the same thing twice. This would spark great controversy as Eddie, our chief songwriter, couldn't understand why the same greatness could not be repeated with every successive play of the tune.

(I just got off the phone with Ed, now living in Nashville, who reminded me that it took him twenty years to understand Kerry's shoulder shrugging attitude and enigmatic smile when queried about this very lack of consistency. Kerry, Ed pointed out, was already bored with the last riff after only a play or two and was stretching his musical boundaries even then. As a guy who has been singing the

same lyrics and pounding out the same notes for twenty five years with Goddo I think that I now get it too.)

Needless to say this lack of shared musical adventure often resulted in childish tantrums and arguments.

The rot had set in.

Soon it was time for Lyndon and Kerry to bid us adieu and they did. Enter Dave Wood and Wayne Wilson, my old pals from The Pyggs. I convinced Schwartz and Flaherty that these two would be the right replacements and I was right. Wilson's guru mentality had a way of showing up in his drumming and Wood, eschewing his latent greaseball leanings had become chemically imbalanced enough on acid to find the various raga influenced riffs needed to fulfil our collective delusion.

We were now Toronto's Avant Garde rock band! All that was missing was the wrong management.

Eddie Schwartz had two friends, who called their fledgling company G&G Productions, managers, and soon we had direction, promo, and snappy new stage clothes. Times being what they were it was decided that collarless Indian caftans of varying hues were de rigueur so this is what we got. I always have a chuckle when I think about Wilson's choice of green fuzzy caftan which looked like he was wearing someone's front lawn.

On him it looked good.

Because of our new Hebrew connection we soon found ourselves playing at the Jewish Community Centre. The Jewish Y we called it. The best thing about these gigs is that Jewish maidens all seem to have big jugs and in those carefree days were only too happy to share them with longhaired WASP-types in caftans. The worst thing about these gigs is that we were usually paired with G&G's other feature act The Chosen Few. These guys, who are probably all millionaire dentists now, stunk. They had lovely matching polyester leisure suits, sort of Elvis Las Vegas, and the best equipment daddy could buy. They did songs like The Four Seasons 'See You In September' and other really wimpy pop. We resented the shit out of these guys because we believed ourselves to be real musicians.

At this time I was playing a Gibson EBO bass through a Traynor Custom Special amp. After seeing Mandala I just had to have an amp with a fan built into it. The high point of The Mushroom Castle's short-lived run was a gig with The Hollies at the O'Keefe Centre. We were scheduled to play with not only them but also Spanky and Our Gang and Grant Smith and The Power who currently had a hit single cover of The Spencer Davis Group's 'Keep On Runnin.' The Chosen Few would also be singing 'See You In September.' The big night arrived and we found ourselves in the O'Keefe Centre.

We would be playing in the upper foyer.

THE UPPER FOYER?!

What fresh hell was this? Our dreams of "big time" glamour were dashed once more. We could see the crowd filing in, programs in hand as they studiously ignored us in the search for their seats. My Mom angled for position as she shot off a roll of time grasping black and white film. We finished to a smattering of applause as the last stragglers made their way into this hallowed concert venue. I had to wonder how The Chosen Few had fared at the opposite stairwell.

And then, the stuff of legends. Spanky and Our Gang cancelled due to illness. The Mushroom Castle would have to play on the main stage after all. My blue silk caftan, only marginally soiled with foyer flop sweat now glistened majestically as I made my way to centre stage.

"Good evening ladies and....blarp," and I could see the beautiful blue electrical arc leave the mic only to plant itself directly on my tender young lips. I was blown back at least ten feet by the improper ground where I landed at the bass drum of my rhythm pal's kit. The sound of two thousand people laughing is still ringing in my ears.

"Ha Ha Ha, did you see that kid almost get electrocuted?"

Nice caftan.

That is all I remember about that gig but Peter Goddard summed up our performance in the old *Toronto Telegram* thusly:

"Similarly, one admired the Mushroom Castle's enthusiasm but not their musical results, their potential but not their performance."

What the fuck was this guy saying? My Mom still dutifully glued this early review into a scrapbook along with the photos.

Another writer, Ned Winapple, saw us this way:

THIS WEEK – SPECIAL REPORT:
THE GROWING MUSHROOM

There has been much interest lately in the growth of the musical group The Mushroom Castle. When they appeared in the Alliston

Ontario arena recently they impressed the promoters with their boldness in pushing their talents with original material. Before the evening was over they had completely won over the packed house.

If any group was growing in popularity it would certainly have to be The Mushroom Castle. I interviewed them and heard them play at Boris's, a coffee house in Toronto's Yorkville village. The leader of the group is bass player Greg Godovitz, who personally doesn't like playing much in the village (lie), but he does like to travel. Some of the boys are in school but prefer working in the band. Although the boys don't know when their first record will be released they do have recording dates throughout April. They play all original material. Greg stated that the best place he has played was Cinecity (a soft seat theatre on Yonge Street with a very good light show). In the future, the group would like to record and establish their name. Dave Wood is the group's lead guitarist. He personally doesn't like to travel but he would like to play with the group as long as possible. Dave digs the clothes he wears, as do Wayne, Peter and Eddie. They all say it represents their music. Dave has been with a few other groups, which gave him experience working with bands. (what?) He says when the group records he would like the first song to be 'Magic Land' written by Greg Godovitz (possibly the worst flower power era song ever written).

Wayne Wilson is the drummer of the group and has worked with Dave for a long time. He previously played with The Pyggs and has gained much of his experience from them. Wayne has been playing with groups for about three years.

Eddie Schwartz, the group's rhythm guitarist and chief songwriter is a high school student. When he records he says he would like the first song to be 'We've Won The War' (can't remember how bad this song was). Eddie has been with other groups but they weren't original so he left. Both Eddie and Peter decided that to get anywhere in the business the group must be original. Eddie writes most of the songs with Greg and says that if you are in music you should be creative. (Let's see now, exactly how much of 'HIT ME WITH YOUR BEST SHOT' did I write... er...none!) Peter, who is the organist and piano player, is also a student but he still finds time to work with the group.

Watch out for this group. They have developed a sound all their own that is well worth hearing. I personally like the music they play and so will you.

Huron Park Recreation Centre presents

THE CHOSEN FEW

THE MUSHROOM CASTLE

JULY 1

8:30 PM   **$1.50**

This Week
THE STATIC JOURNEY
presents
Thursday THE MUSHROOM CASTLE
Friday THE CHOSEN FEW
Saturday The MUSHROOM CASTLE
Sunday LEIGH ASHFORD

Well done Ned Winapple!

Now there had always been an undercurrent of hostility brewing between Eddie and myself so it seemed inevitable that it would lead to us breaking up. Looking back on this group it was a great experience as we were one of a handful of band's doing completely original material at this time. It also taught me a valuable lesson in paying back debts as one of the managers took me to small claims court over the repayment of $100. Peter Flaherty was a witness for the plaintiff who said under oath, "Mr. Godovitz was always borrowing money from somebody."

The Mushroom Castle was finished.

Magic Land
There's a land I know with flowers in the park
And the people there do strange things in the dark

..there's more to this but for the sake of my own sanity I cannot continue. By Greg (flowers in his ass) Godovitz.

The Air That I Breathe
— a John Mayall story

As I glanced over to the stage right sidelines, I couldn't help but notice Bluesbreaker's guitar whiz Mick Taylor checking out our set. The Rockpile was, as usual, packed to the rafters with a horde of sweaty, stoned out hippies all there to celebrate the blues. As we were fast becoming Rockpile favourites we finished our encore to thunderous applause and stumbled offstage. I ran straight into Mick who put out his hand and said, "I really dig your bass playing man, my name's Mick Taylor, do you want to join me and check out the other group?"

Mary Lou Horner, The Rockpile house band would soon take the stage so Mick and I found a seat in the upper balcony and waited for them to come on. It amazed me how young this guy was, a beautiful English kid with a mass of brown curls framing an angelic choirboy face. This kid had replaced Eric Clapton in John Mayall's famed band. We talked small talk, his girlfriend Rose lived in London, Ontario and he told me he would be leaving Mayall in two weeks to join another band but didn't mention which one. After a few tunes by Mary Lou Horner, Mick invited me up to the dressing room for a drink. The Rockpile dressing room easily accommodated five or six people so the twenty already in there made for a very cosy atmosphere. Mick handed me his famous Gibson SG and asked me to show him the chords to one of the songs we had just performed. I could not believe this, this guy was a guitar god and here he was asking me to show HIM something.

All of a sudden the relaxed vibe was shattered by the sound of a huge fart. Conversation died, my fingers froze on the strings. Not ten feet away was the door-less toilet and sitting on the bowl, bigger than life, was John Mayall. Slouched over, arms resting comfortably on his knees, he eyeballed the room and then...BRAAACK...another fine effort. The people in the room, mostly hangers-on and groupie types, began rising and leaving the room, perhaps to allow the great man his privacy. I sheepishly handed the sacred instrument back to Mick who immediately had the chord changes memorized and began to play them note perfect as I arose to take my leave. Mick just laughed and said, "No, man, stay, he does this kind of thing all the time to wind people up."

That was all well and good but at the same time it was beginning to get a bit rank in there so we exchanged phone numbers and I split to watch their performance.

Two weeks later Mick Taylor was a Rolling Stone.

— *set five* —

Sherman and Peabody

Douglas (Buzz) Shearman was gaining a reputation as the hottest new front man in Toronto. As a soulful vocalist with soul spinning dance moves, he, like so many others at the time, aspired to be the next George Olliver. His band, The Bo Street Runners were an R&B outfit from Streetsville who had been voted Toronto's best non union act and, in his purple outfit with six inch Spanish waist band and matching cape, Buzz was a whirling dervish of fevered soul passion. With the recent demise of The Mushroom Castle I found myself back jamming with BJ, Wood and Wilson. For some reason Peter Flaherty was still along for the ride as well. Probably because his younger brother John humped equipment for us. Still under the G&G management flag one of them decided to pair us up with the aforementioned whirling dervish and of course I sulked mightily, thinking that I should take over lead vocalist duties.

John Bjarnason tells it like this...

"We wanted a front man and you wanted to be the star. Your time wasn't right yet. We started rehearsing with Buzz in Peter Flaherty's garage. You were still "The Kid" to the rest of us."

Being The Kid was great for pulling chicks and half price movies but lousy when it came to getting respect. I grudgingly accepted my demotion but I had to admit, we did sound good with Buzz out front.

Buzz was the perfect guy to front our new group and we were soon christened Sherman and Peabody Ltd. in deft homage to the cartoon heroes of the same name. Our set list covered a lot of the same blues material we had done with The Pyggs but there was a psychedelic soul element now in place with songs like 'Sookie Sookie' by Steppenwolf, The Chamber's Brother's 'Uptown To Harlem', and 'Killin' Floor' by The Electric Flag.

Buzz was never afraid to drag up his R&B roots and the odd knee-drop and soul-spin worked their way nicely into his onstage repertoire of moves. The best thing about the new band is that nobody mentioned matching suits so we quickly adopted individual hippie styles currently fashionable in 1968. Silk scarves had replaced love beads, striped jackets for caftans. Sunglasses all around. Everybody was jamming. Fuelled by LSD we would lock into a groove for hours, from up-tempo to take it down low, from paint blistering loud to pin-drop dynamic. No one was bored, audience and musicians locked together in a free form spiral of psychedelic delight. At points BJ, Peter and Buzz would exit the stand while Wood, Wilson, and I blistered through a lengthy Cream-styled 'Spoonful.' The Village scene was still happening and we stepped up appearances at The Flick and El Patio. I remember one night having to escape The Flick as three different girls, all of whom I had professed undying love to, had shown up at the same time to see me. Wilson placed his hand on my shoulder and sagely intoned, "You better get the fuck out the back door man, better to leave with none than to have three beating your ass."

Discretion being the better part of valour I did a quick duck out the back and never saw any of them again.

The old Masonic Temple, once Club 888 and greaseball central had now become The Rockpile, a stoned-out Hippieland where like-minded individuals, or out-of-minded individuals could watch or butterfly dance to the great bands of the Flower Power era. With a great San Francisco-styled light show of swirling oil and water projections it was the perfect place to expand your consciousness while grooving to some serious sounds. The place held about twelve hundred comfortably but was usually jammed packed, standing room only most nights. As musicians, we just strolled in the backstage door, avoiding the prohibitive cover charge of $2.50 to see artists like Spirit, Freddie King, and a galaxy of touring American and English soon-to-be superstars.

We soon found ourselves playing in support of Albert King,

Kensington Market, John Mayall and just missed out on a chance to open for Led Zeppelin because Dave Wood was at the Ex and nobody could find him. I went to the show anyway. The buzz was all over town about ex-Yardbird's guitar player Jimmy Page's new group and the hall was under siege with musicians and fans alike trying to get in. I ran into Ed and Brian Pilling out back who didn't have tickets.

"Here Godo, do us a favour and go tell John Bonham that we're out back and we can't get in, there's a good lad," said Ed and I dutifully trudged upstairs and knocked on the dressing room door. With visiting English pop stars in town the groupie level was well up and the legendary Zep drummer reluctantly tore himself away from this evening's distraction and came to the door.

"Can I help you?" he asked, eyeing me suspiciously.

Over his shoulder I saw Jimmy Page, cigarette dangling from smirking lips, fingering a guitar, while an absolutely to die for girl paid rapt attention to every musical noodle.

"Brian and Ed Pilling are out back and..."

"WOT?" he shouted as his face lit up.

As he grabbed me by the scruff of the neck he screamed in delight, "WHERE ARE THEY?" and with that we leaped down the stairs three at a time where much hugging and back slapping would shortly ensue. It turned out that Bonham had been a friend from the old Birmingham club scene and this certainly seemed to be the case. Robert Plant was another story, for if legend has it correctly, it was he who borrowed the look and certain effete stage mannerisms from one Edmund Pilling.

I was still somewhat pissed off at not having the opportunity to play before this electrically charged audience, and feeling somewhat of a fifth wheel I made my way backstage to check out the new gods. The curtains parted as Zeppelin slammed into an old Yardbird's warhorse 'Train Kept a Rollin' and I was watching it from just beside Page's amp. Shitty English white boy blues, I thought, and, after a song or two more, I made my way out and over to the crowded Village streets. It was many years later, when I finally came to terms with Zep's genius, that I realized what a missed opportunity this had been to see history in the making and from a great vantage point onstage to boot. The Pilling boys had a good time though from what I've heard with Bonham and Plant sharing their couch in Scarborough after the show.

Now all this time, I was still attending high school. The music scene there had grown as well and our school in particular would eventually spawn a number of great music business luminaries like record exec Bob Roper, bassist James Morgan, engineer Hayward Parrot, drummer Marty Morin and keyboard virtuoso Gord McKinnon amongst others.

For me there was no time for most classes; the auditorium stage was perfect for fine tuning dreams of stardom and, with the help of the audio visual crew, you would soon find yourself bathed in magenta light and in full musical flight with a full PA system to practice on. I knew that my academic career was finished, and my folks, obviously disappointed at this turn of events, were now prepared to face the fact that I had another destiny in mind.

I needed however to make one final musical statement and it soon came to me courtesy of my old pals, The Beatles. 'Hey Jude' was the happening song of the day and would be my departing statement from high school.

We began rehearsing this great piece of music for the upcoming Christmas assembly. I had never resolved my differences with the music teacher who had kicked me out of class for having long hair but now I needed his orchestra. It was time to offer up an olive branch. Through pianist Gord McKinnon, always clean cut and a genius musician, we introduced the outro of 'Hey Jude' to the music dude, convincing him that George Martin's score was indeed worthy enough for his lofty consideration. With myself on guitar, Gord on piano, Marty Morin and Jim Morgan on drums and bass respectively the W.A. Porter senior band now backed us and the sound was awesome.

The assembly day soon came and all was in readiness. Our little quartet was set up on a riser off the main stage with the school band just off to the left. With the first two words of the McCartney lyrics barely out of my mouth the squeal of recognition from the gymnasium full of students was all that I needed to give this great song the full on treatment.

"And anytime you feel the pain, Hey Jude, refrain, don't carry the world upon your shoulder," I sang and the little girls ate it right up.

As we hit the outro the audience, two thousand strong, teachers, parents and students alike, broke into the "Na Na Na Na Na Na Na" chorus as the brass and woodwinds faithfully reproduced George Martin's simple genius. I truly believe that even that music teacher could see his folly, caught up, as he was to be part of such a production. The feeling that I had of uniting everyone in that room through song ranks in my top ten great moments on stage.

Right or wrong, my opinion at the time was that I had everything I needed for my future in my guitar case. As far as math was concerned, I really only had to count to four to get a song started and, as for geography, I would see the world soon enough.

The audience had swallowed us up for what they had just witnessed and with the cheers still ringing in my ears I quit school for good.

Now it was time for a change of address. Things were somewhat stressful at my folk's house what with my academic career suddenly screeching to a stop, so I decided to leave the nest. A communal situation for the band was what was needed. The times we lived in demanded it.

A hippie pot farm on the outskirts of the city perhaps?

A Victorian manse on Admiral Road in the Village with a wood burning fireplace in the main dining room where the band could practice in style?

An artist's loft on Spadina Avenue perhaps?

Hey, how about the basement of a run down store on Queen Street in the east beaches area? No running water, no toilet facilities, no place to cook or sleep and the rent is way more than we make collectively.

Perfect! Today this place is a pet store, back then it was a zoo.

After painting the windows black for privacy and throwing some mattresses on the floor in the basement, Buzz, Wood, Wilson and I moved in. It was my first home away from home. It was cosy. A complete shit hole. It was da blues man. We could eat, sleep, fuck, get stoned and jam to our hearts contents in our own little clubhouse. The group would rehearse upstairs and sleep in the cellar. "Crabhouse" is what we should have called it as very soon we were all crawling with those horrible little monsters. One has not lived until you've examined one of those gross outs while peaking on a tab of very potent Sixties acid. All claws and tentacles and it's fucking smiling at you while you're screaming for somebody to come and look at it and say it's not really there! They don't make horror movies any scarier.

"Hey man, where did you get these mattresses from man?" someone yelled out in the night.

"Buzz and I found them in the garbage, man," said Wilson.

"THE FUCKING GARBAGE, MAN, NO WONDER WE'RE ALL CRAWLING!"

But these kinds of things did little to deter our shared vision. I say shared but you will notice that BJ and Peter Flaherty were not with us. No scratching for those boys. They were safe in the warm bosoms of their respective families, seeking higher education and clean sheets. The unfortunate thing is that sometimes things can happen under those circumstances.

For instance, BJ fancied himself a very adequate second guitar player. The boys in the hole, especially Wood, disagreed. We voted, after the evening's chemical of choice had kicked in, that BJ was far too good a harp player to be burdened with the extra responsibility of having to play any guitar at all. The guilty party, an old Harmony solid body, was hiding in its case behind the furnace. After a brief trial it was decided that the guilty party should be sentenced to death.

These things must be dealt with delicately. Remembering the desecration of Troiano's legendary Tele at the hands of Mellow Carmello it was decided that burning this instrument of evil would be a wise and just thing to do. Amid much cackling and side splitting laughter the guitar was dutifully set ablaze, a touch of Ronson's here, a dash of fluid there, adding a nice glow to the squalor that was our new home. Somebody mentioned that marshmallows would have been a nice touch.

After the fire died down we checked for signs of life and although it was charred like a bad steak the guitar still looked too good. The degree of damage sought was not the degree of damage attained so I had an idea. While the charred remains of this once lovely instrument was held down on either end I gently placed the pole from a mic stand under the strings and with a mighty yank ripped off the strings, bridge, and part of the headstock in one grinding mess. Mission accomplished!

There was nothing to do but replace the ex-guitar lovingly back in its case and leave it for BJ to find at our next rehearsal. Needless to say, BJ was not pleased at all that somebody had broken into our space and ruined his guitar, but we all swore revenge on whoever had done this dastardly deed and BJ never played rhythm guitar again.

Drugs

My first LSD trip had been in the company of my old childhood buddy Phil Joyce. We bought it in the Village and soon the quaint streets of Yorkville were a veritable kaleidoscope of swirling lights, strange sounds and even stranger looking people.

Unless you have experienced acid there is absolutely no way to describe what happens to your mind as it is being altered totally out of shape. A red light becomes fire, simple car horns turn into echo-drenched symphony brass sections and really good-looking people start to grow strange disfigured appendages out of the middle of their foreheads. The most interesting things could suddenly become quite terrifying. As I still did not wear spectacles the whole thing appeared to me as a giant distorted light show.

I ended up somehow at my folks house where my Mom wanted to know what I'd been up to. I was lying on the floor grooving away to something that sounded quite unlike I had remembered it before the trip and as I took my arm away from my eyes was quite disturbed to see that my Mother's head was now six feet in diameter. Mumbled excuses about not feeling too well and down to bed where I lay awake watching swirling psychedelic pinwheels dance on my once normal ceiling.

One morning, in my folk's basement, I awoke to find Phil Joyce sitting on the end of my bed carrying on quite an animated conversation with Wayne Wilson about his drums. One problem though, Wayne was not there at the time.

Phil was talking to my bass amp.

My brother Gary, sleeping in the next bed, noticed this even if Phil did not, shook his head in disgust and gave me a look like it was better he didn't know what was going on. We had been to my pal's house across the street the previous evening where large green capsules of horse tranquilliser had been passed around. This had seemed a bit extreme even for the sixties so I spit mine out at the first opportunity and went home. Phil, being somewhat of a drug Christopher Columbus had swallowed the pill, walked barefoot through the snow, opened our side door and whistled his way downstairs in search of stimulating conversation with inanimate objects. My Mother, getting up to see what was going on, was somewhat surprised to see this barefoot vision calmly wishing her good morning as he stumbled out into the frosty morning.

Another time I sat watching the most amazing tropical fish in a huge aquarium while Jimi Hendrix's just released album 'Are You Experienced' played endlessly throughout the night. The fish, which were brilliantly coloured to begin with started to look like alien beings and at points I thought they were communicating with me. This combination of sights and sounds resulted in a wonderful trip.

The scene in the hellhole we were living in at the Beaches was that we did acid nearly every day. If you got up one morning and you wished to try and get through a day straight somebody would invariably spike your drink and within an hour you would be looking at the culprit and uttering, "You prick!" as you began lift off for the next ten hours or so. It got to the point where we could literally do everything during the course of the day while in a state of hallucinogenic disarray. Pot and hash were always around to buffer those nasty acid comedowns but booze in those days was the drug of choice for our parent's generation and totally out of the question. It's surprising that under these conditions we ever accomplished anything at all musically but the level of creativity was astounding during the many acid soaked sessions we had then.

Tommy's Lunch

Now I have already mentioned that there were no facilities in the band's fort so it was very important for us to find some place close by where we could make potty and brush our teeth. The little greasy spoon across the street was our choice as victim...er...sanctuary. We had purchased enough coffee in the joint that we could be regarded as regulars but the owner, Tommy, always had an eye out for us, like he didn't trust us or something.

Every morning we would traipse across Queen Street and file past the working citizens having breakfast so that we could wash up in his public rest room. In reality it was not much better than the one we had at our place but his at least had warm water. He also had toilet paper, another luxury item missing at our place. On the way out we were always careful to order at least a coffee so as to show support for Tommy's lovely little business. Everyone was careful not to lift too much and life went on.

We got a big boost when Tommy finally had enough of working ninety-hour weeks and hired a Newfie named Ralph for us to play with. Ralph couldn't read or write, and his ciphering was probably on a par with Jethro Bodeen, so he was a natural to become best of chums with Buzz and myself.

On Sundays we would hold an open house and girls and boys would come over to hear what new songs we had been working on that week. With the amount of pot being smoked it wasn't long before everybody had the munchies. With Tommy out of the way Buzz and I would stroll through the doors of the cute little greasy spoon, hail our new pal Ralph, and take right over.

"Hey Ralph, twenty vanilla milk shakes man, I'll handle the burgers," and Buzz would do a great job of flipping those breadcrumb laced patties.

As I poured the frozen chips into the year old grease all was right and fuzzy with the world. Ralph felt wanted and we were his new buddies.

"I never had celebrities for friends before," he would say as his drool found a clean spot on his work shirt.

After everything was all packed up Buzz and I said goodbye to our old matey Ralph and made for the door.

"Hey guys, whose paying for all that stuff?" asked Ralph, all innocent and real cute.

"No sweat, Ralph my man, we'll just do what we always do and sign for it," Buzz said confidently.

Buzz was a true artist. Of the con variety.

We obligingly signed the markers and told Ralph to hide them under the cash register until our royalty cheques came in and, off we went to feed our stoned out friends. Now this show of faith set events in motion that would prove disastrous for poor old Ralph but once this situation was in play Buzz and I could not stop.

We had became very good fry cooks.

One lazy Sunday afternoon, weeks later, there was some rather frantic pounding at our door. It was good old Tommy, of Tommy's Lunch over to pay us a surprise visit.

"I want to see Buzz and Greg, RIGHT FUCKING NOW!" he yelled and we thought that this was very rude indeed, seeing as it was the Sabbath and all. In his hand was a huge pile of yellow restaurant receipts.

"I found these under my cash register and there's about $500.00 worth of meals owing to me here from youse two," he said, pointing with great confidence at Buzz and myself like he actually had us.

"Can I see one of those?" asked Buzz all innocent like.

Tommy grudgingly handed Buzz one of the chits.

"There seems to be some mistake here as this receipt is signed Buzz The Jerk sir and my last name is Shearman," said the very innocent Jerk, "and the other signature is from Greg The Goof, and Greg's last name is Godovitz."

"I FUCKIN' KNOW THAT!" Tommy screamed, "THEY'RE ALL SIGNED LIKE THAT!!"

"Well there's nothing tying us to those receipts so I suggest you have a word with your man Ralph over there," and with that Buzz closed the door on Tommy as he stormed across the street.

Ten minutes later Ralph was standing in the band's fun house and saying all kinds of stuff about getting fired because of Buzz and I. The poor guy, who had idolized us as musicians, let us brush our teeth where paying customers washed their hands, and had fed our friends when finances had been a problem, was now out on the street and in search of a sympathetic ear.

Buzz, firm hand on Ralph's quivering shoulder, his head nodding in silent understanding says, "You can stay tonight man because you're stuck, but tomorrow you'll have to split."

A true humanitarian.

Ralph slept on the floor upstairs and was gone the next morning.

We would need new lodgings ourselves shortly.

Willowdale Avenue

For some strange reason three of us were smitten by the love bug at roughly the same time. I had met a young Scottish lass named Helen, Wilson had Gina, and Wood fell for Francois, who was a former fling of mine. All three girls in their own cute little ways were complete psychos. Helen once threw an iron at me as I tried to leave her and knocked me out cold. Francois was a serious mental case who I had picked up on a beach one afternoon and balled at Brian Pilling's parents' apartment. Because Wood knew this there was a constant resentment brewing which this French cretin would constantly use to her advantage. The only thing going for her was that she was a total tramp with a great body. Her level of conversation on a good day would be like talking to a fish. Gina was sort of Olive Oily and okay on her own but when these three were together we could always be assured of much unrest.

The obvious solution of course was to have all of us live together in a semi nice house in suburbia. Buzz would live there too as the lone bachelor. At one point, Ray Daniels, who had just begun managing a new local trio called 'Rush' (he still manages not only Rush but Van Halen as well) lived with us and helped out on occasion at gigs. I recall Alex Lifeson, Rush's guitarist coming by once in a while but whether he joined in on the jamming is lost to time.

Soon the neighbours could not only enjoy the extremely loud musical offerings from the basement but also the knock down, drag 'em out domestic disputes from a bunch of zonked out hippies. The basement was full of broken bottles, the toilet was constantly plugged and there was something so unbelievable backing out of the bathtub that a smarter man would have charged admission to see it. There was never any solid food in the fridge and we would amuse ourselves playing poker with the loser having to eat a spoonful of mustard, mayonnaise or even chew on something from the ashtray in lieu of money exchanging hands. As I had always been a bit queasy in the old stomach department, I soon became a fair poker player.

I remember one summer day using absolutely anything left in the cupboards to concoct a sort of stew-ish type dinner. As we tucked into it, Wilson spooned out and proceeded to show around the table either (a) an average size beetle or (b) a large cockroach, causing me to run to the toilet, further adding to the backup.

Wilson, ever the realist, merely placed the offending bug beside his plate and kept eating.

The Electric Circus

There was now a new concert club in town to rival The Rockpile, called The Electric Circus. Housed in a large former office building on Queen Street east of Yonge, (and soon to be the original CHUM-CITY TV studios), this place was a godsend for acidheads. Various rooms catered to your psychedelic needs, including a room with a soft foam floor that would give you the impression of walking on marshmallows when you stepped through the entrance way, and another room that looked like a bee hive with circular tubes in the walls that comfortably housed two people for a little quiet reflection or making out if so desired.

Strobe lights and black lights were everywhere, adding to the disorientation and the music was pumped at mind numbing levels into the various rooms. The main concert area was awash in a vast array of lighting and featured at times a very strange fire-eater who was most sinister to look at while he did his bit. Dressed entirely in black with a pompadour of snow white hair, his skin tone was like a dead man's and, with a dark Dracula-esque voice that smacked of eastern Europe, he scared the shit out you when you were tripping. I was once dispatched to fetch him something from his loft and the girl and I who entered his home were absolutely freaked out by the black magic icons and shrunken heads in the place. We did not stay there long to snoop but found whatever it was that had been requested and split fast.

Soon we were playing gigs there as well and once backed Country Joe and The Fish just after the Woodstock movie was released. I had seen original Woodstock posters, thousands of them and now each worth a lot of money, on every wall, store front and telephone pole in the Village and even though the group line up was impressive, never thought to take one home. Anyway, Country Joe was everything you might have expected, they stunk, the only song of any note being the ubiquitous 'Fish Cheer.'

"Gimme an F, gimme a U, gimme a C, gimme a K"

"What's that spell??!!" and the hippies would try and figure it out.

I would see other great bands like Rhinoceros, Teegarden and VanWinkle, and The Foundations in this venue. After hanging out with The Foundations, whose 'Build Me Up Buttercup' and 'Baby, Now That I've Found You' had been huge hits, and jamming with them, they invited me back to England with them, convinced that I had a great future there. Putting it down to the fine pipe of opium we were enjoying, I declined the invitation.

I also remember this very strange group from the Sarnia area called Zoom who played the room once. The handful of us in attendance there got off not so much on the band's music, but the sight of the guitarist/vocalist dressed in cowboy chaps made of shag carpeting careening about the stage like a demented puppet. Kim Mitchell even then was a memorable presence.

> In February of 1969 *The Toronto Telegram* reported:
> *Mainstream Records out of New York swept through town a few weeks back and signed up just about everything in sight including Nucleus, Cathy Young, The Yeomen, The Male Bagg, and Sherman and Peabody Inc. Presumably what they have in mind is the initiation of some sort of Toronto scene promotion campaign which could just boost some of our local bands into the North America spotlight. And so it goes. It's becoming clear that we're now involved in something of a boom period for the Canadian recording industry. Let's enjoy it while we can.*

Shel Saffron was the man behind Mainstream Records and he was indeed signing up everything in sight. I've never heard of The Male Bagg, and although familiar with The Yeomen had never actually seen them. Nucleus, on the other hand, was a great band and the record that they would create would perfectly encapsulate the hallucinogenic flavour of the times. Cathy Young was a great Earth Mother of a hippie folk singer. She was a well-liked Yorkville troubadour who would pull out her acoustic guitar at the drop of a tab and soothe your frenzied psyche with her gentle, introspective

TRAVELS WITH MY AMP

Sherman and Peabody Inc.:
Left to right: Peter Flaherty, Dave Wood, Buzz Sherman, John Bjarnason,
Greg Godovitz, Wayne Wilson.
Photo: Frederic Lewis

songs. I spent many wonderful hours in her company, and, as I lusted after her older sister Chris (which, alas, was never realized), we remained good friends with no affairs of the "hard" to interfere with our friendship.

I remember once Cathy and I going to The Purple Onion on Yorkville to see The Influence from Montreal, an amazing band that featured Canadian guitar legend Walter Rossi. At some point his vintage Gibson Les Paul went missing and suspicion fell in the general direction of Cathy and yours truly as we had been in their dressing room while they went on stage. I had nothing to do with the theft of his guitar and I sure hope that neither had Cathy but years later when I was reintroduced to Walter on an early Goddo visit to Montreal I told him about this story. His reaction was "So where's my guitar man?" I waved him off and that was the last time I ever spoke to him.

Sherman and Peabody Inc. were a great live band, but with the exception of a couple of early attempts at bad song writing we were basically just a white trash blues band doing "covers." Shel Saffron probably figured we could sell a couple thousand units to our core audience and signed us regardless. Nothing ever came of our New York record deal, which probably hurried along the end of the group.

Things were changing in the Village as well. The Aquarian Age ethics of peace, love, and understanding were being replaced by rip offs, violence, and paranoia. One night BJ, Buzz, and I were casually strolling along Yorkville when this very tough looking dude comes out of the shadows and ominously intones, "Hey hippies, show me your fingers." Being pacifists by design and cowards by choice we dutifully comply. As BJ and I wore no rings we were quite certain that we were relatively safe.

Buzz, however, was unfortunately sporting a lovely little bauble.

"That's a nice ring man, it's now mine so take it off!" said the hoodlum who I suddenly recognized as a guy from where I grew up. There were three thugs from my old neighbourhood who the mere mention of their names would leave you shaking in fear. This guy was the worst of the three.

"But my dead Mother gave me this ring," lied Buzz. A good try though.

"If you don't give me the ring now you're gonna be joinin' her," and I knew he meant this.

It was time to make my move.

"Hey Danny, how you doin' man?" I stammered.

"I know you?" he said, sort of taken aback.

"I'm Greg Godovitz from over on Westbourne and I used...," I began but was quickly cut off with his finger wagging near my cute little face.

"You just mind your own business, and YOU!" he said, snarling at Buzz, "Give me the fucking ring, NOW!"

Which Buzz did.

(I ran into this guy at a public school reunion a few years ago. At first I was tempted to dress up but I quickly figured out that there was nobody there that I really had any need to impress so I wore shorts and a t-shirt and took my daughter which was accomplishment enough. Everyone there was of course dressed to the nines and stories of tremendous success and other bullshit wafted through the summer air. Danny was there. He had not changed at all and I assumed that prison life had been good to him. He made a point of insulting my station wagon. He had done so well that he was driving a real flash car. He was sporting nice little baubles on his chest and fingers. Just like the one he stole off Buzz those many years ago on Yorkville Avenue. I was going to bring this up but he wouldn't have understood. He would have beaten me to a pulp in front of my daughter. I soon left and realized that of course he probably had no idea of what I'd accomplished since public school. He probably couldn't read.)

Buzz's ring did look nice on him though.

Morale-wise, things were in downer mode as we were making no money, playing the same tunes over and over to the same audiences, and everyone was pretty much fed up with everyone else's old lady as happens in the close knit confines of a rock group.

The end came after we opened for The Jeff Beck Group at The Electric Circus. I am relying on BJ's memory here as I personally don't recall this gig. The acid I dropped that night must have been excellent. Apparently Buzz, suffering from Lead Singeritis was being deluded with the old "you don't need those guys, go out on your own" routine by his cronies and, with one glimpse of Rod Stewart in action, our fate was sealed.

Now I was really fucked. I had to support not only me (who I sort of liked), but also Helen (who I was quite bored with) on a salary of... well...nothing.

Helen and I moved into one of the great old houses on Admiral Road in the Village. It was one of those shared communal efforts that were very much in vogue in those days. Any food that you left in the smallish kitchen would be stolen before you could get around to eating it and with upwards of twenty hippies living there at any given time the chances of ever having a hot shower were pretty slim to none. Helen, who was of Scottish decent, was also of Scottish temperament. She could throw a punch with the best of them at the slightest provocation, and soon our pacifist neighbours were regaled with the sounds of our nightly skirmishes.

As I've mentioned earlier in my sad tale the one time that I tried to walk out on her I was hit in the back of the head with a perfectly hurled laundry iron. I awoke to see a crying Helen and sundry concerned hippies staring down on my comfortably prone body on the hardwood floor. My only thought was how to kill this witch and I managed to utter, "You'd better get the fuck out of here," before lapsing back into unconsciousness. She redeemed herself by getting a daytime job, leaving me free to practice my new Gibson SG guitar, eat loads of Kraft dinner, and fuck everything that moved.

For instance, one day I was sitting on the veranda minding my own business, absentmindedly noodling on the guitar, when I noticed a rather well endowed hippie girl, in a see through blouse, on the adjacent front stoop, smiling at me.

I nodded back.

"You wanna come over for a while," she cooed.

I was not in that room five seconds before she was pulling down the shutters and tearing off her clothes and mine. (A couple years later I ran into this chick at San Francisco International Airport where Barbra Streisand and Robert Redford were busy filming *The Way We Were*. She didn't remember me at all.)

Another time this Amazon of an English lass named Liz stopped by for a spot of tea. As I was fresh out of tea at that moment we had no recourse but to peel off and get it on. The whole thing was over for Liz and myself in about two seconds as I was absolutely freaked that Helen could return at any second. I personally enjoyed our brief time together nonetheless but for some reason it was the last time Liz ever talked to me.

At this time my gig situation was very strange. One night I found myself doing a York University pub night with a pick up band that included bassist Don Elliot of Mandala fame. I was sort of impressed but was too chemically removed to really get the picture. I somehow raised the money to rent a guitar amp at Long and McQuade (L&M) and set off for the gig with my trusty SG and my two lead guitar licks. The obvious thing to do in light of the situation was to drop acid and see how it went, which is precisely what I did. I'm pretty sure that we sucked at that gig but the punch line to this story is that I forgot to bring the amp back afterwards. By the time I remembered and went back to get it, the amplifier was long gone. This smart move landed me on the famous L&M "WHEEL," which meant that my credit was screwed and their collection man would be hot on my trail.

After Sherman and Peabody disbanded Buzz went off to form an amazing band called Flapping with two of the greatest guitar players this country had ever seen. Kerry Shapiro and Ron Merrinelli. Ron had the dubious distinction of leaping on stage at an early Hendrix gig at the Grande Ballroom in Detroit and making off with Jimi's guitar strap. Years later he would eschew such worldly treasures and shave off his own Afro to become a Hare Krishna disciple. Legend has it that his mantra chanting was on a par with his guitar playing. Kerry was an Eric Clapton look-alike who took me under his wing. (Flapping-get it?)

One night I was in the mood to visit Kerry at the band's pad on Spadina Avenue and being in no condition to walk on a lethal combo of gin and Seconal(s) I "borrowed" a bicycle from one of my house mates and proceeded over to their place. At one point I crashed into a fence and bounced off a car where I decided wisely to abandon my vehicle and stumble off on foot. Noticing that their window was slightly open I proceeded to slither through the portal in search of their front room. What I had failed to notice was that the owner of this particular hippie crash pad was walking around the corner at that very moment with his attack trained German Sheppard. Soon I had the most unpleasant feeling of my ass being turned into ground meat. My screaming awakened my friends who soon came to my rescue and notified the slumlord that I was a very welcome guest indeed, whether it be through the front door or window.

I had formed a group called, not surprisingly, Sherman and Peabody with myself on guitar, Gil (Triumph) Moore on drums, a guy called Henry on bass and good old Dave Wood as lead guitarist. Except for Gils outstanding Ed Sullivan impression, we stunk. The last thing Gil said to me when he kicked me out of my own band was, "You make it your way man, and I'll make it mine."

Little did I know at the time how powerful that Ed Sullivan impression would prove to be.

BJ and Wilson formed Whiskey Howl which would be a great white trash blues group in the fine tradition of well...er...Sherman and Peabody, only rootsier.

The times were definitely achanging.

(By the way, I remember my Mom one day asking me if I'd ever heard of Bob Dylan. "Of course I have, why?" I asked. "Oh, he's been sitting in after hours at the club (Friars) with Levon and the boys, jamming all night." My Mother had seen Dylan with The Band at their first rehearsals.)

My Own Private Altamont

Things in the house on Admiral Road were getting very strange when a really scary thing happened. There was this large black guy staying there who was dealing heroin out of the place and drawing some really undesirable people into our orbit. Voicing my concern one day that if it didn't stop I would call the cops myself, I was none too surprised when this monster came a calling on our door. Stealing myself for a quick and brutal death I grabbed a large piece of wood, which for some reason was in the room and approached the door.

"You open this door now and you'd better not have anything in your hand when you do," my new friend with the x-ray eyes said in a voice not unlike Isaac Hayes. Placing the weapon down I gently unlatched the four or five locks and peered out into the hallway.

"Now you listen here boy, I just got out of prison and I don't want to hear no talk of police. Do you understand me?" and with that he walked off.

No further explanation was necessary.

There was another guy, who I'd met in the Village, who was storing pounds of pot in our room, in exchange for a buck or two storage fee. Of course we were liberally helping ourselves to his fine product now and then to help supplement Helen's income, figuring that he was totally oblivious to our little scheme. Imagine my surprise when one day I come in the front door and just as I was starting up the stairs I was suddenly confronted with the sight of a very large and cocked handgun being pointed in my face by this maniac. Just as I was about to start crying and confess the pilfering of his profits he un-cocked the gun and said, "Hey man, cool piece, eh?"

I couldn't agree more and excused myself to the second floor toilet.

Now Helen had a friend named Heather who was living with this rip off artist named Benny. Benny was a real creep. One night Helen got into a verbal with both Benny and Heather, which escalated, to the point of Benny backhanding my girlfriend. Now while I quietly applauded his efforts I had to do something so I quickly sprang into action and punched the shit out of him. I ended up throwing him down the stairs where he gently counted sheep until arising to a fabulous headache.

Later that night I was standing out in front of El Patio on Yorkville Avenue when I was jumped by Benny and three of his polo pals who proceeded to kick me around like a World Cup soccer ball. I rolled up into a tighter ball than when I was living in my Mom and prayed for a cop to arrive. One of the Jones and Gerrard boys who had been with me at the time was suddenly conspicuous by his absence. As the local cop pulled me to my feet, friend Andy K was nowhere to be seen. Neither were Benny and his brave pals. The cop let me go with a warning.

A WARNING?

Perhaps next time I'd try to be beaten in a more acceptable fashion.

When I stumbled across Andy later, I simply had to ask him why he had abandoned me in my hour of need. He lifted his shirt to reveal a nasty looking handgun. I guess he had figured that it wouldn't have been proper etiquette to waste Benny and The Gits over the minor point of my having been outnumbered.

The writing was on the wall.

I had to get out of the Village.

Axel and Bobby were speed freaks who were east-enders and big fans of Sherman and Peabody and they offered to take Helen and me in. Out of the frying pan and into the fire.

Have you ever lived in a house full of east end speed freak greaseballs? You haven't? Lucky you.

Their nondescript house in the Greek section of Toronto was a haven for the worst drug abuse I have ever witnessed. I once stood in the kitchen washing dishes as the cops crashed through the door, guns drawn, and proceeded to bust the place. The guy who was shooting up the crystal Meth at the kitchen table actually slapped the cop's gun away and told him to "Fuckin' just cool it, man, 'til I've had my hit!" That guy is now dead. I was shitting myself. Not being a speed user, never was, never will be, I didn't understand the speed freak jones. These guys would take a bloody bullet before giving up the needle. Insanity. The cops had a good laugh at my expense when I informed them that Helen and I would indeed be getting married at some point. I was convinced at the time that they could drag us downtown for living in sin. They left with our names and a cheery, "We know where you are, speed freaks. We'll be back!"

Very reassuring.

Another time there was this guy visiting who had ripped off the local chapter of a notorious biker gang in a drug deal. As I was talking to him in the kitchen he all of a sudden started crying like a baby. I checked my last utterance to make sure that I had not said anything to set him off so when I noticed that several bikers had entered the house and were making their way towards this poor guy. We heard later that they took him out and broke both of his kneecaps.

My credo to this day is, "A place for everything and everything in its place."

I have always been a neat freak and I would clean up day and night for these guys. Speed freaks are not into good housekeeping and one morning

I awoke to a scene of carnage that was beyond belief. Mongol hordes would have been tidier. Making my way to Kenny the fat fuck's room I started to lose my mind.

"I SPEND ALL OF MY TIME CLEANING UP THIS PLACE AND YOU FUCKING SLOBS SHOW ABSOLUTELY NO APPRECIATION FOR MY EFFOR..."

My tirade was cut short by the very loud and messy crash of a whiskey bottle exploding about two inches beside my head on the wall.

Kenny, if nothing else, was a great shot.

I ran for it.

Almost as if by magic my Mom sent my two older brothers down to talk to me. We met at the beach and they stated a case which I really didn't need to hear. I was quite prepared at this point to give up the lovely Helen, take a bath, and return to the nest.

As Dorothy would have it, "There's no place like home."

— *set six* —

Fludd

*Rosicrucian subtleties
In the Orient had rise
Ye may find their teachers still
Under Jacatala's tree.
Seek ye Bombast Paracelsus
Read what Fludd, the Seeker tells us
of the Dominant that runs
through the cycle of the Suns
Read my story last and see
Luna at her apogee*

– Rudyard Kipling (Consequences)

And he never even saw us perform!

The gymnasium at Cedarbrae Collegiate was packed to capacity, the guys in attendance generally hanging along the edge of the hall or standing in the back, while the mostly female fans were seated in front of the makeshift stage. FLUDD was definitely a "chicks" group. It wasn't hard to see why as we were all in our early "pretty" twenties, with slender shirtless bodies radiant with a sprinkling of gold or silver glitter dust and bedecked in the height of English glam rock foppery. Feather boas, satin and velvet suits with optional multi coloured platform boots or ballet slippers, the better to mince around in.

Our shag cut hair was made all the more spectacular with crazy colour highlights in blue, pink, or yellow. Even our roadies got into it, one having his jet black hair treated with white accents down the centre of his head, giving him the look of a rock and roll skunk.

The band was pumping out one of its rockier radio hits as the lights pulsated in time to our massive sound. Each band member had his own core of fans with Ed, as front man, commanding the lion's share of attention from the ladies. No problem, you only needed one or two after the show to make the evening's performance a wholly satisfactory experience, so I focussed my leer on some nubile victim buying into this and rocked out in her general direction.

All at once I noticed that nary an eye, including those belonging to my own little beauty, were focused on me, but had shifted to centre stage where Ed was bumping and grinding while brother Brian ripped into his guitar solo. All I could see was row upon row of wide-eyed virginal innocence with their jaws dropped open in absolute astonishment. Checking out Ed a little bit closer I casually noted that his satin pants had split and his entire panties-less package had dropped clearly into view. Nonchalantly I turned my back and shimmied sideways until I was directly in front of the over-exposed singer.

Looking him directly in the eye I mouthed the words, "Ed... your...cock...and...balls...are... hanging...out!"

With a smile so devilish you wanted to make for the nearest church, he looked back at me and said, "I... know... get... the... fuck... out... of... the... way!"

Ed Pilling. Photo: Ed Pilling

Cock On

Anticipation grows, the crowd is overflow
On stage the lights are bright, the scene is dynamite
The band they hit the stage, they really rock the roll
The singer splits his pants, the girls all lose control
I said it's C-C-C-C-C-Cock On
It's C-C-C-C-C-Cock On
It's C-C-C-C-C-Cock On
A picture in the nude, the kids all think it's cool
Some parents must complain, the band is banned from school
The boys pull up their pants, this up-yours attitude
Reflects the way they feel, it keeps them in the news
I said it's C-C-C-C-C-Cock On
It's C-C-C-C-C-Cock On
It's C-C-C-C-C-Cock On
Girls Like It!

Written by me for FLUDD but recorded by GODDO
(WHO CARES)

"Testing, testing, one, two, thwee."

Fludd was performing at Midland Collegiate this evening and their young roadie was testing the microphones.

"One, two, thwee," he repeated, his voice echoing through the empty gym as my eyebrows began to rise up.

"Check this guy out," I said to the girl sitting next to me on the bench, "Elmer Fludd," and we both chuckled softly but cruelly.

I found out later that Bruce "Bwuce" Duncan had been wobbed of his ability to say the letter R due to cobalt wadiation tweatment as a child. This was to be a source of great amusement and concern for Bruce and all who know him to this day. I remember Bruce and I trying to hustle these two chicks after a Fludd gig up north one night. One of the girls asked him his name.

"Bwuce," he softly replied.

"Pardon me?" she said.

"Bwuce," he said once more.
"What did he say?" she inquired again in frustration.
"His name is BRUCE!" I finally said.
"Thanks Gweg," said Bwuce.
The girls now understood and chuckled softly, but cruelly.

A lot of girls, especially on the east coast, thought that Bruce was English, which of course was a jolly good thing for him and ensured a full dance card for the little wabbit. The men may not know, but those fishermen's daughters always understand.

Anyway, with the stage set, and the audience now in place, I settled back to check out Fludd at this, their second gig. With the addition of my new round John Lennon styled glasses I could actually see without massive squinting for the first time in my life.

The first thing that struck me when the house lights dimmed and the band kicked in, was the transformation of one Ed Pilling. The last time that I had seen Ed on a stage, he was sitting behind his Ringo Starr Ludwig drums with The Pretty Ones. Even sitting down he had appeared taller than me. Now he was Enormous and fronting a very loud and colourful quintet of characters called Fludd. All long hair and English Pop Stars to a man, I sat transfixed throughout their performance. The kids were eating this up, the chick I was with was eating this up, and I was eating this up. I can't recall a single song they played that night but I knew that it was destiny that had brought me to this gig.

Brian Pilling had found the missing chord in his playing, and looked not unlike the 'White Album' era Lennon but with a cocky arrogance all his own. Guitarist Mick Walsh chopped his Union Jack painted Fender Jaguar in wonderful counterpoint. The young drummer, John Andersen, literally attacked his kit with a power not unlike John Bonham, yet with a finesse that comes of years of slavish practice. The bass player, a bowlegged chap with strange eyes by the name of Graham Kuntz, would have to go.

And gone he was. The wheels were set in motion almost upon completion of the gig. It had not been Brian's intention to merely show off his new group to me, he had invited me here to show me my future.

I was at drummer John's house to begin rehearsals within the week and was present when Graham took his leave. Much sorrow and condolences as he was given the sad news, followed by much laughter and merriment as we counted off the first tune. Rock and Roll is a living thing.

Cruelty is second nature.

We learned the 'Mean Mr. Mustard/ She Came In Through The Bathroom Window' medley from Abbey Road, 'Gypsy' from the Moodie Blues, 'Reflections Of My Life' by Marmalade and 'Hey Grandma' by Moby Grape. I even got to spread my lead guitar wings with an extended version of Neil Young's 'Down By The River', where three licks went a long way.

But for me the real pay off was learning songs from the 45s that Ed and Brian had brought back with them from England. Songs like 'The Eagle Flies On Friday' by The Exceptions and Elmer Gantry's Velvet Opera songs that were miles above the more well known material that we had been rehearsing.

> 'There's a flame burnin' in my heart, and it's gonna grow
> A flickering love light, burnin' up my soul
> Flames, growin' higher
> Your love's got me all on fire'
>
> — *'Flames' by Elmer Gantry's Velvet Opera*

Great, obscure British pop songs brought to life by a group of musicians who would do them justice.

Two weeks in the Andersen's basement and we were ready. The funny thing about rehearsing in the Andersen's basement was that John was always the last to show up. The rest of us would come from great distances by bus, car or thumb and be in place at a previously designated time, only to have to wait for John to crawl down from his room, mere yards from the scene of the festivities. The other thing was his annoying habit of keeping us waiting even longer by eating his morning breakfast of wheat germ, which used to drive us nuts, to a man. His Mom would always stick up for her tardy son's nutritional needs, and, as we were practicing in her basement, we would always find some sense in the twisted logic.

This was the era of the high school dance and soon we were playing them all. High schools were great mostly because we were still young enough to pull the chicks that were having it. It was always a first order of business to scout out a quiet little nook somewhere backstage for the obligatory knee trembler. The amount of times that I was almost caught in flagrant delicto by a teacher or janitor was amazing. You'd be freshly zipped up and marginally dishevelled as the principal, suspecting full well the worst, would gently ease his young charge out of the backstage area. It was the very thrill of being caught with your pants down that made it fun in the first place.

Years later at a Goddo gig in Cambridge I was escorted to the principal's office and admonished for saying the word "shit" on stage. The principal's point being, "We have impressionable young girls out there, Mr. Godovitz."

My parting response, before getting up and ending the meeting, was, "Yeah, and do you have any idea what those impressionable young girls do, man?"

One thing soon became obvious and that was if you scored before the show your energy level was somewhat diminished, and if you scored after the show there was a good chance that the other less fortunate lads would leave you behind. Catholic schools were especially great because the nuns didn't want anyone to have any fun at all, so it was doubly adventurous when a close encounter of the sticky kind could be arranged. I know that certain feminist types are going to get upset at these kind of stories but it was a different climate in those days and I personally know of very few musicians who weren't in it for the girls in the first place.

They didn't coin the phrase Sex, Drugs, and Rock and Roll for nothing, you know.

One night at Alderwood Collegiate certain locals took offence to our effect on their women. As we sat out back waiting for the last of the gear to be loaded up an army of toughs rounded the corner and soon surrounded us. Now, in all fairness, most of the assembled had come simply to enjoy the sight of a rock group being shit-kicked but nobody in that throng took into consideration the Pilling brothers' idea about bad odds. The ring leaders had just started in on the verbal abuse, feeling somewhat fearless with the large crowd behind them, when Brian bounced out the front door and immediately began pounding one big mouth into submission, while Ed was out the back door and was quickly holding the other guy in battering ram position, trying repeatedly to put the fool's head through a giant plate glass window. Either the guy's head was very soft or the window was very strong as nothing shattered and peace was soon re-established as the Principal, teachers, and dance committee members rushed out to restore order. This was funny for us as our manager, Skinny, had been busy all evening putting the moves on the chief dance committee member, a beautiful girl named Dawn, whom he would eventually marry.

TRAVELS WITH MY AMP 81

Skinny

"Lighthouse plays for peace, Mainline plays for money, but Fludd plays for the chicks."

*William "Skinny" Tenn.
Why managers do not make good rockstars.*

*September 1971
William "Skinny" Tenn at Pacific Sound in San Francisco*

William "Skinny" Tenn was Fludd's manager. As a fast talking AM radio disc jockey out of Regina, by way of Saskatoon, he had been known as "The Slimmer Thinner Skinny Spinner." He referred to his listeners as "Boppin Boogalooers." I called him "Wild Willy."

Whatever else, Skinny was a really good manager, a 98 lb. dynamo of artist friendly representation. He also had the best nickname in Canadian rock. When we met up with him he was in partnership with Ray Daniels in a booking agency/management company called Music Shoppe International. Ray handled affairs for Rush and Skinny handled Fludd. Ray certainly made more money off of his charges but I'll wager that Skinny had more fun. Before managing us, Skinny had handled affairs for Witness Incorporated, which was a great prairies group featuring a young Kenny Shields, who would go on to further fame as lead vocalist for Streetheart, a group that would also include guitarist Paul Dean and powerhouse drummer Matt Frenette, both future Loverboys.

Even though Skinny paid little attention to my developing talents, he was slavishly devoted to Brian and Ed, and by virtue of this I got my first taste of what being a rock star could be like. With management in place, we were soon playing all the time.

Soon our set list was peppered with Brian and Ed Pilling originals. Even back in The Pretty Ones days the brothers had shown a certain skill in song writing but their new efforts showed a remarkable growth and maturity that belied their tender years. The songs now featured memorable hooks, catchy lyrics, and wonderful three part harmony parts that were perfectly suited to our abilities. It would only be a matter of time before we secured a recording contract, so we arranged a demo session at Toronto Sound Studios, and with expatriate Brit Terry Brown as engineer, we cut our first sides. I had borrowed a Fender Tele bass for this session and recall Terry getting me a beautiful sound, especially on the Pilling brothers 'Hollywood'.

> Hollywood is the place I want to go
> Hey, can you see me there?
> Movie stars, limousines and big cigars
> Hey, can you see me there?
>
> – *'Hollywood' by Brian and Ed Pilling.*

It wouldn't be long before we were really California bound.

Scarborough Fair

Our first big gig was at an outdoor event held in Birchmount Collegiate Stadium in the heart of darkest Scarborough. Hence, Scarborough Fair. We shared a bill with, among others, Paul Butterfield's Blues Band, McKenna Mendelson Mainline and Woodstock vet, Richie Havens. It was a gorgeous summer day with not a cloud in the sky. The stadium was packed and we tiptoed down the hill in our summer frocks to tear up that home to track and field. The highlight of our set and for many years to follow was a savage drum and bongo duel between Ed and John called 'Aston.' The title of this primitive marathon was a sly tongue-in-cheek homage to the poor black district of Aston, a suburb of Birmingham, England, where Brian and Ed came from.

Nobody had laughed when Keith Relf played bongos in the Yardbirds and nobody would laugh as Ed attacked his during this percussion duel. The festival audience ate it up and after briefly basking in our fleeting moment of fame we were herded up, as we had another gig later the same day. We packed up our gear and headed north for the Aurora Community Centre, thirty miles north of Toronto.

Upon arriving at the venue I happened to notice a new amp in the backstage area. A brand new Fender Reverb amp, with the legend 'Richie Havens - New York' stencilled in white lettering, had somehow made its way into our lives.

"Bruce!" I shouted, "Where the fuck did this amp come from?"

"Oh shit, Godo, we must've packed it by accident," pleaded the innocent one.

Innocent or not, at the end of the Aurora gig Bruce and I drove flat out to return the "misplaced" piece of equipment. The Fludd Bus pulled into the backstage area with minutes to spare before Richie Havens would take the stage.

The Fludd Bus

After travelling around for what seemed like ages in two borrowed station wagons, it was decided that the group would invest in an old yellow school bus. We looked at this ancient conveyance with an air of wonder and soon plans were underway to convert this dilapidated pile of junk into the tour bus from heaven. A coat or two of sea blue paint was the first order of business with the new Fludd logo emblazoned on each side in white letters three feet high. The seats were all torn out and two folding couches were installed in the front that met in the centre when folded down. A wall was built separating the band from the equipment with a handy fold down table on the passenger side, the better to lose your paltry earnings playing poker en route home from some gig up north, or to eat a fast food meal in the dead of night while the other lads slept.

As the bus was compartmentalized the heater was more than adequate but there were numerous sleeping bags on board for those draughty winter nights. If nature called, and a pit stop was impossible, you could open the hinged passenger door a bit for the old "Wiver Wat," as Bruce called it, while motoring down the road. The best feature of all, at least to a non-driving sex maniac like myself was that you could fire up the engine, with its aforementioned heating, using a flat head screwdriver for a bit of moonlight funata. And chick magnet it was. Much like today's luxurious tour buses, this primitive forerunner was just the thing to entice the ladies.

Even though there was absolutely nothing on board to get excited about, people in general, but mostly girls, couldn't wait to climb on board. There wasn't much privacy mind you but that never seemed to stop anybody from a bit of naughty fun. I remember Brian and I each supporting the leg and ass cheek of some chick that Ed had picked up at The Belgium Club in Delhi while he gave her one standing up as we roared through town. Her legs were wrapped around the metal posts as you entered the passenger compartment and, as it looked sort of uncomfortable, Brian and I offered our services. We also offered our participation but this comely lass was not having any of that.

"What do you think I am, a pig?" she asked, and that seemed reasonable enough at the time.

Things could get a little claustrophobic at times in the bus and I remember a trip up north, after a Paul McCartney and Wings concert at The Gardens that was memorable in a wholly different way. I had dined at Harry's Steak House on Church Street prior to the Wings' show. The garlic quotient at Harry's was enough to insure many years of vampire-free existence from the cheese bread alone. Garlic to me was a flatulence-inducing time bomb. By the time we were snug in our beds, head to toe like so many sardines,

I was chuckling away quietly while unleashing a torrent of noxious fumes at my friends and band mates. Their pathetic cries of, "Fuck off Godovitz!" "Knock it off Godovitz!" and "I'm warning you Godovitz," only heightened my resolve to destroy whatever peace they might have had while we motored northwards. At last, tiring of this game, I drifted into the false sense of security that sleep brings.

I knew almost at once that something was amiss when I woke up with the feeling that my air supply was in jeopardy.

Something, or someone, was covering my nose.

"Okay, hit the lights!!" someone yelled.

The interior lighting was dutifully ignited by bus driver Bruce as my eyes adjusted to the horrific sight of someone's truly horrible, pimply ass, positioned right over my deeply breathing nostrils. With the light came the terrible blast of hot air as Brian farted directly in my face. Much laughter and backslapping accompanied my somewhat modified "Wiver Wat" as I puked up Harry's gourmet meal on the 400 highway while cruising along at eighty miles per hour.

I had been taught a valuable lesson in travel etiquette.

There was a very strange occurrence another evening as I awoke out of a sound sleep with my head just behind the driver's side. Bruce, who was probably half asleep himself behind the wheel seemed to be driving more in the lane designated for oncoming traffic and as I looked over his shoulder I noticed that two rather bright lights were heading our way.

"Bruce," I said quietly but calmly, not wishing to disturb his rest while he drove, "move a foot or two to the right will you."

Bruce slightly shifted the wheel in the desired direction and the transport truck roared by, tearing off our side mirror in a shower of sparks as metal was destroyed and glass shattered. Had we stayed where Bruce was originally driving we would've hit the transport head on. There was something very strange about that incident and not a word was spoken again about it.

As dependable as the ancient bus was it was not without its share of mechanical problems and I remember the worst case scenario developing one night, hundreds of miles up north, en route from Timmins to Sudbury. Canadian winters being what they are, it was decided to leave directly after that evening's show, drive all night, and find rooms in the next city. The band could sleep all night, Bruce would stock up on hot coffee, and whatever else it took to get the job done, and we could assure ourselves of making the next gig. There was one small problem though; after consulting a map, we decided to take a rural route of sixty odd miles over the better-marked roads, cutting our travel time but putting us totally at the mercy of the elements.

We were advised by the locals that it was policy to inform the police what time we would be travelling along this road, Highway 144, so they would have an idea when we would make our connection to the relative safety of the main highway. It was further advised to check in with the local OPP detachment upon completing the crossing. As young rock and roll outlaws we figured it best to just take our chances with Mother Nature and the less to do with the police the better. And off we went. When I awoke sometime later the bus was not clanking along all cosy like and it became painfully clear that it was now extremely cold in the passenger compartment. We had broken down. I don't know how long we had been stopped but you could already see your breath in the night air and it was getting colder by the second. Bruce, who had been driving, had squeezed into the sleeping quarters and was now shuddering along with the rest of us under the ineffectual sleeping bags.

Soon the heavier sleepers came to and there was much discussion about how we were going to die this very evening. I have never been as cold in my life as I was that night. Much like the incident in BJ's windowless car a few years back, it was now time to get warm any way that you could and soon we were a mass of hidden hands, tucked in toes, legs and torsos and, under any other circumstances, a very gay scene indeed. Two things were then decided; one, that if we did nothing but get to know each other better we would indeed freeze to death, and two, Bruce had better get out and fix the engine. So Bruce grudgingly bundled up and stepped out into the fresh night air. Ed, being the most mechanically minded member of the group got up to join him. The rest of us cowards, feeling bad for our doomed friends, immediately go for their pillows and blankets.

The first order of business outside was for Ed to get a fire going, which he proceeded to do, and with Bruce's hands now all nice and toasty, and armed with his trusty spanner, Bruce crawled under the bus to repair what turned out to be a frozen gas line. Gasoline anti-freeze being somewhat unknown to us in those days Bruce simply set aside his wrench and, using his mouth, blew out the offending gas fur ball. Soon the sound of much merry making filled the good old Fludd Bus as the heat was restored and we continued on our journey. Bruce and Ed had saved the day, our very lives even, and we vowed to a man to treat them with the utmost respect for the next hour or so.

Adam Mitchell

The Fludd demo tape of four Pilling and Pilling originals had been expertly shopped around by Skinny and it wasn't long before we had some serious interest. Adam Mitchell was a carrot topped Scotsman who had enjoyed some success as singer/songwriter with The Paupers, a psychedelic folk rock group who were managed by the great Albert Grossman, who also handled Bob Dylan, Janice Joplin and Peter, Paul, and Mary. The Paupers had recorded two wonderful albums entitled 'Magic People' and 'Ellis Island', and had been invited to their big break south of the border by performing at The Monterey Pop Festival. The only problem was that their guitar and bass amps blew up thirty seconds into their performance. End of American dream.

Now Mitchell was a record producer, his first charge being a very young Linda Rondstat, whose first LP established her as an artist to be reckoned with and Mitchell as an up and comer. With his stateside connections we soon had two Warner Brothers artist and repertoire types flying north to experience the group firsthand and, with a good live showcase to drive the point home, we soon had an offer to consider. It was decided that legendary San Francisco attorney Brian Rohan would handle the group's affairs and the small details were hammered out by all interested parties.

Mitchell, in the mean time, convened with the group in the Andersens' basement and began tearing apart everything socially and musically that the record company had liked in the first place. At one point Brian Pilling confided that Mitchell wanted to fire and replace Mick and John immediately, but thought that I could stay only because I could sing harmony and the three-part blend was alright. A real confidence booster was old Adam and I pretty much hated the sight of him from that moment on.

Mick and John, having been likewise warned, pulled up their musical socks and it was decided that perhaps, as nothing was truly broken, then perhaps nothing needed fixing. They could record with the rest of us. Mick Walsh was by no means a great guitarist but he had a very English style all his own, which suited the group, and he certainly had the right accent. Mitchell's assessment of John Andersen's drumming ability baffles me to this day, as John was, and is, one of the greatest rock drummers to ever come out of Canada.

The record company wanted to know what we needed in the way of an artist advance and, being the big thinkers we were at the time, we decided that the princely sum of $12,000.00 was all that we required. This sum also represented the approximate price of a new PA system that we had been eyeing. The money, a fortune to us but chump change to the record company, was no problem at all and the deal was quickly finalized. The problem turned out to be in getting the bloody advance from Brian Rohan in California. Calls were made, lots of them, but nothing was heard back from him or anyone else in his office. In desperation, (we really wanted that PA, man), it was decided that Ed, Brian, Bruce, and Skinny would all pile into Skinny's brand new Camero and drive to San Francisco to pick up the check.

Picking Up The Check

Once more I was left out and this time I was really pissed off!

Five guys in a sporty new Camaro or four, what was the big difference? I even offered to ride the hump from Toronto to San Francisco.

"I never get to do nothin'!" I moaned.

"You guys are always pickin' on me!" I moaned some more. I moaned a lot back then. (Skinny recently pointed out that I was a huge pain in the ass in those days, but he was drinking wine when he said it.)

They pointed out that, as I couldn't drive, I had nothing to contribute and no, being cute wasn't good enough. Nothing I said worked so Ed, Brian, Bruce, and Skinny were soon California bound, without me.

Here's the story in a very small stream-of-consciousness nutshell:
They drove virtually non stop all the way...it got so hot in the car with no air conditioning that they all stripped down to their undies for the Nevada desert leg of the trip...they of course got stopped by Nevada State Troopers who were so impressed with their underpants that the cops threw the only set of car keys into the trunk and locked the lid...now stranded in the desert in their assorted underpants Ed had to pull out the back seat to get the keys...at a diner Skinny heard and really enjoyed listening to Dylan's new record 'Watchin' The River Flow'...they finally managed to reach Brian Rohan by telephone and told him in no uncertain terms that they were en route to pick up the check...they were told that the check was in the mail...they didn't care they said...they were coming anyway...they made it

TRAVELS WITH MY AMP

to San Francisco and got the check but first they wanted it certified...while the check was being certified they were taken to the set of *Bonanza*, where they were introduced to the entire Cartwright clan..."Hoss" Cartwright turned out to be just as nice as he appeared on tv...Brian Pilling bought a Fender Telecaster with the name "Gary Garretson" inlaid in the neck in black mother of pearl...the lads were given an ounce of high quality pot and the certified check...they turned the car around to face Toronto and, without further delay, rolled some joints...they had so much pot that giant roaches were only partially smoked and discarded without care...as they reached the Canadian border it was wisely decided that the pot was far too good to just throw out so the remainder of the pot was hidden in an eight track tape container... the certified check was deposited and we bought a new PA system.

Left to right: Brian Pilling, Ed Pilling, Greg Godovitz, John Andersen, Mick Walsh.

San Francisco 1971

And it came to pass that Skinny, Brian, John, Mick, Edmund and I winged American Airlines to sunny California. Five thin rock wannabes and their even slimmer, thinner, skinny, spinner manager arrive in the United States in a blaze of satin, leather and suede.

It was my first time on an airplane. I was twenty years old and I was in San Francisco to begin recording my first record with my friends.

Oh yeah, in all my excitement remembering this, I almost forgot, Mitchell was with us too.

Life would never be better than this. The sun was different; somehow brighter than it had been back home mere hours before. The trees, alive in a rainbow of colours, provided exotic backdrops for our instamatic cameras. The palms, swaying in the gentle California breeze brought everything at once into focus; we were certainly not in Scarborough anymore, Toto.

Soon we were met by Brian Rohan's female assistant, who had brought along a great big black limousine. This fine car, just like the ones that The Beatles and The Stones used also came complete with its own uniformed, mental case chauffeur! He even had a real chauffeur's cap!!

My first airplane ride, my first recording session, and now my first limo ride!

I lied a few lines back; life could get better than this!

Now the assistant was pushing hundred dollar bills into our hands and she's telling us to have fun tonight in San Francisco. Yes, with a limo and a handful of U.S. currency we can have much fun in San Francisco and off we go to have it!

We'll call the driver "Johnny." Not because I forget his name, I do, but because he reminded me of a guy whose name should be Johnny.

"You boys ever been to the Bay before?" asked our new pal.

"No, first time," someone in the band offered.

"I drive around fuckin' rock stars all the time," says Johnny, adjusting the rear view mirror to catch our reaction. As we are too busy in the back, giggling and tickling each other with our recent good fortune, Johnny continues, "I had Sly and The Family Stone last week. Buncha' fuckin' animals! Chicken bones all over the back seat!"

We were just not interested, lovely though Johnny's description of Sly Stones's table manners was.

Johnny, now sensing our total lack of interest in his shit story, decides to appeal to the animal in us.

"You boys want a little excitement?" he asked, and now we are listening.

What could it be that Johnny is offering?

Loose hippie chicks in the Haight?

Some serious Vietnam bud fresh from a recently returned body bag?

No, nothing as mundane as that.

What Johnny has in mind is to DRIVE US OVER A FUCKING 500 FOOT CLIFF IN HIS GREASY CHICKEN BONED LIMO AT 100 MILES PER FUCKING HOUR!!

If you have seen any movie of San Francisco there is always a lovely shot of The Bay and The Golden Gate Bridge taken from a cliff high above this idyllic scene with no barriers around it as barriers would be futile in the event of being out of control anyway, and this was what we were now looking at while accelerating rapidly towards the edge!

Our giggles had now turned to screams as we hurtled toward the fatal precipice. All at once Johnny applied not one but both feet to the brakes as the giant car fishtailed wildly out of control, tires screaming as rubber burned, stopping within inches of the cliff. The doors flew open as we spilled out of the car, the dust settling gently on our soiled rock star clothes.

"Nice view huh boys?" sneered Johnny. "Welcome to Frisco."

Pacific Recording/San Mateo

The first order of business after Johnny's San Francisco initiation was to book into our new home for the next two weeks which was a small hotel with kitchenettes, about two blocks from the studio. The rooms were small but tidy and, had any of us desired to cook, there were cute little appliances on which to do so. Pretty much everyone in the group now showered and those that wore underwear changed them in honour of our near death experience earlier. It was time to take up Brian Rohan's assistant's generous offer of fun in San Francisco and it was decided that Sausalito was where we would find it. With the fun loving Johnny at our disposal for the evening, we headed to the world famous Trident restaurant for dinner.

The Trident is a wonderful place, overlooking the Bay and Alcatraz, and in one of Woody Allen's movies he gets up for a better view and walks smack dab into one of the full length mirrors that completely surround the place. As I peeled my nose from the glass, much laughter and merrymaking erupted all around as patrons from all over the world enjoyed my most recent humiliation. Next we went to see Taj Mahal, the singer, and his blues band at a very dark and funky bar. I had played many Taj songs during my blues guy period so this was a big thrill and I managed to enjoy the show without further harm to myself. The drinking age in California at this time was twenty-one but somehow I had a very nasty morning after, just in time to start recording.

(*Two things*: 1. Adam Mitchell would not agree to budget in an airline ticket for good old Bruce so Bruce hitched a ride down with Kathy and Linda Minidis, our two fans from Detroit from The Pretty Ones era who took their summer holidays in order to enjoy this historic event. The girls worked for The Hilton Hotel chain and as such got a tremendous rate at any Hilton Hotel. So Bruce the roadie stayed at the swanky downtown hotel while the rock star guys shared accoms in San Mateo. 2. We had rehearsed like crazy prior to this trip but something very strange happened when Ed developed singer's nodes on his vocal chords and needed an operation followed by six weeks of complete silence. It was great arguing with good old Ed at this time, as he could not answer back. I won nearly every argument we had and I was always right! This arrangement suited my needs perfectly. We had purchased the dear boy one of those reusable plastic writing pads and if Ed had a good point and wrote it down you merely closed your eyes when he passed it to you, insuring your winning point. It was during this period of inactivity that Brian, Mick, John, and I recorded the famous Fludd Rock Opera about a man who awakens to discover the loss of his own name and identity. The four band members recorded a series of amazing songs in one night in Mick's living room. Mick was a technical wiz at recording and soon all the instruments were patched into an ancient mixer, directly into the two track reel-to-reel tape recorder. The drums were various sized cardboard boxes with mics on them and John used real hi-hat and crash cymbals. As everything was directly mic'd, the neighbours had to wonder what was going on at five in the morning when a huge splash of cymbal broke the early morning peace. Two of the songs, 'A Man Like You' and 'Easy Being No One' would make the cut for our debut LP.

I'm hoping that this will be included in the back of this book as a bonus CD or even DVD. Mark your place right now and see if it's there. If it is say, "Hey, Greg pushed that great idea through making less money for himself but really giving the person who bought this book a fabulous bonus!" or "Those cheap pricks at (insert publishers name here) wouldn't spring for Greg's idea. When are they going to wise up to the cat's obvious brilliance?" if it isn't.)

Pacific Recording in San Mateo was a state of the art sixteen-track studio where we would be recording. We selected this studio not so much for its technical qualification's as for the fact that engineer Fred Catero would be twirling the knobs. Fred Catero was a legendary figure in recording as he had engineered projects for artists such as Steve Miller, Santana, Joplin, Sly Stone, Simon and Garfunkel and the Al Kooper version of Blood, Sweat, and Tears. While awaiting Fred's arrival on the first day of recording, I passed the time chatting with studio Girl Friday Ginger Mews who asked me to describe Fred sight unseen based on his musical reputation.

"Oh," I said, "he's about five feet three, very skinny with a greaser goatee and oily black hair."

At that moment this man mountain walks past me, California tan with decidedly North American Indian features, very long hippie hair pulled back into a pony tail, blues jeans tucked into knee high suede boots. Movie star handsome.

"Who is that?" I enquire.

"That would be Fred Catero," laughs Ginger.

We set about recording as soon as introductions were made. Fred had the wonderful ability to put total strangers immediately at ease, often taking the blame for the artist's poor performance with a gentle, "Hey man, we had a technical problem with that last take, could you do another on us," a producer's white lie that I would borrow from him and use forever. Mitchell was efficient and workmanlike but never very forthcoming with any sort of encouragement. Besides playing bass, I also got to play the grand piano on the very Penny Laneish 'Birmingham', and a small lead guitar solo on 'Easy Being No One', which had been originally written for the little rock opera recorded in Mick's apartment. This was my first experience with the old studio lie "Don't worry kid, we'll get it in the mix." The guitar solo had no volume or sustain and having voiced my concerns Mitchell said they would fix it later. "But surely you can't alter the sound from clean to distorted once it's been committed to tape?" I reasoned. These days you can do that but then you couldn't. I was basically told that, as this was my first recording session, better not to question things too much and with that, the case was closed.

San Francisco proved to be an eye opener in other ways as well. We had little or no experience with the gay community in Canada and here we were in an openly gay city. One day while shopping on Polk Street we entered a boutique that for all appearances seemed to be run by very heavy looking biker dudes in black leather. As we looked around I noticed these two guys walk in, hand in hand, and whispered to Ed that it should be interesting when these bikers check out this activity. This monster in leather approached the two lovers as we steeled ourselves for the bloodbath that was surely to follow.

"May I help you ladies?" lisped the biker; his hands flitting upwards like gentle butterflies. All was clear.

Coming from an environment where we feared for our safety just for dressing differently it was refreshing to be in a city where normally socially unacceptable behaviour was considered commonplace.

The free love aspects of the Haight Ashbury were still being practiced as I found out one night while bar hopping downtown. I was approached by a lovely hippie girl who offered to look after me for the night and make sure I was back at the studio in time for the next day's session. Her pad was straight out of a movie, all black light posters, incense and no moral issues to get in the way. A great night was had that would have grave consequences for me. Two days later I had the clap.

We finished our first LP in our allotted two weeks and it was back to face another fall and winter of touring the frozen north. At the airport while waiting for our plane I already told you that Streisand and Redford were filming and that the Toronto hippie chick who seduced me on Admiral Road didn't remember me. What I haven't told you about was that, as we were having a drink in the airport lounge, we soon became aware that the Marine sergeant on the other side of the bar was making light of our flamboyant dress and suspect sexuality for the amusement of his troops. His comments could clearly be heard by one and all but as these guys were Vietnam bound and trained to kill people it seemed like a good idea to ignore them. Imagine my surprise, then, to see Ed get up slowly and make his way over to the other side of the bar.

"Here, General," said Ed in a very threatening tone, "one more word out of you and I'll do you in front of your Boy Scout troop!"

As I loaded up my pants, preparing to die, I watched that Marine sergeant back down from the daintily clad lead singer.

Eastern Tour

Soon our first single, 'Turn 21', was doing lovely business at radio across the country and the demand for live appearances increased in markets where we had previously not performed. It was deemed necessary to travel to the eastern provinces, in the dead of winter, in order to break this new territory. The band travelled by train to Moncton, New Brunswick, which was fairly uneventful save for travelling at one point through the remains of a recent derailment. We moved through the wreckage at a snail's pace, with smouldering train debris and cargo strewn everywhere. The sight of dead animal carcasses and tons of rotting produce was unnerving to look at. It was like I imagine war to be.

We shared our travel time with Syrinx, a progressive electronic group that featured Moog synthesizer pioneer John Mills-Cockell, who were also on tour. While we boozed it up, socialized and tried to score the few girls on board the roadies drove the bus down. I say roadies, as we now had Pat Ryan on board to help Bruce. Pat was a Cockney and, with that responsibility, he brought to the group a wonderful sense of camp humour that could unsettle the most liberal of sexual thinkers. Pat had been a mate of Mick Walsh's in England and had made his way to us after finishing a stint working the oilrigs of western Canada.

Prior to that he was in the Merchant Navy and would regale us with ribald tales of lonely nights at sea, the deprivation of women, a lonely watch in the crows nest accompanied by the Moroccan cabin boy.

"You're joking right, Pat?" we would say.

"Don't knock it til you've tried it, mate," Pat would offer, all worldly like but no one ever knew for sure if he was serious or not. Pat was as much a lad as the rest of the boys but at a gig in Pembroke, where we were given the key to the city, Pat sat out a celebratory orgy afterwards at the local army base in order to get to know his future wife in a more platonic meeting of the minds.

"Hello luv, do you mind if I join you?" he'd asked.

"Not if you expect what's going on upstairs!" was his disgusted wife-to-be's answer.

He's still with her to this day.

Now, if we were freaking people out back home with our street apparel, the easterners were simply not ready for the sight of seven "queers from Toronto" invading their beloved fishing grounds. All manner of snide comments and outright hostility were the order of the day with every pit stop or hotel booking we made. The sheer volume of our touring party managed to avert any serious problems but it was uncomfortable all the same. The girls liked us, though, and wanted to know where they could get clothes like we wore. We played mostly high school gyms, armouries, and the odd club, and, as we were getting airplay, the crowds weren't too bad either.

One memorable night saw us driving from Halifax across the bridge to Dartmouth, normally a twenty-minute trip. This was not "normally" however as we were in the middle of the worst storm in Nova Scotia history and the snow was piling up so fast that the bridge itself was virtually inaccessible.

Pat, at the wheel, was busy making the tollbooth guard very nervous by telling him how much he adored a man in a uniform. The guard took our fifty cents and wished us luck. The Fludd Bus was stuck within twenty feet and the only way to get to the gig was for the rest of us to get out and either push or shovel. The gig was at a local high school, which was unfortunately at the top of a rather steep hill. There was no way that the bus was going up there but we hadn't endured this much hell to give up and Pat convinced a snowplough driver to clear a path up the hill. With this accomplished, we played our show to the hundred kids who had braved the storm. Stopping off at a very famous local fish and chip shop afterwards, we all loaded up on the local take-out fare and had a nice hot meal while slowly making our way back to our hotel. The next day everyone in the band had food poisoning, with the exception of Ryan and myself. The boys were sick, the boys got better, the weather didn't improve, and we made no money.

We had conquered the east!

England

It was time to visit England again. I say again as Ed, Brian, Ray Daniels and I had gone over briefly the year before. We rented a car at the airport and had driven through a hideous fog to the Pillings' hometown of Birmingham. Ed only smashed the car up once. We stayed with good old Auntie Hilda and Ray and I basked in the warm glow of English pub hospitality. What we soon realized was that in general the English hate Americans but they love Canadians. It's a Commonwealth thing I'm sure. Free drinks were coming fast and furious as we fielded questions about Toronto, where a lot of the local's friends and relatives had settled.

On that trip we visited the brothers' old stomping grounds, nightclubs like Barbarellas and The Rum Runner, where the boys had honed their musical chops alongside the other great Birmingham musicians of the day.

The highlight of the trip for me, silly as it seems now, was getting the tips of my hair dyed silver. This had not been seen in Canada before but after I'd witnessed a girl in London with vibrant blue hair I just had to have something done to freak them out back home. This little follicle experiment would be the first in a long line of hair enhancements that would eventually reduce me to being a chrome dome.

My next English adventure was on my own when I travelled to London solo. I booked into the Shaftesbury Hotel on Monmouth Street and went crazy, shopping at Kensington Market, where you would see all sorts of pop stars buying velvet jackets, satin trousers, and a brand new item, multi-coloured platform boots and shoes. I saw but didn't approach Dave Davies of the Kinks and Brian Connelly of Sweet. London, being the hip capital of Europe, was too cool for words and so the most famous film and rock stars could walk around, doing their business, virtually unmolested. The days of Beatlemania were indeed over. I managed to chat up a beautiful girl who worked in the hotel bar who told me that dating the guests was strictly taboo. Less than three hours later we were shagging our brains out in some dark London alley, in her Mini Cooper.

I brought back a wonderful assortment of very trendy clothing and it was almost a turn around for me as Skinny, Ed, Brian, and I were back in London within the month just to shop. Our first night there we were all in the mood for a bit of fun and, as it was much too late to hit the clubs to try and pull, it was decided that prostitutes would be the answer. Never had one of those, I thought; this might be interesting. I was sharing a room with Ed, who latched on to this horrible old crow he'd found in deepest Soho. She had awful peroxide hair that looked like bouffant candyfloss and she stunk of cheap booze and even cheaper perfume. I was having none of it, well, her at least. I'd put the word out to the concierge, whose name was Ooja, but thought nothing more of it as I joined Ed and his "date." After she had finished blowing him, (with a rubber on no less, even back then!), I could hear Ed pass out almost instantly, his drunken snores filling the tiny room. This was her ladyship's cue to get up and start rifling through our stuff. In the darkened room she jumped out of her skin as I yelled, "HEY, OLD PROSTITUTE LADY, YOU'LL BE LEAVING NOW!!"

She cursed me for scaring her and I showed her the door.

About an hour later I awoke to a very gentle but persistent tapping at our door. I figured the old hag had probably returned to retrieve her teeth but it was only good old Ooja standing there.

"Good evening Mr. Greg," he said in the most pleasant of singsong Indian tones.

"Hi Ooja, what time is it?" I yawned.

"It is three thirty in the morning and I have with me your special request!" he smiled.

"A HOOKER!!!" I screamed and put my head out into the hall while Ooja motioned for me to not yell out.

Standing to the right of the accommodating concierge was a remarkable looking woman, possibly in her mid twenties, and dressed in a diaphanous powder blue, floor-length gown. Her skin was milk white and her hair a mass of flaming red curls. She was absolutely stunning. I thanked Ooja five, maybe ten times, maybe more, and led my new pal into the room. I can't recall her name but the moment she opened her mouth I knew that she was French.

French!!!

Oh Boy-Oh Boy-Oh Boy!

"You are zo young and beautiful," she cooed. "Why would you have to pay for a woman?"

"Well, it was late when we arrived and my buddy Ed over there picked up this old boot when we went down to Soh...," and she put the loveliest of perfumed fingers to my lips to shut me the fuck up.

"You are not what I expected at all. Phone your friend at ze front desk and get him to bring us a bottle of Scotch whiskey," and with that said she floated out of the room.

When she returned the Scotch had already been delivered and she picked up the tray and motioned for me to follow her. As we entered the communal bathroom in the hallway I instantly noticed that the ancient tub was full of steaming water and that a few candles had been lit.

She undressed slowly, always looking me straight in the eye, although I didn't have a clue as to what colour her eyes might have been. Her body was magnificent. She drew me to her and guided me into the water.

"I am not going to charge you for this," she said, and I'm glad that she didn't because that bottle of Scotch had cost me two months allowance. She then proceeded to roll two perfect hash joints, which we smoked while sipping the fine whiskey. I can't remember what happened next but the other lads asked me over breakfast later that morning if it had been me screaming, "DOWN PERISCOPES! DIVE! DIVE!" just before sunup.

But sex you could get anywhere; it was the clothes that kept us coming back to London. Alkasura, Granny Takes A Trip, Biba's and the ever popular Ken Market. I once bought a blue and red velvet toreador outfit with an outsize black velvet hat trimmed in fur. I wore it out in the street and no one looked twice. Velvet pants with elaborate stitching or mirrors down the leg. Canary yellow satin suits with hand painted canvas shoes featuring Beatrix Potter rabbits. Over to Biba's for a jar or three of Crazy Colour.

And the makeup, darlings!!!

Something new was happening in England and it was called Glam Rock. Nothing nicer than a platform'd satin doll with a bit of blush and polish, dear.

The girls were dressing up too.

London was buzzing with Bowie and Bolan and we were there before the word got out to the rest of the world. I clearly remember coming home from a solo trip and it was straight from the airport to some rural high school gig. All of my freshly purchased treasures on display in the dressing room.

"Five minutes, ladies!" according to Pat and the band was at it again.

I cried for days afterwards, when upon entering the dressing room I noticed that something was missing.

MY ENTIRE FUCKING NEW FRUITY WARDROBE WAS STOLEN!!

One afternoon we spotted ex-Move Roy Wood at Ken Market and Ed and Brian and I approached him. Fludd were BIG Move fans. Roy told us he was putting together a rock orchestra but was having trouble finding string players. I told him about this great new group back home called Lighthouse that had strings AND horns. He didn't seem too impressed.

After all, He was English!

His idea went up to eleven!

I always liked the Electric Light Orchestra, though.

One night I checked out Elvin Jones at Ronnie Scott's and then, just to put everything into perspective, Status Quo at The Marquee. It was so packed in The Marquee that at one point I lifted my feet off of the ground and didn't sink. Elvin Jones was too out there for me but Status Quo were straight out of The Gasworks back home. They rocked.

My one and only visit to the world famous Speakeasy club was on another solo trip to England. This time I had our newly released '...ON!' LP with me and the club's disc jockey played it all night. He also played a hot new tune called 'Walk On The Wild Side' to death as well. As I stood in the club's men's room, the unmistakable baritone of Long John Baldry came in regaling a very drunken Ronnie Wood about forming a group of "Giant Queens! Ron, think about it!" There had been this very strange seven-foot guy with a helmet type hairdo doing these weird robotic dances this very evening and it looked like Long John had ideas. "And how is Mr. Gosling, then?" Baldry imperiously asked the Keyboard Kink as he joined the line.

Chris Squire from Yes was at the bar and I thought to myself that this was a very good place to be hanging out. The live band was from Liverpool and the guitarist told me that Paul and Linda were over on the restaurant side at that very moment, having dinner, and would I like to meet them? I couldn't even go peek at them. Just being in the washroom next to Baldry, Wood, and the Kink had freaked me totally out already. No, I decided right then and there to wait another seventeen years before I would allow the McCartneys to meet me.

HEY!!!!....THIS JUST IN
Last night (Thursday, January 28, 1999) TRAVELS WITH MY AUNT was on TV! This wacky 1972 romp starred Maggie Smith as the light-fingered old broad hoping to separate her naive young fool of a nephew from his less than deserved inheritance. I actually saw this at the show back in '72. At that time, I shit you not, I turned to my date and said, "You know, if I ever write a book I'm going to call it Travels With My blah, blah,..." and we laughed and laughed.

TRAVELS WITH MY AMP

1972 ...

The "Arthur" making a point.

Go West Young Band

We had gone east, now it was time to tour out west. Once more the crew drove the Fludd Bus out while the group and Skinny flew. I loved flying and was never nervous on planes. We got smashed and flirted with the flight attendants and arrived, none the worse for wear, mere hours later. The road crew, on the other hand, got smashed and flirted with each other for days on end until they picked us up. We landed in Kelowna, British Columbia and it was our first experience dealing with mountains. The Canadian Rockies are more than mountains; they are the thrones of God. For a guy used to the flatlands of southern Ontario, I was suitably freaked out to be standing amidst snow capped peaks and breathing in the cool mountain air was like breathing for the first time again. Drinking from freezing-cold natural springs at the side of the road was almost otherworldly to us. The travel was constantly interrupted with us jumping out of the bus to click off roles of instamatic film. In the early morning hours, Bruce would sometimes wake me up to share and enjoy the sight of dozens of wild deer or reindeer casually slowing down our progress, while they gracefully shared the highway with us.

We played mostly high schools, small arenas, and the odd club. The single had charted out here as well so once again we were drawing fairly decent crowds. One thing did not change, and that were the girls. The dressing rooms, bus, and hotel rooms always had a steady stream of available beauties, which was great as Fludd was a very horny group. One night in Vancouver Skinny found himself in the company of four very eager participants from Detroit, all blocked on the local acid and looking to expand more than their minds. The girls had been somewhat dismayed to show up at the after-show party, only to discover that the Fluddies were not to be found. Skinny, with no competition in sight, had offered his services to all four girls. The "Don't worry girls, I'll do you all" boast is one which every guy says at one time or another in his life, and actually means at the time, but seldom lives up to it, given the opportunity. The boys in the band, perhaps bored with too many easy conquests, went searching for more interesting distractions. In other words, we had taken up an invite to a local gay bar.

Just curious.

We were the belles of the ball but we all left with our virginity intact.

Even Ryan.

We went, we checked it out, we left.

Bruce arrived back at the hotel and upon entering his room, which he was sharing with Skinny, was pleased indeed to find at least three unfulfilled candidates. The over boastful manager, fully satisfied with one close encounter, was, in true guy fashion, itching to bail on this scene when the Calvary arrived in the shape of one, Bruce Duncan. Bruce more than kept up his end of the bargain, so to speak, and the girls left the next morning in very good moods.

Now it's been a while in my little story here since good old Ed had just cause to beat the crap out of someone. "Just 'cause" usually meant "just 'cause he was there," but one fine Vancouver morning we awoke to sad tidings that some rogues were taking liberties with the trusty Fluddmobile and were at that very moment trying to tow it off the lot directly behind the Tropicana Hotel. The two scoundrels were going happily about their work when Ed, Pat, Skinny, and Bruce went down to investigate. Well, one thing led to another, as things often do in these circumstances, until one of the tow truck drivers said the wrong thing to Ed and suddenly found himself being used as a human battering ram into the side of the bus. From the fine vantage point on our balcony, high above the scene, the rest of us enjoyed the fine morning air while the sound of much mayhem and the shattering of glass could clearly be heard for blocks below. I say the shattering of glass for, in his zeal to show the tow truck guy the inside of the bus, Ed accidentally put the guy's head through the front door. Some mornings it really is better to just stay in bed and leave the cruel workings of the world to others better equipped to handle those kind of things.

The wounded driver's partner, perhaps fearing a similar fate, picked up a large piece of wood which was lying about and began making threatening gestures with it. Pat, no fool, did the only thing he could do; he egged the guy on to take a swipe at him but kept a safe distance while doing so. With all sorts of distractions taking place Pat slipped off, opened the hood of the tow truck and ripped the battery cables out. Now, nobody was going anywhere.

Things were cooled down somewhat with the arrival of the local constabulary, who quickly took stock of the situation. The tow truck drivers argued that they wanted justice for their disabled vehicle, Skinny countered that as the Fluddmobile's front door glass had been shattered that it was we who had suffered at the hands of these ruffians. Nobody addressed the point that had Ed not put the tow truck driver's head through the door then this would not be a point up for debate. All fines were duly levied and paid and our first western tour ended with much laughter and fine memories as we flew home the next day.

Here's A Brand New Feature In The Book Where You, The Reader, Get To Pick Out What You Read Next!

Your choices for the next story today are:

1. Mr. Booth's Homemade Italian bread recipe.
2. Balloon art in the new millennium.
3. More senseless violence and sex at a gig in small town Canada!

Now here's how it works...
If you choose:
Story #1 – simply place your left index finger up your left nostril and give it a good dig.
Story #2 – turn to the person seated on your right and tell him/her/it that the person seated on your left wants their $20.00 back.
Story #3 – place your thumbs in their respective ears, wiggle your fingers, and begin clucking like a chicken.

If you are on public transport and people are looking at you then you may either:
a) Mark your place and wait until you get home or
b) Freak everyone out by going for it.

Votes are now being tabulated.
Please turn to the next page for the results, and good luck.

TODAY'S WINNER!...
STORY # 3

More senseless violence and sex at a gig in small town Canada!

I Abhor Violence.

It's not from being a coward, you understand, it's more to do with the fact that no matter how well you do in a fight the chances of being hit yourself are quite good. Whether it's a good solid head butt to your breathing apparatus or a well placed boot to the goolies, there are many other things that a body could be doing that might not be so painful. I have always subscribed to the fine old axiom that "the man who throws the first punch is the man who has run out of ideas." I have lots of ideas.

Brian Pilling, back in The Pretty Ones era, used to sing a great Kinks song called 'I'm A Lover Not A Fighter.' I should have sung that song, as that was more my thing. And so it was that one night I made the near fatal mistake of crossing that fine line between last idea and first punch with the guy least likely to lose a fight.

Ed

Now I have already gone to great lengths extolling Ed's legendary ability with not only his fists but his sexual magnetism with the ladies as well. He was the undisputed heavyweight champion of our group and any other group for that matter. But on occasion, every once in the bluest of moons, a girl that he was eyeing would want me.

The Jubilee Pavilion in Oshawa was another pre-war wooden dance hall by the lake. It was reputed that the owner's sons Jerry and Dennis Edmonton, had gone on to fame and fortune as members of Steppenwolf. The Jub was always packed and this muggy summer night was no exception. We were in between sets and Ed was doing his best to seduce this beautiful girl with much Englishness and "C'mon then, luv, give us a kiss" and, "Wot's yer name then, Twinkle?" and other charming panty removers. Unfortunately for Ed, this one wanted me and, as he took his leave to attend to some matter of nature, the young lady stood up and grabbed me by the hand, leading me off through the myriad of dressing rooms and storage rooms that existed underneath the venerable dance hall. It's quite true that a hard cock hath no conscience and so it was that I found myself in an empty room with this fine young thing who set about doing what she'd come to do and I'm sure had done many times before.

I was busy looking around the empty room and generally enjoying myself when who should burst through the door but good old Ed himself. The young lady quickly recovered her dropped eyelash, or whatever else she had been frantically searching the floor for on her knees and raced for the door. I tried to tuck myself in as best I could, given the circumstances, as the irate lead singer grabbed me up by my silk lapels and with one mighty hand lifted me off the ground until the toes of my white ballet slippers looked like Nijinsky himself was performing in them.

The smell of heated beer breath washed over me as Ed cocked his right hand over his head in my general direction. Now giddy with fear at my imminent demise, I did the only thing that seemed right under the circumstances, I had an idea.

"Ed, think about it, man!" I begged, "Think about your great big ugly fist smashing in my cute little face! Think about it, Ed!"

Ed thought about it for a second or two, lowered his fist and pushed me none too gently away.

"You're not worth hitting," he said and I couldn't have agreed more.

The rest of the gig passed without incident and was forgotten by the time we encored. I never saw the young lady again and had learned a valuable lesson in band sexual politics.

By the way, you should have chosen story two as it was much more interesting.

And Then There Were Four

As the amplification grew larger and more powerful and Brian's lead guitar abilities began to overshadow those of Mick, it was decided that Mick Walsh should leave the group. I have nothing against Mick, he was and still is a great guy, but in those days Mick, like most Englishmen, loved his beer. I often felt that his failure to grow with us as a musician was partly due to his brew intake, and as the rest of us hadn't yet discovered the dubious joys of alcohol, the pot/acid heads in the group couldn't understand the attraction. It soon became us vs him.

Fludd was like that. There was a great sense of brotherhood and all for one but if the party line was questioned then all hell broke loose. The Pillings were very good at convincing you that life as an outsider just wasn't worth living and that your only hope for success was to maintain the status quo. As Mick was much older than the rest of us, he was also much more settled in his ways, therefore, his playing style was already firmly established in his mind and he probably saw no reason to practice night and day like the rest of us. Mick was offered a technical job with the band, most notably mixing the sound, and he indeed stayed on in that capacity. Pat Ryan left and a new fellow named John Glover came on as a third roadie.

For a few months a former member of Brian and Ed's Birmingham-based group, The Wages Of Sin, was flown over as a replacement for Mick Walsh. In typical shifty Fludd fashion Mick Hopkins was brought up to a gig to observe while Mick Walsh played on, unaware that his fate was sealed. Mick Hopkins was an owlish looking imp who could play amazing guitar. He was so good, in fact, that we quickly featured him in his own solo spot with the aptly titled 'Mick's Boogie.' He brought some fresh ideas to the mix and would share his skills with any interested party. The thing I remember clearest was the backwards sounding phasing technique that he showed me, which I eventually passed on to Gino Scarpelli in Goddo at the beginning of 'Cock On.' By letting your finger run up and down the A string of your guitar, while butterfly picking, you could create an otherworldly effect without the use of gadgets or foot pedals. We recorded a new song called 'Get Up, Get Out, & Move On' with Adam Mitchell, which was Mick Hopkin's only vinyl appearance with us. The record charted immediately and Mick toured the eastern provinces with us until he got very homesick, having been somewhat of a momma's boy, and left the group to return to England. He was a good lad and would be missed.

One of our first gigs as a quartet was opening for Ten Years After in Winnipeg. Now, it had only been a year or two since Woodstock had firmly established Alvin Lee as a guitar god so it was no surprise to find a near-sell-out crowd in the arena that night. Fludd had received steady radio support in this market so it was considered wise to take advantage of an arena full of people and possibly sell a few more records. And so it was that we all flew to Winnipeg for a one nighter. I remember running in to Anne Murray at the airport, who kindly posed for a picture in a very stylish patchwork suede jacket. It was my first time playing Winnipeg, Rock Capital of Canada and a city that I would happily return to time and again during my touring days. We rocked the arena like there was no tomorrow; the band dressed flash and we were not intimidated by the size of the venue at all. We earned our encore, closing with The Beatles version of 'Roll Over Beethoven.' We didn't even stick around to see Ten Years After. After the show, the band got familiar with the local girls at a hotel party that raged 'til dawn. The next morning we picked up the local newspapers at the airport.

Showy is the best adjective to describe the warm-up group from Toronto called Fludd. The four musicians dressed in flashy outfits and performed co-ordinated callisthenics. The group had a tight sound and good vocal harmony. The lead singer, whose actions were reminiscent of Mick Jagger and the late Jim Morrison, writhed and jumped about on stage, displaying his navel. – Susan Janz (*The Tribune*)

The group causing all the commotion was Fludd. I was caught off guard by the band's dynamic stage presence and straight ahead rocking and rolling. – Andy Mellen (*Winnipeg Free Press*)

"*...displaying his navel.*" You've really got to be paying attention to detail to notice this in an arena. We had raped, plundered and pillaged Winnipeg in the space of twenty-four hours and we flew home on a cloud.

1973 ...

Brian Pilling and Greg Godovitz

Photo: Barb Pilling

TRAVELS WITH MY AMP 109

1973 ...

Brian Pilling and Mick Hopkins warming up in Moncton, N.B.

Photo: Barb Pilling

Greg Godovitz and Ed Pilling

Fludd roadies Pat Ryan and Bruce Duncan

The Maple Music Junket

Our next major show was a brilliant attempt by Australian writer Ritchie Yorke to bring the world to Canada for the Maple Music Junket. Ritchie had been a contributor to Rolling Stone magazine and Billboard and was so pro Canadian talent that he should have had a Maple Leaf tattooed on his ass. I loved the guy. Along with Ronnie Hawkins, Ritchie had spearheaded John and Yoko's War Is Over campaign, which saw the duo globe hopping, at the Lennons' expense, to deliver posters of peaceful intent to a mostly uncaring world.

Along with Crowbar, April Wine, Mashmakan, Lighthouse, Thunder Mug and others, we would be given the opportunity to play before a select group of foreign press and talent scouts at Massey Hall in Toronto. This was our great chance to secure a world wide recording deal.

What to do.

New stage outfits!

Fuck rehearsals, we needed a bit of flash and at that point there was none flashier than John Gibb's store Long John's. Gibb was an English guitarist, friend of both Page and Beck, entrepreneur extraordinaire, and the owner of the trendiest boutique in Toronto. His coterie of friends were all dedicated followers of fashion and his store was the Mecca of the very hip and the very wanna be hip. Gibb didn't care who the fuck you were, when you were in his store you were in HIS store and he thought nothing of taking the piss, even at the expense of his customers. It was totally John to side over to you while you admired yourself in some velvet frock coat and utter to the room at large, "Here, Godo, exactly what is it you see when you look in the mirror?" followed by much guffawing and merriment.

It was like having Oscar Wilde for a tailor.

John's saving grace in those days, and still is, his beautiful wife Shirley, who would always put him in his place with something like, "John, you should have more clothes in the shop like what Greg's got on." Gibb didn't like that one bit and he would simmer until the next opportunity to have a go at you. He also had the most amazing girls staffing his store and the flirt factor was in overdrive with every visit.

I decided that a florescent pink velvet suit with brocade lapels and leg piping would be suitable and ordered up the same. Ed chose a more revealing canary yellow chiffon affair with wings that gave him the look of a rock and roll Big Bird.

The big night arrived, much madness prevailed backstage with the cream of Canada's groups looking for their big break in a jammed-to-capacity Massey Hall, for my money, The place to play in Toronto.

There is nothing worse for a vocal harmony group than when the PA system totally refuses to play along and resplendent in our never before seen suits of light we stormed on stage, only to have technical problems for three of our scheduled six songs. We never recovered.

The girls in attendance, as usual, were definitely buying in but there were more catcalls than cheers from the guys in the balconies, mostly directed this evening at a very fey Ed Pilling, and we blew our chances for that big European deal. Looking like sweat soaked harlots we dejectedly sulked offstage to lick our wounds while April Wine, Crowbar, and Lighthouse tore the roof off the place. The critics saw it somewhat differently though.

Surrounded by other dreary groups, they emerged with flash and style...what happened to The Rolling Stones in seven years has happened to Fludd in seven months. – Peter Goddard (Miss Chatelaine)

They were one of the few groups on the bill attempting creativity with their music-an almost lost art with today's musicians. – RPM

None of the groups really accomplished much as a result of the Junket but Ritchie Yorke had proven his point about Canadian musicians by presenting one of the greatest rock shows ever. Good on ya, Mate!

Lori, Kim, and Paula

Lori and Kim were sisters. Paula was their little Japanese girlfriend. She had gigantic breasts for a little Japanese girlfriend. As no one could get organized as to who liked who best, it was no big deal to date all three of them with no jealousy involved, and we all became great friends who hung out on a daily basis. The girls were amazing shoppers who supplied me with most of my wardrobe at that time. The most casual remark regarding a red satin jacket with emerald green lapels and it was yours within minutes. I rarely had to dip into my pocket; and come to think of it, neither did they.

One night they arrived at my townhouse in lovely fur coats, just, fur coats! The advent of glitter rock had opened the floodgates on sexual experimentation, and things that had seemed taboo a year or two before were accepted as common occurrence in the early Seventies.

Eventually I gravitated to Lori who was tall, beautiful, and smart. We were inseparable. The best thing about our situation was that her parents were amazingly hip and understanding to having boys hanging around who wore more makeup than their daughters. Her Dad, Norm, was a high roller who lived every day like it was his last and once came home early from a business trip to find me asleep, naked, next to his first born, also naked. Norm was a big man and as he hadn't dragged me out of bed and pounded the crap out of me, I sheepishly got dressed and made my way into the kitchen where I made my intentions clear regarding his daughter. After that I was sort of accepted into the family as the third daughter they never had and proceeded to learn about the good life.

Norm had a charge account at a posh downtown steakhouse called Harry's and upon arrival we would be guided to the best table by maitre'd George Bigliardi, resplendent in our rock star finery to dine on scampi, New York steaks, and always washed down with the finest Pommard and Poulet wines on the menu. Massive consumption was the order of the day and I seem to recall Brian Pilling hurling six orders of escargots and Chablis out of the back window of Norm's Lincoln as we cruised up Church Street.

Summer months were spent at the family cottage on Chandos Lake where the girls would sunbathe topless while the Fludd PA system would blast the latest T Rex and Bowie tunes at ear shattering volume over the lake. One particular "two-week-a-year" cottager would race over to try to restore some peace in his vacation, only to be met with the sight of semi-naked goddesses and androgynous rock types cavorting on the dock.

"TURN THE MUSIC DOWN!" he would scream.

"WHAT?" we would yell back.

"TURN THE GOD DAMN MUSIC DOWN FOR CHRIST SAKE!" the silly man would scream.

"WHAT?!? WE CAN'T HEAR YOU, THE MUSIC'S TOO LOUD!" we would shout back as the luckless vacationer roared off in his boat, shaking his fist in our general direction all the while.

One night Norm invited me to see Tony Bennett at the Royal York's famed Imperial Room. I was very pleased to get this invitation, relishing the thought of expanding my musical horizons. I called Norm to thank him for the invite and asked if a suit would be required.

"Of course you have to wear a suit, you stupid Pollack, it's the Imperial Room."

Now I am definitely of Polish lineage but I am certainly not stupid.

That night I picked up Lori and her Mom, Mary, and settled into the back of the limo to gauge reaction regarding my choice of apparel. The suit I had chosen was a red and white checkerboard affair but with no shirt and tie. They were not thrilled.

Oh well, damage done and much too late to turn around we checked our coats and made for the elegant dining room.

The look on maitre'd Louie Janetta's face was a wonderful panache of horror, astonishment, and disgust as he caught sight of me. The dress code at this restaurant was just short of tuxedo and I will lay odds that under normal circumstances you couldn't get past the door without a tie on, much less no shirt. Mary, who was well known to Mr. Janetta, simply muttered something about me being their guest and we were quickly deposited at a ringside table.

Norm, when he arrived, was not amused. Can't blame him really but I never liked the stupid Pollack thing. All night long a parade of well wishers, including legendary voice of The Leafs, Foster Hewitt, were introduced around the table. Introduced to everyone but me that is.

I was never much into hockey anyway so I enjoyed my dinner, lots of wine, and good old Tony Bennett. He was great.

After the show as we travelled north on Yonge Street I casually mentioned to Lori that we should go clubbing. Norm, who had been pretty tolerant about the whole thing finally snapped. "She's coming home with us!" he snorted, "and so are you."

"You can drop me off over there please," I said and with that I found myself at the front doors of The Level Crossing, a club where much music and fun could be had. I said my farewells and got out, but so did Norm.

Uh Oh!

"If you come near my daughter again I will...," said Norm all dark and menacing like and I knew that he meant it but before he could continue I blarped, "Look man, I'm going to marry her and all you're going to do about it is pay for it!"

With nothing more to be said regarding this perfect logic, Norm drove his girls home and, I'm sure, pondered the thought of life with a son-in-law who wore blush.

West

And so it was that our four intrepid scoundrels found themselves on the west coast one more time. It was the usual; travel hideous distances, play, fuck someone, travel another ridiculous distance, play somewhere else, and fuck someone different.

At one stop I amused myself by applying Biba's lipstick to a young willing who proceeded to make my cock look like a barbershop pole, all this while Brian, my room mate, feigned great indifference to the goings-on from the next bed. In all fairness, our drummer John was a bit more sensitive than the rest of us when it came to the debauchery. Although he rarely voiced his disapproval to our carryings-on, he was more into the conversational aspects of courting, a trait that I'm sure served him well when he was...er, drumming for Allanah Myles in the gay 90s.

After a tour of the British Columbia interior we raided Vancouver, which was still hippie-fied but still ready for a good dose of something interesting.

Pharaoh's was a subterranean club in Gastown, The Greenwich Village/Yorkville Village of Vancouver. Girls in flowing floor length dresses twirled and fluttered like so many hippie butterflies to our music while a new faction of dolled up glitter queens stood lasciviously within inches of the stage, making their intentions quite clear with much suggestive body language and eye contact. I had this beautiful French Canadian vision in a see-through blouse raising her arms above her head and shaking them mere inches from my face while I attempted some semblance of cool. The roadies had it down pat and with one offstage glance she soon knew not only what hotel to visit but also what room.

We played this club for the last week of the tour and virtually crawled legless on to the plane flying us home. It always seems like the most sexually satisfying part of any tour is just before you have to go home and pretend like you were a pillar of virtue the whole time away to your wife or girlfriend. Most times I got off a plane, my dick looked like chopped liver.

Once again the local press were vocal in their summation of our shows.

Fludd is as exciting as any group to come down the pike in some time, and that includes the Rolling Stones.
– Jack Wasserman *(Vancouver Sun, 21 Jun 1972)*

...a beautifully engineered mechanism with a remarkably precise, unfaltering movement, Fludd is uncompromising as well as uncomplicated. The feel is rhythm, and it can be addictive. – Jeani Read *(Vancouver Province)*

One day about two weeks after this tour ended there was a knock at my front door. My girlfriend answered it and told me that it was someone for me. Imagine my complete and terrified surprise to find the little French Canadian groupie from Vancouver standing on my doorstep.

Obviously the roadies had given her more than my hotel information. Lori left her in the front hallway and very coolly told me to call when I'd worked things out. What to do. What to do. I figured that the best thing to do, given the circumstances, was take a shower with the poor travel-weary girl and then buy her a one way plane ticket to Montreal. It's amazing how good old-fashioned common sense prevails during those little times of crisis.

With a second album's worth of material ready to go, we now had to look ahead to rehearsing and recording. Our future with Warner Brothers U.S. was tentative at best, due to lack of radio or sales south of the border. We arranged to have their head A&R (artist and repertoire) man fly up and attend a high school gig in Thorold. The group was in top form, the audience was in top form, the A&R guy was in top form. The only problem being was that he couldn't pull himself away from shooting hoops in an adjacent gym to even check us out. It had probably been nothing more than a formality at this point but we were soon label-less.

But not for long.

1972 ...

The "Arthur"
Photo: Myron Zabol

FLUDD...ON!

Frank Davies was an aristocratic Englishman, now residing in Toronto. Francis, to his mom, was a gentleman through and through and you just knew that he could always be counted on to use the proper fork during dinner. His Love Productions had recently scored heavy radio and retail success with A Foot In Coldwater's debut single 'Make Me Do Anything You Want.'

Although our contemporaries at the time included Mainline, Crowbar, April Wine, and Lighthouse, there was always an element of tension when it came to Foot, as they shared home turf with us. The Scarborough quintet, with its emphasis on swirling Hammond organ, moody lyrics, and heavy guitar and bass sounds was a favourite with the biker crowd but still managed to grab a hold of the ladies as a result of the Robert Plant affectations of lead vocalist Alex Machin.

Frank signed us to his Daffodil Records label, which was distributed by Capitol in Canada. It was at this time that talk turned to adding a fifth member, but as our track record with guitarists hadn't been so great, we now considered a keyboard player. A classified ad in Rolling Stone magazine, of all places, produced one Peter Csanky.

An electronics wiz, Csanky came equipped with much more than mere technical know how, he had TWO Mellotrons. The Mellotron was a curious English keyboard instrument that utilized pre-recorded tapes of cellos, violins, flutes, and voices, and in the hands of the right player/operator could give your little combo the added dimension of a small orchestra. Think 'Days Of Future Past' era Moodie Blues or the obvious Lennon application to 'Strawberry Fields Forever.'

Although limited as a player, much like myself during my wagon toting Wanderer's days, Csanky at least looked the part in long hair and walrus moustache and he certainly had the right equipment. Rehearsals were exciting once more as this exotic new sound drove us to musical heights only hinted at before, and Brian and Ed's new songs sounded more English than ever.

We were now booked into Manta Sound Studios with Lee de Carlo as co-producer/engineer with Brian. With almost a month of booked studio time ahead of us we could spend all the time we needed to realize Brian's vision. Great songs like 'Homemade Lady' and 'Down, Down, Down' would now have the balls missing on the debut album. Studio owner Andy

Hermant was deputized into adding a little banjo hook to 'Cousin Mary', a natural single that would eventually earn itself an award for over 100,000 air plays.

Csanky's "less is more" piano and Mellotron noodlings actually enhanced the songs beyond anyone's expectations and John Andersen and I had developed into a formidable rhythm section with hints of R&B fatback thrown into the McCartney/Starr style that we had previously favoured. Brian and Ed shared lead vocal duties, quite often trading verses while I was content to act as their Graham Nash, fleshing out the three-part blend with my "fifth" harmonies on top.

It was during this period that I took to wearing nothing but sleepwear at sessions. Pajamas and slippers, with a terry cloth housecoat or satin robe seemed much more comfortable than ball-squeezing satin trousers. At one session, band, roadies, management, studio staff, and assorted guests all wore those one-piece pajamas with the trap doors in the seat. In shades of pink, powder blue, or yellow we looked like a menagerie of gay birds as we went about our recording work. Many pictures of this session were snapped, with the exception of Lee de Carlo, whose Dad had been a major New York crime figure, thus rendering him somewhat camera shy from habit.

The album soon developed a life of its own although the obvious influences of The Move, The Beatles, and others could clearly be heard in the final mixes.

During one break in the proceedings I was sitting in the lobby when Laugh In regular Arte Johnson strolled by. He was in town recording a Christmas special and certainly had no idea who I was. "Well," he said to his producer as he passed by me, "at least we're getting better results than this bunch over here," pointing in the direction of our studio.

"Hey man, why don't you go fuck yourself!" I said to the diminutive TV star who thought better of pursuing the issue and instead ducked into studio "B" to try 'Jingle Bells' for the umpteenth take.

With the sessions completed it was now time to concentrate on Fludd's real reason for being, causing trouble!

118   GREG GODOVITZ

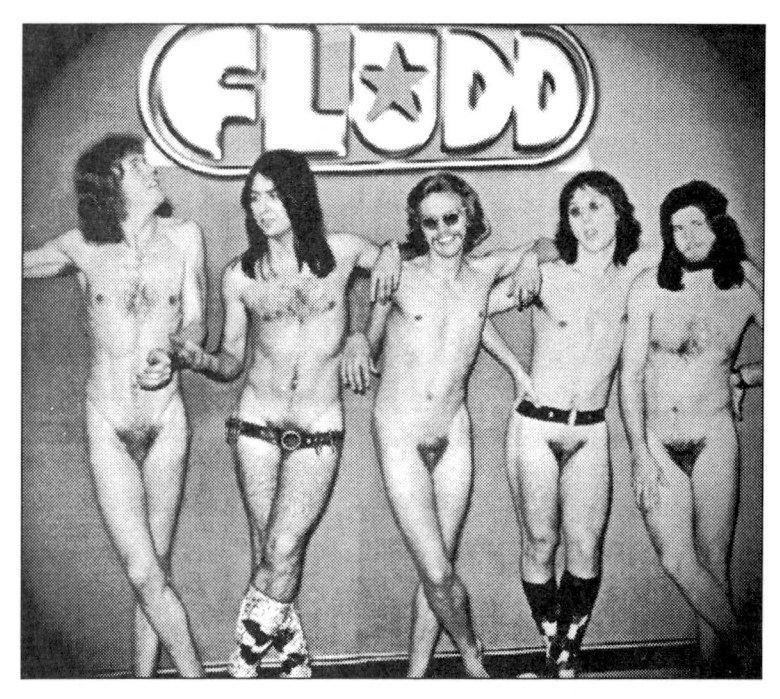

The controversial censored LP cover for the "Cock On" LP ... restored here by Unidisc in the 1990s. Photo: John Rowlands

1972 ...

Daffodil Records label copy of the censored "Cock On" LP.

Fludd In The Nud

The original title for our second album had been Cock On, a Cockney expression meaning "precisely." The Canadian record industry, being somewhat cautious, said no way. The LP was eventually released as ...ON!. When we finally held the finished product in our hands it looked like a Christmas present with the cover a sparkling metallic red with gold lettering that looked more like ...ONE than ...ON! owing to the graphic used for the exclamation point. The gatefold included individual shots of the five band members including a very camp photo of yours truly sporting a tear on my cheek made of glittering stars. I cringe to this day but as I was only twenty-one at the time, and probably high, I put it down to the impetuousness of youth. Csanky, with only mere weeks in the group, was already questionable as a permanent member and was thus given the foldout in the middle rendering him creased in the face whenever the album was opened up. He still didn't look half as goofy as I did with that stupid teardrop on my cheek though.

The group decided that what we needed to do was to generate some good old-fashioned controversy to coincide with the album's release and the obvious choice was to take the piss out of the very blinkered Puritans who wouldn't let us title our record as we saw fit in the first place. If it couldn't be Cock On!, then it would bloody well be Cock Off!

Early in December we gathered at the offices of Rainbow magazine, which was published by rock writers Ritchie Yorke and Martin Melhuish, to pose for a series of revealing semi-nude shots. Tucking the other members of the band firmly between our legs we posed naked save for the odd pair of flash boots or strategically placed belt, for renowned rock photographer John Rowlands' camera. My tongue, as is evident in the published photo, is nothing if not firmly in cheek but my own shortcomings with a straight razor caused me a bit of a set back when I attempted to shave my pubic hair into the shape of a heart. The result was far from heart shaped and I would advise the help of a trusted, no, make that very trusted loved one should you ever have the need to replicate the same on your own person.

After the indoor session we decided to take this a step further by posing in a nearby park and so we all donned our long winter coats and proceeded to the secret rendezvous point by limo. Csanky decided that he would drive his own car, and being somewhat slower arrived after a roll of film had already been surreptitiously shot of the four of us. In so doing his fate was already sealed and in true shifty Fludd fashion we had the photographs to prove it. All the members gave curious bystanders on their balconies behind us one quick flash as we raced off laughing to the warmth of the limo, which raced away before the cops arrived. This stunt would be repeated some twenty-five years later by Toronto's Barenaked Ladies in a photo but I've never had the courage to seek one out.

The subsequent poster was released in the December 18, 1972 edition of Rainbow and was quickly the locker pin up of choice for high school girls everywhere. The backlash was immediate as Fludd was banned by various high schools for their habit of "taking their clothes off," as one principal wrote in a widely circulated letter. The attendant publicity was wonderful, to be sure, and in due course we would be back corrupting the minds of youngsters everywhere in dimly lit high school gyms and auditoriums throughout the province.

The record launch party in the posh Centennial Ballroom at The Inn On The Park Toronto was a gala affair attended by every music journalist, scene maker, and groupie that could find a way in.

Press kits were distributed to one and all in brown paper bags with the Rainbow poster drawing much enthusiastic approval, especially from the more liberally minded in attendance.

Dressed in the height of glam rock finery we played a live set that included most of the new album and our radio hits from the first record. Members of Edward Bear, A Foot In Cold Water, the John Gibbs, Ritchie and Annette Yorke and many others took full advantage of Frank Davies' generous hospitality. RPM publisher Walt Grealis was heard to remark "Fludd is the most exciting group in Canada today," and believe me, he would know.

With Christmas less than two weeks away, we flew to England to shop for new stage clothes. The streets of London were ablaze in Christmas cheer and we spent our time noisily celebrating our good fortune with tankards of ale while fat snowflakes transformed the streets outside into scenes straight out of Charles Dickens. At the ATV publishing offices I was given an advance copy of Paul McCartney's new single 'Hi, Hi, Hi.'

The first single from ...ON! was 'Always Be Thinking Of You' which was top ten in Edmonton, or in other words, a stiff. The next single, 'Yes', fared somewhat better and with Ed's penchant for splitting his trousers during the high stepping chorus we were back in the news for corrupting the youth of Canada.

As things so often happen in the tight confines of a rock band there was a growing resentment from myself towards the Pilling's tight reign over the song writing and its attendant royalties. One of my new songs, which chronicled the Fludd in the Nud episode, was dismissed without so much as a "by your leave," prompting me to quit the group. Ed came over to talk to me and dutifully informed me that they had lined up a replacement in only hours.

Gulp!

I hadn't expected that.

It was then agreed upon that my songs would be given the same input as theirs and all was forgiven for the time being. We rehearsed 'Cock On' and it sounded great, with a much Whoier dynamic than the version that Goddo would later record. I don't think that it was ever played in public however and it sat on the shelf until it resurfaced on Goddo's 'Who Cares' LP.

Another notable change at this time was the retirement of the Fludd Bus, which had served us very well indeed in its day in favour of a brand new stretch Cadillac Limousine for the group and a half tonne truck for the gear. Now if the bus had been a chick magnet then the limo was the ultimate panties remover and much debauchery was had behind its tinted windows.

Bruce had his own agenda with the new truck as one night he completely missed a gig after he was arrested lifting lobby furniture from the apartment building next to our townhouse. He was caught red handed loading it into the band's truck which was clearly marked 'FLUDD' in blue letters four feet high on each side. As everyone in the apartment building knew that we lived right across the street it only took a matter of minutes to figure out who was doing some creative decorating and Bruce was hauled off to spend the night locked up.

One night Bruce and I took the limo barhopping and ended up at a club where an old friend of mine was always holding court. Brian "Beau" Stewart was the flashiest guy in the music business. His younger brother Alan was a drummer and had been a life long friend of mine and Beau had always helped us out by loaning us bits of equipment when we first started out.

His office/dressing room upstairs in The Running Pump had to be seen to be believed. While the owner of the place did his business in an adjacent hovel of a room, bereft of the most humble amenities, Beau had transformed his area into a Playboy magazine styled lair of black leather, deep wooded panelling with the thickest shag carpeting and a personal bar that was better stocked than the one in the main club.

Beau had always had a penchant for the finer things in life and he loved showing off his latest toys. He was the first guy I knew that had a spring mounted record player in his convertible, and this was in the early Sixties. Legend had it that he had backed up teen idol Bobby Rydell in the fifties and he now fronted his own group, comprised of some of the city's top musicians, when it suited him.

With girdle tightly in place under frilly shirt and tuxedo, this diamond-pinkie'd, rug-wearing lounge lizard would hold court in an almost imperious manner as one of his stooges prepared his guests a "little taste."

Representing a new age of rock star we were always feted by Beau and his entourage and it was in his office while enjoying this hospitality that someone came up to ask if the limo parked outside was ours. We nodded that it was and continued with our "tastes."

"Well you boys had better drink up because there's someone out there stompin' all over the roof of your car."

With that said Bruce and I ran out of Beau's office and leaped down the stairs where we were suddenly confronted by the sight of some asshole jumping up and down on our car. Spotting us the culprit jumped off the roof and proceeded to run down the hill. I yelled for Bruce to follow in the bruised limo as Alan and I gave chase on foot. Now, "on foot" is sort of stretching things, as I was wearing three-inch platform boots and it was the middle of winter. For some reason I did not slip but seemed to make great time down this treacherous course until my prey diverted off the road and began to run along a partially frozen creek bed. I say partially frozen as he had barely given us the slip when this awful creaking sound occurred and he went through the ice and into the water.

Bruce, having parked the car by the side of the road, now helped us pull this asshole out of the freezing water.

"Please don't hurt me, I'm sorry," our new pal begged.

"What do we do with him," I said. "I don't want him in the car soaking wet like that," and with that Bruce popped the trunk and we dumped the shivering fool into the back.

We went back to our "tastes" and had a hearty laugh or two with good old Beau before eventually calling the cops. When they arrived, we explained what had happened and then opened the limo's trunk to hand over the nearly frozen to death roof crusher who was then roughly handcuffed and whisked off for a night in jail. Feeling sorry for the stupid clod, we didn't press charges, figuring his time in the trunk was penance enough.

Rocko

It was mutually agreed upon that Peter Csanky just wasn't working out. The combination of bad Mellotron tuning and suspect playing abilities made his stay in the Fludd fold rather short lived.

For the time being we were down to being a quartet again until the right person passed the audition. It was at the Jarvis House that I first caught sight of Peter Rochon. With hair and arms flailing wildly, he attacked his keyboards like a man possessed while still managing to play brilliantly.

Skinny and Brian went down to see him the next night and we began rehearsing him within the week. Peter was a bilingual native of Ottawa whose claim to fame was having played with A Mythical Meadow.

He was an odd shaped duck, (think Jake The Snake Roberts), who had a lovely set of tits that the older boys abused in Catholic boarding school. Or so he said.

He spoke fluent French and could dance The Funky Chicken unlike most white men that I have ever seen.

His left hand was a brilliant combination of bass percussive ness and fluent melody and soon we were doubling lines to produce the fattest bottom end that the Fludd sound had not previously enjoyed. He was a patient teacher and my playing improved considerably under his tutelage.

Everything and everybody now seemed to be in a perpetual state of rush in preparation for our upcoming recording sessions in England. The current emphasis was on new material, which would be recorded on our upcoming third LP.

On Sunday, March 11, 1973 we all flew off to England to start work at a new studio called The Manor.

The Man Who Broke The Bank At Monte Carlo
– a Richard Branson story

The close proximity of a fine dining restaurant, a mere cobblestoned courtyard away, was the difference between half cold delivered pizza or a quickly fetched order of escargots, piping hot onion soup and a carafe of French wine. Feeling a bit peckish, I pulled a bathrobe over my flannel pajamas and headed over to Gibby's restaurant which was not fifty feet from Listen Audio Studios in the heart of Old Montreal.

It's not like you often see a grown man padding around in his night wear in the middle of the day but nobody seemed to mind as I made my way over to the counter to order the above mentioned French delicacies to go. The staff was quite used to musicians ordering thusly and would even send someone over to the studio to pick up the dishes later.

As I picked up the tray I could here an unmistakable English voice saying, "I know you," somewhat unsure and then louder as he grew more certain.

"I KNOW YOU!" said Richard Branson, all huge Richard Branson grin and twinkling eyes as he wagged his finger in my general direction.

"Hello Richard, I'm Greg from Fludd and we recorded at The Manor a couple years back." I said.

"Yes, that's right," said the Knight-in-training, "You lot owe me ten thousand pounds!"

The Manor...before we get to The Manor story, let me first tell you a story about how I got to tour the Royal Yacht Britannia, which is owned by the lady who would someday knight Richard Branson

Six Months In a Leaky Boat
– a Queen Elizabethian Boat story

I had the feeling that I was visiting a huge floating cottage. The furniture that I was peering at, albeit distantly through a rather large plate glass window, did not give off the impression of royal splendour at all but more like someone's idea of simple country comfort. With the exception of the million dollar jewel-encrusted elephant, courtesy of the Sultan Of Brunei, on the coffee table, the place looked like someone's rec room, perfect for a night of poker, brewski, perhaps the odd loud fart.

I was invited to tour the Royal Yacht the previous evening after being introduced to two ship's officers who were feigning admiration for my rather beat up Gibson Grabber bass, then on display at the Skydome Hard Rock Cafe.

After a Springsteenian version of 'Gloria' with the Hard Rock house band, it was decided that I could bring my entire family down to tour the yacht, providing of course, that I wore a jacket and tie. I had a lovely Beatles acrylic already in mind.

I'm not going to name the officer who set this up as he stands a pretty good chance at beheading but let's just say that he was up there in rank.

The first order of business was a drink in the officer's own private pub which looked like every other British pub that I've ever visited with the obvious exceptions that this one was:

(a) floating
(b) featured autographed portraits on the walls of the Royals at play
(c) drinks were on the house.

It's almost like they want you to get a bit pissed so you don't notice how normal it all is.

"Look mate, you're one of the few that I've invited on board that hasn't requested a souvenir," said the officer after our tour.

"Well, my request would be a bit...er...unusual...," I stammered.

"I've heard them all mate, what'll you have?" he said, confident in fulfilling my wish.

Spoons and mugs were for the less debauched, I had bigger trout to flounder.

"I...uh...I want some toilet paper from Her Majesty's Private Bathroom!" I burst out, unable to restrain myself. The look on his face was priceless.

"I haven't heard that one before," he started, "but here's what I can do..."

He went on to explain to me that with Charles and Diana due on board the next day, it was impossible for him to accomplish this task at this time but after the boat dry-docked for maintenance back in England the precious paper would be spirited out of the Royal Privy and flown Her Majesty's Post to my then current address where I examined it closely.

Having fantasized triple ply purple velvet sheets with gold embossed crowns to catch the corn I was somewhat taken aback by the cheapness of the Royal Wad. In my hand was nothing more than single ply pink sandpaper, suitable only for the most common of backsides.

Hardly befitting the girl who used the greatest throne of all!

...the cork blarphed as much as popped from the freshly squeezed Bordeaux. My crusty gums, now barely in control of my teeth found the well chewed plastic straw and pathetically sucked back the rich grape's life...

Another dream...shattered!

The Manor

The matronly lady in the bookish glasses was learning the Funky Chicken dance at thirty five thousand feet with two Fludd stickers firmly adhered to her pendulous, sagging breasts. With a cackle of laughter, keyboardist Peter Rochon, resplendent in hot pink satin pants and lurex Nehru shirt offered her yet another Bloody Caesar, fuelling her once extinguished fire as she did her thing in the middle of the jet's cramped aisle.

Rocko, as he had now been christened, humped and whirled, finger-popping to the funk that only he could hear in his head. The stewardesses, as they were known in those days, had only thought that they had seen it all. With our usual level of audience participation the Fluddies had managed to convince everyone on board that this was indeed the place to be and it was a very drunken in flight party that landed at London's Heathrow Sunday March 11, 1973.

Not a punch had been thrown.

Located in the village of Shipton-on-Cherwell, some five miles to the north of Oxford, The Manor was the brainchild of Richard Branson, Virgin Everything's King Midas who had purchased this ramshackle seventeenth century stone manor house and converted the barn area into a then state-of-the-art recording studio. The musicians and studio technicians shared accommodations in the fifteen-plus bedrooms, which also boasted a staff of live-in maids, cooks, and groundskeepers. It was reputed that Henry the Third had built the place as a hunting lodge and that Oliver Cromwell had slept under its roof. As they were both long dead, rock musicians could now record loud music at all times of the day without ever having to bow or curtsey.

TRAVELS WITH MY AMP

I had seen an ad for The Manor in an issue of Melody Maker some months earlier and had pointed it out to Skinny and Brian. Before you could say "We can't really afford this but it would be quite indicative of our rock and roll delusions if we went there," we were standing in the front hall of this beautiful mansion and being designated rooms.

My room, just at the top of the stairs, featured its own fireplace, four poster bed, and en suite bath. Perfect for those after-session sessions. The staff, mostly young English hippie-types with long hair and wanton smiles were quite shocked that the visiting colonials were not squirrel-eating lumberjacks but fully realized rock stars in satin and velvet with more of a penchant for English beaver. The female staff, it should be noted, outnumbered the men. After settling, in the first order of business was getting laid, of course, and with a nice drink in hand I soon found myself in the company of one very French and one very German chambermaid, sitting on the well worn but comfy living room couch, fire ablaze in the giant open hearth and Donovan warbling innocently on the record player.

1973 ...

The "Arthur" at the Manor.
The most
natural of poses.

Photo: Peter Simpkin

"This place is quite old," I slurred. "It's not haunted is it?"

"Yes, zere is a ghost who haunts zee upstairs after dark," cooed my little French cupcake.

"Arghhh," I screamed and burst into crocodile tears, "I'm so sensitive to ghosts, please don't leave me on my own tonight!" and with that the ladies took me upstairs, tucked me in and started a fire in my chamber that wouldn't be extinguished until dawn, when they both left.

Mr. Sensitive was recording in England.

As our rented gear hadn't yet arrived, we had the first Monday off to explore the canal, farm fields, and adjacent church and cemetery on the edge of the grounds. The groundskeeper was a wonderful old character named George who was just stopping off on his way to walking the British Isles top to bottom before he died. At about eighty odd years old and in possession of no teeth to speak of, George cut quite a figure and was always smiling away as he puttered around in the gardens, talking to no one in particular.

Mid March in England is Daffodil season and the flowerbeds were bursting with yellow petals. Meals were prepared in a gloriously ancient kitchen and served in a huge dining hall with open-hearth fireplace and massive L-shaped table. The staff ate with the groups at the same time and the food was fresh and excellent. Bottles of fine wine appeared from the cellar below and conversation was bright and animated during dinner. The whole scene was reminiscent of The Rolling Stones Beggars Banquet and it was good old Ed who supplied the laughs one meal by leaping from the wooden table, only to break his foot in the process. That'll slow him down, I thought, perhaps now I'll take a run at Maggie the chambermaid, seeing as he can't catch me.

Dinner was usually followed by a trip to the Jolly Boatman Pub down the road and in order to get there we would pile into either a vintage Rolls Royce or Bentley. It was during this trip that I began a long and dangerous affair with crawling out the back window of a fast moving car, sliding over the roof to the other side and crawling in the opposite window, to the great amusement of the other drunks riding with me. It was all very Clockwork Orange and the drivers revelled in my escapades by joining in and swerving from side to side in the hopes that I would be shaken off and crushed to death by the following luxury vehicle. No such luck though and it was all matey and no hard feelings as the drivers would have another opportunity to kill me the following evening.

One of the houseguests this particular week was Graham Bond; famed British blues great who's Organization had once boasted such alumni as Jack Bruce and Ginger Baker. Now firmly in the grips of the monkey he took an immediate shine to me as I had a pretty good blues background and also because I knew who he was. He offered to play Mellotron for us should the need arise but it never did. Many nights I would pick up a guitar and with Graham on organ, John on drums and one of the studio engineers on bass we would jam the blues for hours. Learning later that it was also me who was playing bass on the tapes, Graham took me aside and offered me stardom if I would remain in England at the end of the sessions. Happy though I was with the offer I declined and was glad that I didn't accept, as some short months afterwards Graham's body was discovered cut in half under a British Railways train, one half facing up with the other facing down. It was rumoured to be a black magic ritual death.

As if there were not enough distractions already, a Scottish group called Giraffe, who had recently recorded at The Manor, had an actual full grown giraffe flown in for a cover shot. A huge truck backed down the winding driveway carrying a thirty-foot box marked Property Of Scottish Zoo on its sides. Clad in my robe and jammies I spent the foggy morning chasing the terrified beast all around the grounds while imploring it to be friendly and pose for a photo with me. At one point I awoke Ed and Brian to come and have a look just as the giraffe poked his head through their second-storey window. That caught their attention and hangovers were soon forgotten as we all went out to check out our new pal.

The same day, Richard Branson gave me a beautiful English gentlemen's top hat which, coupled with my ever present nightwear, gave me the look of a rock and roll Harpo Marx. A fresh Daffodil each morning in the hat's band set it off perfectly.

With Lee de Carlo at the board once more we got down to laying the bed tracks. The drums and bass sounds were huge and quite different from those achieved in Canada or the States. We even recorded two of my songs, the Ray Daviesesque 'Good Good Life' and perhaps the most stupid song that I have ever written 'English Spaceman', a glittery tribute to David Bowie. With lyrics like "Phobos and Delos, when he is romancing he can gaze at them both," this song was a barf fest of inanity, and would mercifully never be finished. Phobos and Delos by the way are the names of the two Martian moons, which of course Bowie and his Spiders From

Mars rock group would look at on their way home from work.

Tubular Bellows
– a Mike Oldfield story

Now all the time that we were supposed to be recording but were in effect carousing, wenching, and drinking there was this hippie guy sneaking into the studio and using our gear to record this album that he was working on. We were introduced to him as Mike Oldfield and in fact, he was.

There was something about myself in particular that young Mike didn't like.

Was it my flamboyant use of sleeping attire?

Was it my green tongue from too much Creme de Menthe?

Was it the fact that I was fucking my way through most of the female staff, and that his then girlfriend was part of that staff and, as such, an obvious target?

Whatever the reason, and perhaps it was only that Mike was a "serious" musician and didn't need any new pals, he studiously ignored us at all costs. One night I happened upon the youthful Mozart as he composed in the Manor's living room. The music that he was working on looked nothing like standard notation but resembled strange chicken scratches, or to the untrained eye, kindling.

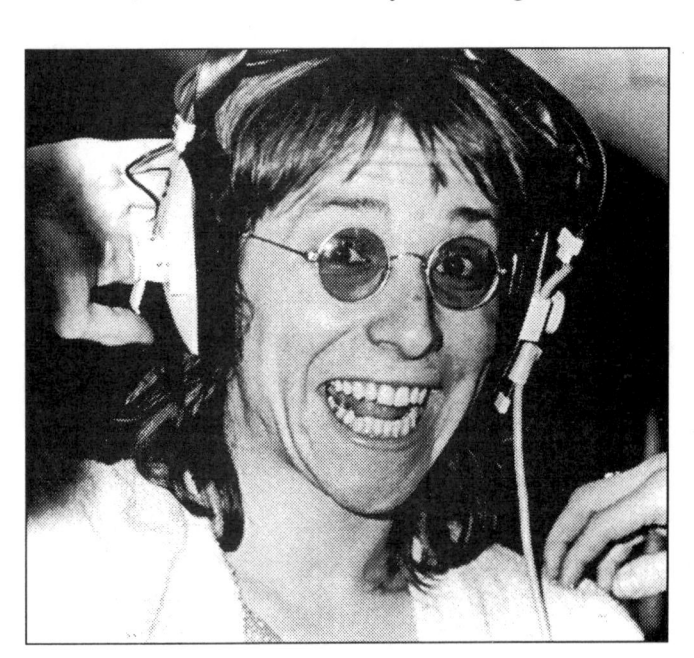

1973 ...

The "Arthur" at the Manor.

Photo: Peter Simpkin

"A bit cold in here, eh Mike?" I said in the spirit of true friendship.

"Mmmmrmph," snorted Mike, ignoring me.

"In that case I believe I'll start a wee blaze," I said, not taking the bait. "Let's just pile up this dry old wood here nice and high."

"Mmmmrmph," snorted Mike, ignoring me and diligently composing away.

Now Mike was starting to get to me just a little bit so I thought that a little practical joke might be in order. Something harmless but effective, cruel but fair.

I HAD IT!

I would light his musical score on fire!

Perfect, I thought.

"Well Mike, the old fire's ready to go but there's nothing for kindling so I'll just reach back here on the table and use a piece of this paper here..." and with that mumbled I took a sheet of the original score of Tubular Bells and lit a match to it.

The sound that now came forth from Mike was somewhat reminiscent of Linda Blair's possessed demon child in *The Exorcist*, a movie that would eventually use a piece of this very Tubular Bells for dramatic effect.

"ARRRRAGGHHAU!!" Mike screamed as he leaped over the coffee table to retrieve the precious manuscript from the hearth.

With a lovely little jig he danced the flames out.

The smouldering paper now safely in his shaking hands, I took my leave of Mike with these words, "Oh, I'm sorry man, was that your sheet music that I just set on fire?" I chuckled softly, exiting the room. Yes, what I had done was uncalled for in the extreme, but a valuable lesson had been learned here. Never, I repeat, NEVER leave your brilliant manuscript in reaching distance of an asshole armed with matches.

For the rest of our stay Mike retreated whenever I drifted into his orbit.

Later that same week...

"Comfy Ed?" I asked innocently as the wounded singer relaxed in front of the roaring living room fire, book in hand, broken foot propped up on pillows.

John Andersen snickered at my side.

"Yeah Godo, very comfy," was his reply.

"Fire nice and toasty is it?" I asked politely, the spirit of brotherhood coursing through my veins.

"Toasty!" confirmed Ed.

Actually, it wasn't the spirit of brotherhood coursing through my veins at all, it was too much wine. John and I had lifted the wine cellar key from Skinny and had made ourselves useful down below with corkscrew and glass.

Maybe a touch too useful.

"Can we get you anything Ed old pal, some eggs perhaps?"

"Eggs?" said the now confused vocalist as the first volley of God's perfect creations hurtled towards their reclining target.

The heretofore late night quiet was shattered with the anguished cries of the betrayed as Ed lurched forward, now covered in the sticky rooster goo.

"You fuckers will pay for this!" Ed raged as we tossed a few more at him, a couple at the ancient tapestry over the hearth, and a couple into the flames themselves where they crackled away with a good morning sizzle and smell.

The Manor kitchen staff had stockpiled dozens of like projectiles just outside the kitchen door and it was there that Andy and I had hatched our plan. It wasn't a real plan as such, more like two inexperienced drinkers getting very experienced in a short space of time and coming up with a great stupid idea. As I was clad in my terry cloth robe I was capable of carrying up to a dozen or more eggs without reloading.

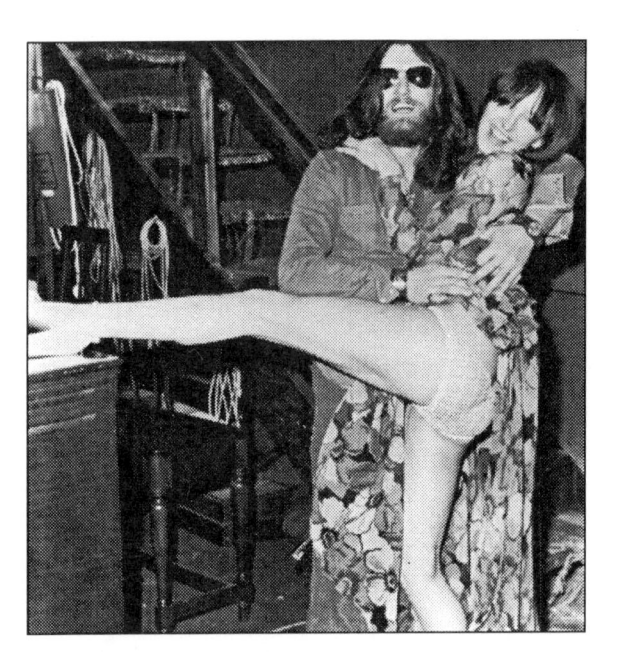

1973 ...

Brian Pilling checks for dust with Maggie the Maid at the Manor.

Photo: Peter Simpkin

Our next stop was Brian's room where we burst through the door and let him have it while he was in the middle of letting one of the chambermaids have it. Covered in various sticky goos, he swore revenge and was soon in hot pursuit, armed with a jug of very cold water, which soon found its mark on my back. While John and I reloaded I smashed a couple eggs into the back of his head and ran screaming through the kitchen as eggs flew helter skelter around my ears, crashing against the walls.

Now it was every man for himself as doors were kicked in and innocent victims were either pelted with eggs or drenched with garbage pails of freezing water. The staff were now running around, not really joining in as much as trying to protect things while we pelted them with anything we could lay hands to.

There was one beautiful area where a mezzanine overlooked a hallway below; this became a favoured snipers nest as two or three garbage pails of freezing water were dumped on unsuspecting enemies below. Skinny, our manager, the voice of reason itself, was roused from his slumber with a pail of cold water all over his sleeping form. The madness continued well into the early hours, there would be no eggs for breakfast this morning. Soaking wet and covered in chicken embryo, I made my way to my room and gently pushed back the door.

Expecting the worst I was shocked to see the fire burning brightly in the hearth, with the candlelight dancing on the walls. My sheets were turned down ever so gently and all that was missing was a mint on my pillow. My room, possibly because I hadn't been in it all night, had somehow escaped the carnage. Slipping out of my wet pajamas I towelled off as best I could and then, exhausted and totally drunk, slipped into bed.

I slipped into bed all right.

Something was dreadfully wrong.

Something warm and very sticky was all over me.

Throwing back the covers I could make out in the warm fire's glow that someone had gone to all this trouble to make my room seem nice and cosy, and then had deposited a huge load of shit in the middle of my bed.

Brian!!!

I pulled the sheets up and instantly passed out.

The next morning I awoke with that awful feeling of having absolutely no recollection of the previous evening's horrors. I smelled awful and was disgusted to realize that I'd shit myself whilst I slept. And then, even worse, the awful realization that it was someone else's shit!

After showering I trudged downstairs where not a good morning could be heard, instead the sight of everyone cleaning egg from murals and tapestries, carpets and furniture. As I walked through the kitchen door in search of some morning air I saw Richard Branson getting out of his car and heading my way.

Trying to make believe that I was invisible, I backed through the door as he sang out, "Here Greg, might I have a word with you?"

My shoulders were so stooped in shame by this point that a career in bell ringing wouldn't have been out of the question as I slowly made my way over to our gracious host's side.

"I understand that I missed a bit of fun here last night?" he said cheerfully as I stared intently at his shoes.

They were nice shoes.

"Yeah, I guess so..." I lamely began.

"Well, next time you plan another night like that please let me know so that I can join in!" and with that he walked past me to inspect the damage.

And that was all that was said about it.

Truly great men are born that way.

After a night celebrating my twenty-second birthday, which included a cake shaped like a huge breast we partied down at the Jolly Boatman and later attempted some drunken vocals. The next day I went to look at Rolls Royce Phantom limousines at a dealership in Oxford. I was in the company of one of the chambermaids who, although in her twenties, favoured schoolgirl outfits, in and out of bed. The very proper English salesperson, reminiscent of John Cleese, upon finding out that I was staying at The Manor, was only too delighted to pour us champagne in the back of the most expensive car on the lot and even managed a chuckle as I began to shoot sparks at him from my toy space pistol, which at one point fell out of my belt onto the car's floor. Eccentric behaviour from young rock types was actually encouraged in England and, as many very rich rock stars lived in the general vicinity, there was no doubt that my intentions were honourable in viewing this wonderful car with the possible intention of having it shipped to Canada. Of course my intentions were merely to have a laugh, a drink, and, if we could shake Mr. Fawlty, perhaps a quickie in the back seat with the young lass. I had to settle for the laugh and the free bubbly.

The recording aspect of our time in England seemed to be spent more and more on drinking, screwing, and generally doing everything but serious work. It was strange but nobody ever said anything about this and the clock was ticking away on our allotted time here.

Mike Oldfield's project was coming along smartly, though.

The next day we piled into the Bentley and headed down to London to shop. Listening to children's stories on BBC 2 on a warm spring English day was perfection itself as the luxury car descended on the King's Road. Alkasura was one of the trendiest boutiques and it was here that I scored a beautiful red and white candy-striped satin suit. All of the boys were busy trying on great stage clobber when I caught sight of Rocko trying on a beautiful purple satin jacket. Inquiring as to matching pants, the porcelain-skinned salesgirl pointed out that the matching piece for that particular jacket would be a full-length dress. Rocko looked to me for some much needed advise and of course I convinced him to go for it.

When he emerged from the dressing room a line had been crossed. Up to that moment I had been the most outrageous dresser in the group but there was no way that I was going to wear girl's clothing. Rocko won knickers down. When we got back to the Manor we all tried on our new stuff and Rocko got the best reaction with his new gown, which was now accessorised with lurex evening gloves, a touch of makeup and three-inch platform boots. He cut quite a dashing figure although of what no one could be sure.

The next day we posed for group shots using various archways, bridges, and the two luxury cars as backdrops. The band really looked great and it was these photos that really captured Fludd at its best.

In the afternoon, our English publishing company, ATV, arranged a press reception but not one of the invited journalists showed up. Perhaps they had had enough of us at The Maple Music Junket the previous year. I spent the evening playing the blues with Graham Bond. Things were winding down now; we had certainly made our presence felt without really having accomplished anything but a load of great bed tracks, which would never be finished. Brian and Ed went off to visit relatives in Birmingham while Rocko took off for Sherwood Forest. The rest of the boys went to London to catch flights home.

A group of African musicians from Osibisa were now booked in to begin recording and, on Graham's recommendation, I'm asked to stick around to record a track or two. The entire atmosphere at the Manor now changed completely as these funk warriors took up residence and the staff

1973 ... March 11-28

*Fludd at the Manor.
Left to right:
Brian Pilling, Bjorn Andersen, Ed Pilling, Greg Godovitz, Peter Rochon.*

Photos: Peter Simpkin

adapted to a whole new set of rules virtually overnight. Girls who had once been draped over us were now smoking huge spliffs with guys named Remy, Dell, and Chilly. I was feeling quite uncomfortable and spent as much time in my room as possible waiting for Rocko to return so we could catch a flight home. The session that I was involved with was a fair disaster as I was just not cut out to play funk bass and they probably rerecorded the lines the moment a suitable player could be brought in. I did get to hear an almost finished version of Tubular Bells well in advance of its eventual release and it was revolutionary and brilliant in structure and execution. Rocko finally returned from Sherwood Forest now sporting an oversized Robin Hood cap and with that we bid a fond adieu to all at The Manor. I drove down to London with my schoolgirl pal and booked us into a hotel in order to rest up for the trip home. For some reason I was very tired at the airport as she took her leave and I joined Rocko, Ed, and Brian only as Mick Walsh and John had missed the flight.

The flight home was great as British rockers Wishbone Ash and Vinegar Joe were also on board. These two acts would hook up with Gentle Giant in Toronto at Massey Hall for the start of their package tour. Our travel time was spent exchanging road tales, drinking, and, of course, chatting up the stewardesses, who were young and digging it. I managed to find a girl flying solo back to Canada and before you could say Mile High Club we were the best of friends.

The next night we attended the concert and my diary reports the scores as follows: Wishbone Ash*, Vinegar Joe**(even with a young Robert Palmer on vocals), with Gentle Giant**** the clear winners.

It was just after our return from England that our drummer, John, decided that he'd had enough and wanted out of the group but, in true Pilling fashion, he was convinced to hang in until after our rapidly approaching western tour. He began, however, to not give a shit and his playing, once a source of great pride, took a dive while the rest of the band rallied to get on with it.

At a college gig two nights later, I was attacked by what turned out to be the school bully, who took great offence with my choice of stage wear. John had seen me getting done and had jumped on the guy's back, which was very nice of him, all things considered, only to get lumped for his trouble. Fortunately for us but not so fortunate for the school bully, Ed poked his head out of our dressing room, quickly appraised the situation, and then beat the bully into a fearsome mess. We were astonished later to receive a letter from the college, commending Ed for dealing with this guy, who was well disliked, even at his own school.

Westward Ho The Limo
– Showdown in Kirkland Lake

It was now into the limo for a trip to Vancouver. The last single to be released from the ...ON! LP was 'Cousin Mary', which had been very radio friendly indeed and stayed top ten long enough to warrant another tour. Our current single was the very Beatle-eque 'Yes', which would pop up on AM radio as we made our way westward.

Our first stop was Kirkland Lake and it was here that something very crazy happened that would affect the rest of the trip. We had made a wrong turn somewhere up north but before we backtracked to find the right road we stopped for lunch before continuing. The sight of a bunch of long haired weirdo's in a flashy new Cadillac limo in these parts could only lead to one obvious conclusion; we were the much-rumoured drug dealers that the Ontario Provincial Police, aka OPP, had been expecting. Two OPP helicopters were soon following us, although we ourselves were completely unaware of the situation. As we arrived in Kirkland Lake, we were pleased to see a number of police cruisers surround our car, lights flashing.

A police escort! An excellent entrance.

Now, a police escort to the gig would have been mighty impressive indeed but instead we were directed to stay in the car and follow the officers to the local police department where we were hustled out and shown into an empty office. While we were thusly sequestered the boys in blue made merry by tearing the inside panelling of the limo out, searching for the STUFF!

I was summoned out soon after and questioned about the inordinate amount of pill bottles that had been found in my luggage.

"We got a serious bust with this one," smirked the hick cop as I pointed out that although there was no denying the quantity of the drugs, they were all legally prescribed and then I took great joy in popping a Valium right in front of them.

The Valium had been prescribed for stress and these fellows were making me nervous.

Quickly rejoining the lads I was told that we were being taken out one by one and strip-searched by these fools. There was also a police sniffer dog being brought up from North Bay and "...if there's anything to find you can bet she'll find it." There was a low chorus of "oooohhhh's" from the group as the red-faced cop split. We could now hear a ruckus outside as the local fans gathered in front of the precinct and began demonstrating our detention and the possible cancellation of the concert.

"WE WANT THE BAND, WE WANT FLUDD, POLICE SUCK," seemed the popular choices.

There was however, one little problem, and that was that Skinny had a huge tour-sized chunk of very potent hash, not only in his jacket pocket but also in this very police office.

We needed a distraction.

Now it struck me funny that it took five cops to oversee the strip searches but only one was on guard for the rest of us. Ed and I asked to use the facilities but Barney Fife here said, "Oh no you don't, you're not dumping anything down there, I'll be watching you the whole time. The rest of you just sit here 'til we get back." With that said the cop followed us into the bathroom and almost had his face close enough for spray while Ed took a leak.

I couldn't go, on account of this guy looking so intently at my dick, it was a pretty homo kind of situation, and I froze.

As the dog hadn't arrived and everyone's assholes were free of bags of high quality shit, we were released to play our show while Skinny was held hostage. As we hopped into the limo, I said to Brian, "What did Skinny do with the hash?"

"He opened up a file cabinet and took his sweet time finding the right criminal's folder before dumping the hash in and closing the drawer," he said laughing and the image that I conjured up had me bent over in hysterics.

The show went great and soon afterwards the hostage was back with the group. We were all concerned about the famous drug sniffer dog from North Bay but Skinny said that the stupid thing was more interested in wagging its tail and humping the furniture and it eventually came up empty-pawed.

The ultimate drag was that these cops, pissed off at the lack of success in their big bust, now began calling up precincts that we would be travelling through and we were soon being hassled every hundred miles or so. The next day Ed got a $75.00 ticket from some cop just as we pulled into Winnipeg. On Monday April 16, 1973 we performed at the beautiful soft seat Playhouse Theatre for CBC Television, to be included in a series of upcoming music specials involving some of the country's hottest groups. The production was amazing, certainly more lights and PA than we had ever used but, despite the nervousness at having the show recorded live, we rose to the occasion and earned three standing ovations and an encore. Ed finished the gig in grand style by leaping from the top of the stacked PA cabinets, bringing the group and the show to a crashing close as he hit the stage. On the finished broadcast this was shown in slow motion for full dramatic effect.

After the show we returned to the hotel where our local record company had set up a party in our honour that included what they felt was an entertainment worthy of our achievements.

I now go on record as saying that the following story is not for the squeamish, faint of heart, and especially my Mother.

Skip to the next page Vera.

This especially goes for my sister-in-law, Sandy.

Okay, I'm still going to do a bit of editing to protect the guilty so you'll just have to use your imagination at times during this next item.

Here are a few helpful words to fill in the space:

...dog...pwick...Who...fucking...suck...boy...load...roadie

Ready?

The record company guys started hustling a group of us out of the main party and spirited us down to a nearby hotel room. In attendance were a couple members of Guess --- and future Lover---s. Everyone was quite drunk, stoned, and very confused until one of the record company guys returned with this gross looking chubby girl who had brought along her pet ---.

"Okay -----, you can start your show now," said record company guy and the room erupted in much laughter, screams, and cries of disbelief.

"Oh, I get it!" one wag pointed out, "It's Lassie cum home!" and the room fell apart.

Now most people have seen a porno movie in their time, some perhaps involving a spot or two of this sort of debauchery, but let me tell you, innocent reader, this is a sick thing to see in person.

In romantic missionary position the two lovers exchanged intimacies, rudely ignoring their guests.

"---- him off!" someone yelled.

"THAT'S GROSS!!" said the featured entertainer.
"Yeah, but ------- him is okay right?" and the room dissolved.
Just then, good old ----- came into the room. Drunk.
VERY drunk.
"Hey, what's goin' on in here???"
With that ----- pulled out his ----- and said "Move over wover and let a weal man in there!"
Now it was getting ugly as the --- had some serious competition from the drunken ------.
The --- hadn't dropped his ---- yet so he was getting pretty upset at this interloper making moves on his gross girlfriend and began attacking good old -----.
The snarling combat of man and beast was more than any of us there could take and, not wishing to see the outcome of this primitive love ritual, we fell out of the room en masse, in search of human companionship. I ended up jamming with the hotel house band and picking up one of the waitresses.
"Got any pets?" I asked her as we made for the hotel elevator.

The next evening we went to see the filming of The Greaseball Boogie Band's performance at The Playhouse. The Greaseballs were a Sha Na Na kind of fifties act and were likewise very entertaining. After the performance we were all invited back to the director's parents' house for a grand party. The house turned out to be a huge mansion in the Osborne Village area of central Winnipeg that was owned by the Grand Dame of The Royal Winnipeg Ballet. The party was in the ballet studio on the main floor, just off the main entrance way with its fountain and crystal chandeliers. There was a veritable feast on the huge banquet tables running up and down the centre of this immense room.

Ron, the director of the television shows, was also a great guy and took us up to his quarters at the top of the house. What a difference from the downstairs as all of his rooms were painted black with snow-white furnishings lit by black light.

An acid-heads delight.

Now there was this girl at the party who called herself Juicy Lucy, which, although hardly original, turned out to be quite accurate as she was currently taking on all comers.

Excuse me.

She was in the process of blowing me when another tour arrived upstairs to smoke or whatever and soon interest shifted to our side of the room, with a line forming to my right.

Now, much like the peeing incident back at the Kirkland Lake Police station, I was finding it difficult to complete this normally easy program.

"Hey boyo," it was Greaseball's Scottish drummer, *Shortass*, "if ye cannae finish then make way for someone who can!!"

Never argue with a drunken Scotsman with a boner. I moved away as the line inched closer.

The next day the boys piled into the limo for the trip across the prairies but I had already had quite enough of the police harassment so I convinced Mick Walsh to go in the car while I travelled with Bruce and John in the truck. The next phase of the tour was playing small arena gigs in interior British Columbia.

Creston, Nelson, Trail, Oliver, Kelowna, Penticton, Fernia, Kimberly, Revelstoke, Vernon, Salmon Arm, and Kamloops go by in a blaze of beautiful scenery, half empty arenas (or is it half full arenas?), naughty girls, hot springs, curried dinners, ghost towns, too much alcohol, and far too much drug abuse.

The main problem as far as I could see was the complete lack of consistency when it came to playing the concerts themselves. From gig to gig it could be brilliant to downright diabolical, all in the space of twenty-four hours. Perhaps if we hadn't drank so much every dinnertime, things might have been better. One of the best moments for me was going to a little movie theatre in Nelson where we saw *Slaughterhouse Five* which began my life-long love for the novels of writer Kurt Vonnegut Jr.

And so on.

Daffodil rush released our latest single which was 'C'mon C'mon' from the ...ON! LP.

We ran out of gas at what seemed like the top of the world. There was snow all around and you could see your breath. Even though the brilliant sunrise made it difficult to see without squinting it was brutally cold at that altitude. You knew that you wouldn't die up there in the majestic Rockies, as sooner or later another adventurer would drive by, this being the only highway into Vancouver.

The dawn had broken on another beautiful day.

Bruce had much better eyesight than I did.

"Hey," he suddenly cried out, "I think I see a town way down in the valley!" I could hardly see the valley, let alone a town.

Easing back into the truck's cab Bruce released the hand brake and we began coasting down the great mountain. With ten miles to navigate down a mountain road the free-fall trip had its moments, but we glided up to the gas pumps and waited until the service centre opened.

God is the warden.

A reprieve!

We were back in Vancouver and playing at The Body Shop for four days. After three weeks of playing the interior, we were all ready for a bit of big city. Things had changed here; the glitter mentality had caught up to the hippie myth. The club was alive with strangely dressed creatures of no fixed sexuality. The hippies still moved with their butterfly dance, transfixed on some beat that only they were tuned into but the come hither looks and sensual undulations of these new night creatures proved far more alluring.

The gigs were great but the after hours parties were bordering on orgiastic as the young dudettes of Vancouver lined up their band favourites. I had my entire head dyed bright orange, with the peroxide burning the hell out of my scalp. When I look back at all the abuse that I put my hair through it's no wonder that there's very little left today.

We stayed, as usual, at The Tropicana Hotel with a fantastic view of the mountains and harbour to groove on. One day, while looking down from the balcony overlooking Robson Street I spied an Indian in full regalia, including chief's head dress, sitting on a curb. I had to check this out and raced downstairs. The old Indian turned out to be Chief Dan George, the famous Canadian actor. Not long before this we had seen him as "Old Lodge Skins," opposite Dustin Hoffman in *Little Big Man* and now he was sitting on a curb right before my eyes. I was kicking myself that I didn't have a camera with me.

"It's a good day to drink, eh grandfather?" I asked in reference to his screen roll as he mumbled back at me, absolutely pissed.

"Mmmmrrmfarf de white man mmmrther," Old Lodge Skins smarfed.

I sat down next to him but when he looked at me I could tell that he had absolutely no idea who, what, or where I was, he was so out of it. I soon tired of this but raced upstairs nonetheless to try to find a camera.

As the other lads looked over the balcony we could see the local police loading him into the back of the cruiser.

By this time we were all accomplished road warriors, well versed in the ways of truck stop etiquette, hotel decorum, and certainly never farting on a slumbering band mate's nose. Our level of musicianship was growing in leaps and bounds, but what some of us were really getting good at was dealing with girls.

Sexually speaking at least.

Not everyone in the group was a sex maniac. For instance, I never saw Mick Walsh even look at another woman the whole time that I knew him, and John Andersen was very discreet on the extremely rare occasions that needs of the flesh had to be addressed. Even Brian, who was now married to a right shrew, was not given to banging everything in sight.

Rocko could get silly, given the right circumstances.

Actually, I lied a few lines ago; it was really only Ed and the roadies who plucked the fruit off the vine, as it were.

And myself, of course.

But truth be told, at least as far as I was concerned, it was never full-on sex as much as getting head. Whether it was in dressing rooms, hotel stairwells, airplane rest rooms, back seats of taxi cabs or wherever, this was a no-fuss recreational activity that quite often presented itself to touring musicians.

The weirdest incident was just after our first single was released and a lovely young thing approached me at a shopping mall and then proceeded to drag me into a very straight men's clothing store. She grabbed a couple of totally out of fashion shirts as she followed me into the change room. Now I had every reason to suspect that the entire male store staff knew exactly what was going on but nobody said or did anything and the young lady in question got what she was after and gingerly replaced the shirts as we exited the store.

On this particular trip to Vancouver the young lady whom I had spent time applying lipstick to on the last tour while Brian was in the next bed visited me. She turned up at our hotel and proceeded to engage me in the most wonderful afternoon delight. After I had finished she took a while longer, seemingly enjoying the fruit of her efforts, before sensuously snaking her way up my body and then very calmly spitting the entire load into my mouth!

Holy shit, this was a new one.

What to do, what to do?

I was thoroughly grossed out but I had options. I could spit it out obviously but I really didn't want to make a mess. Option two wasn't much better, I could take it like a man and swallow it. Sort of recycling, I quickly surmised and, for the only time in my life, I sampled myself what hundreds of former partners had likewise experienced. I grossed myself out but after that I always had a healthy respect for those who thought it pleasurable. Later in the evening she serviced me again but this time I held her head down until I was positive that the coast was clear.

Like I said, a healthy respect.

We finished up the tour by driving back into the interior for dates in Penticton and Kimberly. I once again travelled with Bruce and John Glover in the truck and we even brought along my little friend, who lived in Penticton. Somewhere in the highest Rocky Mountains it seemed like the perfect time for her to do her thing so John held her legs out the passenger side window while she went to work on me in the middle seat of the truck's cab. Anyone seeing us, either coming or going, would be treated to what looked like a beautiful peace sign made out of firm young flesh.

Bruce, normally an excellent driver, was now quite smitten with this young vixen's obvious joie de vie at her appointed task and began paying more attention to her than the road ahead. I casually noticed that he was also driving with one hand. The sound of a wailing car horn momentarily brought us all back to reality as Bruce had drifted into the oncoming lane as we rounded a bend in the road.

Now up in the mountains it is almost futile to have guardrails, as they only slow you down anyway, and so, with that in mind, I grabbed the steering wheel along with Bruce and tried to jerk the truck back into our own lane before the oncoming car ploughed into us head on. The car, horn screaming, swerved around us as we hit the gravel shoulder a mere ten feet from a five hundred foot precipice. We fishtailed wildly before Bruce coaxed the truck back onto the road.

The little princess, busy enjoying herself in my lap, didn't miss a stroke during this entire incident but my dick, perhaps hoping to at least save himself and survive the crash into the valley below, had shrunk to nothingness, and would not return from hiding for several hours.

Another lesson well learned, always keep both hands on the steering wheel.

We finished up our western tour with a great arena gig where my diary shows that we "rock on like fuck," whatever that mean's. After the show we drove all night to Calgary where we caught a flight home. I arrived back in Toronto the next afternoon, owing everyone in the group money from the previous month but I had a million dollars worth of great memories.

Broke or not, these were the best of times.

Fists Of Fury
– another Ed Pilling story

The motel was packed for Super Bowl Whatever. The Fluddies were in the northern Ontario town of Elliot Lake for a concert and we couldn't care less about the "big game." The distance between my room and the Pilling's was about thirty feet or so. If someone tells you that the river is not very wide but there is a really good chance that it is full of man-eating fish and you will be devoured do you take the chance? I was quite bored in my room so I took the chance.

Perhaps it was the black crushed velvet pants with the Indian embroidery, perhaps it was the white ballet slippers, perhaps it was just me, but not ten feet from the safety of my sleep chamber and I was now being held up against the corridor wall by not one but two very drunken football fans.

"WHAT THE FUCK ARE YOU SUPPOSED TO BE?!" screamed the goon as my toes stretched to touch rug.

"LET'S FUCKING KILL THIS FAG!" reasoned his pal.

All at once I spy good old Ed walking towards my new pals and me.

"CHECK OUT FUCKIN' GOLDILOCKS HERE!" said goon number one just as Ed was in striking distance. Instantly I was free as he crashed to the floor, Ed having rendered him blissfully unawares with one well placed punch. Turning his attention to the other guy, Ed cocked his fist as the guy threw up both hands, and begged for mercy as he abandoned his slumbering pal to flee down the hall.

"Godo, either stay in your room or stay in ours until we leave for the show," Ed said as we stepped over the sleepy goonie.

I followed Ed into his room.

My hero!

Bob Segarini on the set of "Musical Friends" (CFCF-TV). The fateful meeting day between Bob and Greg.

Photo courtesy: Peter Kruchelenski

HEY!!!...THIS JUST IN!!!
MARCH 15, 1999

I just got back from Bob Segarini's place north of the city. He lives in a hundred year old log cabin nestled in the woods about thirty minutes from the draggier aspects of Toronto. My wife vacations in India, China, and Australia. I go to Stouffville.

After an amazing roast beef dinner and a good swim in his very well stocked bar we sat around singing Beatles, Searchers, and Hollies songs. Our voices are now the product of too many smoky nights in too many bourbon soaked clubs but there is naturalness to the sound that rises above any loss of range. Bob looks more like Buffalo Bill Cody these days with grey hair tied back in a pony tail, bad teeth, and skin the colour of one too many nights after. I look like my Dad, who at eighty-one is very handsome indeed but hardly rock star material. My forty-eighth birthday is on Saturday.

My point is that I have known Bob for twenty-six years or so, and despite some silliness that would have ended the friendship of lesser beings, we remain true pals. Bob is yet another undiscovered gem. Now you know.

I met Bob when we both appeared on a Montreal based television show called *Like Young* in 1972. He was performing with his band The Wackers and I was, of course, in Fludd. Up until the moment we met I was convinced that Fludd were the only band doing the outrageous glitter rock thing, at least, in this country, but we were all taken aback to see The Wackers in full glam drag at the television studios.

The sight of Segarini and his soul mate Randy Bishop miming their great song 'Day and Night' while sharing a single mic cheek to cheek is an image I can easily conjure up to this day. Fludd, not wishing to look like we were copying, backed off on the heavy use of make up and accessories and instead opted for a more low key presentation that day. I knew I had made a friend for life after Bob and I had introduced ourselves and made off to the canteen for a drink, a smoke in his case, and some shared road adventures. Bob had natural warmth to his personality that drew you in and we planned on continuing our new mutual admiration society when schedules permitted. It would be a few more years until we met up again but I'll get to that.

Pilling vs. Pilling

The day started innocently enough with us piling into a car to drive to the airport where we would catch a flight to Montreal for our second *Like Young* television appearance. The band was fully decked out, including Rocko in a burgundy floor length skirt complete with raccoon styled white-eye make up.

He was also on acid.

Come to think of it, we were all on acid.

Doing a TV show while tripping seemed like a good idea that particular morning. For some strange reason the Pilling boys began to argue, which soon escalated from verbal to physical. The only problem with this was that combatant no.1, Brian, was in the back seat and combatant no. 2 and the favourite to win, Ed, was in the front seat when the fisticuffs started.

Ed was driving the car at the time.

Brian was no shrinking violet when it came to defending a matter of honour, regardless how insignificant. After all, as we have seen, Ed could've qualified as a heavyweight boxing contender had he been so inclined so genetically speaking it was only natural that his brother would inherit some natural born killer qualities as well. Their younger brother

Steve was also reputed to be quite handy with his fists.

Think Bee Gees in boxing gloves.

The car, well over the speed limit and full of screaming rock types was careening wildly out of control while the Pillings made their point. A police cruiser, cherry top ablaze and siren wailing, was keeping pace with us but separated by a road divider, him in the express lanes, we in the collectors. After pointing this out, the combatants went to their corners as Ed figured it best to lose the cop, seeing as we were late for our flight as it was. We actually lost the cop.

Our fellow air travellers were quite amused by not only our outlandish costumes but by our howling at the moon demeanour. None of them had the foggiest idea that we were totally out of our minds.

The TV show taping was fun and the Pilling's both had extra makeup applied to cover their respective punch marks. As we were only lip syncing to our latest record it didn't matter that we wouldn't have been able to function live and the only tense moment occurred when the host of the show, Jim McKenna, invited me for an on air interview about Roy Orbison before an early clip of Roy's was played. I know lots of stuff about Roy, personally considering him one of the greatest vocalist in pop music, but I of course forgot everything I ever knew about the artist when questioned and Jim the host probably began to suspect that drugs may be playing a hand in my reluctance to divulge any information in front of his perplexed studio audience. I was quickly hustled off camera.

The day progressed smoothly until it was time to return to the airport in the studio-supplied limo. Ed, normally a very passive guy unless provoked was very pissed off at the fact that, although we were indeed in Canada, part of the English Commonwealth, all the street signs were printed in French. The acid, coupled with whatever alcohol had been consumed during the day, brought out the very worst in the Rule Britannia lead singer who began loudly cursing the French for their treason with the road signs. I was up front with the very concerned driver, very French himself, and now very nervous, what with the carryings on in his back seat.

The flight home was a celebratory drink fest as we returned to the land of English road signs. The Pilling boys, now coming down from the acid but decidedly three sheets to the wind from the booze, ended the day much as it started by punching each other out while Ed drove us home.

We were playing a high school in Cornwall when Brian collapsed on stage. Back in the dressing room there was naturally a great deal of concern for our friend and brother as he was always the very picture of health, a bull of a man who would keep his problems to himself. Brian had worked for a time as a male nurse in a hospital and was not unfamiliar with various illnesses. He showed us his arms and we were all quite alarmed to see thousands of what looked like tiny black dots. He told us that he was covered in them. As the gig was effectively over we all piled into the limo for our trip home. The silence was broken as Brian informed us that, although he had not yet consulted a doctor, he was almost positive that he had leukaemia. We had no reason to doubt him as Ed and I cradled our dear brother in our arms and cried.

It was only a matter of days before the awful truth was verified that Brian had indeed contracted the deadly blood disease.

Pat Little

May 1973 was spent mostly on the road out west, once again touring Alberta and British Columbia. Brian's health was a cause of great concern to all of us as he had lost a lot of weight and his hair had fallen out completely as a result of the chemotherapy treatments. Although touring was hard enough on healthy individuals he never complained and his very English sense of humour remained firmly intact as he even posed for our amusement wearing his custom-made wig backwards, creating the most surreal image for our cameras.

Upon our return John Andersen quit the group, much to the relief of everyone concerned. John was and is one of the best drummers in this or any other country but his serious devotion to his craft often resulted in tense frustration due to the lack of dedication displayed by other members of the group.

Well, not everyone, mostly by me.

Rocko and Brian were certainly good players who occasionally strayed into my territory as part time rock and roll outlaws but I was much more interested in what to wear and who to take it off with. John may have seen the obvious writing on the wall with regards to the future of the group as Brian's health certainly impacted on his leadership capabilities, and this might have speeded up his decision to abandon ship ahead of time.

Aside from the obvious drag of rehearsing old material for the umpteenth time, a fresh face might prove interesting. And what a face it was. I had known Pat Little since the Yorkville Village days when he was the highly regarded drummer for Luke and The Apostles, one of the cities best blues bands. Pat was a wee sprig of a boy, one hundred pounds of human dynamo soaking wet. He also had no upper front teeth to speak of and was a first-class mixer who single handedly encouraged our feud with the Foot In Coldwater boys to the level of near physical violence. For some reason he really had it in for Foot's very large guitar player, Paul Nauman, whom he baited as "Paul Fucking Newman" at every chance he got, creating mass tension whenever the two groups performed together.

One of his first gigs with us was at Varsity Stadium on a bill with Leslie West, Mitch Ryder, and Humble Pie. Although we were the first act on, we were charged up to be performing in the company of these rock and roll legends and pulled out all the stops which saw our photograph picturing Pat, Ed, and myself on next morning's entertainment front page.

I recall being asked to leave the stage during one Hall of Famer's set after gently refusing his offer of a drink back at his hotel after the show. That kind of thing was always happening to me but I put it down to too much trashy eyeliner.

Taking up a position by the front of the stage for Humble Pie's set I was surprised to see the actor Michael J. Pollard, of *Bonnie and Clyde* fame, standing just to my left. He acknowledged me with a small smile but did not invite me back to his hotel for a drink.

Perhaps I was slipping.

The next huge gig we did was headlining our own show at the Ontario Place Forum, a 10,000-seat theatre in the round complete with revolving stage. Eight thousand, mostly female fans screamed their way through a radio hit driven set that prompted many stage assaults through the Forum's security. With Ed leaping from the PA stacks, and Rocko slipping out of his evening gown to finish the set in fringed panties and lurex gloves, the show was finally stopped as waves of hysterical fans broke through to the stage where mass chaos ensued. With the power cut, performers, security, roadies, and fans alike were now in total darkness. Order was somehow restored but the concert was over as the band was hustled down the tunnel to our dressing rooms where we celebrated our triumph.

Typical of shortsighted Canadian mentality, we began a weeklong gig at The Colonial Tavern the following week, where stringent liquor laws effectively stopped most of our real fans from even getting through the doors. Any momentum gained as a result of the Forum riot and its attendant press coverage was lost as we settled back into being a bar band.

The only excitement that we could conjure up for the week was the near arrest of Pat Little who had mooned a lady driver on the highway going home one night which resulted in our being stopped and questioned by the police. It was funny, to be sure, but hardly like having your clothes torn off by screamies.

The other local Toronto groups were by now all jumping on the glitter rock bandwagon but the band that created the biggest noise in this department was called Brutus. Fronted by a bald-headed maniac named Walter Zwol, who would later go on record as saying he sustained his youthful appearance by drinking and washing in his own urine, this five piece was always good for a laugh in concert. We started playing double bills with them quite a bit at this time which was great for me as one of their roadies had a girlfriend named Debra who would join me in the back seat of the limo while he dutifully did his lighting gig.

Walter Zwol was a commanding presence in full drag who thought nothing of grabbing his guitar player by the balls if he felt a lack of showmanship necessitated such action. If the pain of twisted nuts wasn't getting the guitar player moving, Walter would grab a handful of hair and pull the diminutive string-bender off his feet until his mouth was framing a blood curdling scream. At this point Walter would casually slip his tongue into the guitarist's mouth.

The guitarist was named Gino Scarpelli.

Fludd's Follies

It was at this time that the Fludd limo was retired in favour of a full-size Winnebago. As Brian's health fluctuated it was deemed necessary to cater to his physical comfort and the mobile home afforded him the opportunity to relax on the way to gigs, as well as a private dressing room, should the venue's own facilities be lacking. Most venues had facilities that were lacking. It was also very nice for the rest of us too. On long trips we would gather around the table to drink and play poker while the driver and his shotgun partner did their job, separated by a pull down screen.

One such trip, Skinny at the wheel with Brian keeping him company, we were all freaked totally out by unison screaming up front as the RV lost total control with drinks, food, ashtrays, cards, and money flying everywhere. With the RV now stopped by the side of the road we pulled up the screen to see a very ashen-faced Skinny coming to terms with having almost collided head on with a full grown moose. If the moose had connected with our front end I would not be telling you this little story right now as the card table would have sliced me in half, just under the rib cage. It was bad enough that my first winning poker pot all evening was strewn all over the floor.

About this time Bruce rolled the Fludd truck as he drunkenly drove people home from a club one night. All five passengers, Bruce included, were in the truck's cab when he took a sharp corner just a tad too fast. Our brand new MacIntosh PA amplifier was jettisoned through the roof and landed in a mud pile, where it was retrieved later. Miraculously it still worked, which was a great testament to the fine technicians at MacIntosh.

Bruce was not an excellent driver.

Raymond was.

Good old Bruce was at my 48th birthday gig at The Harp and Crown tonight (March 20, 1999). It was a "No Flies On Frank" gig, a group I play in that also features Ed Pilling. Bob Segarini was there sitting in (you met him a few pages back), and Roy Young (who you will meet later), also sat in. Roy often sang with THE BEATLES in Hamburg. Tonight Roy sang with such gusto that our PA. crapped out. Roy felt sabotaged. Segarini perhaps? Bruce, eternally roadie, had a maglite on him and instantly set about fixing the PA.

It was almost cosmic that Bruce's maglite was there!

Our crew had now swollen to epic proportions. Along with the ever faithful Bruce, Pat Ryan had returned to road manage our lunacy and a new guy was hired to do lights. Barry Harvey was a huge, lantern-jawed character that used to come and see us at a place called the Knob Hill Hotel. The Knobby we called it.

Barry was notable in that he talked very quietly, always had a cigarette on the go, and had the look of somebody that could rip your head off if so provoked.

Having Barry around took a bit of pressure off Ed.

We all figured that the best possible job in the world was being the devoted slave to a rock group's every whim but not for old Barry, no sir, he wouldn't be happy until he managed Gordon Lightfoot.

Which he now does.

One night at the Knobby, after a very satisfactory performance, various band members were invited to try some white powder, courtesy of this creep named Turd.

Turk actually.

Assuming that the proffered lines were cocaine, we greedily snorted back the gift.

"I play bass myself so I cut you an extra taste," said my brother four-string-plucker and I set into two six-inch lines, the longest on the table to be sure.

And oh what happened then was rich!

I began to feel as if my brain was being separated from my body. Holding on to Rocko in the corridor, his slightest whisper became a howling wind tunnel of banshee wails with the most intense audio hallucinations imaginable. I fell to the floor where I saw Ed's enormous head bend down over me and his voice was like some giant slow-motioned super bass boom as he asked me, "Arrrrrrrrre yoooooooooou alriiiiiiight Godoooooooo?"

Was I alright?

With that said my mind travelled to a parallel universe where I was the king of everything. This place actually exists, I'm certain it does. The only way to reach this magical kingdom, where all is fairies and elves, is to ingest an overdose of angel dust, which is what that fuck Turk had slipped us!

I next came to consciousness in the Winnebago where I was treated to the sight of Brian, sans wig, driving us somewhere. He had twisted two little locks of remaining hair into horns at the front of his head and when he turned around the flash of oncoming headlights strobe'd over him giving off the illusion that the devil was at the wheel.

I figured it best not to dwell on this and passed out again.

I awoke the next morning to the persistent ringing of my front door bell. Try as I might, I could not walk and literally crawled on my stomach to answer it. Reaching up I opened the door where two deliverymen stood with my new air conditioners.

They looked confused.

"Hey," said one of them, "you're the Fludd guy!"

"I'm not feeling too well," I said, trying to look as normal as anyone answering the door while lying on the floor might look.

"Please install the units and don't steal anything," and with that said I crawled back down the hallway to my bedroom.

Shortly after John Andersen, was at my door, as his Dad was dropping us off at our rendezvous location for our drive to North Bay where we would play that night.

John had returned to the fold, Pat Little having not worked out for one reason or another.

"Jesus man, what happened to you?" asked the drummer, totally unawares of our drug-taking the previous night.

"I'm having trouble walking, man," I said as John helped me down to his Dad's car.

"Fuck man, tell my Dad that you're sick or something will you!" and with that he pushed me into the back seat of Mr. Andersen's car.

"Hi Mr. A., I'm sick," I said and watched as Mr. A's head grew coloured feathers and antennae owing to the massive hallucinations that were now growing in intensity instead of subsiding. Mr. Andersen thankfully chose to ignore me and dropped us off at the rendezvous location.

I spent the rest of the three-hour trip well...er...tripping in the back of the RV.

The gig was interesting as I was not given a microphone for fear of what I might say during the performance but I managed a credible job of playing the songs while dodging lightning bolts of green, red, yellow, and some unknown lights that were being hurtled down at me from the lighting rig front of stage.

I remained this high for almost two weeks and thought that I would never return to normal.

Perhaps I never did.

Brian's health was slowly deteriorating to the point that a substitute guitar player was required. Gord Waszek was a one-time guitarist for a Vanilla Fudge-like band called Leigh Ashford. He was a dead ringer for a young Anthony Newley and it was he that was called up. As Gord was a proper musician he was reluctant to join a teenybopper group but, like all "real" musicians he wasn't making as much money as we were at the time and so relented. When Brian was well enough to perform we would feature six musicians and the interplay between the two guitars was often brilliant.

The first thing we did was record a new single entitled 'Brother and Me' which was a Caribbean-flavoured pop song that featured John Andersen on vibes, and me gently playing a bucket of water to approximate the sound of waves lapping against a boat. Waszek's country flavoured picking was a beautiful addition to the song and the single charted immediately.

The down side of having Waszek around, at least for me, was that suddenly it was all music theory and technical this and chops that.

I didn't want to know. I still believed in sex, drugs, and rock and roll. Musicality had no place in a rock group!

I'm not joking about that either.

It soon became THE MUSICIANS vs. me. There was no way that I could win, so I basically started to distance myself from the rest of the boys while they discussed musical scales and treble clefs and stuff. John Andersen was right in his element having another schooled instrumentalist around and got heavily involved in playing the vibes. Even Ed was buying into all this nonsense and he only played the fucking bongos for Chrissake!

Peter Rochon

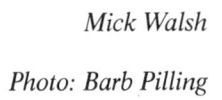

Mick Walsh

Photo: Barb Pilling

TRAVELS WITH MY AMP

John "Jorn" Andersen

Peter Csanky

Pat Little

Thinking that a holiday might be in order, Brian and I grabbed our girls and headed to Freeport in The Bahamas. We gambled at the casino, drank syrupy sweet coconut rum, and went deep-sea fishing where I caught a forty-pound Kingfish and Brian a fifty-pound Wahoo. We were also thrown off a glass bottom boat cruise when we drunkenly commandeered the ship's PA system with filthy songs and general goofiness that ended in a fistfight with some American tourists. The boat pulled into the nearest dock where we were bodily removed in the middle of the night and had to find our own way back. Brian stayed down an extra week as Waszek was covering for him and I had to fly home for gigs that were on the books.

It was en route home that the strangest thing happened. My girlfriend noticed something outside the window of the plane and she excitedly told me to have a look. I couldn't believe my eyes as what I saw appeared to be a gigantic funnel-shaped object that looked like it was enveloped in a greyish smoke, not moving but resting on top of the huge field of very white cumulous clouds. I immediately called for the stewardess who looked out and upon seeing the object muttered a simple "Oh my God!" before racing off to the cabin to notify the pilot. She walked by us several times as we watched the object gradually disappear from view.

Ding, ding, ding went my overhead pager.

"Yes sir, can I help you?" asked the same attendant.

"What did the captain say that thing was?" I inquired.

"I don't know what you're talking about sir," was her firm answer.

"Look lady, you saw that thing out there as plainly as I did and if I had a gun on me we'd be heading back there for a closer look right now!" I protested.

Really stupid thing to say though, don't you think?

Giving me a look that could turn you to stone she dropped her voice and said "If I were you I wouldn't be talking about guns on this or any other airplane!" and with that said, she left for the cockpit again.

When we arrived back home I went to question the pilots but was not surprised to learn that they had left the plane before the passengers.

I am absolutely convinced that we had seen a UFO.

It would not be the last time in my life.

The newspaper's said that there were 50,000 people at our City Hall appearance during the summer. It sure looked like a lot of people from where I was standing. It was a beautiful summer day and the highlight of the show came when Ed sang the 'My, My, My, look at the sky' line in our set closing song 'Put On A Two Step', and directed the entire audience's attention to an airplane dragging a huge banner reading FLUDD WISH YOU ALL A HAPPY SUMMER! flying overhead.

Kind Of A Drag
– a KISS story

"I wan' that guy there removed from the building!"

It was one of the guitarists from New York City band Kiss and he was pointing directly at me. Although I knew little about the group, I did know that none of the four were English so this lisping mid-Atlantic accent, (sort of cross between Bryan Adams and Madonna), demanding my removal from the hall, was confusing. Fludd had been scheduled to open the first three shows for Kiss, one here at the University of Guelph and then two shows at the Victory Burlesque in Toronto.

"I wan' tha' guy removed NOW!" he screamed as security started towards me.

"I play in the opening group!" I protested.

Was it my brand new rose embroidered black wedged shoes that offended?

"NOT YOU!...HIM!!!" and now I realized it was the guy standing next to me that was the source of the guitarist's mounting frustration.

I checked his shoes.

Brown loafers.

That would certainly qualify for getting turf'd, by my standards.

As he was being dragged to the door I noticed that he had a number of camera bags around his neck but not one of them was out and aimed at the musicians on stage.

It was only when Kiss hit the stage a few hours later in full make up that I realized why Paul Stanley had not wanted to take a chance being photographed at sound check. They had wished to maintain their anonymity even at risk of offending the press.

I was impressed.

This was a group who were thinking ahead.

It was another east coast tour and a triumphant return to a packed Ontario Place Forum that capped off the group's summer activities but I had one other little social event on my calendar. Lori and I got married in a society wedding that saw four hundred people enjoying a virtual cornucopia of delights under a huge circus tent. If ever there was a guy who shouldn't have been married at twenty-three, it was me. As we have already seen, my fascination for all things female would most likely not stop at the altar and the marriage was doomed before the "I Do's" were spoken.

It had nothing to do with her, she was wonderful, it was me.

The whole monster-wedding thing had just seemed like a cool rock star thing to do at the time and it was great fun. We had a nice little orchestra fronted by the late Bobby Gimby, composer of the confederation hit, 'C A N A D A' and a host of notable people from the rock world mingled easily with captains of industry. I liked the captains of industry best as they would pull me aside and give me thousand dollar bills. I had a whole pocket full of them.

They also had better quality drugs than my pals but this was a day off for me.

The worst thing about the whole affair was my suit which had been custom tailored at one of Toronto's finest clothiers at my new father-in-law's insistence. When I went down to this shrine of silk it was deemed necessary that the great man whose name adorned the store's marquee would himself measure me up. I was fearless this time, having all the information about which side I dressed on carefully stored in mind from my encounter with the 'Pygg's' tailors.

A hush fell over the assembled craftsmen as Lou entered the room.

"So, this is Normie's new son-in-law?" he said with a big smile, and I could tell that he was disgusted just to be standing in a room with me.

We shook hands and came out fighting.

"Dresses on the left," he said now hunched over and staring at my crotch.

Curses!

That was my big line and he ruined the moment.

His henchmen muttered approval at the boss's keen eyesight.

He was, after all, the guy who made suits for Sinatra.

"Left inseam...32 inches," and so on he went while his minions scribbled down my vital statistics.

There was a little problem though that I felt just had to be addressed.

"Er...excuse me sir, but shouldn't you be using a tape measure?" I asked weakly.

A roar of laughter rained over me as the assembled cried in disbelief, "TAPE MEASURE?!" "Lou using a tape measure?" and so on while until

Lou held up his hand to silence the room.

"Kid," he said in solemn tones, "I've been doing this since you were still dripping down your mother's leg! I DON'T NEED NO GOD DAMN TAPE MEASURE!"

The room erupted once more.

Later that month as I stood at the altar with one arm and one leg too short on my suit I cursed Lou's name.

As I couldn't drive a car yet, and wouldn't for a great many years to come, we departed the festivities in a horse and buggy with me urging on my trusty steeds to clippity clop their way around the corner and out of sight of the cheering guests where we hooked up with Lori's Beetle and off for a week of spending thousand dollar bills in old Quebec City. It was a great time of fine dining, the finest suite in the best hotel and me keeping a sharp eye out the whole time lest we run into any one of dozens of over-zealous French groupies that I might have encountered on previous visits.

The highlight for me was a visit to the world famous Maison du Vin, which had a section, reserved only for those of impeccable wealth and taste, in the deepest subterranean reaches of this finely stocked wine emporium. As I lacked both real wealth and taste and under normal circumstances would have been shown the exit door, I did possess a large wad of thousand-dollar bills, which was just as good, and we were soon ushered into the padlocked holy of holies by a wine expert carrying a huge candle like the ones people use in English horror movies. The only things scary about this place however were the prices but we were young and eager to impress and soon had a little basket of various fine wines that cost a few thousand dollars. The nicest wine in the basket was a Chateau Lafitte Rothschild of some great vintage year that I had read about in a novel somewhere. These wines would of course be lost on me as I couldn't tell you the difference between a white and red in those days. My only rule of thumb was red for meats, white for fish and poultry, and rose for hot dogs.

The most awful thing happened upon our arrival back home a scant week later while attending an "important" group meeting where I yawned and stretched just a little too far and felt something snap in my body. You know that burny feeling you get in your neck when you turn your head too quickly and spasm? Well it was like that but worse. The burny feeling ran from my tiptoes to the top of my head.

Something was wrong.

I had to play that night but by the time I hobbled into the Winnebago I could no longer stand being in pants. Joe Mendelson, of McKenna Mendelson Blues fame, was sitting at the RV's table and asked what was the matter with me.

"My balls are swelling up," I groaned.

Joe, a sage of great wisdom shook his head knowingly and said, "Don't fuck with your bag, cancel the gig and get to a hospital."

I told you he was wise.

The others, although pissed off that the gig was cancelled, were guys after all and sympathized with me, knowing how attached I was to my little friends.

The hospital waiting room was full of misery and woe as I made my way to the nurse's station. The matronly prune behind the desk ignored me for as long as her union allowed and then asked me what the matter was.

"I've injured my testicles," I moaned in a teensy weeny voice.

"Excuse me?" asked the nurse now bending closer.

"I've hurt myself in my privates and..," but was cut short as she snorted, "I can't hear a word you're saying sir, would you mind speaking u..." and with that I yelled in her face, "LOOK LADY, MY FUCKING BALLS ARE ALL SWOLLEN UP AND I'M IN GOD DAMN AGONY!"

The moans and groans of my fellow sufferers were now more like the sounds of gentle amusement as all eyes and interest shifted to me.

"There is no need for that kind of language young man!" she said sternly and motioned for me to follow her.

There was much laughter as the doctor examining me was made aware that we were freshly returned from our honeymoon.

"Must've been quite the time," he said while probing my balls. "Does this hurt?" and with the gentlest of squeezes I hit the highest note a human being could possibly reach.

"Well," said my torturer, "We'll just have to open you up and have a little look-see in there."

It took a second or two to actually register, a little look see shouldn't be too bad.

"OPEN ME UP?" I screamed hysterically, "YOU MEAN MY BALLS??!"

There was no waiting involved and I was "prepped" for the O.R. and wheeled down the hall by an English male nurse and his younger female assistant.

"Nothing to it, mate," the Englishman said with a shrug.

"That's easy for you to say but this guy here had the same operation and look what happened to him!" I said, pointing at the young female nurse beside me.

We all laughed as they wheeled me into the operating room.

When I came to on the operating table the doctor said to me, "It's okay, the operation was a complete success and you'll live to fight another day" as I once more lost consciousness.

The next morning I called Lori and told her to bring that five hundred dollar bottle of Chateau Lafitte, which I presented, to the doctor who had saved my nuts. I spent the next week with my balls resting comfortably on an ice pack.

I haven't had a good yawn and stretch since.

With all the sexist stories in this book, there had to be a few of you feminist-types reading this who really enjoyed that little story of my torture so I will tell you another one from the same era that's even worse!

There were a few of us in the group that developed warts as a result of passing around the same groupies at various social functions. I remember Ed showing me his dick at a truck stop urinal and it resembled nothing if not a cauliflower patch. I wasn't quite so bad but these things had to be dealt with. The doctor who examined me was thoroughly disgusted by my activities and gave me a scathing lecture on morality and monogamy.

"All right, I'm going to give you a little anaesthetic and then we'll remove them," he said as my heart began racing.

"Would you mind giving me the needle in the arm instead of my ass," I asked not being overly fond of needles being injected anywhere.

"It's not going in your arm or your ass," he said soberly and then added, "It's not as bad as you might think," and with that proceeded to jab it into the left side of my dick.

He was such a liar!

As awful as I was now feeling I managed to look down just as he stabbed me in the right side for good measure. My mind was reeling, the pain was unbearable, and now my nostrils were being assailed with the sickly sweet smell of burning flesh as he went about his work.

I did the only reasonable thing available to me and passed out.

When I came to I couldn't get my pants on and I left the downtown office with my jacket covering my ass and a borrowed sweater over my wounded best friend. Ed later told me that his doctor had merely prescribed an ointment, which did the trick.

For any girls that have ever felt like getting back at me, those two stories were for you.

But it wasn't all international travel, limousines, fine dining and needles in your dick.

Fludd had become a source of massive paranoia for me. I was tired of being constantly called up on the carpet for voicing my opinions and it was inevitable that I should leave the group. I got shit for cutting my hair off, for Chrissake!

It was a question of quitting before I got fired.

I was now married and responsible for my young wife and my future was very uncertain.

Years of Pilling brainwashing had indeed convinced me that I faced certain failure without them and I found myself adrift on an ocean of uncertainty. Still, there was a nagging feeling in the back of my mind that the new songs that I was writing were worthy, and as I had no outlet for my sudden creative streak in the tightly controlled Brian and Ed song writing monopoly, there was no other option available to me.

With a heavy heart I tendered my resignation.

Intermission

The dressing room at The Knobby was packed with an odd assortment of musicians, roadies, groupies as well as Myra the Manager, in a cartoonish costume of fishnet nylons and strangely applied makeup. Walter Zwol eyed the crowd with a bemused gaze as he listened with a sympathetic ear to my drunken ramblings concerning my departure from Fludd. I would put together a trio of musicians that would make a difference, I told him, a heavier sounding group than Fludd but with the added bonus of vocal harmonies.

Cream meets The Beatles!

The Brutus front man put a hand on my shoulder and said to me, "Gino's not too happy with us, maybe you should talk to him."

I looked over at the diminutive guitarist sitting across the room, lost in a haze of marijuana smoke and surrounded by the best looking chicks in the room.

Yeah...maybe...

Definitely!

— *set seven* —

Goddo 1975

The Gasworks was the happening live venue on Toronto's main thoroughfare. On this particular night the club was packed to its three hundred standing-room-only capacity with a healthy line-up, waiting to get in, snaking south on Yonge Street. The band, drenched in sweat and in mid-set, was shaking the very foundations of this hallowed rock shrine as the corkscrewed siren made her way to the front of the stage, oblivious to any remarks or stares.

Gina was a work of art, the groupies' groupie, with a body that Venus herself would have coveted and in possession of a razor sharp intellect.

She was The Wholey Grail of wanton lust.

Throwing her lion's mane of hair over her shoulder she had the good sense to wait until the song finished before telling me that Rick Nielsen and Robin Zander from Cheap Trick were at the front door and couldn't get past the bouncers.

"I'll be back in a minute," I said and put my bass down to follow her exaggerated strut to the front door where the Chicago popsters awaited our blessing and instant entry to the club.

With the rock stars safely ensconced at a beer soaked table we picked up the show where we had left off with a new fury. The electricity in the room was palpable. After the set Gina introduced me to her friends and I casually asked, "You guys wanna sit in?"

Rick looked at Robin.

Robin looked at Rick.

"Yeah man!" Rick said excitedly.

"What do you wanna play?" I asked, excited myself at the prospect of these two great musicians sharing our stage.

"I'll do sound!" said the guitarist.

Who's on first?

"I'll do lights!" added the vocalist.

What's on second?

And next set they did sound and lights while the audience sat there completely freaked out.

A 1975 Interview With Ritchie Yorke (RY)

(Some of this you know if you've been paying attention but I'm going to print it in its entirety for the continuity of the piece. This interview will give you a pretty good idea of what an asshole I was in '75. By the time this gets to you, some "know it all" editor will have buffed up his/her eraser and hacked great festoons of text from it anyway.)

RY: Let's firstly get down to some of your reminiscences. Why you became a musician and what have you...

GG: I can remember being thirteen years old, and my mother, who worked at the Friar's Tavern, taking me down there to watch the Saturday afternoon matinees, and sitting in with all the bands. At this time I looked up to everybody and anybody but some of these people, although they were just bar musicians, definitely developed. I sat in with The Band when they were Levon and The Hawks and with The Female Beatles. Some of those chicks are in Isis now but this is going back to 1964. From the very start it was music because I wasn't into sports very much. It was music or nothing and as The Beatles had hit I found some other people and we formed a band. I remember playing a club on Yonge Street called The Rocket a Go Go from nine pm to three am and I was just starting high school then. I went from being an honours student in public school to failing miserably in high school. My teachers couldn't believe the change and it was a drag for my parents because nobody had long hair in this country in those days and it brought with it a fair amount of heat. My Mom was always behind what I was doing but it took my Dad a long time to realize that I might be right.

RY: What drew you to bass guitar?

GG: That's weird. I was sitting one afternoon with Rick Danko (The Band). I'd gone there for a matinee and at this time I wasn't actually playing. I wanted to be a drummer and when I told him this he grabbed my hand and said, "Man, you've got bass player fingers." I've always dug Paul McCartney but I think that because it was a real musician who was telling me this it had a fairly obvious impression on me. Within the week I had a Supro bass guitar and the only amplifier in Scarborough. I can remember going to practice with my amp and guitar on a kid's wagon (remember Danny Cooper from the first set?). The group was called The Wanderers and I was in it strictly for my amp and long hair. I couldn't really play a note then. I even did a gig back then and I couldn't play but I looked the part.

RY: How about your association with the Pillings?

GG: I was in grade nine in high school and Brian was in my class but we really didn't know each other for a while. He still had Vaseline in his hair. We never found our common interest of music until a day when all the freshmen had to come dressed up and (be) at the mercy of the seniors. Well, Brian and I both came as Beatles that day and it started a lifelong friendship. I remember us both running furiously across the football field and fantasizing we were being chased by a horde of screaming girls. After that we got together at Brian's place and learned songs on acoustic guitars. I think 'Ferry Cross The Mersey' was one of the first. At this time Ed was coming back from England and I was very thrilled at the prospect of meeting a real live Englishman. On this particular night Brian and I went over to another friend's house (Don Harbor-The Harbor Roak) and I was confronted by this giant who was busy tapping along to records with drumsticks on his knees. We didn't hit it off that first time and I can see how that could have affected our relationship in the years that followed. So the four of us started our first real band The Pretty Ones and we had mother of pearl cards printed and a real English Bedford van and our fates were sealed. I can remember driving to Kingston for sixty dollars and Ed having an accident with his boss's car that we'd borrowed. We had to rent all our gear for this gig.

RY: Scrimping and saving all the time...

GG: For sure. The scene in Canada at that time was so nowhere that if you got one gig a month you were lucky. It got to a point years later in Fludd where we wanted a night off but you're never satisfied.

RY: How about the Fludd trip?

GG: Fludd started out as a great idea. Five young guys who were really into making it. At first everyone thought the band was English due to our image at the time. Even this new band (Goddo) sounds a little English because of certain inflections in my singing voice but I feel it's okay because that's what my roots were (a serious asshole). I never related to 50's music.

We did very well at first but conflicts of interest and direction blossomed early. There were five heavy egos in the band and everybody couldn't be the leader. Soon people began siding with each other and talking about each other and a bad scene came about. Also, I was very uptight because I always felt that I wasn't able to contribute as much as I could've, especially as far as songs and creative ideas were concerned. I was always comparing and being compared to George Harrison's situation. We played (at being) Beatles too long. (At a recent 'No Flies On Frank' rehearsal Steve Pilling once again pointed out that I was always the George Harrison of Fludd. "Which would've made you the Andy Gibb," I replied and everyone laughed and laughed.)

RY: What about the money?

GG: You can't see someone getting a cheque for ten thousand dollars after you've worked just as hard for the band and not be bitter about it. I mean, those songs were not worth all of that money when they were brought to the band but after we'd sat down and refined them, and I know this is true because of my new situation (cue Doug and Gino throwing darts at a smiling picture of me.) There was also a constant paranoia for me that I would be fired and after hearing about how I would never be anything on my own for so long I believed it. After getting married and having a little dough in the oven I decided that the time was right to split and I didn't hear anything to change my mind. I never wanted to be a back up musician for anybody.

RY: Which brings us to Goddo, your new number. How do you feel about it at this point?

GG: About this band, I had played with Marty (Morin) in a group called Cloud (I did?) just prior to joining Fludd and after years of just occasionally seeing each other we both found ourselves unemployed. We kicked around the idea of forming a band but the guitarist I wanted was in a similar situation to my Fludd one. This, of course, was Gino. Marty and I had been re-establishing our old friendship from high school when one night Gino phoned me up and said let's do the thing. I wanted both of these guys because they fit the bill musically as well as visually. We went into rehearsals and the band came together within three weeks of very hard work. We were all very broke at this time so it was very important to get it together quickly. Fortunately for us our first gig turned out to be great and it's been uphill ever since. One thing about our first rehearsals, we got together and after the first ten minutes we learned two songs. We had just planned on jamming that first night but things went so well that we wasted no time. There was a magic in the air that night that I think will linger around this band. We played our first gig with seventeen songs and at this point we have eighteen originals and six non-originals that we do with new arrangements. As far as recording goes I was in laying them down before the band was formed but now all the songs will be played by the band. However, there's an important thing about making records. You should use the best guys possible to get it down. I mean, if in the future we have a musical groove that requires a certain style and one of us can't cut it I'll not hesitate to bring someone in (who can cut it). After all, it's the group who really profits from the record, not the session men (yeah sure). I'm trying to avoid the mistakes of previous bands by involving the guys in most of the group's activities. For instance, Marty and Gino are both contributing material and we've now laid some of this down. I used to always feel in the dark in Fludd so I call Marty and Gino every night to fill them in on the day's business. The way I see it is if I'm going to be rich then everybody that's working with me is going to be rich too. (Right now the telephone is ringing at the Scarpelli residence. "Hello Gino, it's Doug, do you know what that asshole just wrote in his book?" "Yeah man, that Greg is a real asshole!" "Think we should have his legs broken?")

RY: What are your plans for Goddo?
GG: Right now we're ready to go on the road. I feel very confident about playing with any big band anywhere and doing a great job. So far

we have had excellent response from everyone who has heard us. We're not selling out but we play commercial music in the sense that it's popular and the people can relate to it. I never thought that I could write heavy but I seem to have slipped into a nice groove in that way. They're coming out very naturally. Not only that but everyone in the band is contributing good material. I want people to know it's a band when they see it. As far as the name Goddo goes, well it's my name but I view it the same way as Elton John. When I see Elton I see Nigel and Dee and the whole thing as being Elton John. Same as Alice Cooper. We see the name Goddo as being powerful in print and that really sums up the band live as well.

RY: What about ambitions? What do you want ultimately?

GG: I'm not out to be a virtuoso. I want to be a personality and an all around entertainer. I don't want to ever limit myself to one form of musical expression either. I want people to see my act and leave a hall feeling good about it. Give them their money's worth. Since I was thirteen I've always wanted to be a millionaire. But I'm already wondering if I make that million where to from there (loony bin perhaps?) Now I feel ready for the (next) big step and if one of these initial releases clicks (then) I'm sure we'll be able to handle what will follow. This group has a commerciality that a lot of other groups would like to have and can't. Getting off topic, I also want to open a great gourmet restaurant some day. You need other things to involve yourself in. There's all sorts of things I want to do, but you have to do one thing at a time and right now all I want to be is a rock and roll star!

With all the talk of how wonderful I was and would be in the future I hadn't noticed that Ritchie's smile had turned into a grimacing frozen mask, his eyes devoid of any light as they appeared glazed and unblinking. Reaching out my hand to shake his I was shocked at being pulled violently from my chair where my nose connected perfectly with Ritchie's knee. As the blood flowed freely Ritchie began to punch at me with his clip board and even stabbed me with his pencil while furiously screaming, "YOU TALENTLESS LITTLE CUNT! YOUR IDEA OF GOURMET FOOD WOULD BE AN EXTRA SLICE OF CHEESE ON THE BURGER! YOUR NEW GROUP SUCKS! WITHOUT THE PILLINGS YOU'RE AN INCONSEQUENTIAL PIECE OF SHIT! NOW GET OUT OF MY

OFFICE BEFORE I KILL YOU!!"

Now of course he didn't really do that but he should have.

Instead he shook my hand and wished me good luck, and by doing so encouraged the ego that would destroy so many bridges just a little further down the road, to blindly sully forth on an unsuspecting world.

Transition

For a few months after leaving Fludd in 1975 I became the human pinball. Musically I was game for anything as I needed a source of income and attempted to put together an acoustic act with Danny McBride. Danny was the younger brother of Lighthouse lead vocalist Bob McBride and had cut his musical teeth as a well-regarded blues player in the Rockpile house band Mary Lou Horner during the blues rock boom of the late sixties. Although our voices blended beautifully and our choice of material was compatible it was over before it started when concert impresario John Brower, who was most famous for arranging John and Yoko's appearance at The Toronto Rock and Roll Revival, questioned why Danny would have to split things evenly with someone like me. I had no idea what a major star Danny was and was very thankful to Brower for pointing out my inadequacies.

He was shown the door.

Not wishing to get caught up in another battle of managerial wits I decided to pass on the idea of being the next Simon and Garfunkel. Danny would soon enjoy the good life as Chris de Burgh's guitarist, a gig he maintains to this day.

There was even an idea, fuelled by hallucinogens I'm sure, to front a one-man group called Godo And The Zombats. I still have the notes and diagrams with a stage set utilizing taped accompaniment, toys, robots, and lighting to approximate that big band sound, but the idea was soon forgotten.

Gino Scarpelli was nothing if not loyal and although he was indeed fed up with Brutus, he was in no position to pass on a steady gig and pay check to throw in with me. With a wife and son and daughter to support, a career change wouldn't be practical and I couldn't realistically offer him anything but a dream at the time. I called him up constantly, continually selling him on the idea of a heavy power trio. His absolute devotion to Jimi Hendrix and the thought of being the only featured soloist probably pushed him over the line and soon the meetings were in my apartment where I could play him great tracks by obscure groups that we could cover while preparing original material. It took me a few months, you would think that

I was trying to convince him to blow me, but he eventually agreed to jam and after that I knew that I had him.

About this time rock writer Ritchie Yorke had plans for me to record a number of tracks at Wil Webster's Thunder Sound Studios. A version of Neil Young's 'On The Weekend', Van Morrison's 'Caravan', and a Crazy Horse song called 'Dirty Dirty' were quickly recorded with a studio line up including Danny McBride on guitar, John Andersen on drums, Peter Rochon on piano, with me on bass and lead vocals. During these sessions we also recorded an original of mine called 'Starstruck' and a Kinks-styled version of the Richard Berry Classic, 'Louie Louie.' Gino came down and added a guitar overdub on 'Louie' but although these two songs were eventually released on A&M as a Goddo single it was really just the studio group. Another guy sitting in on the sessions was my old high school friend, Marty Morin. Possessed of an abundance of energy, Marty was a great drummer who sang like a bird and was now writing some very good songs. Plans were made now for Gino, Marty and myself to rehearse and see what would come of it.

Gino had been born and raised in southern Italy in the Calabrese town of Cosenza. Having picked up the guitar at the tender age of four he was taught his first chords by his Zio (Uncle) Rinaldo. By the age of twelve and in possession of a silver metal flake EKO guitar he was by this time proficient enough to play lead guitar in his only Italian group, the instrumental Italo and The Apaches. "It was a solid body with a lot of knobs on it, I applied stickers to it spelling out my name," says Gino adding, "I still have it."

He was a quiet kid who read superhero comic books and developed a ninety-pound weakling fixation on bodybuilding before immigrating to Canada in 1966. The usual procession of basement bands followed including such non-notables as The Indigo Five, The Extensions, and Boo, before graduating to more accomplished groups such as a later version of Motherlode, the R&B influenced Tightass and finally Brutus, which was where I caught up with him.

He was sometimes referred to as Silky Valentino and was very popular with the local groupies. With a very laid back demeanour, fuelled mostly by the ingestion of the finest herb, he would become the group's anchor as both Marty and I had limitless nervous energy and enjoyed bouncing off walls.

Marty had been brought up in Scarborough and had already shared many great moments of music making with me at high school. He had very eclectic taste in music and turned us on to early Kool And The Gang, Commodores, and Miles Davis grooves.

The three of us began rehearsing in a very strange west end facility, where the owners rented small cubicles to musicians while they themselves built gigantic observatory telescopes in another part of the building. They were completing one such instrument to be sent to China while we were there and once took me over to see it after telling them that I had been a member of the Royal Ontario Astronomical Society as a child. The facility was so top secret that the hallways beyond our designated safe area were patrolled by the nastiest Rottweillers and Dobermans that you could imagine, but usually only at night to discourage sabotage.

One day, in search of the owner to pay our week's fee I opened the door to his hallway and proceeded down the corridor. As I rounded the corner I spotted one Doberman and one Rottweiller sitting together, probably discussing telescopes, about twenty feet from me. The animals should have been locked up outside during the day but as I hadn't seen a human around I quickly surmised that the dogs were probably brought in whenever the scientists left the building, regardless of the time of day. Stopping dead in my tracks I carefully breathed in deeply enough to draw my balls up into my body and ran like fuck in the opposite direction. Under circumstances like these I can really run fast and I beat both dogs to the door which I managed to slam shut just in time to hear them both smash into it from the other side. With my nuts safe once more I reasoned that perhaps in future it might be prudent to have someone search me out for the rehearsal room payment.

We concentrated on throwing a set list together that would feature not only hard-edged guitar histrionics but tight, two-part harmonies. Marty and I would sing unison verses and then break off into harmony parts during choruses. The vocals blended beautifully, the music was loud and already tight. It was very much my dream of Cream meets The Beatles.

We learned songs like 'Standing In the Road' by England's Blackfoot Sue, an infectious foot stomper that nobody had heard in Canada. Likewise 'Do Ya' by The Move, a song that was virtually unknown until ELO released it as a single years later. 'The Eagle Flies On Friday' by The Exception was lifted from the early Fludd repertoire and 'Waiting For The Bus' by a new group called ZZ Top. Also thrown in were our earliest attempts at song writing and with seventeen songs we felt ready to get out there and hit the boards.

TRAVELS WITH MY AMP

One minor problem presented itself, what do we call ourselves? As I had started everything in the first place and had written most of our early songs, it was decided that GODO would be the perfect name. The problem was that most people initially pronounced it as GO DO. This drove me nuts so we added another "D" and I reckoned that if anyone asked me "What's GOD DO?" I could always respond that "He's my Father who Arts in Heaven."

The new name looked great as a logo and we were now booked for our first gig.

*Left to right: Marty Morin, Gino Scarpelli, Greg Godovitz.
Photo: Gerrard Gentil*

1975... *Goddo Live at The Gasworks.*

Photo: Gerrard Gentil

The First Gig – The Hollywood Tavern
– March 15 to 17, 1975

The chair arced beautifully through the stage lights and landed directly at the feet of Gino Scarpelli, who up until that moment had been lost in a dazzling display of fretmanship.

It appeared that there was a critic in the house.

Reduced to a bass and drums duo for a few bars Marty and I soldiered on as Gino hurled the chair defiantly across the dance floor, missing the drunk by inches as he weaved his way back towards his table.

Ed Pilling, who was curious enough to be the sole Fludd member in attendance at our debut gig, was now doing what he always did at times like this and was now heading in the direction of the perpetrator to offer him some advice on audience manners. Fortunately for the drunk the hotel bouncer got to him just as Ed did and he was hustled out of the club on his own steam instead of a stretcher. Order now restored, Gino switched the light control panel at his feet from blues to reds as we thundered into our set closing 'Drive Me Crazy.'

While Marty pounded out the drum intro I adjusted the echo unit to approximate the tight tape delay favoured by John Lennon while the dance floor quickly filled. With full time roadies only a dream at this point, sound and lighting would have to be controlled from the stage itself.

Unlike the spread eagle leg stance that would become something of an early trademark, I opted for one in which my left leg was well out in front of my mic, pumping furiously in time to the music, while my right leg anchored my balance behind me. After the set Ritchie Yorke remarked that it was nice to see me "...putting my best foot forward." The club owner, Alex Korn, was the former owner of The Knob Hill Hotel and had pretty much given us this gig as an act of charity. After our last set he shook my hand with warmth and said, "You told me that you guys have only been together for three weeks! I expected shit but you guys are fantastic!"

He had expected right.

We were shit.

HOT SHIT!

The Early Gigs – Cobourg

The weeklong club date at the Plaza Hotel was on the books but it was imperative that promotional material be delivered ASAP. At this point we were all bereft of driver's licences so bopping around the city to pick up photos from the boys was out of the question.

I had to improvise, and quickly.

I had a solo picture from the Fludd days and Marty lived close by enough to bring me a shot over by public transport, but Gino, a west ender by choice, was a definite problem. Spying a Lado Guitars calendar featuring a buxom semi nude lass modeling the latest six string I had an idea. With a bit of glue and magic marker our first poster was ready for delivery. I bummed a ride the sixty miles to Cobourg and stood back to admire the new Goddo poster, now hanging in the club's front lobby.

(The group appearing there that night was a trio called Act III, which featured a very young Rik Emmett of very soon-to-be Triumph.)

APPEARING ALL NEXT WEEK!
FROM TORONTO!
GODDO!
FEATURING FROM FLUDD-BASSIST GREG GODOVITZ!
FROM TRUCK-DRUMMER MARTY MORIN!
AND FROM BRUTUS-TRANSSEXUAL GUITARIST
GINO SCARPELLI!

The club was packed to capacity for our first set Monday night, mostly guys, and mostly there to see Gino's huge breasts. Gino, totally unaware of my creative artwork, long since stolen from the lobby, confusedly weathered the jeers, wolf whistles, and cat calls of "Show us your tits!" throughout our performance.

After the show we celebrated our first road triumph by igniting our dear friend and sometimes driver Neil Gertzbain's toes on fire. The classic hotfoot involves a lighted match placed gently under the toenail of an unsuspecting sleepy head. As Neil was special to us we set one match alight for every toe and then left him to enjoy his well deserved kip. As he awoke screaming we were in the process of getting to know the chubby waitress from the restaurant downstairs. As she wasn't the best of lookers, she gamely agreed to wear the picture of a Playboy Playmate over her face while servicing the entire group.

No big deal, we were only a trio.

Duffy's Tavern was a downtown Hamilton club. I always refer to Hamilton as Little New York as the potential for serious trouble or even violence was a wisecrack away.

Upon our arrival we were pulled aside by this huge beast of a bouncer named "Lucky" who also doubled as manager.

Lucky had some instructions for us. We were all ears.

"How many of youse are in de group?" he smarfed.

"We're a trio," I said.

Noticing the smell of something burning and his eyes glaze over I added, "Three."

Doing some quick math Lucky seemed satisfied the three guys in front of him were indeed the group and proceeded to bark out the band rules.

"Five sets a night, no swearing onstage, and NO DRUM SOLOS!"

Fine rules all, we agreed, and repaired to our dressing hovel under the front stairs.

Showtime eventually arrived and we took our places onstage while Lucky checked IDs for the ten people in the club.

"HOW THE FUCK ARE YOU ASSHOLES TONIGHT??!!!" I screamed, instantly breaking rule number two as Marty went into our first song of the week, a twenty-minute drum solo.

The audience went mild.

Lucky was smouldering behind the bar.

"Well then, now that we've established who's really in charge here, this is called 'Standin' In The Road'," I said as we stormed into the first real song of the night.

By the end of our first set, which would also be our third and fifth sets, plus a bit of our encore, we had won over the crowd completely. Even Lucky, who was dumb, but not stupid, applauded our efforts and gave us free reign to curse, jam and drum solo for the rest of the week.

Port Dover

"Do you know why I picked you up tonight?"

"Uh, no," I replied to the vision in front of me.

"I liked the way your balls moved in those velvet pants."

Simcoe

— Backwards Bob

My eyes were trained firmly on the naked ass in front of me. It's not what you're thinking.

It was ugly and hairy, and it was perched on a bicycle seat weaving wildly out of control as it narrowly navigated the hotel corridor on the second floor of this tobacco belt hotel. It was like an accident scene, repulsive yet strangely compelling. At three in the morning it was unlikely that we would actually mow down any other seriously registered guests, but with various band rooms in total party mode, it only seemed right to stage a naked bike race around the concourse.

Only a few hours earlier I had ordered a drink from the naked loony now in front of me who had made some Cockney slang remark about my stage outfit of platformed wedge clogs, burgundy velvet trousers, black sweater, and Alex The Droog bowler hat.

"Nice whistle, mate," said the waiter, using Cockney slang, obviously taking the piss over my attire.

"You drop a pony?" I asked back in the same language, and with that, a lifelong friendship was formed.

Bob Gray had only been in Canada from Woking, England, a mere month when we connected at The Norfolk. Possessed of a keen sense of the absurd, and an intellect that would eventually find him rubbing shoulders with other such like-minded individuals in the Guinness Book Of World Records, him and I set out almost immediately to wreck havoc on our mutual place of employment.

The old night guard was sound asleep at the front desk when the telephone snapped him to attention.

"There's an awful lot of noise in room 205 and we're trying to sleep, either tell those guys to pipe down or throw them out, NOW!" and I crashed the phone down.

The occupants of room 205 were in actual fact quite laid back and with all available joints long ago having been smoked and the TV purring softly in their room, they were now passing out. It was Gino and his buddy Dave Phelps' bikes that Bob Gray and I had been riding bareback through the hotel corridors. Bob and I, now fully dressed, watched as the night man made his way up the stairs in the direction of room 205. From any room on the second floor you could see the front lobby, stairwell, and corridor.

Running quickly in the opposite direction we unleashed a torrent of shaving cream, completely covering Gino's front door. The old man reached the door and cocked his fist to knock when he realized that the entire portal was smothered in Gillette Foamy. After a hurled abuse and a diligent wall-pound, the door to room 205 drew slightly ajar and a finger pointed in the direction of my room.

A sharp pounding on my door was followed by the insertion of the night key in my lock.

"Wha's goin' on? I'm tryin' to sleep in here," I murmured in my best phoney, just-having- been-woken-up voice.

"Oh! Sorry, Sir," and with that the night man withdrew from my room as Bob Gray ran downstairs to plant a stink bomb under the leg of his chair.

The sulphuric smell of rotten eggs soon seeped under my door.

I knew that the other rooms would catch a whiff as well.

All was right with the world.

I drifted off to sleep.

Later that same week...

It was about three am when I noticed a piece of paper sticking out from under my telephone. Upon careful examination it appeared that some former occupant of my room had written down a local girl's phone number and then had carelessly discarded it.

This, I thought to myself, had the makings of one great practical joke written all over it.

Taking the slip of paper I carefully adjusted my face to straight and went a-knocking on Gino's door. Gino was always good to play tricks on because he never got mad at you for doing so and, especially, because most of the time he didn't get the joke in the first place.

Knock Knock.

"Hi mans," I said all innocent-like. "Some chick phoned my room and left her number for you. She wants you to call her now. She sounded horny."

Gino studied my face for signs of mischief and then went directly to the telephone on his night table and began dialing. I went behind the heavy red velvet curtains and bit down hard on my lip. I could of course only hear Gino's side of the conversation which went like this.

(the girl on the other end – "hello?")

"Hello? It's Gino."

("Who?")
"Gino."
("Who?")
"Scarpelli."
("WHO?")
"Gino Scarpelli."
("WHO??!!")
"From the group."
("WHAT?")
"Goddo."
("WHO?")
"GODDO!"

At that point I assume that she hung up on him as he put the phone down and hearing me snickering said, "You fucking prick!"

I fell out from behind his curtains and made for the door.

Massey Hall

We were rehearsing a new song that I'd written called 'Under My Hat' in Marty's Cabbagetown house when Pat Ryan came flying down the stairs to the basement. I had hired Pat to oversee the band's interests and he was doing just that as he breathlessly told us that we had landed the opening spot on the upcoming Golden Earring concert at Massey Hall. Much excitement ensued as we congratulated each other on our good luck. Golden Earring's recording of 'Radar Love' was a huge hit and a sell out at Massey Hall meant a captive audience of twenty five hundred potential new Goddo fans. We had only been together two months and had not really cut our teeth in downtown Toronto.

The night of the show saw us nervous but eager to get on with it. There was some recognition as we walked on stage as we had all come from well known local groups and the twelve songs we chose for the set list leaned heavily on our original compositions. Aside from the odd sped-up tempo, we were smoking and everyone in the Hall knew it. About eight songs into the set we played 'Under My Hat' for the first time in front of a live audience. Although this song would become a fan fave it was certainly not what we had in mind to close our set with but, as Gino soloed, I glanced stage right to see Ryan gesturing frantically that this was to be our last song. Marty tells me that, although I was livid at being given the hook, he was relieved as the combination of excitement, nerves and adrenaline were about to cause him to pass out. The audience, perhaps also confused at our early departure, started to call us back but were subdued by the house lights and recorded sounds suddenly being turned on.

The next day the papers reported that there was a new gunslinger in town and his name was Goddo. Larry Wilson on CHUM-FM raved for over ten minutes about the group and especially gushed over Marty's songs, 'Already A Memory' and 'Dead of Night.'

Although I was overjoyed at the accolades I have to admit that there was a slight twisting in my stomach that my songs hadn't been singled out.

Belleville
— *Tonight's Dinner Menu*
1. Take one can of pork and beans
2. Turn on hot water faucet in bathroom sink until none hotter
3. Place can under running hot water for approximately five minutes
4. Open can and eat with a spoon stolen from the hotel restaurant
5. Start crying at how pathetic your life is

Thunder Bay

The train ride to Thunder Bay is almost as gruesome as the car ride to Thunder Bay. Limited resources called for just the three band members to travel the fifteen hours with just our guitars and drum hardware and the stage gear would be supplied at the club.

With not much else to do we found some fellow travelers and convinced them that nothing but blow jobs in the train's washrooms would do for the remainder of the journey; at first the girls agreed to this idea, one even going as far as performing the service under the stars in the observation car. While I communed with nature, enjoying the northern light show, the ancient porter silently approached from behind. The young lady, lost in thought, didn't even hear him coming. Quickly appraising the situation the porter asked, "Would the lady care for a pillow?"

"No, I think she's comfy enough, but I wouldn't mind one."

The next day and for the rest of the trip, the girls were hiding from us.

Parry Sound

Marty had just earned his driver's licence. It was mid-winter as we piled into the Volkswagen Beetle for the drive north. The roads would have been treacherous for a seasoned driver and with a novice behind the wheel the loudest sound in the car was not the radio but our collective hearts beating. The weather and the roads got progressively worse as we made our way to the high school in Parry Sound. The bug hit a patch of black ice just as the transport truck came into view in the oncoming lane. Nobody in the car said a word as Marty began frantically turning the now-useless steering wheel while we spun totally out of control into the opposite lane. The truck's headlights now blinded us as the driver leaned on his air horn, the last sound we would ever hear as he didn't even try to brake his rig on the icy stretch of highway. At the last possible second the bug slid off the road where it landed sideways in the ditch. The trucker didn't even stop to check on us as he roared by in the black night, his horn still screaming.

The three of us sat in the stillness for what seemed an eternity, each man lost in his own thoughts as to how close we had just come to death, when we were suddenly aware of fellow travelers running down into the snow covered ditch to offer us some assistance. A short while later, a tow truck dragged the car out and we were soon on our way again. After what seemed like an eternity we arrived at the venue and made our way towards the dressing room.

We were very late.

The school social convener stopped me as I made my way towards the dressing room and said, "You're late! There's no excuse for you arriving late and you won't be paid tonight!"

I grabbed him by his shirt and pushed him violently up against a locker.

"Listen to me you little prick!" I said, not two inches from his face. "We almost died getting here, so don't give me any shit about not getting paid!" and with that I released him.

We played.

We got paid.

Now about this time Bob Gray quit his waiter's job and moved to Toronto to work for the band. I got him a place to stay with a fairly well known groupie but his first night there he was sound asleep in her bed, she was out, when her very large, drunken biker boyfriend came home, crawled into bed with Bob and promptly began making moves on him. I got a call from a very frightened ex-waiter who had managed to stave off the advances of the drunken biker and maintain his virgin status while fleeing his very temporary address.

"Yeah, hello mate, listen," he began, "I just had some fucking cunt try to fuck me at that chick's place. No one said anything about a huge boyfriend and me 'avin' to fuck him."

He moved in that night with us.

Twenty Bucks

The stairs leading down to our rehearsal room in Marty's basement were tricky enough to navigate when totally straight. Drunk or stoned they called for Sherpa mountain guides.

One had to lean way back and support oneself by clutching the walls on either side when descending into the pit.

It was a lovely design flaw.

"Hey Bob," I called out across the crowded kitchen as the drunken party raged on in every room, "you know that twenty bucks you owe me?"

Bob nodded.

We had recently learned how to play backgammon and had graduated from the loser performing menial chores such as dish washing and garbage-outing to actual gambling for money.

"If you jump down these stairs here, the debt is cancelled," I smarfed.

"Wot, just jump for twenty bucks?" Bob asked and with that, proceeded to remove his jacket. Passing me the garment and without a second's pause he dove headfirst down the dreaded stairwell, landing in a non-moving heap at the bottom.

The debt was cleared.

A legend was born.

For twenty bucks I have witnessed Bob run the full length of a dressing room and smash his head into a metal locker, drink a glass of coke spiked with cigarette butts, mustard, bits of food, and other assorted items, and throw himself out of fast-moving power boats only to slam into the water at breakneck speed.

Hanging at full arm's length from the eighteenth floor balcony of my apartment was deemed a reasonable bet for twenty big bucks in the big land, aka, BBITBL.

Once, chemically imbalanced, we watched in horror as he hopped a freight train and disappeared down the line. He returned the next morning on the 8:15.

In his house there is a photo showing Bob leaping from the bridge that separates Paradise Island from Nassau in the Bahamas and subsequent photos of our unconscious kid being fished out of the water below by fellow thrill seekers. Looking on with great admiration I asked him if the standard fee of twenty bucks had been negotiated before the leap.

"Fuck no, mate," he said poker faced, "I got a hundred for that one!"
BBITBL.

Goin' Down
– a Linda Lovelace story

There are a million horny guys in the naked city. I was one of them.

The line snaked its way down Yorkville Avenue and wound around Avenue Road for what seemed like miles. Porn queen Linda Lovelace of "Deep Throat" fame was making a special appearance at a local bookstore and blow-job aficionados of every race, colour and crud were anxiously awaiting her arrival.

With a recording session scheduled and no time for lining up I scrawled out a suitable message and stood by the curb as the stretch limo pulled up. As the chauffeur got out I passed him the note which he dutifully passed over to the gifted starlet as she swanned onto the street to a hearty chorus of catcalls, wolf whistles and general abuse. Instead of dashing into the store, she paused momentarily, read my note, smiled, quizzed the driver as to who had written it, and then crooked a well-manicured finger in my direction, motioning me to join her. After a brief conversation, she agreed to call me later and with that I made for my recording session.

There was a flurry of activity as candles were lit, the sauna ignited, and fine wines were brought in as we all fantasized about what might possibly come of Linda Lovelace and her much sought after blow-job technique actually coming to our session!

The phone rang!

It was Linda Lovelace calling for Greg!

HEY, THAT'S ME!

"Hi Greg," she purred into my ear, "I wanted to call you and thank you for your generous offer but my manager says that we have a big day ahead of us tomorrow so he says I can't come."

She couldn't come.

The guys in the studio were devastated but were nonetheless curious as to the contents of my note, which got her to phone in the first place.

The note read: "Linda, I am going to be so famous someday that you should get to know me now!"

HEY!!! THIS JUST IN...

I've just returned from Ronnie Hawkins Manor up north and I am drained. At sixty-five The Hawk is more like a vampire than an aging rock icon, as he sucks the energy from your body, feeds on it, and then channels it into the funniest Arkansas anecdotes and one-liners that leave you shaking your head and gasping for air.

"...we never had orgies! That sounds nasty. We mighta had fifteen or sixteen people in love a few times..."

"...these two motherfuckers came off like Heckle and Jeckle, or that Simon and Garfuckel!"

"...He'd do things to her that would make Caligula ashamed!"

Looking around the beautiful living room at the wealth of historical material, from Ronnie posing in the oval office with President Clinton, to Jerry Lee Lewis and Carl Perkins honouring the man at his sixtieth birthday, to the vast array of music awards dotting the sideboards, you are truly awed at the sheer volume of history that The Hawk has brought to Canada and the world. Mention of The Order Of Canada came up but he didn't have one of those things yet. I mentioned to the Hawk that Rush had been so honoured. He looked at me for a nano-second before saying, "Yeah, those boys recorded one of their best albums in mah barn."

In his barn.

Let It Rock
– a Ronnie Hawkins story

Skid Row lead vocalist Sebastian Bach was in town so that we might "Save The Gasworks." Now one young upstart and one old pioneer were not going to change a diaper, let alone stop the destruction of one of Toronto's rock shrines, but to me it seemed like a good chance for some national media coverage and cheap press.

I agreed to do it.

Sebastian, a gorgeous hunk of big-haired heavy metal rock god, had recently graced the cover of Rolling Stone and was now sitting on the couch in my living room, singing along to my old songs, of which he knew more of the lyrics than I did.

My wife, who had a crush on the rock star, having seen him open for Guns N' Roses, was very impressed. I later overheard her talking to her friend Michael and saying, "...and he knows all the words to Greg's songs!"

To Greg:
I've been a fan of yours ever since that Chum/City Simulcast from that church.
The Gasworks was a part of our Canadian Metal heritage and I will be sad to see it go.
I will miss the quarts on the patio especially.
Here's to the Gasworks.
And a special Party on to Nile. Hang in there.

Mike Myers

Impressed?

Michael sure was.

I got a good feeling from him that he was enjoying his newfound celebrity and taking advantage of this by visiting his old heroes at their homes.

"I was at Hawkins' farm last night," he said, "and I said to him, 'Hey Ronnie, you know whose place I'm going to tomorrow night?'" Ronnie waited for the information and Sebastian offered, "I'm going to Greg Godovitz's!"

The Hawk, enveloped in a cloud of smoke, sat back in his chair, trying to place my name.

Not to be outdone, he simply said, "Tha's okay boy, Ah know Chuck Berry!"

and later on...

I know absolutely nothing about HOCKEY, the Canadian obsession, except that Andrew (Coney Hatch - Drug Plan) Curran and myself wrote some songs about HOCKEY for radio and television. I am watching game 5 of the 1999 Philadelphia - Toronto series with the bad guys up 1-0 in the first period and the meaning of HOCKEY suddenly came to me.

"It is much better to watch hockey when the players look really old than it is to watch the game and they all look like kids."

Thunder Sound
Wil Webster was a family member of The Montreal Webster's who amongst other...

HEY!!! THIS JUST IN...
May 2, 1999

It had been a while since I had draped myself over the lip of a stage from the audience side to admire someone's playing but for "Donny," exceptions are the rule. Troiano was a few feet from me, my ear at speaker level, as he cut into the Bush classic 'I Can Hear You Callin.'

I suddenly found myself punching the air while offering up throaty accolades.

Troiano didn't hear or see me.

If he did he was ignoring me.

They staged a Toronto Rock and Roll Revival tonight featuring all of my favourite local 60's groups:

The Stitch In Time, Luke and The Apostles, The Ugly Ducklings, Mike McKenna's Mainline, Robbie Lane and The Disciples, Kensington Market, Crowbar, Lighthouse, and the aforementioned deity, known as Domenic (DONNY) Troiano, with George Olliver (The Blue Eyed Prince Of Soul) and Roy Kenner (Roy Kenner and The Associates), both ex-Mandala front men who shared vocal duties this evening.

Fludd, as important as they were in the last 100 pages, were not invited.
Neither was "Subway ELVIS."

Apparently Little Caesar and The Consuls were miffed that they hadn't been invited either.

The "Arthur" does his best Van Morrison impression while Sebastian Bach blows bubbles at GASAID – the "Save The Gasworks" Benefit.

Here is my review:
- Keith McKie and Luke Gibson (Kensington Market), well into middle age, still look and sound and come off as stars.
- The Ducks need me to play bass.
- George Olliver IS the blue-eyed Prince of Soul.
- I was almost convinced that the girl mixing my drinks was a guy.
- Somebody was throwing ice cubes at Robbie Lane while he was making dramatic stage moves.
- Stan Endersby is a good bass player but The Ducks should use me.
- Mike McKenna (Mainline) once turned down an offer to join Paul Butterfield's Blues Band.
- He is still very good.
- There was a lot of balding and greying in the crowd.
- There was a preponderance of fatsos.
- On my fourth or fifth visit to the refreshment station the she-male bar tender was beginning to look good.
- "DONNY" will eventually play in God's personal house band as second lead guitarist but will have to lay back a bit to give God a fighting chance.

and now back to our story...

Thunder Sound

Wil Webster was a family member of The Montreal Websters, which meant that you could own the staid and true Globe and Mail newspaper. As a Webster, it was important for young Wil to not appear to work too hard while living a life of absolute luxury. Legend has it that living a life of luxury does not include lighting Cuban cigars with hundred dollar bills earned by your hard working ancestors, which is supposedly what Wil was doing at a poker game when his uncle and executor of the estate came in. Wil was apparently cut off and soon found himself owner of a downtown recording facility called Thunder Sound. Wil bought us a PA system.

As patron saints Wil and Ritchie Yorke were champions of creative endeavour, and we soon found ourselves the recipients of their collective largesse and in the same studio to lay down primitive Goddo originals. The first sessions bristled with electricity and the music found its way onto 16-track analog tape as earthy, edgy, sexy, and exceptionally stupid. Case in point:

HOT THING
Hot thing, you drag me down to the floor
Scream time, you crash, bam, boom for more
Hot love, rug burns on my knees
Don't quit, until I beg you please
...case closed.

We finished up 1975 with a New Years Eve gig at The Level Crossing on Yonge Street, which grossed the three of us, the unheard sum of $1,185.00!

What a way to start a new year off!
We had a record out that we didn't really record together.
We had snappy new press photos.
We had the princely sum of $1,185.00...and!...we had a future.

Goddo 1976

It was the era of the weeklong bar gig. Three or four forty-minute sets a night for six days with a three-hour matinee on Saturday just to finish you off. If you sang, it was awful. If you sang and smoked, forget about it. As an unknown band in a small town you could look forward to shitty rooms, shitty food, and shitty playing conditions. That was the up-side. The downside was that club owners and management detested you on sight as something sub-human. They used every opportunity to make your stay a living hell by refusing you such life necessities as cash advances and bar tabs, while constantly complaining about the volume of the music and the all-night scream festivals in the band rooms upstairs that were keeping the live-in rubbies awake. You just knew that any girl who would walk down one of those seedy corridors was open for business.

With no money you found yourself depending on the kindness of strangers to buy you a meal, or subsisting solely on canned goods for the entire week.

Daily activities usually consisted of sleeping for as long as you could so as to avoid having to study your squalid living conditions by daylight. As someone who had far too much energy to waste it sleeping all day, I was usually up and out exploring in every town we visited. Just walking down Main Street, Ontario, was good enough to pass an afternoon and there was usually some place to sit and read or write lies on postcards about how well you were doing to send home.

Monday night crowds would find a few curiosity seekers, who, if you put on a good show, would tell their friends and ensure some action for the rest of the week. If you merely walked in Monday's set then you were treated to Tuesday through Thursday as much like performing in an empty bowling alley. You could throw strikes all night but they never hit anything.

Friday nights were usually pretty good as people were looking to cut loose after slaving away all week, but Saturday was always the night. Maybe it was that you were finally getting the hell out of this cesspool of a town, maybe it was because after you paid your drug debts and bar tab there were a few bucks coming your way. Maybe it was because by the end of your last set everyone was finally on the same page. The audience was now in tune with the fact that maybe you weren't shit after all. Sure, you were the guy who screwed buddy Joe's waitress girlfriend, but Hey!...you fuckin' rocked man!

There was still something that seemed cool about the whole thing even though the life style was impossible by normal standards, and you just knew that things would be better the next time you passed through town.

With Pat Ryan no longer around, having recently departed to pursue a career at A&M Records, we were suddenly adrift management-wise. What we needed was some bad advice so we hired Barry and Vince to offer some.

> *diary – wednesday, january 14 – brockville*
> *Barry just called and told me that 11 cities worth of billboards would only cost $6400 / 3 months.*
> *What a deal!*
> *What the fuck did we need an eleven-city billboard campaign for?*
> *I can still see it...*
> *HEY EVERYBODY!*
> *THERE'S A NEW BAR BAND COMING!*

> *A Moment With Myra the Manager As Told By Walter (Egghead) Zwol:*
> *"Say Myra, are you a virgin?"*
> *"NO... Aquarrrrius!"*

Myra The Manager

I have this theory that aliens are living among us but they are disguised as loonies who you really don't want to connect with in the first place.

Their job here is to report on certain aspects of human existence.

There is a crazy looking guy around my area that just walks around all day and night. His name is Wayne and he lives under a bridge. I bought him lunch one day and as we sat on the curb enjoying our fish and chips I saw wormy things crawling in his beard. I gave him the rest of my fish and chips.

One minute you'll see Wayne walking up one street and an hour later you spot him miles away and you know that he couldn't possibly have walked that distance in that amount of time.

He is an alien writing a thesis on the city of Scarborough.

Wayne becomes invisible and teleports himself around the area.

I know for a fact that he is an alien because the girl working in my local liquor store tells me that although he doesn't appear to be working he buys better booze than I do. At first this embarrassed me but I soon confided my alien theory to the girl, who never brought it up again.

Myra the Manager was also an alien and her thesis dealt with Toronto rock groups. She stood about 3'5" with naturally curly hair which she would pull out if upset. Once, after an Ontario Place Forum concert, I watched with raised eyebrows as she pulled out clumps of adorable alien hair while talking to herself in the mirror. When I asked her what was the matter she cried that our maniac roadie Clark "called me a weirdo," which came out "weeeiirrrdo" in her rolled-'r's'-Bela-Lugosi-alien-speak.

Knock, knock.

"Who is it?"

"Open the doorrr, it is Myrrra yourrrr managerrrr and fan club prrresident."

Actually, in light of several bad management choices still to come, Myra would have made a great manager as she actually showed up at her artist's gigs and she didn't ask for any money.

Admitted to the inner sanctum, she was all business. "Therrre you arrrre Grrrreg Godovitz you little rrrrascal!" and it kind of warmed you up the way she said it.

She made you fuzzy.

Once she was trying to get to Fludd guitarist Mick Walsh, who she was convinced was George Harrison, and she slugged me square in the nuts when I stepped in her way. After that I always stood well out of striking range or sideways when chatting with her.

On the way home from a gig one night Walter was stopped by the police and, fearing the worst, he got out of the car to try and explain Myra to the officer. He was told to get back in the car while the officer went around to the passenger side window to question Myra.

"May I see some ID, Miss," said the Cop peering through the window.

"Two forrrrty-fives from the Egghead!" she said waving the new Brutus singles at the officer.

"I tried to warn you, man," said Walter, and was sent on his way.

As she would tell everyone that she was the manager AND fan club president of whichever group was playing that night, on gigs where three or more acts appeared she had her work definitely cut out for her. She was really good at guarding the dressing room door and would not let anyone intrude on her group's privacy.

I haven't seen her in a number of years so I must assume the worst and come to the conclusion that Toronto's current music scene is so pathetic that there's nothing much to write about and her work on this planet is completed.

diary – wednesday, january 21 – penthouse motor inn
Chuck The Heavy (doorman) says he's going to kill me when the week is over. Good. Something to look forward to.

I was always offending somebody at lower management level, usually door goons hired to keep control. With something approaching delusions of grandeur they would call you over to offer some inane criticism and you usually told them where to stick it in return. This did not make for a comfortable work environment but you knew that you were relatively safe until after you'd been paid on Saturday night.

Club management was a whole other thing and soon I was developing a reputation as a troublemaker. It was now common procedure to arrive at the club, insult the owner's wife or brother, offend everyone at sound check by getting loads of ear splitting feedback, insult a doorman, say something totally out of line to the married waitress, argue with the owner about who is really in control, and then go back to your room for some hot water-heated pork and beans.

diary – wednesday, january 28 – richmond hill
The owner, "Big Ben" comes on tighter wound than his TIMEX about us only playing 28 minutes. I tell him to piss off.

It was astonishing that I did not get creamed by guys like "Big Ben" on a constant basis, but it almost seemed like they enjoyed the abuse. I am almost positive that no one in their right mind would dare to say such things to guys like this and it soon became part of the ritual.

Le Studio and Roy Thomas Baker

I had been planning a trip to England to find a producer and my first choice was the man behind 'Queen', Roy Thomas Baker. There is something about English records that just sound better, perhaps an adventurous approach to the creative process that North American productions lacked at the time. This, of course, was not the rule but I was set on an English producer.

Before I undertook this quest it was decided that we would break for a week and I would go skiing in Quebec. I had never skied a day in my life but I had a very professional-looking black and white vertically-striped outfit that at least made me look like I knew what I was doing.

The trip was interesting as Lori couldn't handle the all-night drive, so I found myself behind the wheel of our Volkswagen Beetle even though I didn't have a driver's licence. The Beetle presented somewhat of a challenge as it featured standard transmission and, without any driving experience to speak of, I was taking a hell of a chance getting us there.

As our rooms were not ready upon our early morning arrival we drove to Le Studio in Morin Heights to wait it out. French Canadian musical legend Robert Charlebois popped in and made us espresso coffee, and I phoned music journalist Marty Melhuish in Montreal to let him know what we were up to. I had met Marty through Ritchie Yorke and he would later prove himself a pivotal figure in the group's early development. After outlining my plans to seek out Roy Thomas Baker in England Marty informed me that the famous producer was working with English pop group Pilot ('Magic' was their big hit record) at the very studio from which I was calling.

The Holy Grail had found me!

At noon the great man arrived at the studio with various Pilots in tow and I managed to play him our demo tape before they got to work. After the second track he popped his head over the console and said, "How long did you say this group has been together?" and nodded his head in approval when I informed him that we had been together for less than a year. The next night we were invited to watch him work and the spirit and humour in the room was contagious. Every time he opened his mouth to give suggestions it was like listening to the old ladies in a Monty Python skit, and he spent more time sitting on the couch in front of the recording console than actually turning knobs and pushing faders. Still, it was this very same Roy Thomas who had helped create Queen's wall of sound, so one suspended any criticism concerning his working style.

"Let's put a bit of doubly wubbly on that shall we," he would say and one of the Pilot vocalists would dutifully head out to the studio to double his line.

The next day a lovely English lady who introduced herself to me as Mrs. Baker stopped me on the slopes.

"My husband said that I would recognize you by your outfit," and I began to realize that perhaps I was a bit overdressed for someone who had only graduated from Bunny Class that very morning.

"He quite likes your material," she went on to say, "considering that it's usually quite hard to get him to listen to tapes at all."

With that said I suddenly felt quite comfortable in my new ski outfit.

I met with Roy the next day and he gave me his home number as well as his manager John Reid's number in London. John Reid also managed Elton John. Lori and I finished our skiing holiday and promised the Bakers that we'd be in touch.

March 1-6 Tudor Tavern, Cambridge
March 8-13 The Gasworks, Toronto
March 15-18 Larry's Hideaway, Toronto
March 19 Campbellford High School
March 20-31 Freeport, Bahamas (vacation)

Freeport

My father-in-law Norm was a great guy. He was also loaded, having just enjoyed a healthy bit of luck at the craps tables in Las Vegas, and he arranged for Lori, myself, Backwards Bob and Gino to be flown to Freeport in the Bahamas where we would stay in two elegant apartments for ten days, at his expense. With a steady diet of coconut rum and killer weed to keep us in vacation mode we spent our days in typical fashion, getting burnt alive by the tropical sun, fine dining at the island's best restaurants, and taking in the native shows and glass-bottomed boat tours at night. There was also a casino and it was here that I realized that gambling was not my thing. Every time that I played I lost. I had inherited my father's luck regarding games of chance.

After ten days we were somewhat tanned and ready to rejoin the rat race. Things were looking good until we arrived at the airport only to discover that Gino, for some bizarre reason, did not have a return ticket. As we sat on the plane, watching Gino standing there looking lost by the fence and not knowing what to do next, it dawned on me that if we left him there he would never get home. Lori agreed to give up her seat and soon Gino was sitting beside me while my wife watched us get ready for departure from the same spot that Gino had occupied only moments before. I suddenly felt really bad for her and, uttering curses at Gino for being a dough head, I got off the plane and joined Lori as the Toronto-bound jet lifted off into the sun.

The airport officials, who probably felt a little sorry for us, arranged special transportation for us to Miami and we soon found ourselves flying as the only two passengers on a commercial jet to Florida. After hours in tedious line-ups we finally gave up trying to get home that day and secured a car and hotel for the night.

While station-hopping on the car radio I heard that The Manhattan Transfer was performing at some supper club in Fort Lauderdale. Now this, in and of itself, was no cause for excitement, but one of the group's stars, Laurel Masse, was a friend of ours. Laurel had spent a week living in sin at our apartment with Bob Segarini, who was having a torrid affair with her at the time. On the odd occasion when they surfaced from our spare room we spent our time singing three part harmonies around the kitchen table and a nice friendship was quickly developed. Laurel was a beautiful tall red head and a great singer. I like red heads.

To say that she was surprised to see us in Fort Lauderdale is an understatement but she showed her true colours by quickly organizing a complementary hotel suite for us, with dinner and a ringside table for their performance that evening. After the show, the three of us went off and soon found ourselves in an adults-only store, pumping quarters into a peep show movie machine. The feature film that evening was called *Knights of the Night* and involved a group of very merry men doing things with their fists to each other in a daisy chain that had the three of us scrambling for more change.

We flew home the next morning.

Rod and Ronnie

I was sitting on a queen size bed in Ronnie Wood's fairly plush suite in Detroit when it suddenly dawned on me that nearly everyone else was in the bathroom. Rod Stewart, his then-girlfriend Britt Eklund, Ronnie, and my travelling pal Ewan had excused themselves to powder their noses. Across the room sat legendary songwriter Bobby Womack who had composed one of my all time favourite songs, 'It's All Over Now', which the Stones had covered. He sort of looked uneasy at the sudden rude departure of our hosts and attempted small talk. In the middle of the room was a portable flight case that housed Ronnie's rock star wardrobe, an amazing sound system and about a hundred sound board cassettes of Ronnie's recent tour with the Stones. With Bobby there, there was no way to pocket any so we just made with the small talk.

I had come to Detroit to meet Faces manager Billy Gaff, with an eye to him managing Goddo. Ewan was a transplanted Cockney who was an old pal of Rod and Ronnie's, and had assured me that if I paid his expenses then an introduction to Mr. Gaff was definitely on. I was introduced to Billy backstage at Cobo Hall where Rod and his merry men would be performing that evening. The smallish manager limply shook my hand and then ignored my little sales pitch while complaining about a nasty little smudge on his grey wool slacks. In frustration I offered that perhaps he might cover this eyesore with his backstage pass so that he might listen to my tape, and could not believe my own eyes when he did just that.

"Now then," he began, "about your little group...I have no interest in managing anybody but the greatest rock and roll band in the world, and that would be the group that's on stage this very minute."

I could hear Rod and the lads in the distance. They didn't sound THAT hot.

With that rejection established, Billy gave me a copy of a new artist he had taken on, with the unlikely name of Johnny Cougar, and bade me adieu. There was nothing left to say and I dejectedly left the room and made for the side of the stage where Ewan was pathetically egging on Ronnie.

The highlight was that Ronnie got us a room on the same floor as the touring party and I was now sitting in on a wild party with Rod and his highflying entourage.

Some wild party. Looking around once more I shrugged my shoulders and said goodnight to Bobby Womack. As I closed the door behind me this drop-dead beautiful groupie came out of nowhere and purred suggestively, "Excuse me, sir, but I will do anything to get in to that party, anything at all."

Sir?

For once I just wasn't in the mood and I shook my head "No, thanks." as I turned the key to my room. She was still standing there as I closed the door.

Quebec City

I always loved playing in old Quebec City, because of the food and the groupies. Any meal you ate in Quebec, even in the greasiest of spoons, was always lovingly prepared and piled high. As far as the girls were concerned, they literally had fistfights over you, if they fancied you. French girls never had any original teeth to speak of, and always wore sexy, black push-up bras. They would buy you gifts if they thought it might earn them points. Of course, none of this was necessary, but the false teeth certainly offered up possibilities.

We always stayed at L'Hotel Jean Talon, which was one of the seedier "budget" accommodations, down by the train tracks. It was only a short walk uphill to the club from these modest lodgings and the rooms were paid for, as part of the contract, by the ever-hostile club owners. We had a bit of an edge in the language department, as Marty Morin was fluent in French. Unlike the rest of the country, in Quebec things didn't really get cooking until after midnight, so the first set was at eleven thirty, with your last set at three in the morning. The hotel featured a bevy of haggish working girls and the oddest, coin-operated video machines that ran old musical numbers by people like Paul Anka. For the low price of a quarter, you could watch him sing 'Diana' while twisting down the steps of an airplane. Nobody in their right mind had anything at all to do with the hookers, as the club was a cornucopia of sin and these girls were well past their expiry dates.

I had written my ballad 'Chantal' in this very hotel, during a Fludd road trip, and the hoary old daughters of the night cried when I first played it to them.

Things got off to a strange start when one of the brothers who owned the club was killed on his motorcycle. Just mere hours before, he was glaring in my direction, cursing me in a foreign tongue, and now he was bereft of life. As new employees, we were invited to view the corpse but I declined after figuring out that he wasn't that good looking alive, let alone after a fatal motorcycle accident. The club was shut down in memory of something or other and we had the next night off.

Everyone split up and I went into the night, on my own, to the old part of town to listen to Cajun fiddle music. It was there that I ran into a French girl named Linda, whom I knew from Toronto, and she was back in her native Quebec, visiting relatives. In Toronto she had always been friendly but aloof, but here was a different matter and she could hardly wait to show me her bra. With the Cajun music pounding out its fevered promise of hot lust, and after much wine, we stumbled back down the hill to the good old Jean Talon for an evening of merrymaking.

As I opened the door to my room, I noticed a puddle of water just inside. I couldn't figure out where it had come from but set about cleaning it up with my towel, brought from home. About two months later I was going through some tour photos and came across a snap of one of the roadies pissing through the keyhole of my door.

When Frankenstein's Monster Runs Amok

The rot had settled in. Marty was beginning to become less enamoured with my handling of business affairs and was ganging up on me, through managers Barry and Vince. Record deals were tabled, only to have me make some ridiculous demands that no record company executive would ever agree to in the first place. By this time, although I had been in touch with Roy Thomas Baker in England, I was absolutely convinced that the right producer for the band was me. Roy wanted $50,000.00; I would work cheaper. The roadies were pissing through my keyholes; I had asked Backwards Bob to leave; the managers thought that I was out of control; and Marty Morin announced that he was leaving the group.

> *diary – thursday, april 22 – toronto*
> *First thing I hear is, "Sorry, Greg, but I guess you heard I'm leaving."*
> *Fuck Off!*
> *Gino is with me I think but it all comes down to getting a good drummer.*

The next night we played at a local high school where our second set was interrupted by one of the student council walking on stage mid-set and taking a vote on the group continuing or disco music. Disco 1 – Goddo 0.

Doug Inglis

Doug Inglis was in town to audition with Moxy, an early heavy metal group that featured my old pal Buzz Shearman on lead vocals. Their drummer, affectionately known as "The Heaviest," was one Billy Wade, and he was leaving the group. Billy, who was our first choice for new drummer, rehearsed with Gino and myself, but, for some reason or other, things didn't jell.

Gino at one point assured Billy that, although I was sort of a nerdy geek in real life, I was a much different animal on a stage. As this was mentioned in my presence, my left eyebrow lifted in amazement and I made a note to mentally torture the guitarist at the next opportunity. Returning to Moxy temporarily, Billy reclaimed his drum throne but gave Doug my number, adding that "Someday you'll thank me for this."

Doug knew nothing of the group but drove down to see us play and stayed around to jam afterwards. I put it down to nerves but I personally wasn't convinced that he had the chops. On the phone he had assured me that he could sing, which turned out to be more of a cigarette-ravaged rasp, but he did have a driver's licence and he looked so much like Marty Morin that new promo pictures wouldn't be required until we ran out of the old ones. Gino loved him right off and just asked me to be patient and give him a chance. Doug had cut his musical teeth in Ottawa, playing with Powerhouse, who were also a blues-based trio. At six feet one he towered over Gino and myself, and his dark good looks made him a natural rival as far as the ladies were concerned.

He would indeed thank Billy Wade, he was in.

By the beginning of June, Doug had moved to Toronto where he rekindled an old romance with Second City creator Andrew Alexander's sister, Trudy, and moved in with her while rehearsing with Gino and I during the day, when schedules permitted. Martin Melhuish was calling us up and had introduced us to a Montrealer named Allan Katz who had managed Sylvia Tyson and Nana Mouskouri.

Sylvia, Nana, and Goddo.

It didn't make sense then; it doesn't make sense now.

Meanwhile, Katz had flown in to meet with us and it was all Mumm's champagne and big talk. I liked Katz as he was sharp, successful, and handsome, and I trusted Melhuish to keep an eye on him.

Montreal

Marty Morin left the group and as a parting gift we completely covered his car in shaving cream. I was on a train to Montreal the following Monday where I was met by Katz and Melhuish and then introduced to that city's music scene. The club Thursday's was in the trendiest downtown area and was the hot spot for local and touring musicians. Michel Pagliaro, Walter Rossi, April Wine's David Henman, and countless others gathered at happy hour to drink and talk shop. I scouted potential studios by day with Henman and was wined and dined at night. I was convinced that Katz was the right guy to manage us and felt confident in his ability to secure us our first record deal.

The train ride home was bittersweet as my mind was in a state of turmoil over the week's many developments, the most troublesome being my decision to leave my wife for a girl I had been seeing. Lori took my impending departure like every other thing, with a stoic grace that cloaked the shame and hurt that she must have felt. She wished me good luck and kissed me goodbye as I walked out of her life. She had been a good friend, but my mind was clouded by dreams and excess and there was no point in trying to reason with me.

At this time I was writing songs at fever pitch, one day 'Bus Driver Blues', in honour of Marty Morin's new gig, then the next day 'Let It Slide.' 'Let That Lizard Loose' had been inspired by a Ritchie Yorke quip about a certain fondness for fellatio and it soon became another contender for first album inclusion. Songs first written during the Fludd years like 'Twelve Days', 'Chantal', and 'Cock On' were also considered. Rehearsals with Doug were now going great and we were just about ready to start playing again.

On the 10th of July we played our first gig with Doug on drums at The Pav in Orillia.

We stunk. Things improved however as we played six nights a week and soon the band sounded better than before. Although our sound changed dramatically from a heavy pop-oriented vocal harmony group to a heavier power trio with only one vocalist, it was the sound that would make our reputation, and there was little backlash in the press or from the fans with regards to the new direction. A one-day session at Listen Audio gave Katz the five-song demo that he would need to shop around to the major labels.

diary – saturday, october 9 – deep river
Long haul to Deep River. Bad snowstorm. Katz clinches WAM deal and tentatively start LP on Oct. 24. Gig is weird. We go totally over their heads. On the way home we run out of gas and spend night on highway. Lots of snow up north.

WAM was owned by one Gary Cape, a large man in height and girth, who had seen the group and liked what he'd heard. I believe his contract was signed over a pinball machine. It would be the only time we would ever hear the sound of winning bells while we were with him. It was agreed upon that we would record our debut LP at Listen Audio in Old Montreal. Our engineer was Dixon Van Winkle who had previously worked with McCartney on the 'Ram' album.

The accommodations supplied to us by Cape were worse than any band rooms we had so far encountered. The run down hotel stunk of stale cigarette smoke and urine-soaked hallways, and the weekly residents sat in their underwear with their doors always open and their televisions blaring. We requested that Marty Melhuish come and inspect our new digs and he did manage to find certain charming aspects to this hovel as only a writer with a very active imagination would. However, when he pulled back the drapes he calmly said, "Perhaps you guys are right about this place. I think we should all leave now." Looking past him we stared in amazement as the adjacent building, not five feet from the one we were staying in, was completely engulfed in flames.

"FIRE!" we screamed as we ran down the corridors waking up our neighbours. We didn't stick around to witness the carnage but instead did the smart thing: we headed off to Thursdays to drink. I ended up on Marty's couch with a curtain for a blanket.

The sessions, open-ended affairs that saw us start in the evening and continue through the night, were going well and we had six tracks finished that first week. As we recorded late we could experiment with sounds, like dragging the Leslie speaker for the Hammond Organ into the cobblestoned courtyard at three a.m. and then playing a huge chord at top volume as the sound swirled and crashed off stone walls to give us the sound of a giant church organ. Brilliant keyboardist Dwayne Ford added his personal magic Fender Rhodes to 'Under My Hat' and eccentric percussion whiz Geordie MacDonald, whose Mom I had met on the train and supplied me with his phone number, came in with various whistles, bells, and hand drums. The sessions now had a life of their own, but with the amount of over-the-top partying we were doing it was surprising that anything was getting accomplished at all.

My life at this time was a constant commute by train between Montreal and Toronto. A certain amount of live gigs had to be maintained to sustain our personal needs while we recorded, so it was a constant blur of activity.

I had become less enamoured with the girl I had left my wife for and she had moved out but I soon found a new distraction to take her place. Her name was Rose and although she was very young, she would become a big part of my life as Goddo began its climb.

The Zombats

Clark was one of our roadies. A lantern-jawed guy who could pass for a young Burt Lancaster, he was forever getting into fights with anyone who would have it. He rarely lost and I took to having him accompany me on my daily rounds and especially after gigs when the moon was full and the drunks were howling.

One memorable night I came down from the dressing room to find Clark in mortal combat with no less than three club bouncers who had taken exception to him man-handling one of the female staff. They managed to get him outside where I joined him on the curb. At that moment this wise-ass drunk strolled by and, checking us out, looked directly at me and began to say, "Well, well, if it isn't the famous Greg Godovi.." before his face became a punching bag for good old Clarkie. We ended up in court over that one.

Lorne was a stage tech, a dead ringer for Peter Frampton, and in possession of a dick so huge he was nicknamed "Namu." Girls liked him.

Our other roadie at the time was one Allen Henry, who did lighting and would grow up to become the famous Canadian artist C.A.Henry. He designed the volcano-spewing-lava LP cover for our debut that the record company tampered with so much that he swore he would never do that again, and he didn't. Allen was a gifted boxer and as part of the crew with Clark there was always an element of danger.

The three roadies were called The Zombats.

With our debut LP finally in the can we spent the rest of the year playing six nights a week at every bar, high school, and university pub that we could and screwing everything that moved. With Rose not officially moved in and me playing in a very hot group, my apartment should have been equipped with a revolving door. At one point the upstairs neighbours took exception to a certain moaning "Snake Lady" that Gino and I were playing with and cut off their fireplace flue, effectively smoking us out. As this was at three in the morning I retaliated by turning on the stereo to maximum volume with a Hendrix LP playing over and over before locking up and leaving for the night. When I returned a day later it was still playing.

They never tried to smoke me out again.

The "Arthur" wowing the masses at Nathan Philips Square, Toronto.

Goddo 1977

My old friend Brian Pilling was out of remission and was once more stricken with the dreaded leukemia. Fludd had been soldiering on, despite my absence, with a never-ending parade of replacement musicians, but their days as a chart contender were all but finished and any hope of hitting the big time would have been pure delusion. Still, all through the early Goddo madness, Skinny, Brian, Ed, Rocko, or Bwuce would come to our gigs, or come over for a drink and some dinner and I likewise did the same with them. There was never a group anywhere on this planet that had the sense of brotherhood like the Fluddies.

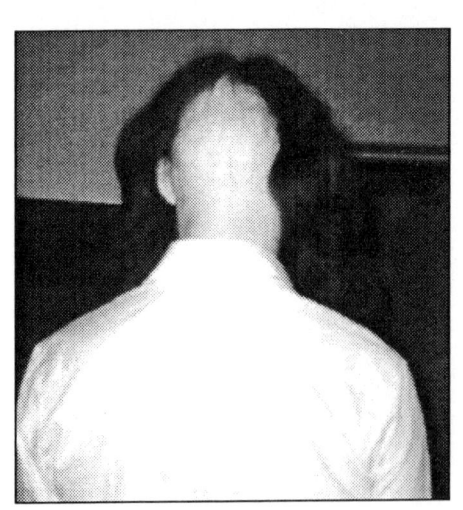

Brian Pilling finally wigs out.

I decided that a benefit to raise money, to lighten Brian's financial load, should be organized and that the hottest Toronto groups of the day would be invited. Fludd manager Skinny was initially unsure as to my motives and perhaps sought to protect Brian from further public scrutiny, but Ed Pilling was all for it to the point that he started running with my ball. I diplomatically talked him down and began organizing the event for Sunday, February 20 at the Tudor Tavern in Cambridge, some sixty miles from home.

Meanwhile, life with the folks upstairs became a living hell as there was no sound insulation and their every fart resonated throughout my entire place. Their baby wailed at all hours and the older kids roared up and down the stairs all day, making any kind of sleep impossible. They viewed me as something sub-human and warned their kids not to talk to me. At one point they said that bringing different women home every night was obscene, to which I countered that I thought it a bit unusual myself that their two oldest kids slept on a couch while good old Dad's choo choo trains took up a full bedroom. This got them arguing.

I had hit a nerve.

The Laundromat billboard where Kim Mitchell and I washed our socks had many interesting items pinned up. This was one that we wrote:

Single white male seeks same for shared accommodations. Lovely Bay window and cosy fireplace. Call Mike at...

The Mike in question was Mike Tilka, the friendliest man alive and bass player for Max Webster, a wonderful group of loonies that also starred Mitchell. As a result of the posted ad, Mike received many confusing calls and actually laughed when he found out who was responsible. The guys in Max were good friends at this time and Mitchell would sit in with us whenever he came to see us play or come over for dinner.

Skinny and I had tried calling Ritchie Yorke at about noon. By rock and roll standards this seemed quite reasonable but try as we might he would not pick up the phone. As we were about to tack up posters for the benefit concert, we wanted the only cassette of the new LP for the journey and Ritchie had it. While I pounded on his door and threw snowballs at his bedroom window Skinny lovingly shoveled Ritchie's sidewalk. All at once the window flew open and a very disheveled Yorke thrust his bleary eyes out at the world.

"WHO THE FUCK IS IT!" he screamed.

"It's Godo and Skinny, and I need the cassette for our trip!" I merrily called back. "Look, Skinny even shoveled your walk."

Skinny had done a lovely job on the front walk.

Ritchie looked at the walk and then turned back to me. I could see that he was not impressed.

"I DON'T GIVE A FUCK WHO IT IS, FUCK OFF!" and with that he slammed the window shut. We had driven out of our way, Skinny had shoveled his walk for free, and we didn't have the cassette for our trip. Skinny pointed out to me that Ritchie looked upset about something. I threw one more snowball at his bedroom window and got in the car. I didn't see or speak to Ritchie again for many years until he had had enough of Canada and was returning to his native Australia.

By this time we had run out of promo shots featuring Marty Morin so we had fashion photographer Gerard Gentil shoot some great film of the three of us on a stairwell in the basement of his office, with Rose's lovely young bum as the centre piece. She had our GODDO logo stitched on the back of her seriously cut-off jeans, which made for great advertising whenever we went anywhere, and Doug could finally sign a picture with his face on it.

1976 ... *Goddo promo photo shoot. Left to right: Gino Scarpelli, Greg Godovitz, "Logo Girl," Doug Inglis.*

A Bruce Springsteen Short Story

"Man, your show was so good tonight that even my ulcers felt good," I said, shaking the rock god's hand in his dressing room at Maple Leaf Gardens.

"A young guy like you has ulcers?" He seemed genuinely interested.

"Yeah, I've been playing on the road for thirteen years," I added.

"Yeah," he said nodding, "that'll do it."

Around this time I wrote a song about this groupie named Wendy who came to visit in the afternoon, had a cup of tea, gave great head, and split. We learned 'Sweet Thing' the same night that I wrote it, in the dressing room of the Queensbury Arms before taking the stage for our first set. We haven't changed a lick in over twenty years of playing it.

The day of the Brian Pilling benefit arrived and I was at the club early in the morning with eleven cases of beer and trays of sandwiches for the backstage area. It was a freezing day but the fans began lining up very early. The bill included Max Webster, Hott Roxx, Wireless (which now included Marty Morin on drums), Goddo, and mentalist Mike Mandel who would become a great friend. The ticket price was only five dollars and the club was absolutely packed. I was a bit surprised that not one Fluddie showed up but the day was a tremendous success and would mark the start for me of years of organizing future charity gigs.

I visited Brian the next day to turn over the money that his friends had raised and I was shocked and frightened by the amount of weight that he'd lost. He also had trouble hearing and his voice had been reduced to a whisper. I was afraid for my dear old friend.

diary – monday, february 21 – gasworks, toronto
Some goof walked by Gino and put a lighted cigarette in his pants. I threw a boot at the guy's head but missed and he was thrown out.

The band was gaining momentum, the debut LP was finally released on Cape's FATCAT label with substantial distribution through POLYDOR. We were now using a hand-painted backdrop of the album cover and even rented an industrial insulating machine that would spew out pounds of confetti from a phallus-shaped hose during 'Lizard.' Radio stations were starting to program tracks off the record and we were gigging to huge audiences every night. We began to get cover articles in various magazines and I was doing radio and newspaper interviews on a daily basis.

I was a BIG star!

I couldn't afford to buy a chocolate bar.

The strangest thing was that we couldn't get any airplay in Toronto. CHUM-FM was pretty much the whole deal back then and they thought the album wasn't good enough. At least that's what one of their DJ's told me when I ran into him on the street one day. I decided to take them on and drew up a home made sign that read:

CHUM-FM UNFAIR TO LOCAL ACTS!
LONDON, NEW YORK, AND LOS ANGELES WERE CITIES WHERE LEGENDS WERE CREATED, NOT DEFLATED!

I picketed in front of their station on Yonge Street where at first the station heads were amused, but with the attendant publicity they soon began to take notice. I also had a great number of their listeners' signatures on a petition. 'Under My Hat' was soon added to their play list.

A Week In Montreal
— April 25 to May 2

- 6:30 a.m. train to montreal
- full page ad in billboard
- no power for lights on opening night at Moustache (4 sets per night)
- Roulette Records A&R in town to see us
- Pete and Darryl from Nazareth see us and offer us support dates over dinner
- snorting coke in executive offices at Polydor (no executives present)
- Gary Slaight phones from Toronto to invite us to 'Stampeders' press bash next week for tv special
- Dick Flohill calls for cover story in *Canadian Musician*
- *CHOM FM* interview
- Dave Friesen from *Montreal Star* down for newspaper story
- Ina and Bill in from New York to check us out
- *Twist and Shout* magazine interview
- Marty Melhuish blows up his hand butting out cigarette in ashtray full of flash powder
- Marty goes to hospital

- shop old Montreal for purple satin pj's as stage attire
- Dixon tapes shows on 1/2 track with two 87s
- *Montreal Star* review is great
- demo 'Carousin', 'Sweet Thing', 'There Goes My Baby', 'Oh Carole' at listen audio
- Cape suggests Doug sing 'Sweet Thing' and I go nuts and storm out of session
- fly back home for gig at Larry's Hideaway tomorrow night

Furniture Surgery

It was Saturday after six p.m. on a holiday weekend, and the brand new rented couch was sitting in the corridor of my new apartment. The furniture rental store was now closed until Tuesday so taking it back was definitely out of the question. It was too long to make the turn to our corner unit, and Rose and I had tried everything to get it in. The roadies had angled, pushed, pulled, and cursed their way around it for two hours and the bloody thing could not be coaxed through the door. Professional movers were called in but after a few feeble attempts they took my money and I could hear them laughing as the elevator doors shut.

"Rose, have we got a saw?" I inquired. She nodded and I asked her to get it for me; I figured that with all the legs cut off we had a fighting chance. I was wrong. It was couch vs. man and the couch was winning.

Drastic measures were called for as I set about remedying the situation.

A month later the guy from the rental place showed up, as he had neglected to get my signature on the contract in his haste to get away that long-ago long weekend. Eyeing the new cushions on the floor, he looked quite puzzled and said, "So where's the rest of the couch?"

"Oh," I said as a matter of fact, "it's on the balcony because it didn't fit in with our plans."

"The balcony?" he said as he made for the door.

He let out the tiniest scream as his eyes adjusted to the brilliant midday sun. The couch was now lying in two pieces, having been neatly sawed down the middle some time before.

Under My hat

Tell me dear brother
What's driving you mad
Have you got the answer
I'll keep it under my hat
This working frustration
Get it off your chest
There's no motivation
No chance to have a rest.
Mechanical feeling
Why there's no such thing
a human endeavor
It has the truest ring

No need to get angry
No ~~one~~ do that
So tell all your secrets
And keep it under my hat
I'll

Now I was wrong
And I'll admit that anyhow
Because a year ago I wouldn't
say what I'm saying now
You better watch out
Because your time's gonna come.
You'll get what's coming
to you and then maybe some

Look out Baby - Because I know
where I'm coming from
Watch Out Little Girl -
Your going back to where you
belong.

Punk

There was something new happening in the press and in the clubs. Not the "A" room shit-holes that we performed in but in the basements of old factories in industrial areas downtown. The "Crash'n Burn" and "David's" now catered to a subculture of very English-influenced "punk" rockers who had suddenly emerged to shake up the "boring old farts." At twenty-six I was now not only considered old, but boring. I have no idea where the farting part came in.

I'm sure that punk rockers farted too.

Most of my musical friends just dismissed the whole thing as amateurish noise played by beginners but I saw it differently. Bands like The Diodes, The Viletones and a newly-formed Teenage Head may have appeared to be aping The Sex Pistols and The Ramones, but they were already writing committed songs while improving their musical skills in front of packed audiences who expected nothing in the first place.

At first my presence at these gigs was looked on as "what the fuck is he doing here?" But soon it became evident that the Goddo "like it or fuck it" attitude was not that far removed from their own message and I was invited in. Outrage was the key element, whether it was language, fashion or public behaviour. Never one to be outdone I can vividly recall having it off with a black groupie who waylaid me in an alley and then taking her into a punk party with her completely nude. The reaction from these anarchists as we entered was more suburban than one would have imagined but it certainly showed them who practiced and who just preached.

Who Cares

We had just returned from another fun-packed week in Montreal where the plan had been to finish our gig at The Moustache and then begin recording our second LP at Listen Audio, with Dixon Van Winkle once again engineering. Something was up, as we had no sooner booked into a beautiful downtown hotel than Marty Melhuish phoned us to say "Pack your bags, we're taking the 4:30 train to Toronto." While heavily into the Beaujolais in first class, Marty confided that Gary Cape's partners had been plotting to steal the group away from him and put him out of the picture. To get us out of town had probably seemed like the right thing to do, so Toronto it was and Sounds Interchange Studios it would be.

It had already been decided that my title of 'If Indeed It Is Lonely At The Top...WHO CARES...It's Lonely At The Bottom Too' would do for the cover and all that was left was for us to record it. Marty and I went directly from the train station to the studio and I could hardly wait to get started. A lovely Englishman was introduced to me as Mike Jones, and he would be our engineer. We would begin recording the following day as Doug and Gino had stayed in Montreal to catch Kiss at the Forum.

The record company had some concerns over the production of the first LP and it had been decided that I was not qualified to produce the group just yet. Granted, the rawness of our initial effort was probably the most honest representation of our live sound at the time, but raw does not necessarily translate into radio, so a "proper" producer was needed.

Thomas Morley-Turner was the right guy.

With an abundance of talent, good looks, an affable charm, and a killer sense of humour he was a lot like myself. In fact, he was so much like me that it was no surprise that he was me. I knew that I could produce the group and made up this legendary, though relatively unknown, English producer to throw the record company types off the trail. With operations in Montreal and us working in Toronto I could go about my business with no pesky interference from Cape or Polydor.

Tom Turner was a much-loved friend of mine who was the father of one of my school friends. He owned a Martin 00-18 guitar, much like the one I cherish, and was only too happy to show both Brian Pilling and myself simple chords when we were just learning. He played in a slow and deliberate style, while constantly puffing the ever-present cigarettes that would one day take his life, and he was a patient teacher. I had continued seeing him for many years, usually Christmas Eve when I was visiting the old neighbourhood, and had recently told him about my run in with Roy Thomas Baker and the record company's concerns about my own abilities.

"How about Thomas Morley Turner then?" he suggested, offering his own name.

Perfect, I thought.

"I'll hyphenate the Morley-Turner to make it more English sounding!" I enthused, and Goddo now had the right producer.

The first track we recorded was 'Drop Dead (That's Who)', which was a title taken from our lighting guy Allen Henry, who had once been asked, "Who the fuck do you think you are!" by some asshole in a club we were playing. The last words the drunk heard before being put to sleep was "Drop dead, that's who!"

The song rocked and the sounds that Mike Jones was coaxing out of the board were fat, powerful and mean. The studio itself was state of the art and huge, a vast change of scenery from the coziness of the Montreal facility. I found a nice simple piano riff of pumping eighth-notes that pushed along the track even more, and I had Rose overdub it. We concluded the first session by committing the dinosaur-stomping groove of 'Too Much Carousin' to tape. I had written this song shortly before, after a night of polishing off one too many bottles of wine with one of our oldest friends and fans, George Holjack. With two bass guitar parts the song rumbled along like a Brontosaurus was pounding your hangover.

The next day, for a complete change of pace, we recorded the track for 'There Goes My Baby' which was pure funk, and I could already envision a mass of saxophones and a wailing King Curtis-style tenor sax solo courtesy of our new friend Paul Irvine. Paul had casually asked to sit in with the band at a recent Knob Hill Hotel gig and had been a welcome guest ever since.

Most records are made with the basic tracks for all the songs being recorded first, then followed by many hours of experimentation and the overdubbing of guitar solos, vocals and any other instruments that would enhance the song to completion. I did not have the patience for that so we recorded in a kind of leapfrog format where two tracks were laid down the first day, followed by overdubs the second with a new bed track recorded at the end of the day to keep us excited and fresh.

For instance, normally the drummer would be finished once the bed tracks were in the can but by working in this fashion he had to report every day to add something to the project. This could backfire on occasion as Gino and Doug would find the down-time all that was required for a little mind expansion, and by the time we got around to actually recording we were dealing with the law of diminishing returns. I wasn't helping as I was popping about 100 milligrams of Valium a day which I carried in a little pouch around my neck. My neighbourhood druggist was also a huge fan and his idea of being my pal was to give me five times the prescribed amount each time I went for a refill. My metabolism at the time was such that instead of putting me to sleep the heavily addictive drug only brought me down to the level of normalcy. The down side was that, unaware to even myself, I was now hooked.

Gary Cape was in town and, having seen our self-abuse firsthand, was cautioning us to concentrate on the task at hand and keep costs down. With that said he would order in a dozen pizzas, which he largely consumed himself. Gary was a big man.

'Cock On' was next and once again Mike Jones did a wonderful job at the board. The song, which had been written back in the Fludd days, sounded like an out of control train coming down the tracks, and with the addition of some English-styled finger phasing it took on an almost other-worldly vibe. We had completed four songs including overdubs in four days. I played the songs for Ed and Brian Pilling the next day and my old friends shared my excitement. We listened to Fludd's Greatest Hits, which was just about to be released, a fitting cap to a great career, but I couldn't help but think that my own adventure was just beginning.

We were all fairly naive when it came to money matters in those carefree days, but sometimes the lack of actual cash in our pockets, considering what we must have been bringing in working six nights a week every week, would become cause for great concern. This problem of our money being handled by other people manifested itself into strange little mind games that had mixed results. None of us had seen a dime from any advances that the record company had negotiated for us but we knew that they existed and all of us were very broke. We decided to strike. With the Monday session scheduled to begin at 6:30 p.m. I made sure that Cape found out about our cancellation at 5:30. He didn't freak, in fact he seemed quite blasÈ about the whole thing.

Had our clever plan backfired?

We were obviously so high on recording this LP that it must have been evident that little things like food and rent meant absolutely nothing to us.

I waited.

I waited and sweated.

I was sweating, and waiting, and hungry.

The phone rang.

It was Cape.

By six thirty we were at the studio with a promise of money for all and Chinese food. We were all quite fond of Chinese food. Gary, of course, would eat most of that. Gary was a big man. After eating the promised Chinese food we got back to work and the basic tracks for 'Tough Times', 'Sweet Thing', and 'Once again' were laid down. The next night Irvine and I did an additional twenty-five takes of 'Once Again', as it's the first time that I've attempted a solo piano tune, and we eventually settled for one take that features one small mistake. Irvine's tenor solo drips honey, and we worked on a four-saxophone section pad that had loads of movement and an arrangement that, under normal circumstances, would've been perfect for a string quartet.

My old friend Dr. John B.J. Bjarnason came down and we recorded 'You Can Never Go Back Anymore', which was my musical shot at Fludd. B.J.'s harmonica part was pure country-blues and it lifted the song tremendously. The next night was spent recording backwards cymbals, guitar overdubs and backwards guitar soloing from Gino on 'Cock On.' Even with this limited amount of work we left the studio at 4:30 a.m.

With 'Oh Carole (Kiss My Whip)' recorded there were just overdubs and mixing to contend with, and after we listened to our efforts a couple of times I celebrated by setting off one of those cold-blast fire extinguishers all over the place. The studio technicians were obviously concerned as to the potentially lethal amount of damage that this might inflict on their equipment, but as it was basically Gino, Doug, and The Zombat road crew who were covered in mist no harm done. We fled the carnage as one man into the night.

Always Have A Chart

Peter Schenkman was the first cellist for the Toronto Symphony. He was also the first cellist that I had ever hired for a session. His guitarist son would find great, though fleeting, fame with The Spin Doctors years later. Peter was at Sounds Interchange to lend his considerable talents to 'Tough Times.'

"Where's the chart?" he asked.

"The chart?" I countered.

"I can't play unless I have a written chart," he said.

"It's only four chords," I helpfully offered, "can't you just jam something?"

"No, I need a chart!" He was starting to get angry. I called out for liquid refreshment.

"How about some Scotch?" I asked, and we started drinking.

Now inspired, I came up with the melody that Peter should play if he had a chart and I hummed it to him. Fumbling around on the cello and not achieving the desired series of notes, now coupled with a fair share of Scotch, Peter appeared to be getting angrier by the second. In drunken desperation I cried out, "Look, you can play that bloody thing, can't you?" As the virtuoso cellist that he is, Peter then proceeded to run off a scale that was truly awesome. When he finished he sat back, very pleased, and smiled at me.

"That was great," I said, "You should have no difficulty playing the simple line that I've shown you."

He played it note perfect on the next take.

The following two weeks were spent finishing overdubs, re-cutting vocals, and mixing the tracks. At one session for 'Sweet Thing', the song's inspiration was invited down and proceeded to service me while I attempted the lead vocal.

> **SWEET THING**
>
> A YOUNG GIRL · SWEET SIXTEEN
> A PERFECT PICTURE FROM A WARM WET DREAM
> C'MON OVER FOR A RENDEZVOUS
> A CUP OF TEA, A LITTLE CANDY TOO
> YOU LIKE THE FACT THAT I'M IN A BAND
> YOU'RE AWARE OF THE ONE NIGHT STAND
> BUT THAT DON'T BOTHER A GIRL LIKE YOU
> YOU GET YOU CAKE AND YOU EAT IT TOO
>   (CHORUS)
> YOU'RE MY SWEET, SWEET THING
> YOU NEVER BITE BUT YOU ALWAYS STING
> YOU'RE MY SWEET, SWEET CHILD
> C'MON OVER AND DRIVE ME WILD
>
> WE NEVER REALLY HAVE TOO MUCH TO SAY
> WE KNOW THAT TALKING JUST GETS IN THE WAY.
> AND IF YOUR MOMMA TRY TO PUT THIS DOWN
> YOU'LL KEEP YOUR MOUTH SHUT BUT YOU'LL
>   STILL COME ROUND

Having just finished a book on subliminal seduction I was curious as to whether this same theory applied to the recorded work and subsequently had the studio drapes separating the control room from the recording area pulled so as to afford a modicum of privacy. As the young lady had never been in a studio prior to this, the disembodied voices now echoing through her headphones might just as well have been emanating from another planet than a room a few feet away. While the vocal mic picked up my somewhat over excited renderings, the other mic - set at crotch level - was busy catching her every moan. The arrival of Cape, with certain visiting Polydor suits, did nothing to diminish our efforts and the guests were just a little confused as to the rather unusual decorating scheme in the studio's control room. Peeking through the curtains, all was made clear as Cape quickly hustled the suits out to dinner while cursing my name. The vocal efforts were deemed of suitable quality and were eventually given a thumbs up as keepers. Things were out of control.

On the one hand we were the hottest pick to click in town, our dance cards were full, and we were gigging every night. On the other hand, we were dead broke and constantly at each other's throats.

The crew hated me.

Gino and Doug hated me.

Katz and Cape definitely hated me.

I had collection agencies hounding me for unpaid TV rentals and furniture surgery, and my phone was cut off. Some muscle-bound guy, who called himself Thor, was sniffing around, hiring the best players and roadies for his new recording project. My Zombat crew, faithful to a man, gave me a week's notice. Gino had even been approached and, with his penchant for at least fantasizing about bodybuilding, was seriously considering leaving. The thought of Gino flexing his muscles while Thor tore telephone books in twain made me nauseous.

My sense of smell became Twilight Zoney, as all I could pick up on was the aroma of soda biscuits.

What I needed was a small nervous breakdown.

It happened in the washroom of the old Imperial Theatre on Yonge Street. One moment, four of us were enjoying the rococo ambience of this grande old dame of a movie house and the very next moment I excused myself to the men's room where I closed the stall door and commenced howling at the moon. Sent to investigate my lengthy absence, my dear old childhood friend, Al Stewart, was shocked to find me blubbering away at the injustice of it all and refusing to open the door. My older brother Ted was called and, being a Pollack of sound mind and perogie, he recommended a little bowling. Channeling my frustrations on the pins, I bowled like never before. While no Archie Bunker or Homer Simpson on the alley, after a couple of frames I was momentarily cured.

As if things weren't bad enough, Elvis goes and dies. Segarini called me up that day, drunk, and encouraged Inglis and myself to join him at Thunder Sound where we laid down Bob's classic 'Don't Believe A Word I Say.' One of the best LP's released in 1977 is without a doubt Segarini's

'Gotta Have Pop.' Having read that last line you are probably adjusting your sitting position and quietly smirking at what an asshole I am but there is not a bad track on that album and it sounds just as good today as it did then. The song that Bob made up on the spot was a deft tribute to the Elvis era and perhaps Inglis's crowning moment as a drummer. Even Pierre Trudeau got into the act when he wore a 'Don't Believe A Word I Say' button on what amounted to a State of the Union television address a year later.

Or so Bob says.

> *diary – sunday, august 21 – toronto*
> *...we later went to David's (a punk club) to see Teenage Head who are a Hamilton punk band. They're quite good. Segarini called me from Thunder to see if I wanted to do some recording. On lousy nights like tonight only werewolves and musicians venture forth. Therefore, I donned coat and hat and went to Thunder. Doug came also and we laid down a Fat's Domino type groove...*

I jumped off the stage, guitar screaming, bent on wreaking havoc with the first few rows.

I did not see the spare lighting pole that the roadies had left in front of the stage.

My left foot twisted and broke but we played on.

Even with five legs we were unstoppable.

A Good Clean Puke

Paincourt, Ontario, was aptly named. The club was at the crossroads of four different cornfields and the accommodations were out of an Heironymous Bosch painting. The rooms were uneven to begin with and the acid hallucinations merely enhanced the lopsidedness. My pants were tucked into my socks in fear that the wasps would work their way in. Being stung to death was not on, so I slept with roadie Lorne. He would protect me from harm.

The next day we booked into a modest motel in Chatham.

At first, the guy in the parking lot had appeared as a ghostly apparition. He wore far too much make-up to be taken seriously, and his strolling-about outfit of slum motel towel gave him the image of interesting. Doug and I stood outside with him. He told us that he was a morphine addict. Nestled between the parked cars he suddenly unleashed a torrent of coffee coloured vomit, a jet stream of exorcised filth. Staring down lovingly at the odorous rivulet, he caught our eyes and said, "THAT! was a good clean puke."

I couldn't help but agree as I backed into my room, locking the door behind me, and placing the solitary chair beneath the doorknob.

Kim Kelly and The Big 10 (aka The Shreeks)

Kim Kelly had promoted a show at an arena featuring The Stacey Heydon Group and ourselves.

Stacey Heydon was a guitarist who had just toured with David Bowie, giving him the necessary fifteen minutes of fame to pursue a solo career. Although a lovely guy and a very nice player, just playing in Bowie's backup band did not immediately qualify you as an arena attraction, and this particular arena we now found ourselves in was empty.

We performed with the kind of professional intensity usually reserved for an audience.

The roadies loved it. Stacey performed well and the roadies loved his performance as well. Kim Kelly, promoter, was last seen back stage slouched over in a throne-like chair, drunkenly mumbling something about arriving by limousine but having to go home by bus.

Even with this financial disaster, he still paid us.

I liked his spirit and his honesty and if he really needed bus fare I would've been happy to lend it to him.

A few months later Kim was on the phone telling me that Long John Baldry's English management team were interested in handling our affairs. They all arrived at the Knob Hill one evening to see us live, and visions of sugarplums and world dominance danced in their heads.

Steve and his wife Jan were a very interesting couple.

Steve was quiet, well mannered, tall, blond, and handsome.

Jan was loud, rude, short, rather rotund, brunette, and to be fair but not cruel, not my type.

She was as funny as fuck, however, and even with her own physical shortcomings, could be devastatingly cruel in commenting on others.

With stories of massive international success, free dinners at the best restaurants, and stoned out joy rides in their Rolls Royce, I was convinced that we had at last found proper management.

I had, however, been proven wrong before.

Goddo 1978

'Who Cares' was finally released and the buzz was out that we had recorded a winner. Radio stations were playing tracks back-to-back and it sounded great blasting out in the car. The print reviews were all positive as well.

At this point we were making about four thousand dollars a week, not bad for a trio, but we were never seeing any money. A girl from Katz's office showed up to collect our earnings every Saturday night as he had been notified that we were actively seeking new management. He couldn't have been too happy with our decision, and I was certain that Marty Melhuish would be devastated by the news, but things had to change. Kelly was now lurking around all the time and Jan and Steve were in constant touch from Vancouver, where they had gone on Baldry business. They promised to fly in for our return to Quebec City the following week.

Upon arriving in old Quebec it was decided that the good old Jean Talon hotel was no longer a suitable home away from home and so it was that the very upscale Leows Concorde, with its panoramic views and room service, became our base of operations for the week. Thirty-dollar bottles of Bordeaux wine were brought in along with packets of cocaine to fuel the after show parties. We dined in the finest French restaurants with little regard to cost. My beautiful Gibson L6 guitar had met a terrible end when I casually threw it twenty feet in the air with no intention of catching it. I would simply get another one. The girls were fighting over the band members and I ended up with this rich girl named Marlen who took me shopping everyday for clothes and records. She would hiss at anyone who approached me at the club, an alley cat staking out her turf, and I was far too stoned or drunk to care. We were fast becoming a caricature of a rock band.

Our return to Montreal the following week was amazing as CHOM FM was playing the shit out of the album and business was brisk at the El Casino. Our opening night was almost a disaster as Gino broke a string during our first set in front of a sold out crowd, which included every major writer and music scene-maker in town. It now seems unbelievable, but at this time Gino had neither spare guitar nor even an extra set of strings so the roadies were quickly dispatched to find a set while I entertained the full house with improv comedy. It worked and the reviews the next day were all glowing.

Doug's father passed away on the Friday but after we met in his room Doug decided to stay with the group so as not to let anyone down. He played brilliantly that night despite his terrible loss. With the press and air play we'd received, the club was packed to capacity for our last night and, with Paul Irvine in from Toronto on sax and flute, we smoked the room. Doug left the next day to bury his Dad while the rest of us licked our wounds and headed home.

> *diary – february 7 – toronto*
> *...on our way to dinner we stopped in at Sounds (Interchange). Met Black Sabbath there. A right load of wankers. Heard a bit of their new LP. Crapola.*

The Sabbath lads had indeed been somewhat rude that first meeting, but I put it down to the fact that they were having great difficulties getting their new project up and running and were looking in all the wrong places for the answers. At one point the carpeting in the main studio was torn out on a whim to perhaps alter the sound for the better. It didn't work. Soon we began to spot the boys every night at the Gasworks where they held court, drank, chased skirts, and dug our music. Ozzy, in a better mood now with drink in hand and wench in tow, extended an invite to join him for a drink back at his hotel. The first time I passed, but later that week Bob Segarini and I joined the old-bat biter at his hotel where Segarini, in the difficult position of tying his shoe lace while maintaining control of his beer, proceeded to liven things up by accidentally dropping his bottle through Ozzy's glass-topped table. While I fell on the couch in fits of uncontrollable laughter, Segarini tried a little half-hearted damage control while Ozzy stood there whimpering about "The hotel's gonna make me hafa pay for that," and "They'll think I did that on purpose!"

The sight of a grown rock star and reputed mad-man worrying about a stupid broken table was too much for Bob and I and we bid Ozzy a fond adieu.

Besides Long John Baldry, Jan and Steve were also handling the affairs for piano man Roy Young and vocalist Kathi McDonald. Kathi was a San Francisco native who had taken Janis Joplin's place in Big Brother and The Holding Company, and had later toured with Joe Cocker's Mad Dogs And Englishmen. She was a wild, free spirit who could rattle the roof with her powerhouse vocals and was no stranger to the follies of the road. Both Roy and Kathi were now working with Baldry and it was decided that I should produce a session for Kathi. We recorded Python Lee Jackson's 'In A Broken Dream' and a Randy Newman song entitled 'Guilty' at Phase One Studios with my old Fludd mate, Mick Walsh, engineering. Gino, Doug and Paul Irvine rounded out the group and although we gave it our best shot, the combination of booze, drugs, and constantly changing arrangements made for a tense session. Despite the chaos of the session Kathi and I became great friends and she would sit in with us whenever she was in town.

We now had a hot LP, interesting management, famous friends, and energy to burn. What we needed was a good old western tour to really get the ball rolling.

The Who Cares Tour
— *April 14 to May 30*

Regina – Calgary – Edmonton – Vancouver
New Westminister – Calgary – Saskatoon – Churchbridge
Winnipeg – Toronto

1999 SOCAN Awards

Much has been drunk, tongues are much lighter, casual conversations and the sound of great merriment permeates the room.

My wife: "You've worked with him. What do you think?"

Anya: "My dear, I have worked with David Bowie. I have worked with Ray Davies. Greg Godovitz stands alone!"

Anya Wilson

I heard her before I actually saw her. She was ever so English and charming and rabitting on about the new record and how much she enjoyed 'Sweet Thing' and could hardly wait to leave New York and come up to meet us all. She had indeed worked with Tony DeFries at Mainman handling publicity for Bowie, and had accompanied the head Kink on a promotional tour. On the British Rail train Ray Davies casually remarked in that wonderful clipped effete lisp of his, "You have lovely skin for an alcoholic." She saw it as a compliment.

Her next job was working for Long John Baldry through Jan and Steve and now she was coming to Canada to assist their other artists.

When I met her at the airport it was instant infatuation. Her natural charm and great beauty coupled with a keen intelligence and a great set of knockers was everything you could possibly want in a publicist. Much to my girlfriend's annoyance, we spent a great deal of time getting to know one another over drinks at every available saloon and wine bar we came across.

I was looking forward to six weeks on the road with this one.

Regina

The tour kicked off in Regina, Saskatchewan. I had flown in with Bruce Duncan as he was, by this point, finished with Fludd; having good old Bwuce around was comforting as he was one of the best roadies in the business; and we had done this trip together many times before. The other roadies were en route by truck with Gino and Doug racing behind in Gino's new Le Baron. Anya would fly out shortly afterwards and hook up with us in another city but at this point I had no idea which one.

The first thing to go wrong, the first thing to always go wrong, was my luggage not landing with me. Seeing as the greater majority of my baggage consisted of prescription pills I was understandably nervous and sent Bruce off to look into it. He came back empty-handed.

The Polydor reps were there to greet us and we were soon whisked off, still bereft of luggage, to the local FM radio station who were co-promoting our show, only to find out that they weren't exactly playing any of our songs yet. Next was the obligatory record store album-signing. This one was especially noteworthy for the absence of any actual Goddo product in the racks, outside of a handful of promo copies. With teeth clenched J pulled the record company type aside and said, "Let's get the fuck out of here shall we," and, with that little humiliation over, we booked into the nearest hotel to "prepare" for our show. Now that the roadies had delivered my travelling pharmacy I prepared for the show by stuffing in a handful of 10mg. Valium and drinking a bottle of French wine. We still managed to not only win over our first western audience but ended up in another club where we danced, jammed, and picked up new friends to take back to our hotel.

The last thing I can remember are Bruce's screams as the lit matches bore into his toes.

A couple hours sleep and off to Calgary. We stopped every so often to photograph tumbleweeds and cowboys. We looked strange, Gino in black leather, Doug unshaven and unkempt, myself affecting the punk look with spiked hair and black eye make-up. We arrived in Calgary at ten that evening and searched out the finest restaurant.

"May I help you?" sneered the maitre'd as we shambled into the steak house.

"Yeah man, table for six, smoking," I said.

"I'm afraid we have a dress code here at El Pretentious," he stated flatly.

"You expect us to wear dresses?" I asked.

The guys were laughing, the maitre'd was not.

"Blue jeans are not allowed, sir, perhaps the MacDonal...," he started before I cut him short with "Look man, the jeans may be blue but they're filled with green so get us a fucking table NOW!"

I had a Big Mac with fries and a large Coke.

I can't remember what the other lads ate.

Calgary

We played in a disco club. They played the dance grooves so loud that you are unable to have children after one night in the place. We were told to turn down before we had played a note. I gave the management non-stop verbal abuse from the stage on a nightly basis. The club was packed every night so they couldn't really say anything. It was uncomfortable. Doug picked up a chick called The Bionic Beaver. I would have to question him at great length about this.

Edmonton

The club this week was the sister disco to the place last week. I walked in and offered my hand to the manager. He looked at me coldly, refused my handshake, and said, "I've heard about you."

"Then we understand each other," I said and withdrew my hand.

Somebody's been talking.

Vancouver

Bruce and I flew into Vancouver and were picked up by the owner of The Body Shop.

He called himself The Worm.

The Worm looked exactly like a real worm but he had a Lincoln limousine full of champagne and coke and, even though he was extremely wormish, we felt relaxed in his company. He took us to the best restaurant in town, which was quite a change from the last two club owners.

It was, however, unnerving eating dinner with a guy who resembled an actual worm.

Angela Bowie

It was a big limo.

It had to be.

It contained three managers, famed rock photographer Dee Lippingwell, and the former Mrs. David Bowie, Angela. The Shreeks, as managers Jan, Steve and Kim had now become known, were now handling Angela's business affairs, and they had all flown in from Los Angeles to see us play. I was trying to be cool but as a long-time Bowie fan I was very pleased to be sharing a car with the lady who helped define the Glam era. As I was filling Jan in on our tour exploits, mostly sexual conquests, Angela began to make rather loud snoring sounds. I told her that she wasn't too exciting either and with that her spiked heel was suddenly part of my chest.

Not ten minutes into our new friendship and she was beating me up!

I let her know in no uncertain terms that this would not happen again and she gave me the beautiful blue Lurex jacket she was wearing as a peace offering.

As we arrived at the Hyatt, a hippie girl selling flowers confronted Jan. Jan bought the flowers and then crushed them into the girl's face. The Shreeks all found this amusing. Angela found this amusing. I was mortified and found myself comforting the flower girl as the rest of them headed off, cackling loudly, to check in. Later that same evening I arranged a nice bottle of Dom Perignon and a late night limo ride around Vancouver with

Dear Greg, I am sorry this has taken so long but I have been running back & forth between New England & Atlanta, between Debbie my girlfriend from College & Sasha who is busy in the last 4 weeks of 7th Grade — forgive the confusion — looking forward to seeing you & Renata & Jasmine & Kai, is your son's name Miles? Haven't had the pleasure of meeting him yet —
love Argyle

Angela. After seeing us play, she was receptive to the idea. I, of course, had more in mind than sightseeing and the thought of mobile sex with Angela Bowie was more than I could have dreamed of. Unfortunately for me, Jan found out about my little plan and, knowing what I was like, she said there was no way this event would take place. Angela was whisked away to her suite while I was left to drink the champagne with the driver en route back to my hotel.

He was not my type.

How Not To Purchase Coca Cola
— *A little lesson in hotel etiquette.*

I had just enough change to get myself a bottle of Coke.

Not a can.

Not a gram.

A bottle.

The old-fashioned dispensing machine was situated in the lobby of The Tropicana Hotel.

I put in my money and pulled on the bottle.

The coins dropped into the box but no Coke.

Ripped off again.

I was pissed right off.

I needed that Coke in a desperate way.

Desperate men do desperate things.

As there was no concierge on duty, owing to the lateness of the hour, I raced back to my room for three things. Rock photographer Dee Lippingwell, a glass, and a bottle opener. As I tilted the very heavy machine forward Dee was instructed to place the glass directly under the bottle and pop off the cap. Necessity being the Mother of Invention and all, it seemed simple enough. I wasn't stealing the desired beverage as I had paid for it. It was man vs. machine.

I watched the refreshing beverage bubble and froth into the semi clean glass when I suddenly had a very disturbing feeling.

"Dee, I can't hold onto this any longer, MOVE NOW!"

Dee jumped back as the machine crashed to the concrete lobby floor in a shower of electrical sparks and smoke. The glass was emptied long before we reached my room.

Word quickly spread that Mrs. Bowie was in town and simply everyone was dying to meet her, dahling. Don't get me wrong, she is still a friend of mine but Angela knew how to play the game. After all, she had helped define the ground rules.

Being somewhat of a sucker for the fans, being one myself, I sympathized with the kids who dotted the Hyatt lobby hoping for a glimpse or an autograph. Angela would not meet one of them. Spying one very cute oriental-looking punkette with blue hair, I did what I could but no luck. Instead, I invited her and her boyfriend out to dinner. Over a lovely plate of Greek food two things soon became quite obvious: her boyfriend, David, was gay; and she was interested in me.

The trick was how to get rid of David and keep Joyce for me. Joyce was her name. Not a great punk handle by any means but handy for introductions. Back in my room I put it to David with great understanding and compassion.

"Look man, you're gay and she wants to stay with me, so you've got to leave!"

Very subtle.

"I am not gay!" he squeaked.

"Are too!" I shot back.

"No, I'm not!" and he almost said it with conviction.

"Gay or not, you are leaving," and with that I showed him the door.

As Joyce and I became better acquainted there came a knock.

It was David!

"I'm not leaving without Joyce!" he pleaded.

"You've already left without her, man," and I shut the door.

Ten minutes later there was another knock at the door.

It was David!

"I came with Joyce and I'm leaving with Joyce!" he said firmly.

He was bold and assertive.

I like that in a man.

"Do not knock on this door again, man!" and I could see actual fear creep all over him.

He never even noticed my boner.

Back to Joyce, now naked and under the covers.

She definitely noticed my boner.

KNOCK! KNOCK! KNOCK!!!!

"Excuse me while I kill your friend," I said and threw open the door.

It wasn't David!

It was her Dad!!

My boner disappeared so quickly that I'm sure he never noticed it.

"Is my daughter in this room?" he demanded.

It was more statement than question. He could plainly see that she was so it was a pretty senseless way for us to get acquainted. I invited him in.

"What are you drinking?" I said.

"What have you got?" he asked.

It's not polite to answer a question with another question but I decided to let it go.

"Beer or rum," I offered. He wanted a beer.

We sat with our drinks on the floor beside the bed where my new friend, his daughter, sat bolt upright with just a sheet to hide herself in. The look on her face at this surreal turn of events cannot be adequately described. Let's just say she was freaked right fucking out.

I know this sounds very strange but, after twenty minutes of rather animated bullshit, her Dad invited me over to the house for dinner later in the week and left his daughter in my bed.

If some asshole ever pulls that line on me I'll fucking destroy him.

The second week at The Body Shop was going great. Anya had arrived from L.A. and I was wining and dining her. She laughed at all the right places but was such a pro that no amount of bullshit would find you in this lady's bed. At one point I even hired a Gypsy violinist to serenade us over dinner but he never showed up. She thought that was charming. Meanwhile, The Shreeks were trying to sue the Hyatt over some small event of non-importance (no salt on the room service cart probably), and there was a wonderful sense of absurd circus surrounding the group.

Terry David Mulligan, musicologist supreme and national treasure, had interviewed me and invited me out for drinks the next day at a posh downtown hotel. The maitre'd took one look at me and refused to let me in. Mulligan, normally a paragon of cool, lost it and threatened to boycott the establishment if an apology to his "guest" was not immediately forthcoming. I would be gone in a week, Terry had to live there but he still defended me.

We have been friends ever since.

Gerry Doucette was riding the charts with 'Mama Let Him Play' and was a frequent onstage guest.

Angela came to the club every night and held court while telling everyone that we were the next big group.

It was on Thursday night that an old friend came to me with news that Brian Pilling's leukemia had caught up with him and he was fading. Words can't describe my utter helplessness at being so far away from my dear friend, and I destroyed one of the dressing rooms with such a vengeance that Keith Moon would have applauded. Anya calmed me down enough to face the crowd but I was seething with anger and looking for a direction to channel it through.

During my guitar intro to 'Let That Lizard Loose' I began my nightly walk across the twenty-foot table directly in front of the stage. There was a guy sitting at the very end and he was giving me the finger.

I had just dialed in the channel.

I saw red.

This guy was about to get beaten.

Without thinking about it I tore off my guitar and dropped it without looking where.

It bounced off the head of some guy who went on to become a music writer. I ran the last few feet of the table, hell-bent on diving into Mr. Finger's face and punching the living crap out of him. The table, which was covered in beer, had other ideas as I slipped off and crashed to the floor. My roadie Mike (Mazola) held me as Marty Pelz, our great mad light man, and The Worm beat the guy out the door.

The audience loved it!

Years later Inglis was auditioning for Bryan Adams, who was at that show. Bryan remarked over lunch that he had never seen an entertainer try to kill a member of the audience before.

diary – sunday, may 14 – vancouver
Today started out sane enough. Got up to get my haircut. Went to see The Last Waltz with Joyce. Bought Nick Lowe's new L.P. and the storeowner told me that our record was sold out. Now the madness begins. Bruce, Gino, The Worm, Joyce and I head to Orestes for Greek food. We get pissed. I'm eating with my hands and wiping the greasy garlic oil through my hair. I'm throwing champagne glasses out the skylight. I'm bending the cutlery. We are asked to leave the premises. Back at the hotel we see Doug (with newly hennaed hair), Marty, Mazola, and Anya in the restaurant. I start pouring drinks over Doug's

> head. Bloody Caesar's, coffee, anything handy. We go upstairs. Gino and I are pogoing to The Sex Pistols. Doug is called. His presence is requested to come and hear the new Nick Lowe but he's now locked in mortal combat with both roadies. I abuse Anya and she hangs up on me. I freak. I phone back and she hangs up again. I decide to visit. The boys are fighting it out. I tell Anya that she's leaving the tour tomorrow. She takes my glasses and demands that I come to her room to discuss this. I decline. We end up screaming at each other in the stairwell. She slaps me and punches me twice in the head, imbedding my earring in the side of my skull. I get my glasses back. The manager tells us to "Shut up!" "FUCK OFF" we scream at him in unison. Gino is destroying his room. (He put his muscle bar through the front door, which I thought was a nice touch). Doug is being put to bed. Marty punches me for abusing Anya and I'm locked out of my room. I end up sleeping on the couch in Anya's room, who I don't even like.
> Just another day on the road.

The roadies had this thing about breaking into the hotel pool after-hours. They would light candles, drink cheap booze, and screw girls in the deep end. Not very healthy but an interesting way to pass time. Returning from dinner late one night Joyce and I made our way down to the pool and the scene was as described. The only difference being the lifeless body of Marty Pelz floating face down in the shallow end.

"Is he dead?" Joyce asked.

"I'll ask him, hey Marty, are you dead man?" I yelled out.

Beautiful echo in the room.

Marty didn't respond.

Now I was nervous.

"MARTY, ARE YOU FUCKING AROUND OR ARE YOU DEAD?!!"

No response.

With that I dove into the pool fully clothed (including footwear) and swam frantically to his body which I grabbed by the hair and turned over.

"Hi Gobbo," he said with a shit eating grin on his face.

Prick.

New Westminister

After the madness of Vancouver this gig was like a week off. The only thing of note was that my right hand got heavily infected and one night doing a windmill a la Pete Townsend, I smashed it directly onto a stage light. The result was the immediate cancellation of the gig and I was rushed to the local hospital where the doctor removed the puss-filled ooze with a scalpel. Believe it or not, it felt much better the moment he did it.

I was happy that my dick wasn't infected in a similar manner.

Calgary

A fourteen-hour drive through the Rockies.
Amazing.
We hit the Rogers Pass under a full moon.
'Long Distance Love' by Little Feat is the soundtrack.
There is a God.

Saskatoon

A ten-hour drive through the badlands of Alberta. Dinosaur country. This is a lifelong dream for me, as junior Paleontologist was high on my list as a kid. Staring out the window, high on Mandrax and grooving to the wonder of the Canadian landscape.

After an in-store appearance we headed over to the Centennial Auditorium, which is a beautiful soft-seat theatre. We have no business being in a venue like this but it's sold out. Our dry cleaning isn't back and it's a half hour to show time. Anya called the cops and charmed them into finding the storeowner. The local police delivered our stage clothes right before the curtain went up. For dramatic effect we decided to make our entrance from the orchestra pit, on a hydraulic riser. The only problem was that the operator started it too soon so we stood there like assholes, bathed in spotlights while we waited for our intro tape to end. The local kids were going nuts just the same. At the end of the show, Anya would not let us go back out.

"If they're still applauding in ten minutes, they get an encore," she would insist studying her watch. Ten minutes later we were pounding into the first encore.

It became a part of the ritual.

TRAVELS WITH MY AMP

Goddo in the '70s:

Letting that Lizard Loose!

Churchbridge

We were heading east from Saskatoon to Winnipeg.

Gino was at the wheel.

The duck was on a suicide mission.

He swooped down out of nowhere and bounced off the right front headlight.

Gino pulled over and the tragic evidence of blood and feathers was displayed for all to see.

Gino Scarpelli...Duck Killer.

"But he had all that other air to fly in, why?" he pleaded.

Gino was beside himself. Up to that point he was only guilty of murdering his own brain cells, and at that he was a serial killer.

Churchbridge was a farming community two hundred and fifty miles either side of Saskatoon and Winnipeg. I couldn't quite figure what we were doing there but soon rose to the occasion as the locals' excitement caught on. The concert was in the local high school and was attended by everyone and their tractor repairman. The three of us appeared in the school band uniforms, which we purchased for five bucks apiece after the show. The orange suit jackets with epaulets and black pants with orange piping were very Sgt. Pepper, and I wore it many times for the remainder of the tour. The show itself was great and we were loose and funny and tight. The audience ate it up. After the show we drank $1.35 champagne and partied with the kids before we hit the road to Winnipeg.

Winnipeg

The ex-con was sitting beside me in the back seat of Gino's Le Baron. My leather jacket was pulled up over my head to keep the sun off as morning broke on the land. I was quite prepared for a shiv in the back at any moment. It wouldn't have bothered me by this point as I had endured his endless stories of penitentiary life for what seemed like my own life sentence. His life of robbery and shit was boring. We were the new outlaws. We were smarter. We never got caught. He was outgunned but he didn't know it. He had just been attacked by a mad dog while seeking gas and we had picked him up on the highway. You can meet interesting people when you travel.

I was jostled out of a fitful sleep about seven a.m.

Our travelling companion was gone.

"Hey man, wake up, you might want to see this."

The billboard at the side of the road was huge.

It read: WINNIPEG WELCOMES GODDO with the Polydor Records logo and the cover of WHO CARES twenty feet tall for all to see.

I'm sure the truckers were impressed.

We were staying in the same hotel as The Orlons (The Bristol Stomp). Paul Irvine had flown in and after jamming with the country group in the hotel bar we ended up partying with the band. We were quite high and not prepared for "nigger this" and "nigger that," but these were the Afro-sheened real deal and that's how they talked. The next morning Irvine and I dressed up like beatniks and were about to go busking for spare change in front of the Playhouse when Anya intercepted us in the parking lot. She had Mazola throw me in a cold shower to sober up.

After recovering, I went to get my hair re-dyed. This amazing-looking chick was in the shop and agreed to join me back at the theatre for the show. The Playhouse looked great. All crushed-velvet seats and rococo trim with a huge stage to play around on. With four lighting towers and 68,000 watts of power, we were ready to rock.

I was standing in the dressing room, reaming out my nose with my left hand and having a leak with my right, when this sultry voice came up behind me.

"I know something that feels a lot better than that," cooed the sultry voice.

I wasn't so sure.

Picking your nose is one of life's little moments.

It was the chick from the hairdresser's!

She was just about to close the stall door behind her when good old bloody efficient Anya comes in.

"Here, you," she started at me. "We'll have none of that. You have a show to do and need your energy!" With that the chick from the hairdresser's was thrown out by security.

I never saw her again.

Kim Kelly was in from The Shreeks and it was limo this, and room service that, and with Irvine and a three-piece sax section, we tore the roof off that beautiful old theatre, which began a great love affair with the good citizens of Winterpeg.

The next morning we headed for the airport, smashed on fine quality record company weed. There were about fifty kids with cameras waiting to see us off and I was so unprepared for this that I got incredibly paranoid and began hiding behind Doug, who was the biggest tree in the forest. As we began to move through the metal detectors my cap pistol set the bells to ringing as the RCMP moved in and slammed me up against the wall. I have no idea why I was carrying a metal cap pistol but I'm sure it seemed like the right thing to do at the time. After a rather professional frisk, I was allowed to continue and caught sight of Johnny Cash, who had just breezed through security. No one seemed to be paying any attention to HIM but he had been checking out the fans going nuts on us. He asked me why the cops had frisked me up against the wall and I told him about my cap pistol.

In that beautiful baritone speaking voice of his, he looked at me and said, "They never check me anymore and it's a good thing." With that he pulled open his trademark black jacket to reveal a shoulder holster stuffed with the business end of a real gun.

Our tour was over.

...we had three days off before we would head out again...

I could see the problem developing before my eyes. The arena in Cochrane, four hundred miles north of Toronto, was packed to the rafters. The boys in the band were hot. Six weeks on tour had sharpened any rough edges that still remained.

The notorious Battered Wives, featuring my old pal John Gibb, had done a great support set and the audience was hot to rock. Gino, who had a habit of playing close to the lip of the stage, now had a very drunken Indian kid hanging onto the leather straps dangling from the headstock of his black Strat. Gently admonishing the fan to let go, the drunk began tugging harder, straining the neck of the guitar and Gino's patience. With Gino about to become one with the audience he raised his right foot and shot the heel of his boot into the nose of his hapless tormentor.

Problem solved.

(The 'Wives' hit a moose on the way home, which totaled both the vehicle and the animal. On a later tour they were driving a Winnebago out west in the middle of the night when a very distraught woman decided to end an argument with her husband by running out in front of their speeding vehicle. The sleeping musicians suddenly found themselves in the ditch with the dismembered corpse splattered all over the road. Jasper, the bass player, went out for a little peek and returned a changed man with his hair standing up on end. The investigating RCMP officers had to pry the driver's hands from the wheel and decided in light of the notorious nature of the band's name and reputation with women's groups that it was best not to say anything to the press.)

Two nights later we played a show with The New Guess Who opening. I searched out my old friend bassist Jim Kale, and told him that I felt weird about having him open for us. He looked at me, put his hand on my shoulder, and said, "It's okay man, this is your fifteen minutes, enjoy."

Brian Pilling's fifteen minutes were just about up. My oldest musical friend was on his deathbed when his Mother phoned me in between sets at a local club just north of the city.

"If you want to see our Brian again you should come soon," she said and I told her that I would be over first thing in the morning.

> *diary – thursday, june 29 – toronto*
> *Brian died last night. When I called his place his Dad answered and I talked to him. I told Barb (Brian's wife) I'd be over after the gig tonight. When we got to the club I asked the manager if we could do one long set so that I could be with Brian's family. He said no but I asked the kids in the audience and they didn't mind at all so that's what we did. The manager wouldn't pay us even though we had played for two hours. I got back up on stage and told the audience, who were quite prepared to take his place apart, what had transpired. (They started breaking bottles and glasses.) The cops even arrived. (I was told by the cops that unless I got the audience back under control I would be arrested for inciting a riot.) What a heartless prick. I went over to Brian's afterwards and Ed and I sat awake talking for quite some time.*

The service was scheduled for the next morning and I attended in my stage clothes from the night before. On the way to the funeral parlour 'Yesterday' came on the radio, which somehow seemed to tie up all the loose ends to a young life cut short.

Brian had been my best friend. Even when we no longer worked together I actively sought out his opinions and his approval. I laugh now when I read about those fools in Oasis because Brian was very much a Noel Gallagher type. Not the greatest guitarist technique-wise but there was something there that smacked of true brilliance. As far as a songwriter goes I smile every time I hear one of his pop gems on oldies radio today. I used to think that the lightning bolts being hurtled down from the cosmos were song gifts from him, that he was helping me out from the beyond.

It's a shame you never met him.

The gigs by this point were all sell-outs and audience reaction was manic. We played our first two shows at the El Mocambo with a four-piece horn section and special guests Roy Young and Long John Baldry. The six hundred-capacity Kee To Bala, an old wooden Big Band era dance hall, was packed to the rafters. The Arthur Pop Festival was a seething mass of ten thousand drunken revelers, intent on enjoying the weekend event and the groups. Just before the end of our set I heard Gino cut out and glancing to my left saw him stumble into the arms of one of the roadies. His head was covered in blood from a thrown beer bottle.

"IF ANYONE SAW WHO DID THAT KICK THE SHIT OUT OF THAT ASSHOLE AND SEND THE REST OF HIM BACK STAGE!" I screamed, and an unconscious body was dragged over the security fence soon after and loaded into a waiting ambulance. Gino, his head swathed in bloody bandages, looked great under the stage lights as we returned to the stage for the encore.

Pure rock and roll.

It was unbearably hot in the backyard patio at Egertons. With its proximity to the Shreek management office it became a handy lunch and beverage spot for the boys. Out of the corner of one half-shut eye I noticed the secretary type fumbling for a light at an adjacent table and grabbing Anya's lighter, I leaped through the air, landing in a glass-shattering thud on her lunch. Flicking the lighter drunkenly in her direction she coolly studied the carnage, watched her cigarette come to life, and then casually remarked, "How gallant" before pushing me off what remained of her salad. My back was full of broken shards of glass as I returned to my amused companions.

Later that night I somehow stumbled into the El Mo, still wearing the blood caked shirt, where 'Saga' were playing a record company showcase and, spying a local groupie, I asked her to fellate one of the Polydor reps under the table. She responded with a well-aimed glass of champagne to my face before excusing herself to freshen up. In her absence I ran to the bar and filled a garbage pail with freezing cold water, which was then poured onto her freshly made-up head as she returned to her seat. I took the stairs five at a time and ended up overdosing on the massive alcohol and drug binge started earlier in the day.

I was totally out of control.

Rochester

Our first show in the States was a great success, with a live FM broadcast one night followed by a club date the next. Standing backstage with assorted hangers-on, crew and management types, I listened with one ear as this drunk American gushed over our earlier performance. Manager Steve was quietly beaming until the hapless fan, spying the rotund Mrs. Steve in an adjacent room, casually remarked, "Hey dude, I noticed you had two trucks parked out back with Canadian licence plates on them."

Very observant I thought.

Steve looked amused.

The drunk, in search of a good follow up remark now said, "I guess one truck's for your gear and the other is for her."

Wrong thing to say.

Steve's left hand shot out as quickly as a snake and grabbed the startled Yank by his windpipe. I'm sure that the fan had no idea up to that moment that Jan and Steve were an item.

Steve's eyes were like red coals as he pulled the guy up on his toes, his cigarette a mere inch from the terrified fan's eyeball.

"What did you say about my lovely wife, you fucking cunt?" he began ominously, and I was deathly afraid for this guy.

"Steve, he didn't mean anything by it, did you, man?" I said. "Tell him you didn't mean anything by it!"

"ARGHHHHH," was all the poor boy could offer as his face turned purple from lack of air.

"I've got a good mind to stuff this fag out in your fucking eye, you fucking cunt!" and I knew that Steve would do it.

"Steve," I implored, "the guy's sorry, aren't you, man?"

"ARGHHHHH."

"See, Steve, he says he's sorry!" and with that Steve released the guy who fell to the floor and crawled out of the dressing room gasping for air.

Jan came in now, noticing the commotion and, eyeing the retreating victim, asked nonchalantly,

"What's up with that cunt?"

"Nothing, my love...nothing," said Steve, lighting up another cigarette.

diary – sunday, september 10 – toronto
Rose and I are both broke. We cash in $3.40 worth of pop bottles in order to buy dinner.

Reading my diary entries I just noticed a horrible reality cropping up every second page. Even though we were working six nights a week to packed rooms we weren't making any money. Where the fuck did the money go?

Clive Davis

The Shreeks somehow convinced an A&R guy from Arista to come and see us play in Niagara Falls. The A&R guy showed up, loves us, and headed back to New York to report to his boss, music legend Clive Davis. Two days later we were told that the great man himself would be attending our show that very night. The club was jammed and jumping, the boys were playing their asses off but no sign of Clive. Towards the end of the night, The Shreeks appeared with the A&R guy in tow and told us that Clive was in the limo outside but would not come in, as he was pissed off at having had to sit on the tarmac at Buffalo International for hours in a holding pattern. He was also fighting with his boyfriend.

I don't know if he was actually there or not but this just represented another beautiful missed opportunity as Arista passes.

With talk of our third LP now on everyone's minds, we had a few things to sort out before we started recording. Polydor was once more footing the bill, thanks to the shrewd negotiating skills of the Shreeks. Studios in Cuba and England had been considered but the Cuban studio was only eight track so that was out of the question, and going to England was cost-prohibitive. I had decided that the title of the next record would be 'SO WHAT, IT'S BEEN DONE BEFORE' and would feature a cover photo of the three of us hanging from crosses while popcorn and hot dog vendors sold their goods to disinterested spectators. Doug would be in the middle in a diamond crown of thorns and Lurex loincloth while Gino and I joked around behind him on our crosses.

Jan, in particular, loved the idea but knew that no record label in their right minds would ever agree to such an outrageous idea. In the end it was decided that Bee Jay studios in Orlando would be our venue and I flew down on a Sunday to check out the lay of the land. Satisfied that it was suitable, I hopped a plane to Nassau, Bahamas, where I would meet Doug and Gino for a well-deserved week of R&R before commencing work on the new LP.

Nassau

1. I lose my money every time I gamble in the Playboy Casino.
2. Doug wins every time he gambles in the Playboy Casino.
3. Gino is ripped off every time he buys pot or coke.
4. Doug snorts whatever it is that Gino bought so that it won't be a total waste.
5. Doug appears to enjoy the company of black hookers.
6. I would also enjoy the company of black hookers but I lost all my money at the casino.
7. The food and weather stinks.
8. Para-sailing is fun.
9. There are no groupies in Nassau.
10. Leaving the island a day early was the best thing about the whole exercise.

An Act Of Goddo
— *A funny thing happened on the way to Orlando.*

There I was, staring off into space, nursing my umpteenth rum and coke, when this huge explosion rocked the airplane we were riding around in and we began an instant drop in altitude. It was like the best roller coaster you've ever been on except that it cost hundreds of dollars for one ride. Immediately I lost interest in my cocktail, which was now part of my travelling ensemble, and turned my attention to Gino, who was fast becoming a Catholic again and frantically crossing himself, while more than likely pumping Doug for a refresher course in Hail Mary's. Not being much of a Catholic himself, Doug could have offered a lengthy discourse on the preparation of Bloody Mary's but looked content to turn white and wait for the airplane to either crash or stabilize.

"Ladies and gentlemen, this is the Captain speaking, and experienced air travelers probably assumed that we just hit the biggest pocket of turbulence ever, but the fact of the matter is that we've just lost our starboard engine. We are quite capable of carrying on with one engine but we're going to turn around for Miami and get you folks on another flight."

This was not a satisfactory explanation!

I was covered in rum and coke, my guitarist was born again, and the guy beside me wasn't my type for one last fling. I reached into my flight bag, wrote one last diary entry and then set to work.

"What are you doing?" said the guy to my left.

"I'm labelling my body parts so that none of me ends up in your bag," I offered.

"THAT'S NOT FUNNY MAN!" was his response and he was quite correct, it wasn't.

After we crashed we went directly to Hell where we were reincarnated as ourselves and soon found ourselves in Orlando, to begin recording our third LP.

Bee Jay Studios was a Christian-run, state-of-the-art facility which featured a Chapel with a lighted picture of Jesus on a dimmer switch, a Dr. Pepper vending machine with those beauty old 16-ounce glass bottles, and a working brothel right next door. This last bit of information was funny as the girls who worked there thought that I was gay.

ME!

I was so busy with producing the record that the thought of sex, let alone costly sex, was the furthest thing from my mind. They also found it a bit odd that I was constantly walking around in plaid pajamas and that my hands were labeled left and right.

I was definitely out of control!

Our personal musical equipment, probably terrified to fly after our recent ordeal, was still in Toronto. This was good, as it gave The Shreeks ample opportunity to sue Eastern Airlines and we just rented the necessary equipment to get started.

It was a totally different set of rules in the south and our interactions with guys from Molly Hatchett and Blackfoot were interesting. Dave from Molly Hatchett sort of found it amusing how I walked around labeled and all, and invited us to their show at The Great Southern Music Hall which was festooned in rebel flags and packed with howling-at-the-moon rednecks.

The guitar player for Blackfoot was a jerk who came out into the parking lot all bent out of shape because somebody had picked up one of his axes.

"Which one a y'all Goddo dudes touched mah guitar, dude?" he asked menacingly.

"It's just a guitar, man," I said, thinking that I'd much rather touch his girlfriend who was flirting with me whenever he was off killing snakes or whatever it was he did.

"Yeah, dude, but it's MAH guitar!" he snarled.

A good point and, as my fuzzy-green slippers were no match for his steel-toed cowboy boots, one well taken.

I immediately posted a "DO NOT TOUCH BLACKFOOT DUDE'S GUITAR" sign in my brain.

The highlight of the sessions for me was the recording of 'Anacanapanacana', which was the classical-styled overture that arranger George Atwell and I had worked on. Utilizing melodies from a number of the album's songs, the piece had sufficient peaks and valleys to approximate a real classical music score. Hiring fifteen people from the Florida Symphony, we commenced recording the song. Arriving for a night time session, the symphony musicians were greeted to candle-lit buffet tables groaning under the weight of rock and roll-styled deli trays and beer and wine in abundance. Needless to say the usually unspoiled musicians took full advantage of our hospitality and were rather impaired by the time George waved his conductor's baton in their faces. They simply could not get it together as an ensemble, which required some serious cutting, pasting and overdubbing from a technical standpoint later on. This marathon session also included overdubs on 'Chantal' and 'Take Care' and we stumbled out of the studio at six thirty the next morning.

Baldry and The Oz had arrived as Long John was scheduled to begin recording his next album after we finished ours. A day at Disney World for the three of us was planned and I was quite excited to be going to this fabled amusement park. My excitement turned to horror as The Oz emerged from the hotel bathroom in a frilly, see-through blouse, white leotards, stiletto heeled boots and a lovely little handbag to complete his ensemble.

Taking John aside, I pointed out that, although I personally had no problem with The Oz's appearance, we were in fact in Dade County, the heart of red neck intolerance.

"Not to worry, Greg, The Oz can look after himself," chuckled Baldry in that wonderful baritone voice of his, and off we went.

Our first stop was Space Mountain.

The Oz wanted to ride.

"I'll get the tickets," I generously offered, but Baldry said just to get two as the "old ticker" might not stand up to it.

So there I was, short haired and dressed in green corduroy pants with a plaid shirt standing in line with Carmen Miranda. The Oz was beside himself with excitement and was loudly proclaiming that excitement to the obvious annoyance of the two hillbillies standing directly behind us.

"I ain't never hit a girl before," one muttered to his buddy, "but you take the one with the short hair and I'll get the other one when we get off the ride."

Just great.

I had probably been with more girls in any month of my life than these two idiots would see in a lifetime and they were going to kill me because they figured I was gay. The Oz had no idea that this was going on and carried on squealing in breathless anticipation of the ride.

I spent the whole time after that plotting my escape as I had no intention of defending either my suspected manhood or the honour of The Oz, who, despite Baldry's hearty endorsement, seemed incapable of nothing more than hitting the two rednecks with his purse.

The rednecks were hot on our heels as we rejoined Long John back outside and I am convinced that we were saved from physical harm only through the giant stature of our musical friend.

Not wishing to go through that again I told them where I would meet them later that evening and took off unnoticed into the mob.

The recording and mixing were on schedule, despite the late arrival of our gear, and we were on our way to Criteria Studios in Miami to safety master our finished mixes. The sign over the front door said "The Home Of the Bee Gees," which seemed apropos, as they had changed the music business by recording their soundtrack to *Saturday Night Fever* in this very facility. We set about safety-mastering, which more or less just means copying the tapes just in case anything funny should happen to the original, when who should pop in but good old Maurice Gibb of The Home Of the Bee Gees.

"Hello, may I pop in?" and there he was, popped in.

We were listening to playbacks of various songs and he was digging it but when 'Chantal' came on he became very excited and ran up to our project engineer, Tim, and began raving that this was "a hit" and "brilliant" and "do you mind if I help you re-mix it?"

"I mind," I said and he ran off to get one of the two legendary SNF producers who listened to the track and said, "It sounds fine just the way it is, Maurice" before returning to his work.

Maurice was now in my face about how I just had to meet Robert Stigwood, and I simply had to stay at his villa to discuss redoing the song with a full orchestra. To this day I will never know why I went out of my way to piss off so obvious a fairy godfather but while he was going on I noticed a tape flutter in our master and yelled out for quiet.

Rewinding the tape we were crestfallen to hear the flutter a second time and I was really off now with Maurice still going on about, "But this is great because now we can record it properly and..."

"Look man, I want you out of here now! I don't give a shit about your fucking plans and I couldn't care less about the disco crap you record at this studio! The last good album the Bee Gees made was Odessa! All I know is that your tape player just ate my fucking master and that really pisses me off!"

Always the diplomat.

Maurice exited the room.

I would not be having dinner with Mr. Stigwood at Maurice's villa after all.

No sooner had he left than Tim discovered an alternate take on the same reel that was indeed our unblemished master.

I had freaked Maurice Gibb out of my life over nothing!

We left for home the next day.

Doug and I were just returning from a quick bite after sound check for our opening spot with Prism at Massey Hall. Spying Prism manager Bruce Allen chatting with promoter Michael Cohl, I asked how many tickets had been sold for the show.

"It's a sell out," Cohl said with more enthusiasm than normal.

"Oh yeah?" I said. "How many for Prism?"

Not missing a step, we chuckled our way backstage while the two remained glued in place, where I am sure at least one of them was hurling imaginary daggers at my back.

We tore the roof off the place and even the staid old Globe and Mail suggested that it was so much our audience that we could have sent down a copy of our new LP in a cab and it would've had the same effect.

A strange thing happened next, in that I was sent an amazing looking representative from an insurance company, who was doing everything short of undressing me to get my signature on a key man clause life insurance policy. The beneficiaries were none other than The Shreeks and I may have been horny, but I was certainly not stupid. I would not sign it.

Standing backstage, sweat-soaked and hyperventilating from the extreme physical output during our show, I was reaching for a drink when someone came barreling through the dressing room door.

"THERE'S A HUGE FIGHT BREAKING OUT WITH YOUR ROADIES!"

The action was centred around the mixing consul, where some asshole had smashed a beer bottle over the faders. Our soundman, Marshall, hit the guy, and Hamilton being Hamilton, it was locals vs. non-locals. As I reached the melee, I looked briefly to my right, and in slow motion saw a guy release the empty beer bottle, which soon crashed into my left cheek. Hitting the floor I was dragged once more backstage, conscious but in great pain.

I was now aware of my glasses, usually held on with elastic bands during a show, rising off my face as my cheek expanded from the injury.

"HOW DO I LOOK? HOW DO I LOOK?!" I screamed, and making my way to the bathroom mirror, I was totally freaked out by the extent of the damage to my face.

The next night was Christmas Eve and The Shreeks sent me down two hundred lousy bucks after six p.m., when all the shops were closed. I couldn't even buy my Mom or Dad a gift. Nobody fucks up my Christmas and gets away with it.

They were gone!

They just didn't know it yet.

We played New Years Eve with Triumph and put '78 to bed.

Goddo 1979

After a quick return to Orlando to remix the new LP, it was business as usual. That is, we played every night of the bloody week, but we didn't get paid. The constant screaming matches with The Shreeks were wearing me out and at one point Kim told me that Steve helped himself to ten thousand dollars of our Polydor advance without asking anyone. When confronted at their rented mansion, Jan, who had taken to referring to me as "Little Hitler," demanded to know who was the source of this "lie"; Steve's eyes turned into little coals and said he would "have the cunt's kneecaps" as Kim sat there all silent-like and white as a sheet.

The Shreeks now expected me to behave like "a star," which, in their mind, meant showing up for openings and such but only staying for twenty minutes before swanning off, or worse, maintaining a low profile and not going out at all.

Fuck that, I wanted to have fun and a free buffet.

With our new LP about to be released we were scheduled for the first live CITY TV-CHUM FM simulcast and everyone in the lack-of organization was up for it. The live show was billed as "An Act Of Goddo In Church" and was scheduled for the old St. Paul's downtown. This whole venture was very professional, with strategy meetings, promo shots, TV ads, live rehearsals, and costume fittings taking place for two weeks before the actual event itself. We, of course, continued smoking dope and drinking right through all this, sometimes in the church basement itself, much to the dismay of certain radio/television types unaccustomed to this sort of thing.

Right up to show time, my custom-made leopard skin satin three-piece suit was nowhere to be seen and I was fit to be tied as the seamstress dashed in with the finished garment mere minutes before show time. The Church pews and balcony were filled with special guests and contest winners and we played with nervous energy for a very live hour. Paul Irvine's four piece sax section looked great in formal attire and the immense pipe organ bells behind us were an awesome backdrop.

NOW I WAS A STAR!

The next morning, while travelling to my folks on the subway, the only mode of transportation I could afford as a big star, a little old lady told me how much she had enjoyed our show the previous evening.

...stardom...anyone?

Take one fresh lemon and bite deeply: By this point we were grossing up to $10,000.00 per week. My pay was generously raised to $250.00.

*Goddo performed the first CITY-TV/CHUM-FM simulcast in January 1979.
Photo: Pat Harbron*

The LB Show

Larry Berringer had somehow wangled an invitation to my parent's house, just prior to the simulcast. With his wife in tow, sitting in my folk's backyard, I had expressed some anger at my parents for allowing these strangers into our family scene, as by this point I was convinced that the fans' place was in the fans' place and not in my backyard. My father pointed out that, as it was indeed "his" backyard, the Berringer's were, in effect, his guests and, as such, should be treated with respect. I was cordial, suspicious and aloof.

By the actual day of the TV show Larry had organized beautiful "Act Of Goddo" crests, satin tour jackets to sew the crests on, free tickets to various Maple Leaf Gardens events, and had earned my trust and friendship. He was now part of our travelling fiasco.

West Once Again
Kirkland Lake – Timmins – Morden – Vancouver – Calgary
Edmonton – Winnipeg – Yorkton – Red Deer – Calgary – Winnipeg
Flin Flon – Winnipeg – Fort Frances – Thunder Bay

Kirkland Lake

We played the local arena and grossed $3,000.00.
The last time here we made $1,500.00 for a full week.

Timmins

A stopover before we flew on to Winnipeg. I went to an art show in the community centre and realized that it was here that Fludd had played a disastrous Boxing Day gig for gas money, many years before. Someone had booked us for a day-after-Christmas concert and, owing to the length of the trip, we had had to leave our families on Christmas Day in order to make the date.

Arriving in Timmins we were somewhat dismayed to discover that there was no gig, the whole thing being someone's idea of a very unfunny joke. Hastily arranging our own show in the local community centre, we managed to make enough money to crawl back to Toronto.

Drinking away the afternoon in the local boozer prior to the show we were smitten to a man by this Amazon stripper named Lena who took an instant liking to Ed Pilling, and after the show Brian, Ed, and myself joined the tall, husky-voiced vision back in her hotel room. I sat on the floor singing the chorus to The Kinks then-current hit 'Lola.'

"Why are you singing that song so much?" asked the dancer.

"Because it's The Kinks and I like it," was my reply, and didn't think anything of it while continuing to hum the refrain.

Soon Ed motioned for Brian and I to take our leave and, after a very soulful exchange of tongues with the exotic one, we made for the door and the band vehicle to wait for Ed. Returning to the Fludd Bus Ed was not his usual boastful self and, instead of a lusty tale of conquest, he took his place under the sleeping bags in silence.

"That was a guy, wasn't it, Ed?" I asked, hoping for the right answer.
Ed confirmed our suspicions that Lena was not all "she" appeared to be.
Lola indeed.

Morden

We were on a "Buddy Holly Special" to Sudbury to pick up our commercial flight to Winnipeg.

It was 2 degrees Farenheit, which is fucking cold, and the airplane moaned and groaned all the way there.

We had only a few minutes to book into our hotel before the local Polydor rep whisked us away for an in-store in Winkler, Manitoba. My throat was fucked from a new cold but people have traveled for miles to see the show - one guy from South Dakota had driven 450 miles to be there - so we gave it our best. The rep drove us back to Winnipeg for an early morning flight to the west coast.

Vancouver

"Are you the police?" the young girl enquired at the check-in counter.

"Do we look like cops?" I asked.

"The Police, the group The Police?" she asked again, and we in turn asked if they were staying in this very hotel.

"Yes they are!" she said smartly and I told the boys that this hotel may be good enough for them but that it was the shits for us, so off we went, in search of better lodgings.

The Police members are all multi-millionaires today, from smart hotel choices.

Calling up the good old Tropicana I noticed a familiar-sounding voice on the other end of the line.

"Yeah, hello, we need four rooms for four days," I said earnestly, the very essence of business-like decorum.

"Who... is this?" came the curious hotelier's reply.

"It's Mr. Godovitz," I said.

The "Mr." part sounded very professional.

"From the... group?" and I realized that it was the long-suffering hotel manager from our last destructive visit out here. Realizing that our long-time relationship with the Tropicana was over, I hung up in his ear. We eventually wound up at the neighbouring Blue Horizon and all was good.

Doug and I ended up at The Commodore Ballroom with its amazing horsehair, spring-loaded dance floor which was now in the process of being given a good workout by The Police's pogoing punk crowd. The Police were in the first flush of their success and a wonderful group. Lots of people were coming up to discuss our date here, and Doug and I split for the Body Shop and The Worm's unique hospitality before slipping off to the hotel.

The next day was a drag: up early as Polydor had five radio interviews scheduled and lunch with my dear pal Terry David Mulligan. We saw the Irish group Horselips at The Commodore later that night but I must've missed something, as I didn't like them.

The next night was our turn but I was sick as a dog and concerned that the show would have to be cancelled. Christian Betty and her Christian Hippie friends attacked my room and smothered me in blankets, breasts and herbal remedies, and by show time I was ready for anything. The spring-loaded dance floor undulated to the massive power careening from the stage and we out-drew both acts from the two previous evenings. I amused myself by flicking sweat from my right arm into the faces directly at the front of the stage. As most of the front row was comprised of dolled-up girls, they soon looked like a row of Alice Cooper clones as their mascara rolled down their cheeks. Even with massive technical problems, the crowd called us back for two encores and the night was ours.

Calgary

Everyone left Vancouver by car for that wonderful eighteen-hour drive through The Rockies but I hung in to talk to "boy wonder" Norman Perry, of Perryscope Productions, about dumping The Shreeks, as he was interested in managing us. McKewan Hall not sold out but the show rocks. Paul Dean and Mike Reno, in town rehearsing their new act, join us after the show.

Edmonton

We played the Sub Theatre, which is a seven-hundred-capacity soft-seater. Sold out. The Shreeks kept calling but nobody was interested in taking their calls.

Winnipeg

About four hundred people lined up to get their albums signed at an in-store. Later we had a group meeting and decided to fire our managers. I called The Shreeks in L.A. to give them the news but did not get the freak out that I expected. More a sort of "who-cares-anyway" attitude. I would've preferred the freak out.

One of the roadies then proceeded to hire his own limo and "bodyguard" to go to the venue; this, minutes after me threatening to fire his ass for similar acts of wanton delusion. The show at The Playhouse was sold out and Winnipeg was fast becoming my favourite city to play.
Afterwards we jammed with a great band called The Pumps, who do 'Sweet Thing' better than we do. With an unhealthy cocktail of pills and wine, I fell head first into a bowl of chicken soup but was soon rescued by the deli's lifeguard.

Yorkton

A ten-hour drive over the prairies. Something for everyone in this country. The absolute best thing about touring Canada is the changing scenery. The trick is not getting too messed up so that you sleep through most of it. From the windswept shorelines of the east coast, the lush forests of northern Ontario, through the rolling wheat fields of the prairies and the badlands in Alberta to the big payoff in The Rockies in British Columbia, there is no other country for touring like Canada. The States have a lot to offer, of course, by way of panoramic views, but there seems to be a major city to play every couple of hours by road. In Canada the distances often involve ten-hour to twenty-hour drives, so it was very thoughtful of God to break up the monotony. The gig was nice too.

Red Deer

Thirty thousand sun-soaked people at the Blind River Pop Festival. The backstage area was a gypsy camp of Winnebagos, stocked with enough booze and pharmaceuticals for the entire audience. No food though. Priorities, we assumed. I amused myself by chatting up a very young and lovely Lisa Dal Bello, who innocently passed over her phone number for dinner, after the tour. We were scheduled for a nine p.m. set, which meant that we would most likely go on after midnight. To add to the general misery of the day a torrential rain blew through the site, destroying any chances for a huge crowd. There were only two thousand soaked and shivering people in a field of mud and debris when we did our headlining set but everyone got into it, and we finished with Doucette, Paul Dean and Donny Walsh jamming with us. We made six grand for our trouble, but the day was ruined with the sight of dead bodies on the road back to Calgary from fans involved in drunk-driving accidents.

Winnipeg

Got hassled by the RCMP for having a pair of scissors in my carry-on bag at Calgary Airport. They half-assedly searched us but came up short so they let us catch our flight. Upon arriving in Winnipeg we were surrounded by RCMP, who promptly whisked us away for a more thorough cavity search.

They didn't find shit.

Even Gino was clean, which shocked the hell out of Doug and me. While we were being detained the officer in charge handed me the phone to talk to his daughter who was apparently a big fan. She was really excited that her Dad was busting us and could hardly wait to tell her friends at school.

We hung out once more with our new friends The Pumps, and Inglis dragged fifty people back to our hotel for a very noisy party.

Flin Flon

Just to show there were no hard feelings, we dropped off a couple of albums at the RCMP office for the officer's daughter. The officer searched us out in departures and basically told us that we would have no more Mounted problems on the tour. Ahh, politics.

We caught a small prop plane for the flight to Northern Manitoba and the gig in Flin Flon was second only to The Playhouse, in terms of audience mania. This was logging country and the mud roads leading into town were packed with rigs, carrying freshly cut timber south to the big city. It was so homespun there that we eschewed the formalities of a hotel, in favour of the promoter's basement-couch hospitality.

Winnipeg

Two days of R&R in Winnipeg was no rest. The phones never stopped ringing at the hotel, uninvited guests showed up with friends at all hours, Limo Lorne was on twenty-four-hour call, and we stayed awake the entire time, partying, jamming, and abusing ourselves. At one point I went to the drive-in by limo and made Lorne sit in the back while my date and I sat up front to watch *Alien*. Afterwards I tried to convince her that I was in fact an alien and, perhaps fearing a flesh-eating monster bursting forth from my jeans, she retreated into the night, convinced that I was somewhat road-burned. I did the smart thing and headed downtown to cause more trouble at a local club. Inglis, ever helpful, joined me.

Fort Frances

A noisy arena gig full of drunken yahoos.

Thunder Bay

Not taking into account a one-hour time difference, we missed our flight back home. We booked another flight and headed off to the best restaurant in town for a little end-of-tour dinner and, what with the surf and turf and champagne and all, we missed the rescheduled flight as well. By this point the only sensible thing left to do was to book into a plush hotel and drink ourselves silly on room service.

No wonder we never made any money.

At the terminal the next morning some guy pushed a piece of paper and a pen under the stall door while I was dropping the kids off at the pool and asked for my autograph. Stardom!

Arriving back in Toronto, a number of things happened in quick succession. My first rather large royalty check arrived and I set about spending the money on clothes, booze, drugs, and fine dining. At The Courtyard Cafe for our coming-home dinner, I caught actor Donald Sutherland staring at me like he was doing film research but put it down to him needing a drink, which I promptly had the waiter deliver, causing the actor to immediately flee the restaurant.

That accomplished, I quickly told Rose about my somewhat carefree lack of fidelity while on tour and she moved out the next day.

After attending the Cheap Trick show at the Gardens, Inglis and I were refused entrance to their after-gig party by a CBS Records flunky. This person went on to say how much "crust" I had, showing up uninvited, although we had spent time with the boys a mere hour or so before in their dressing room and everyone was quite chummy. The only interesting incident backstage was Rick Nielson asking me, "These photos aren't going to end up on the cover of some magazine, are they?" as we posed for the cameraman, having swapped Cheap Trick and Goddo tour jackets for the picture. He had obviously been tipped off to my hidden agenda as I had recently convinced a then-hot Eddie Money to pose for a picture wearing my "Act Of Goddo" jacket. The resulting photo ended up on the front cover of a local magazine.

Next we flew out with The Battered Wives to do the Athabasca Pop Festival, three hours outside Edmonton. After booking into a great hotel, all the bands met in the lobby for the coach ride to the festival sight. The rain came pouring down just as we arrived and with no canopy covering the stage the show was called off.

Great!

We'll just take that certified check for those thousands of dollars and go back to that lovely hotel for some serious self abuse.

WRONG!

The bus was now stuck in the mud and we weren't going anywhere. The driver got out to go see about a tow truck and left us in the freezing cold vehicle with no booze, no drugs, no food, and no women!

What a bloody disaster.

As night fell and it got amazingly cold the scene outside resembled nothing less than a refugee camp with the tent dwellers, now up to their ankles in mud, trying to gain access to our cold but dry environment.

Eddie Money and Greg caught on Candid Camera.

"FUCK THIS!" I screamed and went out in search of the long lost driver.

Noticing a light on in the Winnebago parked directly behind our bus I knocked on the door, which was answered by a very warm, drunk and well-fed-looking bus driver in the company of not one, but two, beautiful girls.

This had been the plan all along!

We all awoke in various degrees of dementia and, as it was still raining out, the whole event was cancelled. Spying a four-wheel-drive vehicle, I leaped out of the bus and offered the guy a hundred bucks to take Gino, Doug and myself back to Edmonton, which he was only too happy to do, leaving The Wives and the other musicians to fend for themselves. After a quick wash up, we caught the first flight home, as we had the CNE Stadium gig the next day.

Canadian World Music Festival

Way back that-a-way, I told you the story of our CNE Stadium gig with The Nuge, Aerosmith, Nazareth, Johnny Winter, The Ramones, Moxy, and Goddo, which was us, and how we got an encore and everything. But what I didn't tell you about was that Gino and his large-breasted girlfriend Gypsy went to visit certain rock stars, with horrifying results. While they were in conversation with the albino guitar legend, for instance, Johnny simply couldn't be bothered with the ten-foot walk to the facilities, perhaps owing to his somewhat limited eyesight, but instead pulled out his dick and pissed in a handy garbage can, in full view of his somewhat shocked guests.

"Ah'll jes' use this here Executive Washroom if you don't mind," and with that, his visitors took their leave.

The Nuge, relaxing in his trailer, was introduced to Gino by an aide who informed him that "this is the Goddo guitar player," as word of our recent triumph had already become the stuff of legends in the backstage enclave.

"And you must be the guitar player," smirked the Motor City Madman, perhaps not so mad after all as he offered his hand to Gypsy while his eyes became one with her heaving breasts. Sensing that a mistake had been made, Gino grabbed her and made his exit.

The humiliation did not end there!

While walking up the ramp to the stage later that night, I heard behind me this gravel-edged voice that could only belong to a behemoth of a roadie, who demanded that I "MOVE WHEN YOU SEE THESE PEOPLE COMING!" 'these people' being a very stoned-looking Aerosmith. I really wanted to point out that, since I didn't have eyes in the back of my head there was no possible way that I could've seen them coming but, thinking better of the outcome of such a remark, I merely stepped out of the way while they swaggered by, without so much as a by-your-leave.

Watching their show from the side of the stage, I was impressed most by the fact that their gently sloping stage gave them the illusion of people actually standing upright, a feat that would've been impossible in their collective condition, under any other circumstances.

Done with mirrors indeed!

Prince George Pop Festival

We flew immediately back to Vancouver to play one gig in northern B.C. As I made my way to my designated seat I saw that someone was already using it and that someone was boxing legend George Chuvallo. We shook hands but did not come out fighting as I opted to upgrade my ticket, and soon Gino and I were sound asleep from too much champagne in first class where we slept it off for the rest of the flight. The boys hung out with the champ while I headed over to The Body Shop where The Worm turned on the hospitality in his office. I soon found myself in the company of a blonde beauty named Beni, who agreed to accompany me to the gig the next day.

On the flight north it turned out that Beni was the adventurous type and, after a bit of overcrowded sorting out, the stewardess on duty at the back of the plane welcomed us both to the famed Mile High Club as we stumbled, disheveled, from the lavatory.

The gig itself was insane, as the first thing you had to go through upon arriving was a search by an overzealous RCMP detachment, who arrested our limo driver for pot possession and dragged him off in handcuffs.

The stage was at the top of a hill, with the audience about two hundred feet away and separated by a fence at the bottom. I jumped off the stage and the spotlights followed me running down the hill, all the while kicking up a trail of dust behind me, which created the most amazing natural special effect. Dragging a very willing audience member over the fence we raced back up the hill where we ended up on the stage in a threesome with my guitar. The audience went berserk. Doucette sat in for the encore, which brought the evening to a peak climax.

Life at The Roadie Hilton

The Terrible Toyota, as Inglis referred to his pick-up truck, groaned under the considerable weight of my earthly possessions and myself as we made our way to my new home. Rose had been back for a while but it was soon obvious that my carrying on with drugs, booze and women were not going to get any better and this time I was the one leaving.

As Doug ran the red light the cherry top was on us in seconds and we were soon parked very professionally by the side of the road.

"Hello there, I'm Granny and this here's Jethro," I hailed, but the cops were not to be fooled and cited Doug for the red light, the dangerous load, and for me sitting on a chair in the back of the truck.

The Roadie Hilton was a lovely three-storey house situated on a tree-lined street in deepest suburbia. Our old pal Bruce was the lord of the manor and the house was full of roadies, hence the imaginative name. The neighbours hated us to a man, as we exemplified all that was wrong with alternative living. Little things like very loud, drunken parties seven days a week, or the Halloween Pumpkin with "GO AWAY" carved on it and kitchen knives imbedded in its poor little pumpkin head, used to scare Trick or Treaters. The guy across the street really hated us so we had sport with him by putting the "For Sale" sign that was supposed to live on our property, on his. We were always very meticulous when we placed the sign on his front lawn but every morning he would just throw the bloody thing in a heap on our driveway on his way to work. We discussed screwing his wife while he was at the office but she was even too ugly for Bruce to consider so that idea, brilliant though it was, was quickly forgotten.

After nailing up my hat collection to hide the rather dubious stains on my new wall I sat down to mend my freshly-broken heart by inviting over a local groupie of no fixed morals. Proudly I showed her the vomit-stained rec room and the stinking sink full of dishes. She seemed quite disturbed with the variety of smells being offered and suggested that the horrors in my room might not be such a bad thing after all as she dragged me up the stairs.

Toronto FM station *Q107* was hosting a "Win Goddo For Your High School" contest and 1,000,000 entries came in.

Good Day Sunshine
– a Bruce Allen story

Wednesday, October 31
11:30 a.m.
Through the haze I could hear the phone ringing and ringing.
Who could be calling at this ungodly time of day?
Keeping the ravages of the night before in mind, I always check to see if I can still speak.
"Testing...testing," I croaked, "hello?"
"Hello, Greg? It's Bruce Allen calling from Calgary."
"Hi Bruce, how can I help you?"
"We're putting together a Canadian super group and your name came up, are you interested?"
"Thanks, man but, I'm already in one," and with that said, I hung up the phone.
Loverboy would have to find another bass player.

Never Accept Gifts From Strangers

As I stood with the boys backstage the crowd was screaming for an encore, when the club's bouncer opened the dressing room door and passed through this amazing-looking girl.

"A little gift for you," he said, as the "gift" pushed me up against the wall and proceeded to perform a tonsillectomy with her tongue. Out of the corner of my eye, I now noticed another stranger standing in the doorway as I continued enjoying my "gift."

As my eyes darted back and forth between the oblivious groupie and the now red-faced stranger, it suddenly dawned on me that although he and I were in fact strangers to one another, it certainly appeared that he was not only quite familiar with the girl pawing me but that he might very well have a vested interest in her.

My fears were soon made flesh as his fist smashed into the side of my face, dislodging his girlfriend and several zillion blood cells from a cut to my lip. The bouncer came back in and, realizing what he had done, immediately began pummeling my aggressor while his girlfriend, no longer interested in me, leaped to his defense.

The three of them fell out the door as Gino, Doug and I made our way out to finish the night.

Fun In Steeltown

I told this story to Dave Bidini for his *ON A COLD ROAD* book, which is a great read, but it bears repeating here in case you haven't got a copy.

There were three interesting guys who used to follow us around in Hamilton. One was a guy named Mac who enjoyed breaking beer bottles on his forehead until he bled; the other guy was this really creepy looking lad who used to enjoy exposing his ass to the audience while making sucking faces at Gino and I, and the last guy was affectionately known as The Lizard Man.

The Lizard Man's idea of fun was jumping on stage during my guitar solo in 'Let That Lizard Loose' and whacking the strings with his exposed dick while I continued to finger the fret board.

Sick? You betcha it was sick, the Hamiltonians loved it.

One night all three of them were at the gig and one thing led to another, and suddenly they were all on stage at the same time. Before you know it Mac, face covered in his own blood, grabbed up the pervy guy and tossed him over his shoulder where he stuffed a stubby up the guy's ass. A stubby was an old-fashioned beer bottle with a three-inch circumference. The howl he emitted at this intrusion not only out-decibeled the group but matched perfectly the dick stroking efforts of The Lizard Man, who was supplying musical accompaniment.

The place went absolutely insane.

Speaking of nuts, life at the Roadie Hilton was very much abnormal as there was a drunken orgy every single night, and people were not above stealing your money and clothes after screwing on your bed.

One night I happened upon my dear friend Frankie Venom, of Teenage Head, giving it to some girl in my room, and I lost it to the point of imbedding a very lethal machete mere inches from Frankie's ass. Without missing a stroke the lead singer looked over his shoulder and said, "Is everything okay, Godo?" but everything was not okay and I started chopping up the steps at the top of the stairs until various roadies disarmed me and put me to bed.

My rebound from Rose saw me even bringing home a girl from Quebec City named Chantal who couldn't even speak English. She stayed for three weeks before I noticed this and I bought her a one-way ticket home.

Backwards Bob and I traveled home from The Horseshoe on the roof of the car in early December, and Bruce and I helped him pack for his trip back to England by filling his suitcase with Cornflakes and sugar. We also rolled up a pile of oregano joints so that he would get busted at Heathrow.

Food fights between Bruce and I left the walls permanently stained with mustard and grease, and the house was a total pigsty.

One memorable night I was ushered into Bruce's room where a "gift" was awaiting me – a to-die-for beauty in full German officer's uniform, complete with garter belts and fish-net nylons – tied up in the candle lit room.

Doug and Gino were constantly arriving late for gigs and I hated their girlfriends, so we hardly said a word to each other. Our schedule for December was nothing but High School gigs every night and we were being supplied full contract riders consisting mostly of booze, which was often consumed before we hit the stage. Joyce arrived from Vancouver to stay for a bit and things just kept getting weirder and weirder, until I finally lost it and cried out to Jesus to save my soul, which is precisely what He did. For about a week.

Doug gave me a Bible for Christmas. Gino, looking over in semi-amused disgust, said, "What the hell are you giving HIM that for?"

"Because he's a born-again Christian this week!" said Doug, who was quite a wit in those days and very tolerant of my mercurial mood swings.

Armed with my newfound faith and peace and brotherhood for all men on Earth, I looked forward to the New Year with hope as I threw another egg at Bruce, narrowly missing his head and splattering onto the kitchen wall, where it would remain well into 1980.

Goddo 1980

Jamaica

Charlie the Cab Man was just into lighting up another spliff as we settled into the back of his souped-up '61 Cadillac limo. Not wishing to bother people on the hotel-supplied bus we opted instead for a rough ride into town and, as we were all still in the Christmas spirit, the rows of decorative lights along the windows and dashboard made for a nice start to our little holiday. Bruce and I, plus Uncle Mike Morin and the Lovely Lu and a new pal Eva, who I had picked up on the plane, all piled in to feast off Charlie's hospitality. I had big plans for Eva but wasn't too surprised that, as we watched Charlie drive off, Eva was sitting very close to him in the front seat of the car.

I had been warned about this sort of thing happening.

Bruce and I shared a few glasses of rum and smoke until it seemed like a good idea to push him into the hotel pool, which I did. Back in our beachfront room, Bruce proceeded to pass out from the cumulative effects of the local smokable vegetation, just as I made the acquaintance of a lovely local gal at the bar that seems to need money for her college tuition. Bruce was obliviously snoring up a monsoon and no matter what the young lady attempted at reviving him her efforts fell short of the mark, in Bruce's case about five inches. As I had now given myself over to Goodness I paid her the tuition money and show her the door.

Our first stop the next morning was Miss Brown's Tea Shack, where Miss Brown and her friend Miss Cool ladled out great dollops of mushroom tea, of which Bruce and I each had three cups. This was not a smart move as within what seemed like mere minutes I was in a darker version of Alice In B!underland.

The whole world took on a decidedly purple hue.

Prince would've loved it.

The rumblings in my already queasy stomach indicated the possibility of a horrible bowel accident and I ran to find a lavatory.

No paper!

Rats!

Finding a grocery store of sorts, I grabbed what look like toilet paper and raced to the front of the line, to the obvious consternation of my fellow shoppers.

"Hey, Mon, back o' de line like everyone else, Mon!"

"Sir, trust me, if I get in the back of this line there will shortly be no line!"

"Ah Mon, you been to Miss Cool dis mornin'? Irie!"

As I nodded, all was forgiven my brash tourist intrusion and the line parted, allowing me to pay for the paper and run for the can.

I just made it!

Two minutes later I was racing back to the same cubicle and mercifully my paper was still on the floor.

This would happen again after that, and once more later on.

Miss Brown's Tea Shack was okay but tomorrow it would definitely be the mushroom decaf.

Back on the beach, Bruce was crawling out of the surf in a turban, screaming "Land Shark" and laughing like it was the funniest thing ever. All of a sudden I started laughing uncontrollably. Three cups of Miss Brown's tea and a bag of fresh psychedelic mushrooms had transformed Bruce into the world's funniest guy! I was laughing so hard that I barely heard the screams of "HORSE, HORSE, HORSE!!!" which wasn't as funny as "Land Shark," but gazing to my right I was somewhat startled to see what appeared to be a mouth-frothing, riderless, mad horsie at full gallop, and he was heading straight at me.

I froze solid.

Bruce continued yelling "Land Shark," perhaps thinking to frighten the horse but with little effect on the charging beast.

At the last possible second to impact, The Horse (who I now capitalize as he didn't kill me) changed course and leaped over a number of sunbathing Germans reclining on lounge chairs.

As The Horse passed it created a strobing trail of hundreds of purple Horses, just like the Hollywood movie versions of acid hallucinations.

As Bruce had his black hair dyed with a bright yellow skunk stripe down the middle and I was sporting blue and pink crazy colours, we were the source of much amusement to the locals who had never seen this before.

"Are you gay boys, Mon?" was quickly followed by "What is your hair made of, plastic?"

Good questions all, to be sure.

What we needed was a kooky female element so I called our agent, who we will call Blue, and within twenty-four hours Joyce's blue-haired, semi-Oriental punkness was standing beside me hand-in-hand on the white sands of Negril Beach.

I didn't care if the locals questioned Bruce's sexuality and neither did he.

We were now the resident rock star whackos and everyone loved us.

"YOU VIL FUCK OFF!"

Well, maybe not everyone.

The fat German in the apartment above us was trying to get some sleep, and was unaware that the entire universe revolved around us and the cassette of vintage Stone's classic's blasting away beneath his bedroom window.

"Can't hear you man, music's too loud."

"YOU VIL FUCK OFF NOW!!" he screamed again.

"Noooo, man, it's gotta sound cooler when you're telling somebody to fuck off, try it again," we offered helpfully.

"I AM CALLING ZE MANAGEMENT!"

The next day the Germans on the beach were rude and wouldn't let us sit in obviously empty lounge chairs, claiming that they were in use. As we were high as kites, we couldn't be sure if this was true or not so we avoided the issue and found some rocks to relax on.

With thoughts of lust and massive drug abuse rampant once more it was only natural that a visit to the local church was in order and so, armed with my Doug Inglis Bible, I hailed a cab to take me to the nearest Sunday School. Fifty Jamaican dollars later, I strode into the service, which stopped dead in its holiness as the congregation glommed onto my bizarre hair colour and wardrobe.

To the spiritually assembled, I represented nothing less than a visitor from outer space.

With the service over in fifteen minutes, the fifty dollars had been a complete waste and I felt especially cheated when the small-town pastor informed me that there were several churches within walking distance of my hotel, some thirty miles away. I thanked him for his hospitality, assured several parishioners that I was not gay, and swore to kill the cab driver when and if I caught him. He wasn't hard to find as he had waited to drive me back for free, probably feeling the effects of a long-lost guilty conscience.

Later that day Joyce and I dined on red snapper at the beach fire of seventy-six-year-old fisherman Mr. Reynolds, which he had caught that very morning in our honour. On the way back to the hotel a kid sold me two dollars worth of sand from the beach, which I still keep in an old Valium bottle. Another kid tried to sell me a hotel room key but I didn't need that so I passed. I should have bought the room key as it turned out to be ours.

We left Jamaica the next day for cloudier climes.

While I was buying sand on the beach in Jamaica, Paul McCartney was in jail for smuggling pot into Japan. I decided to write a song about it.

Stuck In The Tokyo Jail

Flew in from America B.O.A.C.
Didn't hide my stash too well
Customs men were eager to inspect my bags
Then they dragged me off to jail

I'm stuck in the Tokyo jail man
I should've sent it airmail man
Stuck in the Tokyo jail

Been away from Tokyo for far too long
Gee I'd like to be back home
Linda and the kids they must be worried sick
Wish she'd come and keep me warm
I'm stuck in the Tokyo jail man
I should've sent it airmail man
Stuck in the Tokyo
Stuck in the Tokyo
Stuck in the Tokyo jail
Well those customs guys couldn't knock me 'round

I'm far too big a star
But even though I'm world renowned
They went and locked me up, up, up, up, up behind these cold steel bars

Well show me what I gotta do to get on out
Ain't felt this down in far too long
Seven years for seven lids is way too much
Didn't think I'd done that wrong

I'm stuck....

To my knowledge the only Lennon-McCartney-Godovitz collaboration in history. Sung to the tune of 'Back In The USSR', I used Segarini's group to record this little parody, right down to the jet engine noises and Beach Boy-styled falsetto harmonies. The picture sleeve we proposed was the unshaven shot of Paul from the white album superimposed behind bars.

Funny, right?

Wrong!

After sending a copy of the tape to McCartney's lawyers in New York, I received the nastiest little letter imaginable telling me that, should I release this song, then OH BROTHER LOOK OUT KID....

I wonder if Weird Al had this problem at first?

Winnipeg

We flew out west for three dates in Manitoba, and the gig at The Playhouse was another sold out event which saw me smashing a vintage Gibson Flying V to pieces. Mike McLuhan, media guru Marshall's son and owner of Ring Music, had given me the priceless ax with instructions to take it on the road and wreak havoc on it.

Mission accomplished. These original guitars today are worth in excess of ten thousand dollars and that particular one was just kicked off the front of stage like so much junk.

Back at the hotel all of our rooms were open for business and as the party raged in mine I soon sought refuge in the bathroom with Doucette and Chris Burke-Gaffney of the Pumps.

Sharing a quiet joint we are suddenly aware of loud pounding on the washroom door.

POUND, POUND, POUND!

"Whooo is it?" I sing-songed.

"It's the Police! Open up in there!"

"Are you the guys who sing Roxanne?" I asked.

Burke-Gaffney was now freaking as the joint was not going anywhere fast, but the Douce smiled and played along.

"IT'S THE WINNIPEG POLICE! NOW OPEN THIS DOOR!" and quite frankly I was not too impressed with their haughty attitude.

Flushing the joint, I opened the door, releasing a billowing cloud of pot smoke into the fresh faces of two uniformed cops and "Wes," the chief of hotel security.

"What are you doing in here and whose room is this and who are all these people?" Wes demanded.

"We're having a meeting, the room is mine, and feel free to throw the people out," I said, which is exactly what happened next. Wes left me with a warning that this sort of thing would not be tolerated in the Holiday Inn and I was very impressed with his company-man policy as I shut the door in his face.

The next night we performed at the University of Brandon where Communists, handing out flyers, called Gino a capitalist pig as we stepped into the limo. Of all people least likely to be considered that it had to be Gino. A joint, a good comic book and a shared glass of wine were all that mattered to him.

I was a capitalist swine, to be sure, and Inglis liked to count huge mounds of filthy lucre in his spare time, but certainly not good old Gino.

Our third gig was back in Winnipeg, at The Native Club, which was a sold-out "Social" as they called them there. I always thought that socials were debutante balls with tuxedos and evening gloves but, in Manitoba, it's a thousand drugged-up drunks, puking all over each other. I decided to teach old Wes back at the hotel a "who's boss" and invited everyone in the audience back for a party on the ninth floor. At one point I took twenty naked fun seekers down the stairwell to the pool area. With a gorgeous girl on either side and my glasses steamed up from the hot tub I didn't see good old Wes skulk up and loudly proclaim, "YOU AGAIN?!" before throwing my guests out of the hotel.

Hung over, unshaven, and shagged out we caught the first plane home. Business as unusual.

Blue

Too much madness finally gave way to the LB Show and I finding an apartment and fleeing the Roadie Hilton with our meagre belongings. Within days we transformed the two-bedroom-plus-den into a bachelor pad that should've featured a revolving door for the endless parade of willing victims that were soon calling up to visit. Joyce was still around but at that point I was in no position to even consider another steady girlfriend.

Adrift without proper management, we finally settled on David "Blue" Bluestein, a rolly polly bundle of mirth who ran The Agency, which booked our endless stream of gigs. Blue was a one-time drummer, oil-and-water-psychedelic Catharsis Light Show operator, and a dead ringer for Jerry Garcia of the Grateful Dead. Ray (Rush) Danniels was Blue's silent partner at The Agency and was interested in handling our affairs but Ray was sharp enough to know that, with certain previous managers just waiting in line to pick our bones, the mere mention of his name would set off a feeding frenzy of buy-outs and possible litigation. Talks with boy wonder Norman (Perryscope Productions) Perry had ground to a halt and even Skinny (Fludd) Tenn had expressed an interest, which was flattering after what I perceived to be my near invisibility during The Pilling era. Blue, whose keen sense of humour and laid-back business style was the perfect counterbalance to the excessive lunacy of the group he would now be representing, was the perfect choice.

A benefit gig at Massey Hall for our friends Hott Roxx was a great success and the group showed its appreciation by presenting me with a '63 gold Goya metal flake guitar. One-nighters through March were hell as we were pounded by heavy snowfalls, which made travel four times the usual length and dangerous to boot. At a Hamilton gig, Mac smashed a beer bottle on his forehead and then proceeded to tongue my ear while blood oozed down his face. The audience loved it; I wasn't convinced of its entertainment value.

In Montreal we played a standing-room-only date where Myles from April Wine was soon on stage with us. So knocked out was the great songwriter that he arranged for another club to be kept open after our show, where we jammed into the small hours fuelled by an endless supply of cocaine and champagne. He presented me with a Goya guitar coke spoon in honour of my twenty-ninth birthday, and Gino and I rode the empty streets back to the hotel on the top of a very-concerned Marty

Melhuish's new car, where I tried to leap out of an upper floor window while Doug tried in vain to light Gino on fire.

The next day I was hit with a thirty five thousand dollar tax bill, and Blue was notified to withhold any monies payable to me until further notice. Even though I had recently moved into a new apartment, I booked into a beautiful hotel room with a panoramic view of Toronto and drank myself silly in search of some peace and quiet.

May 2-Hanover, May 3-Bolton, May 6&7-The Rondun
May 8-Guelph, May 9 & 10-Nickleodeon
May 12-Recording, May 13 & 14-Hamilton
May 15-Queensbury Arms, May 16-Thorold
May 17-Kitchener, May 18-Minden, May 21-Brantford
May 22 & 23-Headspace, May 27-Ontario Place Forum
May 28/29/30-The Knobby, May 31-Kitchener

diary – friday, may 160 – thorold
...these days I'm not finding much pleasure in anything I'm doing. I'm feeling the same way I did just before I left Fludd. A sense of artistic strangulation and a frustration that's uncomfortable on the way home. The Winnebago that we rented for the weekend broke down just west of Hamilton. We sat in it for 4 hours before the tow truck arrived and then took a cab to Toronto. I arrived home as the sun was rising. Shit.

Ira Blacker

As the founder of ATI Agency in New York, manager of Savoy Brown and brother of Tina Louise, aka Ginger on Gilligan's Island, Ira Blacker had a lot going for him. Having recently discussed a co-management deal with Blue, Ira had flown up from Los Angeles to witness our sold-out show at the Ontario Place Forum. Fifteen thousand kids covered the hills and broke through security on numerous occasions to help us with the best show of our careers. The only problem with this show was that the promoters over-sold the venue by a couple thousand tickets, so the fans who couldn't get in went on a rampage and did tens of thousands of dollars in damages to Toronto's transit system. The same thing happened a week later with Teenage Head. The Head were smart enough to capitalize on a great bit of nasty press but for some reason I opted to play good guy, and a meeting was arranged between myself and various officials from the TTC, Ontario

Place and the police to try and figure out a way for this not to happen again. The obvious solution was to not sell more tickets than bloody seats. Although I was a confident orator and passionate in my drugged out condition we were, along with Teenage Head, banished from ever playing the venue again. Ira was convinced that England was the place for us and we inked a deal giving him two hundred days to secure a contract and gigs in the U.K. Of course nothing ever came of this or somebody else would be writing this book instead of myself. I just thought that I'd mention that I knew Tina Louise's brother.

Studio 306

We recorded 'Homemade Lady' and 'Fortune In Men's Eyes' as a tribute to Brian Pilling. Segarini produced the tracks and we released a picture sleeve 45 to raise some money for Brian's family. Of course good intentions aside, they nor we ever saw a cent.

Westward Ho

Sudbury – Elliot Lake – Thunder Bay – Winnipeg – Saskatoon
Regina – Lethbridge – Edmonton – Calgary – Vancouver
Victoria – Abbotsford – Langely – Edmonton – Calgary
Thunder Bay – Sudbury

Another six-week run out west but the incessant string of one-nighters and our debauched lifestyle was beginning to show. On the second night of the tour I began spitting up blood and my throat felt like it was coated in sandpaper. This would continue untreated for the rest of the trip.

In Winnipeg a friendly sleezeball opened up his massage parlour for our private use and everything was on the house for any tour party member interested in such distractions. Being too drunk to fuck, I amused myself by liberally redecorating the furniture and walls with baby oil before escaping back to the hotel. Such was our reputation in that city that not a word was mentioned the next night at the show when the owner of said establishment and his entourage of girls were ushered backstage.

At breakfast in Regina at a local pancake house, I freaked out my dining partner by slicing open my left wrist in order to prove a point to my waitress concerning the preparation of rare steak. The local law officials gently guided me back to the hotel where I promptly fell, fully clothed, into the pool.

At the end of one performance I threw my Gibson bass into the air hoping that one of the roadies would catch it on the way down. This might have happened had my left foot not been on the chord when I tossed it. The bass went straight up, hit the end of its rope, then proceeded to crash to the stage where it broke in two, abruptly ending the show as none of the support group bass players were keen on me using their instruments. Using a backstage work bench, some clamps and some serious glue, Uncle Mike had the thing fully repaired for the next evening, and showed me a half-inch build-up of salt caused by excessive sweating that had corroded the pickups to the point that the thing hardly worked.

In Regina we got beat by the promoters for twenty-one hundred dollars, throwing our budget into total disarray. To make matters worse, the girl I'd met at the hotel pool and taken to the gig turned out to be only sixteen and missed, as her chaperone for the "horse" show she was appearing at came out of his room drunk and half-heartedly threw a punch at me, which missed. Soon the corridor was full of roadies and chaperones and, after much swearing and carrying on, everyone called it a night.

On the way to Lethbridge in a thirty-seat plane, the little kid sitting beside me, unaware of my extreme hangover, threw up all over himself. With no ventilation I spent the next hour with my face buried in a hastily supplied barf bag and held on for dear life while order was restored.

On the return flight to Edmonton I must've sat in that same little barf kid's seat, as I awoke in a sea of sticky bubble gum.

While the crowd screamed for an encore at the Riviera Rock Room in Edmonton, Gino and I came to near-blows backstage in the kitchen area, over his drunkenness on stage during the performance. The club owner, walking in on the scene, was horrified as Gino, in a fit of rage, sent a tray of one hundred dishes crashing to the floor. Vowing to continue our little discussion after the encore, we played two more songs as if nothing had ever happened and the incident was forgotten as we left the stage.

One hundred plates hitting a concrete floor is an interesting sound.

Comedian Mike McDonald opened for us and his tennis-racket-as-guitar bit was hilarious enough to win over the rowdies. I started out on tennis racket myself but mine was a left handed McCartney model so we had lots to talk about after the gig.

In Calgary, the local rock writer from the Herald walked into the dressing room for an interview, only to happen on a young lady searching for her contact lens in my lap. The interview went on as scheduled.

Rose flew out to join me in Vancouver with a possible reconciliation in mind. If this situation ever presents itself to you, do not do the following. After our show at The Commodore Ballroom we were paid $1,054.00 dollars, which was a joke as the place was sold-out at ten bucks a head and there were over fifteen hundred heads in attendance. I freaked on everyone, save the promoters, who were nowhere to be found. They were pissed that I was over an hour late starting our show, as LB had given me the wrong starting time and I was out showing Rose the delights of downtown Vancouver. With a healthy overdose of champagne, Valium and magic mushrooms, I spent the first night of our second honeymoon baying at the moon and totally freaking Rose right out.

The next day we took the ferry to Nanaimo, where we played to a convention of four-wheel-drive vehicle owners. At one point in the set, the promoter came on stage and said he would pay us in full if we just stopped. The disco music was on and the four wheelers had a new purpose in life as we fled to the comfort of the hotel bar.

The next day was a day off which meant that we could now get silly...er, sillier. A band and crew dinner at our favourite Greek restaurant resulted in all of our food, drinks, plates, and cutlery being thrown out of the skylight. We were immediately ejected from the premises.

Racing down Robson Street I thought that Rose just might like to see me ride on the top of the car. She wasn't interested and restrained me until I leaped out at the first red light and grabbed onto the back of Bruce's truck, which roared off before I could pull myself up. Through the haze I quickly realized that Bruce had no idea that I was thus involved with his accelerating machine and that the band car, now full of appreciative, screaming drunks, was almost certain to run me over should I slip, with my tenuous grip on the back of the truck getting decidedly weaker by the second. As Bruce made a hairpin turn into the parking lot, I let go and soon found myself trying to remain upright as my feet sought to catch up with my body. I resembled nothing if not a poor man's Road Runner. To further cement our newfound relationship I leaped over the twenty storey balcony and soon began to lose my grip on the railing as smartly as my grip on reality. The roadies, now apprised of the situation by Rose's screams, hauled me over the rail, gaffer-taped my arms to my body, and threw me into the bathtub, where I remained for the night. Rose booked into her own room and left the next morning. I never saw her again.

> Dear Greg,
> Hi, I'm only thirteen and I think your fantastic!
> I really wanted to see you guys at Headlines in Hamilton, but my mother (who's a real loser) wouldn't let me go. She's such a space cadet, I swear it!
> But anyways I just wanted to say Hi! and that I think next to Mick Jagger, Frank Zappa and David Bowie, your the Greatest!
>
> Love Always,
> Patricia Sloan
> P.S. I think Doug and Gino are cute too.

...just a little note to aspiring musicians...try to never have any down-time when touring so as not to court trouble with too much free time on your hands...now back to our story...

I flew back to Edmonton to mend my broken heart with a waitress named Sheila. I can't remember what she looked like at all, but according to my diary she was worth leaving Vancouver for. It was here that I met this wonderful character named P.J. Burton who is a schoolteacher by day and a lead-singing, Iggy Pop look-alike in a punk group called The Smarties by night. Blessed with an abundance of charm, humour and the smartest guy I have ever met in a group, we hit it off straight away, a friendship that continues to this day. P.J. also always had the coolest girls travelling with him and was into sharing. After three days of non-carnal activity with Sheila that included us trying to get into gay bars, it suddenly dawned on me: Sheila didn't like boys. Ha Ha. The joke was on me. When I think about what Gino and Doug were probably up to back in Vancouver I felt like a true chump. The last words uttered by her at the airport were, "I hope you enjoyed your visit in Edmonton."

"TO EDMONTON!" my mind screamed in correction as I slumped into the airbus seat.

The limo driver who picked me up at the airport in Calgary told me that his girlfriend Tammy wanted to meet me, so I said sure. When he brought her over my eyes almost dislodged. She was a beautiful cowgirl, complete with ten-gallon hat, and it was obvious that she had more on her mind than an autograph. It was all polite how-do-you-do's, but an hour later she had ditched the boyfriend and was back at the hotel for a different kind of visit.

After three days I flew back to Edmonton as Tina Louise's (or Ginger from Gilligan's Island's) brother called to tell me that Savoy Brown was playing. After a nice dinner with guitar legend Kim Simmonds, I caught their show and soon found myself on stage playing one of his Gibson Flying V's. I was legless on stage and had a foggy deja vu concerning another Flying V in Winnipeg that had met a rather tragic end. Best not to dwell on it, I thought, as I fumbled for a riff.

As I slumped semi-conscious in my return-to-Ontario airplane seat, it soon became painfully obvious that the guy next to me wanted to talk. He was a musician whose band covered five of my songs and he just wanted to say that he blah, blah, blah...

On the flight from Thunder Bay to Sudbury I made a beeline for this black dancer who was sitting on her own and was on her way to Ottawa. By the time we landed she left the plane to buy me dinner and it was over this very same meal that she said, "I knew a guy in Fludd named Greg once and he...," and with that she wouldn't let me sleep. She was a bloody nympho and I ended up hiding in one of the roadie's rooms until I saw her pile into a cab, heading in the direction of the airport.

With the tour now over I decided to catch a ride home with good old Bruce in the equipment truck. After flying everywhere for the past six weeks it almost seemed like a fresh idea. Having had to sign for a cup of tea in the morning I would at least return home triumphant with a few hundred dollars in my pocket, instead of wasting it on an airline ticket. Bruce was high as a kite on some sort of tongue-chewing uppers and I ate the last of my magic mushrooms to help the trip fly by faster.

The weather was diabolical for most of the trip. With massive thunder and lightning showers pounding the roads, our visibility was zero as Bruce refused to take his somewhat leaden foot off of the accelerator. At one point I noticed a rather sharp pain in my left side, which was my portable boom box digging into my ribs. Instead of moving the offending item to the floor I simply opened my window and chucked it out. As later events unraveled this turned out to be a good thing but Bruce was pissed off as he said that he could've used it, but it was gone so enough already. We had a very early morning breakfast at my folks' house, as I had to pick up my keys, and after champagne and eggs, we started the last ten miles of a six-thousand mile trip. As we rounded a corner, less than a mile from my place, Bruce lost control of the truck and now we were heading at a bus shelter containing two very agitated commuters. Grabbing the wheel with four hands Bruce and I managed to narrowly miss the shelter but were now heading for the gas pumps. A quick tug to the right and the load shifted just enough for us to flip over on our side, sending everything in the cab flying and our stage equipment through the roof and across the road. I was now lying on top of good old Bruce on the driver's side when a sudden clear vision popped into my mind.

"Say Bruce, how much gas is in the tank?"

"It's full, Godo," and with that I saw no further percentage to laying around on top of Bruce; I eased myself up and out of the passenger side door, quickly followed by the reckless roadie.

A crowd was gathering and the first guy on the scene was the gas station owner.

"Where's your phone, man?" I asked, and began running for the office.

"Are you calling for an ambulance?" he yelled as I ran.

"Fuck no, man, I'm calling the press!"

A half-page picture in the paper the next day and all local television news coverage that night.

J.D. "John" Roberts reporting on the Goddo mishap for CITY-TV, 1980.

She Loves You On My Wall

For the rest of August after the western tour we did the usual round of local gigs, and I had the music to 'She Loves You' airbrushed on our front hall wall in brown-with-white manuscript. The poor artist had already painstakingly done it once before with brown-on-white, but when he was finished he pulled off the masking tape and the undercoat of paint came off with the tape, forcing him to repeat a very labour intensive painting.

I was juggling French Joanne, Aimee with two ee's, Joyce two, Isabelle, Lorna, Margot, Annie, Hanne, and Miss Nude Ontario Lilly, who changed my attitude towards spandex pants.

There were also girls at gigs to consider.

My lawyer, who we'll call Lawyer Lusti, was now visiting me at my apartment on a regular basis looking for "babes," as he called them, and was content to work off part of our ever-growing legal bills by taking out extra groupies as partial payment. For some strange reason they didn't seem to mind.

I only realized how sick I was by checking this guy out.

The Pretty Bad Boy

Russell was four years old. He was half white/half oriental and as cute as a button. He was Uncle Mike the roadie's girlfriend's sister's kid and I fell in love with him the minute I met him. We went to the Exhibition together, we ate in fancy restaurants, and went to see movies. He knew way more about life at four than your average fourteen-year-old and he was smart. It was like he was an old midget instead of a little kid, and whenever one of my bustier girlfriends would pick him up and cuddle him you could see him copping cheap feels and then winking at you after he'd gotten away with it. The first time I saw him do this was with Lilly the Miss Nude Ontario and she had no idea that a four year old had just perved out on her.

Everyone thought that he was my kid and he sure acted like it.

Los Angeles

Not having racked up any serious waste-of-money expenses in a week or two, it was decided that I should fly to L.A. and visit with Ginger from Gilligan's Island's brother, who would show me studios, introduce me to producers, and generally help me dig myself into a larger financial hole than I was already in. The flight was great and also on the plane, for those taking notes on my name dropping, were Count Floyd, Ricky Ricardo, and Mr. Tijuana Taxi himself, Herb Alpert, who is best known for having that LP cover of the broad covered in whipped cream.

Not wanting to make a bad impression, but incapable of otherwise, I literally fell through the Arrivals lobby door and was pleased to see GFGIB (Ginger From Gilligan's Island Brother) waiting for me. Through what was either my own drunken haze or the local smog, I made out many cool sights from TV and the movies as we snaked our way up long and winding canyon roads until we arrived at my host's comfy little mansion. As I snooped around I couldn't help but notice that there were more locks and chains and bolts on every door and window than Houdini himself could get out of, and I suddenly became quite paranoid. GFGIB of course just wanted to stay in and watch movies on his new VCR but I wanted to go exploring. After waiting four hours for two different cab companies, I finally agreed that going out maybe wasn't such a good idea after all and finally made it to the guest room, where no sooner had I turned out the table lamp than the sound of locks being clicked and bolted began with my door.

I was locked in my room!

Putting it down to some quaint local custom I turned on the table lamp, placed a chair under the doorknob and slept fitfully, in fear for my life. No doubt my hosts were doing the same.

The next day I was driven into Hollyweird and was soon talking to many successful-looking guys who genuinely seemed to like me. I of course was more interested in seeing the theatrical uncut version of *Caligula* and soon found myself sitting in a cool L.A. movie house, resplendent in pink vinyl suit jacket and matching accessories. It was just about the part of the film where Caligula's love for his sister Drusila takes on a more intimate tone, when I noticed the presence of a leg pressing against my own. Looking around me I suddenly realized that there were only two people in the theatre and I was one of them. What could possibly possess someone to sit next to a total stranger in a darkened theatre when they had all those other empty seats to choose fro....HOLY SHIT!!!!

Tearing my eyes away from Guccione's tastefully directed lesbian love scene I leaped to my feet and pointed my finger at this now-startled guy.

"MOVE MAN, NOW!!" I whispered loudly and he skulked off.

I carefully rolled up my pink vinyl suit jacket and placed it on the seat next to me as Caligula dipped his fist in a vat of goose grease in order to help celebrate one of his subject's nuptials.

I managed to secure a date with a real girl who took me out to dinner and then to the Starwood where Michael Des Barres was still re-living glam rock. After a load of pleading appeared to have no meaning on this comely wench, I realized that the night would be loveless and grabbed a cab back to GFGIB house. As we finally made our way down the proper street, the cabbie said, "See that house there?" and I did see a house there. "That's Frank Zappa's place."

"Drop me off here," I slurred and fell out of the back of the cab.

I had a plan!

I would just go up to the door and pretend I was lost and when Frank opened it up and I explained my predicament to him, he would invite me in for cookies and milk and we would go down into his studio and write a brilliant new piece of music and we would become best friends for life!

It was a good plan!

As I rang the bell, I heard from behind the huge door what sounded not so much like dogs but werewolves, and it sounded like they were eating their way through the door to get to me.

Having not one single silver bullet on me, I ran like fuck down the street for my life and the relative safety of my guest room. I thanked my host repeatedly as he locked me up for the night.

My trip to L.A. had been a raging success which was only spoiled when the American Airlines stewardesses cut me off during the flight home for being too out of it.

Renata

Luigi's Trattoria was one of those New York-styled Italian joints favoured by The Mob and any visiting crooner whose name ended in a vowel. The room was candle-lit with chequered red and white tablecloths, and the food was good.

Sinatra ate there.

I was ploughing into another carafe of red wine and keeping one eye on the door as I was on my first blind date. LB and Janice The Woman Who Ruined My Life (TWWRML) were watching me watch the door as I studied anyone coming in.

LB was dating Janice TWWRML and her friend was my blind date.

"Is that her?" I asked as this portly effort made her way towards our table and then suddenly veered left to join her equally portly friend.

"Thank God!" I muttered and this went on for quite some time.

When my blind date finally made her entrance I saw that she was walking towards us but also noticed that I could see her ass coming first. In black velvet toreador pants and decidedly perilous stiletto heels she teetered as she moved, as opposed to walking, and her bum looked like you could balance a champagne glass on it which I had every intention of doing.

"That's Renata," said Janice TWWRML and I muttered something appreciative.

"How do you do," said my date, extending her right hand and smiling. How do you do?

Too Bourgeois for me, I thought, as I fell out of my chair and proceeded to kiss one of her feet under the table. She didn't seem to mind this unusual form of greeting and took her place at the table, instead of stumbling screaming from the restaurant.

After much small talk and more wine and food, I realized that we had a gig down the street and we soon made our way to the club. Wanting to make a big impression I convinced Gino and Doug that starting with my guitar set would surely win her over and, as I was in no condition to consider a rational argument as to why this wouldn't be a good idea, we lumbered on stage where I proceeded to begin playing only to fall off the stage, crashing into a number of fully loaded tables.

As I clambered back on stage I saw the greatest ass I'd ever seen push open the door to Yonge Street and disappear into the night.

At that moment I had no idea of knowing that the future Mother of my two kids had just left the building.

diary – friday, november 14 – toronto
What a great way to start the day. I got a call from Wendy at Bob Ezrin's office. She told me that he wanted me for a session on Murray McLauchlan's new LP. Boy was I nervous. I was nervous because he wanted me to play lead guitar. I got myself in shape (two Valiums) and off I went. It was actually good to see Bob again. He's actually quite a nice guy. He played me the track ('Tell Your Mama She Wants You'), which had a heavy groove. Very different from Murray's previous stuff. I settled into it fast enough but after everything I'd read about how meticulous Ezrin is I felt I was rushed in and out. The playback was good but I felt that I had another one in me. I met Murray who didn't seem overly friendly but the engineer told me that Ezrin was extremely happy with what I'd done. I still had reservations....

In hindsight, Murray may have been somewhat nervous when at one point I looked up from my guitar flailing to see Ezrin holding up a huge sign with "A" minor written on it. Mr. Big Ears here was riffing wildly in A major. Ezrin had his head hung like I was a complete waste of time, which is probably what I was. I kept asking him, "Are you sure it isn't Gino you're after?" but he said that he knew how I played and it was me that was required. The subsequent LP, 'Storm Warnings', was possibly Murray's worst selling effort which I have always taken as my fault entirely. Murray, recalling the recording of this particular song, mentioned me once in his book but you will notice that I mention him six times in mine. That's because his wife, Denise Donlon, let my daughter in to see Geri (Ginger Spice) Halliwell at Much Music.

Hi Denise!

Thursday, November 20/80
Write 'Pretty Bad Boy.'
Monday, November 24/80
Record 'Pretty Bad Boy.'

It's a good thing I was baby-sitting Russell. First of all, his Mom Vicki had him dressed in an "I love Greg Godovitz" T-shirt and secondly, we were stuck in the recording process for a solo idea. A piano solo was no good, great as "Segarini" keyboardist Drew Winters was. Try as he might, Gino couldn't find anything that fit the middle section either. That's when it dawned on me to have Russell do a spoken word solo. I coached him on the timing and, propped up on a chair, he got it in one take. It was like having a cute little furry thing on tape and we all knew that we had the makings of a hit single in the can.

John Lennon Is Dead

"I was shaken at the Lover's Ball
The night the Walrus took his fall"

— *'Shooting Stars' written Dec. 12/80*

Our half of the Double Rinks arena in Hamilton was packed to capacity with a sweaty and pumped crowd as we neared the end of our set. All at once I noticed Uncle Mike, at his workstation stage right, motioning for me to come over. As Gino was just tearing into his solo in 'Drive Me Crazy' I leaned over the mixing desk and could just about hear above the din on stage.

"John Lennon's been shot in New York!" Uncle Mike informed me and all at once I was no longer a part of my own reality.

We finished our set and I immediately hit the pay phone in the lobby where I quickly dialed up my dear friend artist, Olwyn Fleury, who was sobbing uncontrollably. As unaware fans were slapping me on the back in congratulations for a great show, I dissolved in tears as news of the tragedy was passed on to me from Olwyn.

Without a word to the audience we returned for our encore which was our only ever performance of 'Come Together', which must have mystified the crowd not used to us playing Beatles songs. The bitter reality was brought home when we dialed up the car radio and 'Across The Universe' was playing. Trying to accept the finality of his brilliant life cut short, I cried inconsolably for the rest of the trip home.

Even though it was far too early for a real tree, LB and I had set up our Christmas tree that very morning in the hopes of beating the winter blahs, and now I crawled under its brightly lit branches, stoned on magic mushrooms, and sought some solace in its promise for the festive season to come.

The dream was indeed over.

We spent the rest of December recording the Pretty Bad Boys LP at Studio 306 in Toronto.

Make Believe Gardens

"No tickets or passes, Hello!" was how I spent the entire day answering the phone as everyone and their giraffe called to get on the guest list.

I was going to play the Gardens and it was New Years Eve!

Max Webster headlining with B.B. Gabor opening and us in the second slot.

No sound check, no back lighting and only 70% front house power.

I had a good mind to call up Kim Mitchell and give him what for but cooler heads prevailed and I resolved to steal the show at any cost.

Max had Geddy Lee as a special guest but big nose...er, deal...we had the ultimate secret weapon.

Russell!

As our overture was played the sight of thousands of points of light from lighters and matches brought to mind every concert that I had ever seen in the famed arena. It was different from the backstage side of the black scrim and I drank in the sights and sounds like it was my last night on earth.

The Beatles had stood on this very stage and the roar from the crowd was deafening when we took up our positions and thundered into 'So Walk On.'

When the audience caught sight of Russell in his sunglasses and tuxedo, striding purposely to his mic, they erupted in a standing ovation that pushed the music back onto the stage. I could see right away that he

Maple Leaf Gardens New Year's Eve, December 31, 1980

TRAVELS WITH MY AMP

was momentarily frozen in terror, so I gently nudged Russell's behind with my boot and he began twisting to the obvious delight of the crowd.

"I'm just a pretty bad boy," he said and the show was his.

The Websters were great and the audience went nuts when Geddy sat in but the evening belonged to a four year old in a rather smallish tuxedo!

Leaping off the roof of our limousine into the arms of Big Nick he gently deposited me into the back seat, champagne bottle in hand, where I immediately passed out.

And with that 1980 was laid to rest.

Goddo 1981

Goddo Music Inc.

diary – friday, january 9 – toronto
...I was sort of in a rush so I never read anything I signed, but I'm sure that things will go well for us this time...

What an absolute imbecile!

Here we were meeting in Lawyer Lusti's downtown office with all principal parties to sign a proper partnership agreement and, as I was named PRESIDENT of Goddo Music Inc., I figured why bother reading over boring legal details when my time would be better served picking up Springsteen tickets.

In our career, we signed more bad paper over pinball machines, restaurant tables and booze-soaked bars, effectively giving away the rights to any chance to really make any big money, and never took the time to read a word of any of them.

January

Ottawa – Lindsay – Toronto – Hamilton – Oshawa – London Oakville – Hamilton – Mississauga – Toronto – Jarvis – Toronto Hamilton

MUSH YOU DOGS!! MUSH I SAY!! FEEL THE STING OF MY WHIP AND KEEP MOVIN'!

Now through all of this fresh new-years madness, I still had a house full of girls to deal with but I was starting to realize that Renata was creeping into my life, slowly but surely. Even though Gina, Cheryl, Michelle, Chris, Natalie, Tracy, Anita, Lisa, and even Rose were visiting, things were coming to a ...er, head.

At one point Kathi McDonald moved out of Baldry's Hamilton mansion and moved in for a bit with LB and myself. It's a good thing, as one night I returned home out of my brains where I proceeded to fall into the bath tub with my fur coat on and promptly passed out under water. Even though I must have weighed three hundred pounds completely soaked, Kathi crashed through the door and saved me from drowning. With loads of company to choose from, I decided that Renata would join me in Jamaica for two weeks but at the last minute told her that she couldn't come. Her travel agent phoned me up and said that I couldn't do this.

"I play rock and roll, I can do what I like," was my response.

I was now convinced that Renata would ruin my holiday and there was no fucking way she was going to Negril.

Jamaica
– January 25 to February 6

"Your friend is already in your room," I was told as the desk manager handed me the key.

Now life had been so strange for the last couple of years that I didn't even think to ask who or what this friend was, but was very pleasantly surprised to see a very mushroom-headed Bruce Duncan sitting on the spare bed laughing hysterically at nothing particularly funny, but laughing nonetheless.

The next day we eschewed a proper nutritional breakfast to eat the sweet-flavoured "ganja cakes."

"Hey Bruce, Mon, Bruce!!"

It was Steve, a local dealer of no fixed scruples.

"What choo got dere, Mon?" he asked as he peered closely at our treats.

"Ganja cake!" was Bruce's reply.

"DOG SHIT, MON!" said Steve, bending over in laughter, "YOU EATING DOG SHIT!"

Now what we had failed to mention to good old Steve was that this was the second cake that we were now eating and, although I suddenly lost interest in the local beach cuisine, it seemed a little late to repair any self-inflicted damage.

I have no idea what the ratio of actual ganja to dog shit is but soon we were higher than kites as Steve picked up our now discarded delicacies, which he was busy forming into one large, freshly-baked retail product. Washing the fine-powdered beach sand off in the ocean Steve was now offering the cake to a new tourist as we stumbled off in search of coconuts.

FACT!!!...if you tape record ambient night sounds in Negril, the insects sound like very loud Brian Eno noodlings, yet they are barely audible to the human ear...

Renata arrives after a week and I'm actually horny...happy to see her.

Winston The Light Bulb Eater

The floorshow at The Negril Beach Club featured this wonderful maniac named Winston who traveled to his gigs by tying on roller skates and then latching on to the bumpers of passing cars.

Stoned on an assortment of "shrooms" "ganja cake" (yes, we were still eating it, despite its dog-ass connection), "lambs bread," wine, and rum, we watched this guy roll around on shards of broken glass and then eat light bulbs while we howled with delight. Later I hired him to come to our room for a private show.

The Winston The Light Bulb Eater Interview

Me: "So I noticed that we had another blackout tonight. Do you sneak around and gather light bulbs for your act when this happens?"

W: "Yeah Mon, I like to sneak around and 'eep (heap) up de light bulbs ya know."

Me: "Is there any difference in taste between a 20-watt light bulb and a 60-watt light bulb?"

W: "No, mon, when I eat de light bulb it tastes de same y'know."
Taking a 60-watter from my night table, I offered this fine delicacy to my new spiritual adviser and watching closely he cracks the bulb and begins chewing, seemingly lost in his own thoughts.

Me: "It sounds very crunchy, like really fresh potato chips...does it have a taste?"
W: "No, mon."

And on it went.

This guy made those three Goddo fans/maniacs in Hamilton look normal.

I paid him $10 JA. which was approximately $1 U.S. and showed him the door.

You can only take so much of a good thing.

Blue phoned with news that Attic Records was fronting us $35,000 for our next two records. I celebrated by giving my acoustic guitar away to the guy in the B.B. King Calypso Band. This particular B.B. sat on an old wooden box, which he banged with a stick while singing 'Yellow Bird.' He had a vague recollection of another B.B. King but couldn't remember where from. The next morning I was convinced that my guitar had been stolen, only to be told of my drunken Elvis-giveaway the night before. I ended up giving the same guy all of my extra strings as I now had no acoustic guitar to use them on. The guitar ended up in a Jimmy Cliff video.

56 Hope Street

Dressed in yellow clogs with red hearts, striped purple satin pajamas, and with blue hair, I stood outside the front gates of Bob Marley's compound watching the action within as dozens of people slowly cleaned up the forecourt or huddled in small groups to enjoy the local horticulture.

"Hey musician! C'mon in, Mon!"

A huge Rasta, holding an even bigger joint, was hailing me with a gesturing motion.

Soon Renata and I were being given a guided tour of the Marley mansion, which included the Tuff Gong record store off to one side and a studio in the basement. Famed reggae producer Erroll Brown was busy putting a local band through their paces, and the air was heavy with pot smoke as a massive bass-heavy mix boomed from the studio speakers. Not being much of a pot smoker I declined various offers of the local home grown citing medical reasons, but received contact high, not unlike acid hallucinations, just being in the room.

"Is Bob here?" I asked, hoping to meet the great songwriter.

"No, Mon, Bob is in Germany with de cancer."

None of those present would see him alive again.

Back in Toronto, we got back to work on the new LP with help from Segarini co-producing. We recorded during the days and played gigs at night, an impossible schedule fuelled by drugs and booze. Things were happening too fast, as first my old friends John and Robin Bjarnason were involved in a head-on accident with a drunk driver (but survived the ordeal), and the very next night the club in Hamilton we played at burned to the ground after our concert. The following night we almost killed two drunks fighting on the highway, and lost control of our car trying to avoid them. The winter was brutal with record snowstorms and we were travelling every night under the worst conditions.

We needed a lift.

Best Seat In The House – Goddo Lighve
Roxy Theatre – Feb. 15/16

1981 ... Goddo's Best Seat In The House

All nervous and tanned from Jamaica, we began a two-night stint at The Roxy Theatre in Barrie to record a live LP, even though we were in the middle of a new studio effort. Q107 had done an amazing job of presenting the show and fans were lined up before noon for the sold-out concerts. Segarini was in the mobile truck and was doing his best to convince us that our obscene stage volume would not make it to tape. Trusting his judgement we toned it down and, after completing a lengthy sound check, we settled down until show time over dinner while the theatre filled up to overflow capacity. Famed photographer Pat Harbron was shooting everything in sight having remotely to do with the event, from the fans in line to the opening act we had chosen.

Ahh...the opening act.

I had seen Jim Carrey perform his wonderful impressions at Yuk Yuk's Comedy Club and decided that he would be the perfect opening act as we couldn't have a band play first, as they would disrupt the recording levels. A comedian needed a mic and perhaps a stool. Even as a kid Jim was amazingly funny and although his Steve Martin and Sammy Davis bits were a bit old school, you could see that he was passionate about what he was doing. We settled on $100 per show and that was that.

From the dressing room area I could hear through the walls that something was up, and soon found myself standing at the back of the auditorium where the Goddo fans were hurling verbal abuse and a healthy selection of popcorn and garbage at the well-dressed comedian. Most of the bands that opened for us also got this sort of treatment, but here was a guy on his own, armed only with his youthful energy and his "show must go on" professionalism.

Roadie Uncle "Mike" Morin with Segarini   *Roadie Marty Pelz with Segarini*

As he left the stage I took the mic and proceeded to give the audience shit for treating him so poorly. I told them that he was going to be a big star someday and that they would tell their friends about this night. He was totally crestfallen when I saw him in the dressing room later, and wouldn't return to open the next evening's show. Years later during his first real flush of success with "In Living Color," Jim was being interviewed on Q107 and the disc jockey asked him what his worst experience ever was playing on a stage. Without missing a beat he said, "Without a doubt, opening for Goddo when they did their live album in Barrie."

He makes $20,000,000 a movie now.

The way I see it is that we saved $19,999,900.

Jim Carrey opens for Goddo at "the Best Seat in the House" live recording in Barrie, Ontario.

Photo: Pat Harbron

With no peace to be had I did my usual downtown-hotel-thing and booked a suite where I was accompanied by this extraordinary Amazon of a brunette named Aimee. Even LB didn't know where I would be staying, and after viewing several different hotels we ended up at the Sheraton where the desk clerk could barely conceal his contempt at my appearance, my condition and my date. Upon checking in, we realized that we had been issued an invalid room but sought to make good on the various bars which were installed in several areas around the suite. At dinner later that night I stumbled, literally, over a severely inebriated Gordon Lightfoot, who was semi-passed out in the washroom of Harry's Steakhouse.

So it wasn't just me.

Even though I was not supposed to be found I soon received two phone calls. Renata tracked me down and told me to get rid of the girl I was with, and Aimee's friend Buzz called me to tell me that she was not nineteen but sixteen, and that her parents were going ballistic.

SIXTEEN!!

Calling up a roadie friend, he came over to whisk her home and I passed out, more exhausted than when I booked in.

diary – wednesday, april 22 – thorold
...we step outside to discover that someone has stolen our band car...

The Big Bust

I had no idea that this guy that we'd met in Jamaica was a heavyweight dealer until I awoke with a gun pointed at my head, and these two huge guys were telling me to get up as they were here on business. At first I thought these two were in my apartment to do a hit, but it turned out that they were serious narcs and my phones had been tapped since I returned from holiday. Turning over our apartment I knew that I was safe, as they studied my vial of Jamaican beach sand, a few slippery elm bark lozenges and some sea salt that shared space with assorted toys and other neat stuff on my roll-top desk. My bed had little stars and a crescent-shaped moon cut into the headboard with a string of red Christmas lights draped around it. The cops were disgusted and spent more time looking at pictures of my various girlfriends than thoroughly ransacking the place, totally missing a full gram of coke which was underneath my opened diary.

"I'm going to put some music on," I said as I made my way to the stereo.

"We don't like that shit you play!" said Mr. Bad Ass.

"Neither do I, I was thinking more of a Beethoven String Quartet," which I then proceeded to put on.

The two cops assigned to me were now confident that I had nothing while the other two were busy in the LB's room. At one point one of them opened his hand to reveal some pot and magic mushrooms.

"You know what these are?" he sneered.

"Sure," I offered helpfully, "but they're not mine."

"They're your buddy's and he's under arrest."

The LB Show was notified of his rights and the cops left us with the mess.

"We'll be seeing you around, and tell your scumbag friend Tony he's next," and, with that, they were gone.

I just knew that, given time, Tony would warrant a mention.

Winnipeg – Edmonton – Calgary – Vancouver

Attic Records was doing a bang-up job of promoting our double Lighve LP, and it was deemed necessary for their promo man, Lindsay, to whisk me around the western provinces for three days of radio and print media. Being totally out of my mind certainly didn't help matters but as Lindsay was never far enough away for me to big-mouth my way into any serious trouble, the only real damage was self-inflicted. Lindsay was a pretty reasonable sort who did a good job but all that changed upon our arrival in Vancouver.

Booking into the Hyatt after a hell day of interviews, we soon discovered that our rooms had been sold to other parties and we both lost it on the desk clerk. He notified the manager who said that they did have a suite, priced at roughly fifteen hundred dollars a night, which started us off again with the screaming.

"However, as you gentlemen have been inconvenienced by the Hyatt we will let you have the suite for the night at the normal double occupancy rate of one hundred dollars."

And with that said we were soon in a private elevator where we were whisked up to 3304, more commonly known as THE BLOODY PRIME MINISTER'S SUITE! The whole floor was the suite, which needed a bicycle to get from one end of to the other. A library, fully stocked bar, marble bathtubs, Chippendale dining room, and the biggest bed that I'd ever seen in the master bedroom. After the bellhop left we ran around like two kids and eventually flipped a coin to see who would get the master.

I won!

Lindsay was a poor loser and complained that he was the record company guy and that Attic was after all paying for the trip, but I countered that I was the star and that I had won the coin toss after all.

"Look man," I began, "we're never going to have this opportunity ever again so let's be smart and order up some expensive champagne and fancy hors d'oeuvres while I call some women!"

Seeing the logic in my idea, room service was notified of our needs while I got photographer Dee Lippingwell on the phone.

"Hi Dee, it's Greg Godovitz and I'm in town, watcha doin'?"

I was as cool as a cucumber.

I was in total control.

"Hi Greg, that's great. I'm just doing a shoot for Vogue with some models but I should be finished soon, where are you?"

Vogue models?

The Arthur in the Hyatt, Vancouver, living it up like the Prime Minister.
Photo: Dee Lippingwell

Did she say V.O.G.U.E. M.O.D.E.L.S?

"LISTEN DEE, WE'RE STAYING IN THE BLOODY PRIME MINISTER'S SUITE AT THE HYATT AND THERE'S A BAR AND CHIPPENDALE FURNITURE AND A HUGE BED AND CHAMPAGNE AND FANCY SANDWICHES AND CAN YOU BRING THE MODELS WITH YOU?????"

Mr. cool strikes again.

Within an hour we had a wonderful party raging all over the sumptuous suite as drinks were spilt and cigarettes were snuffed out on lovely Oriental rugs. Dee brought along her camera and got a shot of me on "the" bed, surrounded by the ladies.

Later we all went to The Cave to see Three Dog Night and, after a jam session at Gary Taylor's that went on until four in the morning, I fell into "the" bed for a few hours before we started another day of interviews.

diary – thursday, may 21 – vancouver
Lindsay comes rushing in at noon to tell me we only have fifteen minutes. I'm totally out of it still so I'm stumbling around trying to get ready and flailing. Lindsay says that the maids will move everything so off we went. First a luncheon with CBS rep Dave and CFOX program director Don Schaffer. I'm out of control. I couldn't eat. Schaffer orders a Chivas and water and gets a plate with four cherries on it and a glass of water. I consume lots of liquids and drink his water while he gets his order straight. After lunch a series of interviews with newspapers and radio and finishing on air at CFOX. I did what I was supposed to do. I was a good boy. Lindsay and I have not only been moved to another hotel room but our stuff is "exactly" as it had been in the suite. (My dirty clothes were in the same ball at the foot of the bed and the toothpaste tube was in the sink exactly as I'd left it in the suite. Now that's what I call a good hotel.)

With only three hours to kill we went over to the Worm's new club to see Red Rider and Tom Cochrane asked me to sit in, but at the last minute I dashed out for the airport to catch a flight home. The RCMP hassled me over a "Calgary Jr." cap pistol I was packing but let me board the Toronto-bound jet, where I alternated between my first class seat and eating sushi and drinking champagne with the crew on the flight deck of the 747.

The next week was spent putting the finishing touches to the 'Pretty

Bad Boys' LP mixes. Segarini did a great job but there was a bit of a fuss when Attic's president brought in two disco producers to help out. I did not get along with these guys at all and made life very difficult for them by not cooperating in the slightest. A summit meeting was called in a downtown hotel boardroom where Al Mair kept turning down the lights in the hope that I would remove my sunglasses. I wouldn't, as they afforded me the edge of being able to observe while not being observed myself. Of course this was utter rubbish, as I was being stared at by everyone around the table.

"I will not sell out!" I ranted.

"Greg, you're not selling out," Bob began, "you're buying in!"

"I will not have a couple of disco guys mess with my songs and that's all there is to it!"

With that they played the edited singles version of "Pretty Bad Boy."

I could hear the sound of money fluttering down.

Even though I was convinced that the disco lads had indeed improved my song there was no way that I was about to agree with everyone, and I left the meeting in a complete huff. To keep from laughing out loud at how good it sounded, I had bitten a hole through my lip.

Being an asshole was tough and demanding work.

Lighve Tour June 10 - July 11

Toronto – North Bay – Timmins – St. Eugene De Gigges
Cochrane – Sudbury – Sault Ste. Marie – Thunder Bay
Winnipeg – Regina – Vancouver – Richmond – Vancouver
Edmonton – Calgary – Kamloops – Vernon – Calgary – Edmonton
Toronto – Winnipeg – Sudbury – New Liskeard – Minden

By now Goddo was at level three as far as delusions of grandeur were considered.

Level 1   Hiring a guy for slave wages to help lug in and set up stage gear.

Level 2   Having more road crew on the payroll than actual guys on stage.

Level 3   Travel mostly by plane while crew travels by van, car and transport truck.

Young Russell had a grampa named Vic who owned a giant semi-transport truck. This was the kind of CB-equipped vehicle made for long distance hauling and scaring the crap out of fellow motorists, because these guys were the kings of the road and would squash you as soon as look at you if the wrong road etiquette was breached in their right of way. I found it an interesting new way to travel and Vic certainly had a way with a story, so high as I kite on Mandrax I bounced along with him and Uncle Mike in the cab for a change of pace.

The first couple of gigs on this summer tour had been so-so efforts on our part, and little things like headlining The Concert Hall in Toronto or the Hell's Angel trying to feed us speed off of his knife blade during our set were all getting boring. Lovely though the biker was, we needed fresh areas of possibility to explore.

Just two days into the tour and Doug had been found unconscious on his hotel room floor, the roadies had been questioned for grand larceny by the Mounties, and Renata was developing a nasty habit of tracking me down and ruining my day by telephone, something she has kept up to the present day, as a gentle reminder of our early dedication to each other.

So far I had travelled by jet, bus, train, and prop plane, and now I was making out like a peach pit in a blender as we roared across northern Ontario, in search of fun and profit.

Profit?

There was no profit. The gigs were bigger and the crowds were bigger but the biggest thing of all was our egos, which were demanding a steady stream of better ground transportation, more crew, more equipment, better hotels, and on and on until every last cent was sucked up and out of reach. Our whole reason for being was like some silly frat house contest to see who could drink, smoke and ingest any and all potentially hazardous substances, and the last man alive would win.

Feel like you're going to be sick on that bumpy prop plane?

Easy, just book the row directly behind one of the lads so that when you do throw up at least you're contributing to the spirit of fun. It does not take long to find the tour groove, which consists of never sleeping, always being out of it, and not eating anything remotely associated with nutrition. Soon your very guts develop calluses and you are now ready to entertain the paying customers.

In Winnipeg, Renata flew in to join me for a few days so I did something which I'd never done before or since. As I have a rather loose reputation with the good ladies of The Peg, I decided it best that the crew and Gino and Doug will stay in one hotel, and Renata and I will book into another hotel, under assumed names, to avoid any embarrassing reunions. This worked out splendidly until we took the limo over to pick up the boys, who were in the middle of about a dozen of Manitoba's loveliest.

"Now I know why we're booked into another hotel," said Renata as I became one with the back seat lest anyone recognize me.

I don't care who you are, even in the throes of new love never take a woman who is not a part of the tour on the road!

They will not get it!

We opened for Rush at the Pacific Coliseum with no sound check. I was pissed off enough to give a great show and we earned an encore, with Geddy watching our entire set from the side of the stage. The next night was more of the same in Edmonton at the arena where my finger was bleeding badly and the audience was eating it up.

In Calgary we were joined by Anvil and England's Girlschool at the Max Bell Arena. The Girlschoolers were real cute and went down well but it was "the bad boys" that the crowd had come to see and we had hit our stride in the tour. With the huge PA system screaming and more lighting than we've ever used, there was a sense of event that translated into merchandising revenue. With Renata now back in Toronto I became friendly with Girlschool's drummer, Denise, who was blessed with a beautiful ass which she insisted on shaking in time to the music while lying on my hotel room floor, listening to our new studio LP. Eventually she said goodnight and I passed out curious but innocent.

Dates in the interior of BC were pretty but not as well attended. The Payolas opened and were nice guys, but we had more fun back at the Vernon Lodge, where the parties were out of control and the damage level from the roadies warranted hotel and police intervention. I spent my after-show hours jumping from my balcony to the oversized arm chairs conveniently situated below my window.

"It's Stampede time, folks, so we're just getting' ya ready!" was how the Captain of our plane announced our arrival in Calgary. With a couple of whoops and hollers thrown in for good measure, he brought the aircraft in safely through the massive turbulence created by the high winds coming in off the Rockies.

Removing this buxom groupie from my room in Edmonton, she began crying that she came all this way for nothing. I told her, "Don't worry, the way you look, you won't get ten feet down the corridor before someone picks you up." As I closed my door, I watched her being dragged into Gino's room.

The next night as we made our way down to the hall, but with the overture already playing, we suddenly realized that Doug wasn't with us. Pounding on his hotel room door, we finally heard the sound of moaning inside as he opened up a crack and, sticking his unshaven mug out, drunkenly informed us that, "It's okay, I'll catch the next flight."

Taking Doug's cue and having a rare day off, I booked a Toronto-bound flight and limoed north where Renata was staying at a cottage, but within twenty-four hours I was back in Winnipeg, where original Guess Who bassist Jim Kale joined us for an encore of 'Shakin' All Over.' The after-show party got so out of control that I switched rooms and had my phone cut off.

We played two more arena dates and returned home for three whole off days before being sent out again.

Saskatoon – Red Deer – Lethbridge – Edmonton – Medicine Hat
Regina – Calgary – Red Deer – Calgary – Vernon – Penticton
Kamloops – Vernon – Nanaimo – Victoria – Vancouver
Winnipeg – Thunder Bay – Sudbury

It was great seeing my old pal, Barry Harvey (now Lightfoot's manager), at Toronto International.

"Hey man," I half-yelled by way of greeting, "where you off to?"

With his lantern jaw firmly in place, he looked at me and said, "I'm joining you on tour for the first couple of dates to make sure nobody gets killed."

I knew exactly what he was talking about.

Some months before I had taken it upon myself to jump on stage at the Gasworks to give the howling audience an encore. The only problem was that it was not my gig but a local pop quintet called Toronto. It seemed to me that they were taking their sweet time so I strapped on one of their guitars and nobody in the crowd seemed to mind. The group members were not amused and their bass player arrived on stage to tell me to knock it off and put the guitar down.

"Fuck you, man!" was my immediate response but, as no one was joining me, I put the guitar back and headed off to the dressing room to see what all the commotion was about.

Toronto the group were comprised of two girls and four guys, which must have been hell during certain times of the month, and it must have been that time as everyone proceeded to tear a strip off of yours truly as I stumbled into their inner sanctum.

"What's the big deal, Godovitz?"

"You got a lot of nerve, Godovitz!"

"That was my old lady's axe, man!"

Trying to focus on any one verbal assailant I managed to focus on guitarist Brian, the biggest guy in the group, whose girlfriend's guitar I had recently strapped on, and slurred, "OH, IS THAT WHAT THAT WAS?" thus cementing an instant rift and possible physical retribution.

Now I was waiting to catch a plane to Saskatoon where I would be spending a month touring with these same Toronto's.

Things were strained to begin with, my throat being rawer than my dick, but the powers that be decided that a tour of one-nighters, doing forty-minute opening slots for Toronto, would keep the cash cow mooing away.

My old pal through many a rock war, Bwuce, was now doing sound for the headliners and was told he couldn't help us at all.

My bass was completely out of tune as I took to the stage for our first show.

Sooooo....it was going to be like that was it?

It wasn't.

The Toronto audience was younger and far more innocent than any we had encountered and having us as the opening band was akin to The Who opening for Herman's Hermits. As we stunk our way through the first two shows and posed no obvious threat to the headliners things began to change. Within twenty-four hours I was in party mode with Sharon Alton, the beautiful guitarist and then- wife of guitarist/songwriter, Brian and we quickly buried the hatchet...or axe, if you prefer.

I celebrated our newfound camaraderie by crushing a banana and a ham sandwich between the sheets of an unsuspecting Doug Inglis's bed, before retiring for the night. I figured if Doug didn't notice it straight away, he could always have breakfast in bed the following morning.

The next night after the show I got into my new obsession, Bailey's Irish Cream, which was supplied as two forty-ounce bottles on our contract rider, and a further $100 worth at the hotel bar, which turned me into the kind of jovial buffoon who was then threatened by a still banana-smelling Doug, the club bouncers and some girl who wanted to punch me for insulting her on sight.

En route to Lethbridge, I decided to become ELVIS and spent the remainder of the day and that evening's performance in total ELVIS mode.

Speech, stage moves, makeshift cape = ELVIS!

Consuming tumblers of Bailey's straight up, I was starting to beef up to the point that my clothes appeared to be shrinking. The audience ate it up and we hit our groove for the rest of the tour.

As we returned to the stage I reached for my beautiful Gibson L6 and it was gone. Somebody had taken it right off the stage in the darkness preceding the encore. I got it back by a miracle, as the fool who stole it was bragging to his buddies in the washroom about the theft while one of the uniformed cops hired by the promoter was moving his bowels at that very moment. The officer finished his business and arrested the somewhat shocked perpetrator.

I got my guitar back.

The next night we took seven thousand people at the Edmonton Forum on a silly ride and sold twenty dozen tour shirts for our efforts. I traveled with our new driver, Rick Hoeg, who I dubbed Red in honour of his hair colour and the fact that I was still totally in ELVIS mode. I tracked down Roy Young at a local club and spent the night jamming with his great band.

Following an eight-hour drive to Medicine Hat we stunk the joint out and then it was directly back into the van and off to Regina before Toronto even hit the stage.

In Regina, the roadies and I amused ourselves by filling the bathtub in my room with dry ice and then letting it seep down the corridor until it resembled London fog, totally disrupting room service and the maids. After the show we repaired to the hotel lounge, which was conveniently situated beside the hotel pool. Fully clothed and carrying a champagne glass, I casually walked off the deep end and continued my journey underwater to the shallow end. The tour party were enjoying my little show, the lounge entertainers who had been there three weeks finally opened their eyes, and the desk clerk was freaking. As I made my way, soaking wet, to the elevator the night manager suddenly confronted me.

"ARE YOU A REGISTERED GUEST AT THIS HOTEL?!"

"Yes, madam, I am," I slurred, passing her the champagne glass now filled with pool water, "and I wish to use ALL of the facilities!" before falling into the open elevator.

The high points of the review in the local paper concerning our performance focused on our "contemptuous attitude" and made reference to our music as "Cro Magnon rock."

A fine review.

diary – thursday, september 29 – regina
...we play for only twenty minutes. Nobody is amused, including ourselves. Next we get down to some serious drinking. Gino and I start a hassle as I'm doing some interview and he's disrupting it. A very drunken Doug and I go fetch Annie (Holly Woods - Toronto vocalist) and head over to see Roy Young at Sahara Nights. We all become the epitome of R&R obnoxiousness. Inglis almost gets murdered by the bouncers, Gino gets attacked by some guy, I try to ride the roof of the van back to the hotel, and Inglis spits up peanuts all over me. Gino and Doug end up in a fight and Gino locks him out of their room. Doug kicks the door in. I go off to sleep.

With a night off in Calgary Doug and I sat in with blues legend Dutch Mason who proclaimed, "Not too bad for white boys." Our gig at The Corral the following evening was amazing and we pulled out all of the stops in front of six thousand maniacs, who interrupted our overture by letting off rockets at the back of the arena. The taped intro was stopped, I offered the assembled crowd a few well-chosen words of obscene welcome, and we thundered into our set. After the show, I managed a return visit to see Dutch but the rest of the tour party was refused entrance by a Lucifer's club manager who hated my guts from when Goddo last played there. A lovely fight broke out, with everyone being ejected while I blissfully bent strings on the bandstand until closing time.

Passing through the majestic Rockies en route to the British Columbia interior, I was constantly reminded by the sheer spectacle before my eyes of what a complete asshole I am.

To prove this I spent the following evening fully clothed in the hotel whirlpool and then practiced leaping from my balcony to Gino and Doug's instead of walking the ten feet and simply knocking. Uncle Mike carried me to my room where I proceeded to roll off the bed, and awaken the next morning in the space separating hotel wall from mattress.

Sharing a dressing room in Penticton, I was blissfully changing out of my soaking wet stage clothes when I heard the sound of female giggling.

The partition separating us from the female 'Toronto' members wasn't low enough to hide our lower appendages and the girls were laughing at my dick, which was shrivelling up in the cold and was now pathetically small by anyone's standards.

"You fuck people with that little thing, Godovitz?" Holly cackled as Sharon chuckled cruelly.

"Say what you will girls, but, just don't get it angry," was all I could think of by way of witty rejoinder, and I made a mental note to screw both of them before the tour ended.

It never happened.

After an overnight haul to the coast, during which I shared a bunk with Holly in their Winnebago, we ferried across to Nanaimo for a one-nighter in the same hall where Goddo played for the four-wheeler enthusiasts the year before. This show was completely different as it was sold out and people were actually paying attention. The only down-side was that I had fallen off a chair in my hotel room earlier in the day, trying to put a blanket over the window to keep the sun out, and had sprained my thumb which throbbed like hell during the entire set.

The next night we accepted a small bribe to jam with Doucette after our concert at a club in Victoria but Doug was drunk, Gino couldn't get a sound, and I was more concerned with inhaling blow in the Douce's dressing room. We jammed, we pocketed the spare change, and we stunk the joint out.

Vini Vidi Victoria.

Four thousand fans at the Pacific Coliseum (Maple Leaf Gardens west) in Vancouver. The highlight of the evening was the arrival of my old grade nine friend, Ted Salmon, who lived in a plastic-wrapped shack on Malahut Park Mountain and who resembled none other than TV's Grizzly Adams; he ate a huge piece of blue cheese...cheese...not cheesecake, backstage, from the deli tray, smearing it through his beard, and completely grossing out everyone in the process.

We went to see *Caligula* afterwards and the irony was not lost on our tour-fried brains. The exploits of the mad Roman Emperor were very reminiscent of our own. Gino in particular dug the lesbo scenes.

Arriving in Winnipeg on the festival of Succoth, we checked into our favourite downtown hotel and ate a bag of B.C. mushrooms, thus ensuring no sleep and massive mental problems for our first of two shows at The Playhouse Theatre. In spite of our worst show ever in Winnipeg, we were greeted with the banner headline "Goddo Steals Spotlight From Toronto!" in the *Free Press* the next morning, which I immediately assumed meant that someone in our crew had actually stolen a spotlight from the headliners. As Bruce was working for Toronto and not likely to even stoop that low himself, I read on to discover that we could play like utter crap in this city and still be the golden boys. Inspired by the review, we actually planned on making some sort of effort for the second evening's performance. On day two we really got into it and the evening ended with Bruce and I getting cream-pied on stage before wrapping up the Toronto part of the tour by making a map of Canada out of a mountain of cocaine and then proudly singing our national anthem, in between toots.

Sharing a flight with The National Ballet Company the next day, we were shocked and disgusted that it took only a drink or two to turn these poseur assholes into their own version of loutish rock stars. Doing stretching and tippy toe exercises in the aisle during the flight disrupted the bar service to the guys who really needed it most, which would of course be Doug, Gino, and myself, all three massively hung over and in need of hydration from our efforts of the previous evening.

Stepping off the plane in Toronto, clad in expanding jump suit and almost thirty pounds heavier from the massive intake of Irish Cream, I was Elvis.

I, ELVIS!

As Renata greeted me at the terminal the look on her face said it all but, to drive the awful truth home, she said by way of greeting, "I sent one guy out on tour and got two in return."

With the tour over we enjoyed three whole days off before being sent out yet again. There was a definite pattern developing here.

The Alice Cooper Mini-Tour

Through the absolute din on stage, I could hear what sounded likes boo's coming from the throats of seventeen thousand people in a packed Maple Leaf Gardens. Taking the stage to thunderous cheers from the hometown crowd, this unexpected chorus of negativity was somewhat confusing and, having just finished the always-popular 'Sweet Thing', we were into our new hit single with a tuxedo-clad Russell in place for 'Pretty Bad Boy.'

It should have been bedlam but not the kind we were now experiencing. Figuring 17,000 to 1 fair odds, I took the offensive and started screaming at the audience, which only succeeded in antagonizing them further. We still earned an encore but the booing continued and I left the stage in a fit of rage. The first person I saw, upon entering the dressing room, was my Mother who asked me why I was yelling at the crowd.

"Are you kidding me?" I started. "Didn't you hear them booing us?"

"They were booing because the PA system cut out," was her reply and all was suddenly clear. The monitor system was so loud on stage that we couldn't hear the front house speakers cut out and that's what got the crowd started. It would have been nice if one of the crew guys had informed me of this, but, as nobody had, I took the bull by the horns and gave the audience shit for nothing at all and, in the process of doing so, alienated everybody out there. Still, it was the Gardens and we had gone down great regardless of the technical problems.

Then it hit me: the previous evening we had started the tour in Sudbury at the arena and had earned an encore in front of the capacity crowd there, a shock to even Cooper's band, who said that opening acts never got called back.

Sabotage?

With no privacy in the crowded Gardens dressing room I stripped completely off and parted the visitors as I made for the showers.

My Mom was shocked and asked, "Don't you have any shame?"

"None at all," I said as I stepped into the adjacent locker room.

The next night, we played the Kitchener Auditorium, where the security force did its best to ruin anyone's chances of a good time by literally beating down any fan that stood up. Invited to join Cooper's band on the tour bus and not having seen him yet, I watched his show from side stage and then waited backstage as the final encore ended.

"You the guy riding back to the hotel on the bus?" asked this creepy-looking guy now by my side.

"Yeah, why?" I asked.

"Alice is coming off now and he doesn't like anyone looking at him."

Before I could argue the point that this pampered asshole has just been stared at for two hours by an arena full of drug casualties, I saw two beefy security guys, one on each elbow, carrying the stick-figured lead vocalist down the stairs and directly onto the bus.

"Okay, he's on the bus, let's go," said the flunky, like what I've just witnessed was the most normal thing in the world, and we are soon heading for the hotel in the extreme comforts of a fully-stocked tour bus.

At the hotel I stopped to talk to the drummer inside a side entrance and heard a sudden audible moan as Alice disembarked and, spotting a complete stranger - me - runs away.

"What the fuck's up with him?" I asked.

"Way too much blow, dude, he's totally paranoid," was the reply, and we booked in and headed for the bar.

The "Pretty Bad Boy" Russell Nakashima checks out Maple Leaf Gardens

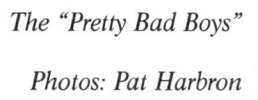

The "Pretty Bad Boys"

Photos: Pat Harbron

Inglis had now joined us and, as was his wont, proceeded to invite all and sundry to party in our room. With huge amounts of booze, pot and blow consumed, I helped in the redecorating of this particular Holiday Inn by moving furniture from various open rooms where it was set up in the corridors, and later by gluing peoples rock star boots to their night tables.

We finished in London with three guys giving me the finger from the front row. Thinking that we probably deserved it, owing to our seriously impaired condition, we blundered through our set and said our goodbyes to the Alice gang before limping back home. The following morning I flew to Montreal and then Ottawa for radio, print and television interviews for the new LP.

With the Pretty Bad Boys single firmly on the CHUM Chart we celebrated at Attic Records' president Al Mair's Christmas party. His beautiful home was immaculately decked out in festive decorations, and was full of the famous and nearly famous artists on his label and other record company hot shots. Everyone was clearly on their best behaviour including the Goddos, until Garwood Wallace from the punk-pop group Twitch' knocked over Al's Christmas tree while excitedly searching out a copy of Phil Spector's Festive Season LP. Most of the rockers in attendance split shortly afterwards, before ideas of topping old Garwood's accomplishment could be initiated.

We closed out 1981, headlining the Concert Hall with Oliver Heaviside, featuring the great Chris and GP Partland, and 'Frank Soda', a great guy who blows up television sets on his head. The sold-out club was packed to bursting and tempers were short as we had to stop the show three times to try and stop the fights. I weaved and bobbed through two hours on the sweat-soaked stage, and narrowly avoided being hit by two flying bottles hurled from the adoring crowd.

With an actual hit single charting across the land we put 1981 to bed and rocked into the New Year, intent on taking the group all the way in the next twelve months.

The Pretty Bad Boy photo shoot.
Photo: Pat Harbron

Goddo 1982

I began the year with a dream in which Morley Safer of *'60 Minutes'* interviewed a parrot that talked about a kid who enjoyed eating June bugs. I was not personally in the dream but I did see the kid eat a June bug and found it disgusting. Later I found myself on a train with Jagger and Bowie, who excused themselves to share a moment in the bathroom together, but didn't invite me to join them. At first I was pissed off as I was sure that they were snorting up some quality blow, but soon realize that perhaps they may be getting to know one another in more of a biblical sense. This caused me feelings of relief and bafflement.

> *diary – thursday, january 7 – toronto*
> *...and it was with much glee and club and nay to knocking on the pearly door and gnashing of teeth that he smiled in his drunkenness for his grape's sake. Bruised and used and spent though his body be he felt quill of plastic in hand and scribbled the scribe that would confuse even himself in saner days...?????*

Headlining a sold out show in the prestigious Great Hall of Hamilton Place got us off to a great start gig-wise in '82. It was a brutally cold day but we dutifully signed copies of our new LP and lots of old ones before settling into a lengthy sound check in this very plush soft seat theatre. Musicals and classical symphonies were more the order of the day in this venue but tonight the steel town fans would get a healthy dose of ear splitting power trio. The union boys were there as well and oh so precious about their jobs. Grabbing a mic stand I was soon confronted by an elderly "jobsworth" instructing me that any moving of mic stands would be done by him and only him, understood?

"Knock yourself out, man," I sneered, and kept him hopping for the better part of a half hour before the mic stand ended up exactly where it had been positioned in the first place.

The union rules also called for everyone, that means EVERYONE, to vacate the hall after sound check but wishing to make my peace with the theatre, I snuck back in and enjoyed the quiet in the completely empty room while thinking about how far we'd come. Five seconds later I was back in the dressing room, drinking.

With keyboards and a full sax section, we ripped through our show and the kids, by now fuelled by their own drink and drugs, began to get violent as chairs were slashed open and people were getting sick. The show was a great success and we were banned from Hamilton Place forever.

Baby Blues
– a Badfinger story

"You're not a homo, are you, Greg?"

The question was emanating from the lips of ex-Paul McCartney look-alike and only original Badfinger member Joey Molland, sitting across from me in the tiny club dressing room.

"Fuck no, man," I slurred, "I'm not even 2%," making a dairy reference that this Englishman would never get but causing ripples of laughter throughout the room as I said it.

What had happened was this...

Hearing that Badfinger was playing for two nights at the same clubs that we played meant that a) I could waltz in for free and, b) I could stumble out Apache-dance-style-drunk on free spirits.

With the band held up at the border due to work visa problems the first gig was cancelled, which saw the quick formation of a Badfinger/Beatles tribute band featuring the scheduled opening act and myself, that lurched on stage for rather sloppy versions of their respective hits.

The next night, the boys had made it and, fortified with various stimulants, we drove to the west end club to see them.

What I saw and heard was a bloody insult to the memory of Badfinger songwriter and suicide victim Pete Ham, as on stage was a vastly under-rehearsed bunch of hack bar musicians feebly trying to keep pace with Molland, who did a handful of the classic hits and far too many fifties cover songs.

Feeling no pain I immediately decided that something was missing and, realizing that that something was me, I stepped onto the stage, took the guitar from the surprised rhythm player and joined Molland at the mic for a spirited run at 'Slippin' and Slidin'.' The crowd was now going nuts and, sensing that the show had just taken a turn for the better, Molland just let me continue until the end of the set. Back in the dressing room and feeling the old adrenaline flowing I slipped directly into complete asshole mode and went for the jugular.

"This fuckin' band you got here sucks, man, it sounds like you rehearsed them on the plane."

I started as easy as I could so as not to offend. The back-up musicians, who should have used my head as a door opener, just mumbled amongst themselves while I continued to rant.

"Look, Joey, come back to my place and we'll talk about putting a great band together that can do justice to Pete's songs."

It was then that he asked me if I was a homo and, after pointing out my dairy preferences, I stumbled laughing out the door.

The next night we played at a high school where a teacher told me that she'd heard that we had recently cancelled a date because the school wouldn't sell "our" drugs to the students during the show. Staring a hole through her and fearing for the education system, I assured her that this was not the case but that it was actually bootleg booze and guns that we were interested in peddling through their front office, and left her to ponder that as we took the stage.

diary – thursday, january 21 – toronto
"Hello." *(croak, cough, splutter)*
"Gregory?" *(omigod-Lawyer Lusti!!)* "What are you up to?"
"I'm sleeping." *(nod, eyes closing)*
"Just thought I'd phone to congratulate you and the boys on the wonderful job Blue did on negotiating the deal with Erdman (Peter Erdman- Polydor-Montreal), and of course I don't want to tell Blue, for fear his head will get bigger, just what a wonderful job he really did."
"You did a good job too, man." *(cough, cough)*

Yes I did, I've got to tell you that their lawyer really didn't know what he was doi..."

What this refers to is that our management and lawyer managed to secure a cheque from our former label, Polydor, for $30,000.00 for royalties owing and a future royalty rate of $1.63 per record sold for our first three LP's. The down-side of the whole thing was that when I went down to the office after the cheque arrived I was somewhat taken aback to see Bill the Platinum YoYo in Blue's office who asked me to please close the door behind me. The nickname Platinum YoYo was bestowed on this guy by my old girlfriend after we witnessed this spoiled oaf twirling an actual yo yo made from real platinum at a party at Ritchie Yorke's one evening. The YoYo was reputed to be related to the guy who owned a local hockey rink and an investor in not only our booking agency but also my very existence, as it turned out.

The YoYo proceeded to point out that as it was all well and good that I was the "Peck's bad boy of Canadian rock," as he so quaintly put it, but if I didn't sign over the cheque I wouldn't work again in this country. The deal called for $3,000 to the lawyer, $4,500 to Goddo Music Inc. (at which point the Platinum YoYo laughed out loud, which made me want to punch him more) with an additional $1.00 per record sold being paid to our/his agency until the balance of $57,000 was recouped. As the cheque was made payable to Goddo Music Inc. it was necessary for me to sign it over, which I reluctantly agreed to.

We were making a small fortune working six days a week and I owed this asshole money?? To this day I'll never understand my reasoning for signing over the money, probably fear that the powers that be could actually stop me from performing, but I left the office with a commission-sized cheque for myself and the promise of the same for Doug and Gino.

I just got off the phone with Blue who reminded me that the $30,000 had been fronted to the group in the first place by these silent investors in order to buy off Gary Cape who owned the first two lps...there were a number of guys who thought that we had a chance to go all the way but didn't want the headaches of having to deal with me on a daily basis...as per the fact that we were not taking home much money on a weekly basis in spite of substantial grosses - somebody had to pay for the airline tickets, fancy hotels, restaurants, limousines, and other silliness *that we were racking up at an alarming rate as our collective delusions of grandeur intensified...my opinion of the platinum yoyo has not softened with the passing of time.*

The Dough Dough Birds

Needing a bit of a busman's holiday we performed as an opening act playing blues numbers and old rock standards like 'Gloria', with my old pal B.J. on harp as Dr. Claude Balls, Gino on bass (of all things) as Gyno Cologist, Doug as Chance Garfield, and me on guitar in the guise of Al LaMode. The Dough Dough Birds opened up for a motley crew of ex-Goddo roadies calling themselves The Coathangers. Both acts played to an enthusiastic but confused audience at Larry's Hideaway. We would appear once more in this fashion, opening a gig for Rick Derringer, but this time we would pencil on thin Frenchmen-style moustaches and wear berets. Not breaking character once, we ignored the cries for Goddo songs and played nothing but Chicago Blues for the confused patrons.

> *diary – tuesday, february 23 – toronto*
> *...Jonathan Gross (Toronto Sun writer) and film crew arrive to tape a TV interview. Seems we've been nominated for a Juno for "Most Promising New Group." Gross sat in my Andy Warhol plastic hand chair while I remained in bed with my Xmas lights on.*
>
> *"Well, after five albums, seven years together, and five million gigs, how does it feel to be to be nominated for most promising new group?" he asked, dripping sarcasm.*
>
> *"Well Jon, it could be worse, we could've been nominated for best new female vocalist!"*

Not So Cheap Holidays In The Sun

England – Egypt – Greece – Italy
March 7 to 28

London

Standing in front of Paul McCartney's office building at 1 Soho Square, London W1, with its almost spit-polished attention to detail, I suddenly realized that I looked completely the opposite, having just survived the all-night red-eye flight into Heathrow and the continental breakfast furnished by British Airways. Hung over, unshaven, unkempt, and with only an hour or two of sleep, I was the guy you did not want pushing your doorbell.

I was, however, the guy bearing limited edition prints of John and Paul and, upon holding them up through the window for inspection, I was soon standing in the reception area. Acting the proper rubber-necked tourist and obvious Beatles fan, I studied everything within eye shot, on the off-chance that the "cute" Beatle may later wish a game of "I Spy," and boldly requested a piece of MPL letterhead which I placed unfolded in my travelling pouch.

The carpets and drapes all appeared to be finely woven musical manuscripts in red, white and blue that were, in fact, original Lennon-McCartney compositions. Having my own 'She Loves You' wall mural at home, I was nonetheless quite impressed.

"Paul's not around, is he?" I asked innocently but the receptionist, well versed in dealing with fans and probably a little more on guard in the wake of Lennon's death, simply said that Paul was out of town on business and quickly excused herself to answer one of the never-ending phone calls coming in.

"No...Linda's over at George Martin's looking at some Italian tiles and Paul's at Abbey Road," she said to someone that she couldn't lie to and, red faced, gave me a little glance up to check my reaction.

"Don't worry," I said, passing her the prints, "we won't be bothering him," and with that, my new girlfriend and soon-to-be Mother of my children Renata and I cabbed over to the lovely Tara Hotel and booked into a very nice suite where I would amuse, befriend and piss off the English music press for the next few days.

...on Thursday December 7, 1989, I would realize a lifelong dream by meeting Paul and chatting with him in his dressing room for almost a half hour. My friend Olwyn, who had drawn the prints of John and Paul which I had delivered to his office as described above, had now prepared a beautiful portrait of Paul and Linda as a gift. Running into a ticket-less Doug Inglis outside of the Skydome, I told him that we were on our way to meet the great man and Doug said, "I'm with you."

After a bit of silliness, where Paul's personal assistant tried to pass off an autographed copy of Linda's veggie cookbook and Olwyn threatened to not turn over the original painting unless we got to see Paul, we were grudgingly ushered into the McCartneys' private dressing room. For some reason, seeing him standing right in front of me, I cooled out instantly upon realizing that he was such a huge part of my life that it was like seeing an old family member and not the world-famous Beatle. So accustomed was he at setting the pace during these awkward moments that we were soon chatting away on a wide variety of topics like old friends. Taking the proffered picture of him holding up his old Hofner bass at ear level, he took the pen out of my hand and slipped easily into cute-one mode by offering, "Oh, that's an old picture of me tuning me bass." Being a cute bass player meself I knew exactly what he was doing in the photo and let his remark pass.

As I began to say something I was somewhat startled that my program, which I had found on the floor outside their dressing room, was now torn from my hands by a rather aggressive Linda McCartney, who was now scrawling an unsolicited autograph and I couldn't stop myself as I pointed out, "Hey! you're tearing the page!" which sort of freaked her out as she shot me a dirty look and handed back the program. Doug was having his own problems.

"What's your name then?" Paul asked as he prepared to sign Doug's picture.

"drumph," was how I heard it, a low inaudible throat-squeeezing sproink.

Paul looked at me quizzically and then back to Doug, caught in a moment of Sahara Desert-like dry-throated panic.

"Excuse me?" said Paul.

"drumph," Doug repeated.

"His name's Doug," I offered upon realizing that Doug was so freaked out that he was having trouble with his own name.

"Thanks, Greg," said a smiling Paul McCartney as he signed the picture.

I couldn't help but notice that the militant vegetarians were both staring at my hand-painted leather shoes.

"What are those made of?" asked Mrs. Like I've Never Seen A Picture Of You In A Fur Coat Before McCartney.

"Plastic!" I shot back, probably further pissing her off, but she had now turned her attention to Olwyn's vest which looked suspiciously like...LEATHER!

Much small talk ensued with only one Beatles question being asked, a good one too that Paul said, "It's interesting that you brought that up as...," and Linda hovering around with gentle reminders to the girls of "not too tightly there, sweetheart," whenever one of the gals present tried to hug her husband.

Shifting from foot to foot Paul finally said that perhaps they should change as they were keeping a few people waiting, as the roar from the fifty thousand people out in the stadium made its way to us through the thick concrete walls. A quick photograph to capture the moment and off we went on a cloud.

When the house lights went up Paul saw Olwyn and I sitting third row directly in front of him and, smiling broadly, gave us a personal thumbs up. Looking to my left at Olwyn, I managed a "He knows I exist," before crying like a schoolgirl.

After much rum and coke celebrating in The Hard Rock Cafe after the concert, we pulled out onto Yonge Street where the police had set up a drunk drivers spot check, or R.I.D.E. program as we call them. As I pulled down my window the young girl officer asked me where I was coming from, while trying for a nose full of booze breath.

I was on my way to jail.

I needed a quick diversion.

Grabbing my autographs I fumbled, "WE JUST MET PAUL AND LINDA McCARTNEY!"

Left to right: Karen Hepburn, Paul McCartney, Doug Inglis, Linda McCartney, Olwyn Fleury, Heather Hepburn and Greg Godovitz backstage at Toronto's Skydome, 1989. Photo: Karen Hepburn

The cop, now totally freaked and out of control of a sure bust, yelled to her fellow officers that her car had people in it that just met the McCartneys and soon our vehicle was surrounded by curious cops with questions not about my alcohol consumption but about the McCartneys. We were soon on our way.

...I make light of this story but I was deeply saddened when Linda passed away, feeling great sorrow for Paul...

Meanwhile, back in London...the next day I sat in the living room-section of the suite doing interviews with writers for Kerrang!, Melody Maker, White Lightning and, from Sounds, an old friend, Paul Suter. Paul's brother had made life somewhat uncomfortable for me upon arriving at Heathrow the day before, with much talk about searching me for drugs, before confessing to me who he was. Drinking record company champagne and eating very spicy Indian curries I was in heaven, even though it would all be eventually charged back to me as recoupable expenses. After a trip to The Marquee, where we were treated to this great band with the unlikely name of 'Wipeout' that was a 1962 version of the Stones, we hopped into one of London's famous cabs for a late-night tour of all the sights that I'd never taken the time to see before, safe from the constant drizzle in the back of the immense vehicle.

The next morning we attempted one last shopping expedition up Kensington High Street but, with a transit strike in full bloom the city was gridlocked and, not wishing to miss our flight to Cairo, we booked out early and headed for the airport.

Cairo

The flight from London to Cairo was full of drunken Irishmen to a man, insistent on smoking cheap cigars. Almost coming to blows with the guy sitting beside me, he grudgingly stubbed his out as his four friends in the aisle directly ahead of us turned around and gave me a face full of stale smoke. With no place to run and many hours to spend cooped up together, I suggested a round of drinks and soon we were all arm in arm, blarping the songs of their forefathers whilst completely enveloped in a life-threatening cloud.

Bitter realty came as we disembarked the relative safety of our British Airways jet and were herded onto a bus straight out of the movie *Midnite*

Express, by bayonet-fixed soldiers with dead eyes who looked more like kids than the nation's defense. You could tell that you were some place different just by the smell in the air, which was not altogether unpleasant but had a heaviness about it that made it an almost tangible thing. The high-pitched keening of women in that Arabic-meets-Yoko-Ono shrieking-style, amidst the cacophony of the over crowded terminal, was such a surreal sound that I immediately began taping the ambient noise on my portable recorder. After clearing customs, we hired a cab and with only the mention of the word "Hilton" the driver tore off into the black night, one hand constantly on the horn, the other on the steering wheel, dodging cars and carts in the dense, late-night traffic.

The sight that greeted us from the balcony of our hotel the next morning was as strange as one could imagine, with scenes from ancient times interspersed with the technology of the modern world. Carts laden with produce and pulled by donkeys jockeyed for position among thousands of cars, buses and trucks, their horns screaming in the morning symphony that the locals call "Egyptian music." A solitary row boat made its way across the Nile while cruise ships, laden with tourists, set off for Luxor and the treasures of Tutankhamen, or the Aswan high dam project far to the south. Hiring a Mercedes and driver for the day, for less than the cost of a subway ride back home, my heart raced as the top of the great Pyramid of Cheops came into view on the Giza Plateau. A boyhood dream was about to be realized as I stepped out of the car and into the hot sun to survey one of the true wonders of civilization. Exchanging the Mercedes for a camel, horse and donkey we traveled into the Sahara, where I was invited to join our new guide, "Mo," on his mount, front or back.

I could tell that Mo was aptly named but declined his gracious offer, even though he told me that he had appeared in the film *Lawrence of Arabia*. The David Lean epic, starring Peter O'Toole, is my favourite movie of all time but, after doing a quick bit of math, I figured out that our guide hadn't even been born when this great movie had been made.

"Would you hold hands with me then as we ride?" offered Mo. "It is the custom."

When in Rome, I figured, and, mounted majestically on the Arabian Stallion our brave guide – all three hundred and fifty pounds of him – took my hand while I sought a comfortable position on my donkey below. All the while I could hear Renata giggling away as her camera captured young romance blossoming in the hot desert sun. In a country where it is illegal for men and women to hold hands in public, guys run around kissing each other like downtown Frisco.

Knowing that the rotund Mo would have a bit of trouble squeezing up the causeway leading to the burial chamber, we left him to abuse the beasts while we attempted the 90-degree ramp up into the pyramid. Finally entering the burial chamber and its oppressive heat, I leaned over the sarcophagus to study it closer, only to have a local teenager rear up and scream in my face.

At The Sphinx, two girls approached me from Montreal who had seen us play there during one of our early tours. When I remarked on the amount of beggars in this country they shook me off, saying that they had just returned from India where you couldn't walk down any street without being hassled. The first words I learned in Egypt were "mafeesh baksheesh," which, loosely translated, came out as "piss off camel breath, you'll be getting no money from this Yankee!"

"Pssst...tourist...want to see the mummy?" Momentarily distracted by the museum guard and bending over an empty sarcophagus, I was suddenly aware of a hand on my ass. As my girlfriend was being similarly molested not ten feet away by another guard, I looked up into the smiling face of my admirer and asked him to remove his hand before I beat the snot out of him. This happened in every room of the Cairo Museum we visited and it was always the same. Even though Renata had a wonderful ass we were, in fact, tied for the number of suitors vying for our attention. Perhaps it was the way my bum felt in my silk pajamas, but these boys just wouldn't leave me alone.

After an afternoon of shopping for perfumes and jewellery, we heard a giant whistle blow and suddenly found ourselves being swept along in a tidal wave of human beings getting off work. We were literally in no control of our own destination but, spying a horse and buggy, I shouted "Hilton" to the driver who began furiously whipping the people around us and cursing them in his native tongue while we scrambled aboard. Now in the relative safety of the carriage, he put the whip to his horse and off we went into the mostly human traffic, the driver continuing to beat anyone silly enough to get in his way. At one point a tank, crawling with armed soldiers, even stopped, giving the buggy right of way.

Back at the hotel we were confronted by more serious-looking soldiers, who wouldn't let us pass but insisted on searching our bags.

"WE'RE FUCKING REGISTERED GUESTS, ASSHOLE, MOVE

OUT OF MY WAY!" I screamed, having had enough of the locals for one day. At that moment Renata was being bodily searched by another soldier and, momentarily losing it, I turned my attention to him, pushing him in the chest and away from her. The freshly-cocked machine gun muzzle was now firmly under my chin as I was pushed up on my toes against the cool hotel wall.

"You can search her, man, just don't touch...understand?" I threatened anyway, and he could see my point as the gun was lowered and we were allowed to enter the hotel. A group of politicians had booked in and, this being terrorist country, they were not taking any chances.

The train station was packed with thousands of locals and tourists, pushing and shoving in a scene of virtual bedlam. After a few minutes, I figured out where to buy the tickets to Luxor and set out in a beeline across the carpeted floor, which was strangely empty considering the sheer volume of travelers, for the ticket window.

"ALLAH!!!!! ALLAAAAAHHHH!!!!!"

I was halfway across when it suddenly dawned on me that I was merrily walking across a sea of prayer mats...in my brand new "infidel" sneakers, no less. With over-zealous Muslims screaming the name of their one true God, closing in on me from every angle, I simply threw my arms up in the air, began yelling, "Stupid tourist! Stupid tourist!" and tippy-toed quickly off the holy ground, all the while giving my forehead a slap for good measure.

Now in front of the ticket window, we were being pushed and shoved in the general confusion of rush-hour commuters with absolutely no manners at all, all the while tightly gripping our handbags as the number of thieves within striking distance was uncountable. At that precise moment the Cavalry arrived. Two Scotsmen, pissed drunk and out of patience, saw our dilemma and pushed their way violently over to us.

"Ya cannae get near the counter with these fuckin' ignorant bastards pushin' ye about, cannae?" one of the lads said and, without waiting for an answer, he and his friend began throwing people left and right; all the while their fists were cocked in alarming readiness until the four of us were at the head of the line.

"I've had enough of these rag-headed bastards!" sneered Jimmy, squarely facing the screaming throng behind him while I purchased two first-class tickets to Luxor.

I say first class because that's what it said on the ticket; however, one had but to lift one's feet off the floor and you were back on a camel. The bumpy train hugged the fertile Nile, making whistle stops at many small villages as we headed south into Upper Egypt. Clad in silk pajamas, the locals took quite an interest whenever we disembarked to stretch our legs and, being a nation of folks in pajamas themselves, played touchy-feely with my travel apparel.

Curious as to where a heavy amount of smoke was emanating from, I casually poked my head into an open car at the back of our train, where the "economy" travelers were stuffed in with donkeys, camels and sheep, and were preparing food on little portable stoves in the boxcar.

Back in the relative cushiness of first class, we tucked into a dinner of exactly the same meal we had been served for lunch and would be served again as a snack later in the evening. Lovely though the chicken and rice was, I made a mental note to bring sandwiches the next time, and we settled in to Van Morrison on the headphones while consuming the sweet Stella beer as the panoramic view of life on the Nile rolled by.

Luxor

The Winter Palace Hotel was one of those old pink, sandblasted Colonial efforts where Howard Carter had stayed before excavating Tutankhamen's treasure. It exuded old European charm, and you half-expected ladies in feather boas and men in tails sporting handlebar moustaches to glide into the dining room with brandy snifters and crystal champagne glasses in hand. The courtyard gardens were magnificent in their presentation and vast array of lush plant life. Everywhere one went the gentle chirping of birds filled the air and, with so much ancient stone, the sound was amplified like a choir singing in a cathedral. The hotel's proximity to Luxor Temple and Karnak Temple, the largest and oldest place of worship in ancient Egypt, put us within walking distance of its thousands of huge columns and corridors of sphinxes. The two balconies in our antique-decorated suite afforded us a view of Luxor Temple from one side and a clear view across the Nile to The Temple of Hatshepsut on the other. You could smell the sand in the air and my favourite time of day was sitting on the balcony, sipping the horrid local wine and writing in my journal, as the sounds of evening prayers drifted across the courtyards from the tinny Mosque speakers.

Hiring a guide and three donkeys, we set out on a four-hour trip up and over the cliffs to the Valley of The Kings. At certain points we had nothing but a rock face to lean against and a sheer drop of one thousand feet on the other side, on a path less than two feet wide. The heat from the scorching midday sun beat us mercilessly as we stopped at an oasis for water and food. Descending the stairs into the tomb of Tutankhamen was one of the highlights of my life but further wonders awaited us in the tombs of Seti I and Ramses III and VI, with their still-vibrant reliefs and hieroglyphs painting a story of life long ago. That night we saw the Son et Lumiere show at the temple and it was while waiting for it to begin that two dime-sized balls of light traversed the entire horizon, soundlessly in tandem, in less than thirty seconds.

UFO's?

Arriving the next morning at the ferry docks we were dismayed to discover the heavily-laden boat just departed, people crammed on like sardines, some literally hanging on the side of the vessel as it lumbered its way across the river. Spying a second ferry I negotiated a fair price of two Egyptian pounds (about fifty cents), and soon we were overtaking the other ferry as the sole passengers on the immense boat, eager to spend another day in the tombs.

The strangest thing happened later in the day back at Karnak Temple, when a wizened old man approached us and, with only gestures, bade us follow him into an area marked "NO UNAUTHORIZED PERSONS BEYOND THIS POINT." Curious, we ducked under the barbed wire where we were soon staring at massive fertility reliefs. As the old man

Lawrence of Scarberia with his henchmen. Egypt 1982.

began strange incantations he had us hold hands while placing Renata's left hand on the Pharaoh's erection and my right hand on the pregnant belly of the Queen kneeling before him. I began taping his voice and after he had finished he walked away from us without asking for a handout, something I hadn't experienced since arriving there. Later that night I awoke after having orgasmed on top of my wide-awake girlfriend.

"Did I just do what I think I did?" I asked, now fully awake.

"Yeah," she purred, "you should stay asleep more often."

We didn't know it at the time but that somnambulistic affair was the beginning of our son Nile. I've never had those tapes translated, fearing that we might have spawned the evil one.

Never Shake Hands With a One Armed Arab

"I need to find a washroom," said Renata as we strolled the Luxor bazaar.

"Right over there," I offered helpfully.

"I don't see it, where?" she asked.

"Over there!" I said, pointing to my right.

"There's no washroom there!" she huffed, now a bit pissed off.

"Look there!" and finally she saw what I'd been trying to show her in the first place.

Squatting in the street, his robes pulled up over his knees, was a gentleman having a good old crap in broad daylight at the side of the road.

"There you go; ladies to the left," I said laughing.

With a couple of Americans in tow we ended up back at the hotel, drinking the crap local wine on our balcony. You could not get a decent imported wine, even at the best hotel, but as the local fermented sand was there I drank it until it seemed like a good idea to hang over the balcony railing, to the utter delight of our guests and the utter disgust of my girlfriend, who had to drag me back over before I slipped and killed myself.

Athens

I was sick as a dog, with a massive headache and stomach cramps from drinking all that shit wine, as we made our way through the paperwork needed to leave Egypt. The airport was crawling with soldiers and every two minutes someone wanted to see your papers. With shaking hands, I was the most suspicious-looking guy there and the forty-five minute flight from Luxor to Cairo was spent with my nose in the airsickness bag.

Switching to Austrian Airlines we enjoyed the great service and landed in Athens in late afternoon, where it was mild, sunny and far too urban for my tastes, considering where we had just come from.

Exploring the Athens Hilton, I stumbled across a lounge band rehearsing and ended up sitting in before cabbing down to the fabled cobblestone streets of the Plaka, where dinner was by candlelight, with live Greek music, and finally a decent bottle of wine. The lounge back at the hotel was crawling with chisel-featured Gucci types who looked on in shock as I turned up the volume for a dirty version of 'Gloria' with the band.

Hiring a car and driver, we toured the city in style, stopping at the Temple of Zeus and The Acropolis before visiting an 11th century Byzantine Church full of gold this and gold that, priceless artwork, and gorgeous hand carved antiques. Stopping by the sea for lunch, I told the waiter to bring me the largest lobster available. The sight of two busboys carrying what looked to be a small body on a stretcher, was in, fact a $500.00 giant lobster that the waiter thought I might want to see before I got the bill. Settling on a much cheaper, two pound effort instead, we were soon driving the coast road, under sparkling skies, overlooking the azure waters of the Mediterranean Sea, to the most southern point of Greece to visit the Temple Of Poseidon at Sounios. We should have called first, as Poseidon wasn't in, and, after a brief look around, made our way up the other coast and back to Athens.

The next morning I awoke to a feeling not unlike what I can imagine as having someone plunging a corkscrew in your guts, twisting it around a bit, and then extracting said guts while you're alive. The pain was so intense that I repaired to the marble-tiled bathroom, where I lay down and began smashing my head on the floor, in the hopes of knocking myself out. Succeeding only in awakening my travelling companion, she complained at the noise my head was making and grudgingly called up the house doctor. As I lay moaning in bed, this oily-skinned creep was openly flirting with my chick, both of them laughing away, not a care in the world, and I could've sworn that he winked at me, as the near lethal injection of Demerol sent me into noddy land.

It seems the strange food and wine in Egypt had given me an intestinal infection, so my corkscrew theory wasn't so far fetched after all was it?

And those were definitely UFO's we'd seen in Luxor!

While I slept, Renata took to the streets, ostensibly to buy me a birthday gift, but instead found herself being followed by the locals, some of who were actually leaving work to try and hustle her. She returned shortly thereafter without a gift, and proceeded to complain about her ruined shopping trip, all the annoying guys she'd met, and especially about her lavish room service dinner while I sipped a twenty-five dollar bowl of consommÈ soup with a weak tea chaser. I kept wondering what she'd look like with a corkscrew sticking out of her.

Rome

After a delightful breakfast of more weak tea, we boarded a giant 747 for a quick trip to Rome. It was my thirty-first birthday and, while I made repeated visits to whatever washroom was handy, I reflected on what a charmed life I'd led to date, instead of reading the local newspapers.

Our hotel suite overlooking the city was choclablock with wonderful antiques, musical prints and paintings, and four balconies, each with a spectacular view of the city. The high ceiling'd bedroom featured hand painted murals of Renaissance Italian life and had massive, full-length red velvet drapes that blocked out the sun.

After a quick walkabout, we got hopelessly lost but eventually found ourselves at Badington's Tea Rooms, beside The Spanish Steps, where we drank even more tea. I was becoming quite the tea expert but my guts were starting to come around a bit. My birthday dinner was in a lovely Ristorante, in the heart of Rome, where Renata started a fight, to ruin a perfectly lovely day. It was at that moment that LB's Christmas-past gift, of two pairs of boxing gloves, finally sunk in.

The next morning, being the first day of spring and a Sunday, we enjoyed a sumptuous breakfast including blood orange juice, which I'd never tried before, and then took a buggy ride over to St. Peter's Square, where the Pope was doing his thing.

THE POPE!

It was really exciting seeing God's messenger on Earth in person, although he was little more than a white spot leaning out a window, but everyone was singing and laughing and crossing themselves, regardless. As he didn't say one word in English I didn't have a clue what was going on, he could've been ordering take-out for all I knew but I went along with it and shared my roasted chestnuts with the buggy driver, who was himself overcome with good will as he charged me double the going rate for his services. Inside the church itself there were a number of dead Popes in glass cases and they were all green and extremely mouldy looking. Now I was hungry and we negotiated a deal with Signor Buggy Man, who took us to the Piazza Novana where we were soon enjoying pizza in a cup.

After the prerequisite Pantheon and Sistine Chapel visits, I realized another boyhood dream when we arrived at The Coliseum. In 1962, I had won a public speaking trophy for my speech on gladiatorial combat in ancient Rome, and now I was standing inside its historic architecture.

"Ladies and gentlemen, boys and girls, teachers and Mrs. Oakes (the principal), over two thousand years ago in the great marble Coliseum in Rome..."

As I stared off into space, I could see the ravenous wild beasts tearing apart the Christians, and I tried to imagine how my current girlfriend would look down there amongst them.

All You Need Is Lunch

"Waiter, there's a worm in the cheese you just put on my spaghetti."

"Ahhh," he said smiling while removing the creature with his fingers, "thassa good luck!"

I couldn't help but notice that a group of kids were staring at us as we lunched one afternoon by a lovely fountain in one of the city's quaint piazzas. Mentioning it to my charming lunch companion, she shrugged it off that I was being paranoid. Looking up from my now wormless food, there was a guy nervously standing next to our table.

"Excuse me, but are you Greg from Goddo?" he stammered. Blushing beet red, I said yes and he immediately began yelling to his friends to come over, as they were all huge fans, from Winnipeg, who then proceeded to snap pictures of my red face while I signed worms and stuff for them, before returning to my lunch.

I was not paranoid. I was, however, broke and, after much international kerfluffellry, Blue wired me an extra whack of holiday cash, which I bounced down the Spanish Steps to sign for at a local bank. Now flush with money once more, we maintained our suite in Rome and left our luggage there while we packed lightly and headed for the airport for a visit to Renata's Mother's home town.

Venice-Pordenone

I should have noticed that something was amiss when we boarded the plane, as we were issued seats well away from our fellow passengers and, at one point during the flight, this guy came out of nowhere and, instead of taking a seat a few rows away, sat directly beside me. Having experienced much homo activity in Egypt, I just put it down to him being interested and we ignored him for the duration of the flight, lost in animated conversation as we were. Imagine our complete surprise, then, to disembark last down the steps in the rear of the plane and straight into a whole pile of police, machine-gun-toting soldiers, and bloody dogs!

Someone thought we were drug smugglers!!!

Having left our luggage in Rome and travelling on Egyptian visas, we were instant suspects and were hustled straight away into an office where we were grilled and searched, then searched and grilled. The officers in charge were in no mood for my lip but, as I knew we were both clean, I gave it to them nonetheless.

I showed them!

No I didn't. They made us miss our connecting train and still tried to get me to give them copies of my records that I was carrying for Renata's relatives. Not a bloody chance.

After a quick look at Venice, we caught the next train north for a short visit to Pordenone. After an eight course dinner, prepared by Berto, the landlord and lover of Renata's Aunt Gianina, I was introduced to something called Grappa, which was like drinking liquid fire. Consuming nearly a full bottle, on top of glass after glass of potent homemade red wine, I awoke with my head throbbing and my stomach turning.

It was time to go visit the dead.

"I am the fucking dead," I reasoned, but they dragged me up to go look at flower-covered crypts and then off to visit people with no legs, and paralysed guys and stuff. I was in no condition for any of this.

The next day we returned to Venice and visited the St. Marcos Cathedral, which featured a wall made out of solid gold and encrusted with zillions of dollars worth of precious stones.

They charge you to look at it. In a kinder world, this one wall, melted down, would feed a starving nation for a year.

We flew back to Rome where we shopped 'til we dropped, buying leather shoes, boots, jackets, and handbags, ensuring that every last penny we had was spent. The next day we got the last two seats on an overbooked flight to Toronto and settled in for the twelve-hour trip home.

I haven't had a decent holiday since.

On April Fool's Day my recent travelling companion phoned to tell me she was with child, and she wasn't fooling!

Back at home we go into full rehearsal at The Roxy Theatre, the scene of our live album recording, in anticipation of our first U.S. tour.

First U.S. Tour
– April 7 to 22

Fort Erie – Detroit – Lynwood – Shreveport – New Orleans Baton Rouge – Mansura – Houston

"My dog killed three hundred and thirty-eight gooks in 'Nam, dude. I've got the papers to prove it!" Sitting at the U.S. border and waiting to clear Customs and, my current encounter with a U.S. citizen looked to be memorable.

"They'd be screamin' and screamin' while bein' torn apart!"

After a bit of confusion with the check from our previous evening's gig, which we managed to cash on the Canadian side, we were now waiting for Irvine, who would be joining us on sax and flute, and our new sound man, Ettore, who was a dead ringer for Rod Stewart. The truck carrying the crew had already cleared and was making its way to Detroit.

After more charming descriptions from this Serpico look-alike concerning his Doberman's eating habits, we were cleared into the United States of America and it was US vs THEM.

Arriving in the early morning hours, the seedy area of Detroit where Harpo's Concert Theatre was located looked more like a war zone than a business and residential area. Bars and steel doors were on every storefront and customer and vendor were separated by bulletproof glass. This area of Detroit also housed the densest black population in the city and the racial tension was palpable. As we searched for our hotel, I flashed back to a summer long ago when, accompanying my Dad to Detroit for a day, we found ourselves in the middle of the city's worst ever race riot. I went off on my own, in search of hippie delights in the Plum Street district and watched the glow from vandals' fires as sirens roared through the night. Walking in my seemingly crazy Canadian invincibility, I passed gangs of black youths who didn't pay any attention to me.

I was invisible. Just a crazy long hair out for a hot summer's night stroll. I shuddered to myself as I studied the view outside the tinted van's window.

Harpo's was a three-levelled, ex-movie house with an eight foot high stage and spectacular sound and lighting. Surprised that Uncle Mike and the crew were not already set up, we booked into a hotel where we were notified that the roadies had called.

From Toledo! What they were doing in Ohio is anybody's guess but one thing was certain, they were going to be late. Arriving at ten thirty, the gear was hastily assembled and we hit the stage to a bigger response than I would have believed possible. It only dawned on me later that, because of Detroit's close proximity to Windsor, we would naturally draw from the Canadian side. Our first gig in the U.S. was a great success. This was going to be easy, I thought, as we made our way into the van. Famous last words.

Lynwood, Illinois was a suburb of Chicago and three hundred miles from Detroit. Travelling was no problem because we were (a) used to driving hideous distances, (b) used to horrid weather conditions and (c), riding in Billy Reed's fully equipped van that he had won in a contest and that Blue had somehow managed to talk him out of. With the LB Show at the wheel, fuelled by a never ending supply of coffee and cigarettes, Gino, Doug, Irvine, and myself could read, get silly, drink, or sleep the long road trips away.

The first night at the Pointe East club saw us playing to another packed house and some enthusiastic drunks were reaching up and putting money on the stage. I was sort of pissed off at first until I bent over to pick up a bill, only to discover that it was a twenty. Quickly warming to this charming local custom, I pocketed the tribute and encouraged other like-minded individuals to continue. The club owners, totally knocked out by the show, offered us a second night, as an opening act for a well-liked local act that sounded like Styx. We played but it was an altogether different clientele from the previous night and not a penny in spare change made it onto the stage. We split right after the gig, laughing and scratching as LB pinned his eyes open for the twenty-odd hour drive to Louisiana. Fuelled with an assortment of beer, wine, pot, and sleeping pills we turned south and into the night.

The sensation of waking up in a moving vehicle, with someone's elbow on your face and foul smells permeating the air, amid a chorus of wheezing smoker's hack and snoring, is one of life's little treasures and the sole domain of hockey teams, carnival workers, and touring rock groups. Stumbling, bleary-eyed into the trucker's cafe in somewhere Missouri, we avoided the snide remarks, ate quickly, and were sound asleep, back in the van, within an hour, waiting for the eggs to work their gastric magic on our sleepy companions as the miles rolled on.

The next time I opened my eyes, we were ten miles from Memphis and that meant ELVIS! Now at that time, there was no such thing as a paid tour; that was scheduled for June, so we simply parked the van and made our way on foot through the famous music gates and up the hill to Graceland. We couldn't go in the house but a guard let us look around and, with birds chirping away in the trees, under a beautiful spring sky we snooped around the grounds and nobody seemed to mind. Just standing in front of the house gave me wonderful hope for the future: you could achieve great things in life if you take the right drugs and eat really bad food.

The Graceland Centre shopping plaza across the street was nothing but Elvis stuff, with a smattering of Pope items thrown in, just to be on the safe side. I pointed out to a clerk that the Vatican gift shop, just off the Sistine Chapel, featured only Pope and Jesus merchandise but nary an Elvis item was to be had. She simply looked at me like I was crazy.

Choosing wisely, I purchased an Elvis waving hand for the back window of the van, an Elvis coffee mug with Greg written on it, an Elvis Graceland pennant and a large Elvis pillow that would come in handy during the trip. I passed on the limited Pope Soap on a Rope but settled instead for a Tennessee Turd Bird, which was an actual piece of lacquered poo, supported by pipe cleaner legs with feathers and googly eyes. Laughing at the counter like a drooling imbecile, I said to the check out girl, "I can't believe you sell something like this!"

"And ah can't believe I jes' sold another one," she chirped in her Southern Belle voice dripping of chitlins or something or other as the cash register ate my $5.00 and went KERCHIIING!! Back in the van our travelling merchandise vendor, Scott, produced a deck of Elvis playing cards and we played on into the night, me eventually losing $60 to Inglis as we pulled into Shreveport, Louisiana at midnight. We had been on the road for twenty-four hours.

With the exception of Irvine repeatedly kicking my bed during the night, because of my roof-rattling snoring, I awoke to a gorgeous eighty-degree sunny day and all the "Y'alls" one could humanly handle.

"How y'all doin' this mornin'?"

"Y'all need more coffee heah?"

"Where y'all from?"

Southern fried hospitality and nice weather, a perfect combination.

Stuffed with spicy local fare, we followed our opening act, a folk singer, of all things, onto the small Steamboat Annie's stage and give the smallish crowd a blast of Toronto power trio. The results are instantaneous and gratifying as a large number of bountiful southern gals grab us coming off stage, with whispered promises of "layin" some sugar on ya, honey child." My final "y'all" of the night was from my neighbour back at the motel, who said, "Y'all realize it's three in the mornin'?" None of the rather large group of mostly female guests in the pool seemed to care.

By midday we were en route to New Orleans where we would open for Humble Pie.

Normally a scenic contemplator, I was now watching America roll by from the inside of my eyelids as the "ludes" kicked in. Driving through the heart of Bayou country we saw heartbreaking scenes of abject poverty, with shotgun shacks sharing space on vast stretches of swamp land as a solitary crop dusting bi-plane performed an aerial ballet, probably for the pilot's own amusement as he went about his work.

> *diary – wednesday, april 14 – New Orleans*
> *...arrived about 8p.m. in New Orleans. Got cleaned up and we all headed for Bourbon Street. It didn't take us long to find it. No cars on the street. Blocks and blocks of every kind of vice you could ask for. The sound of live jazz everywhere as well as the occasional rock, country, or blues band. Most of the good restaurants were shut down but there were take out places where you could get a shrimp kabob with rice and a beer. Strip joints everywhere. Gay bars with transvestites, transsexuals and bits of both. Tired looking hookers offering up the menu. Disneyland for adults.*

With someone sick in Humble Pie, we were cancelled, which meant a night off but this also threw a big hole into our budget. The owner at Ritchie's 3-D Club shot us $300, which we divvied up, and we headed down to the French Quarter once more. The street was rocking this night and we pushed our way through the crowds, feasting on as many sights and sounds as we could squeeze in. The street hawkers were offering up a wide variety of sin outside the strip clubs.

"Right this way gentlemen for gorgeous girls, girlish boys, girls who used to be boys, and a little bit of both!"

Drinking sweet Hurricanes, you could leave one club and stumble, drink in hand, into another, providing you purchased a drink there as well. The famous Preservation Jazz Hall Band, youngest band member in his sixties, was going through the motions with 'The Saints Go Marchin' In,' for a mostly younger college crowd.

Renata called to tell me that we lost our Juno Award to Saga. MacKenzie brother Rick Morainis tried to pick her up after the show and I gave her shit and swore I'd talk to him about if I ever saw him.

It was a short hop to Baton Rouge, where we were scheduled to perform in a huge barn called The Attic. The nervous promoter admitted that he hadn't actually advertised the show and that it was house policy, as the premises were not licensed, for the after-hours patrons to bring their own booze and the group would supply free beer.

Excuse me? The group will supply free beer?

The one thing that never ceases to amaze me about touring is the sheer volume of totally fucked up situations that are constantly being presented to you. You are hundreds, maybe thousands of miles from home, and some shady asswipe is saying that you've got to pay for the beer. With no proper contract at our disposal we negotiate a fee of $200 and he will spring for the suds.

"Oh yeah, your show is from three to five a.m.," he says smiling, before slithering off.

Excuse me?

With Inglis having bonded with a red necked Texas trucker over a bottle of Jack Daniels, we played like shit, got our money, argued like hell all the way back to the seedy motel, and passed out as the sun came up. Tomorrow would be better as we were opening for Uriah Heep in the middle of four cornfields.

Kyrles Encounter was a hall situated at a crossroads, literally in the middle of four farmer's fields. The nearest town of Mansura, Louisiana was right out of a Depression Era movie and featured a general store, a drug store, the Roy Theatre, and a few elongated bars. We arrived to find our crew and the Heep crew in heated conversation as to who was getting what, and who couldn't use this, that, and the other, and a pretty good Mexican stand off it was too. It got really silly when their road manager said that Doug would have to give up his customized drum riser to Heep's drummer and play on the floor.

Excuse me?

Returning to the gig later on we were pleasantly surprised to see that it was packed to the rafters. Hundreds of cars parked everywhere, like everyone for miles around had given up a night of sex with a favourite cousin, just to be there. It was the backwoods social event of the season!

Meanwhile, the Heep group members were now pissed off that there was no adequate dressing room facilities, this in spite of the fact that they were travelling the country in a fully equipped Silver Eagle Tour Bus. The Goddos were content to change into our stage frillies beside the van and play a short opening set of rockers to an appreciative crowd. I can't remember who used the drum riser. Doug can though and he will tell you about it now...

"I refused to give up the riser for Heep's drummer's use. Heep's roadies set up their drums, leaving three feet of stage depth for my drums. There wasn't even enough room for me to use the riser. The Goddo crew saved the day by supporting the front of the riser with empty road cases."

*Goddo –
Deep in the
Heart of Texas*

Not the most exciting story, but then, that is how drummers think. Next up was Texas.

Not being a big fan of strip clubs, I have to admit that at the time Caligula XXI was the yardstick. As advertised in Penthouse magazine, our resident voyeur and porno expert, Gino, suggested a little outing for band and crew alike. The plush interior faced a beautifully lit, all white stage that billowed dry ice while ten of the most beautiful girls that I've ever seen undulated in varying states of undress to a massive sound system. Even the normally cynical Uncle Mike was impressed. Closing the place down, we soon found ourselves in an Oriental cathouse, in an area the locals called "sin city" but we were too drunk and too broke to do any more than window-shop.

The next trauma for the happy minstrels was the news that our dates in San Antonio and Dallas had been cancelled. This meant our budget was now totally fucked and the first order of business was to leave the relative comfort of the local Holiday Inn for the absolute squalor of some crap motel, conveniently situated by Cardi's, which is where we would now be playing for the next three nights.

The first night went great and, as Texas was renowned for embracing Canadian hard rock bands like Moxy, Triumph, and Rush, we soon proved our little point and the free drinks started appearing at our feet. The next night we opened for sixties popsters The Grassroots, who featured one original member, probably the drummer. Pairing us with them was like having Motorhead open for The Archies and the older audience were soon slack-jawed as we turn their ears to mush.

After the show, this amazingly ugly chick offered me that most elusive of forbidden fruits and, being something of an explorer, not to mention three sheets to the wind, I invited her back to the hotel where I promptly snorted a bit, left the room to pee and spun through the shower curtain, knocking myself unconscious. Surviving the ordeal in true indestructible fashion, I was somewhat dismayed to discover, upon regaining consciousness, that my money, clothes, and prescription drugs were gone, along with the amazingly ugly chick who kindly left me to die in the bathtub. Rousing the long-suffering LB from a deep sleep, I remembered where the amazingly ugly chick's car blew a tire and we arrived at the service station just as she and my stuff were about to leave with the attendant.

The look of utter shock, surprise, and terror on her face at seeing me again, mixed with her amazing ugliness, was not a pretty sight and soon my stuff was back in the van. The next day I enjoyed an apple-sized lump on my head, where I'd smacked it against the wall and we stunk the club out with a thoroughly lacklustre performance.

Irvine and I booked two Air Canada seats home where the stewardesses were thrilled that I was on their flight and they celebrated by wearing Pretty Bad Boy buttons for the duration of our time together while I behaved like a complete drunken asshole. I had hit a new low.

After booking into a private hospital room for a series of poking, prodding, and generally unpleasant tests, but what was in reality a last ditch effort for some time off in the midst of this never ending insanity, we began a series of one nighters that took in twenty-one venues in thirty days. The hospital tests came back with the attending doctors all in agreement, my throat was fucked.

> *diary – monday, may 17 – oakville*
> *Got a call from Bwuce. He picked up 'Motorheads' new guitarist and says the guy wants to jam with us. The guy turns out to Brian Robertson formerly of Thin Lizzy. We pick him up at his hotel. The club is slow but we get our rocks off jamming. He bleeds all over my SG. Gino and Doug thought more of his playing than I did.*

Truth be told, I was jealous as fuck. He looked cool, he played cool, and he played us the greatest solo LP that I've ever heard. My only consolation was that he was going from Thin Lizzy to Motorhead.

TORONTO SUN – THURSDAY MAY 27
DON'T RUN OVER A ROCKSHOW

Keep your eyes open as you drive the QEW today. Rock group Goddo played Niagara Falls a night ago and managed to drive back to Toronto with the equipment truck tailgate open. Several amp racks, CO2 bottles and lights took a tumble on the turnpike. If you've found something strange on the Niagara Falls-Toronto run in recent hours, Westbury Sound and Lighting would be delighted to get it back.

Uncle Mike rarely made mistakes but, boy, when he did.

The Summer of '82
– a Mick Ronson story with a cameo by Bryan Adams

"You fucking Canadians are a load of wankers," blarped famed Bowie sideman Mick Ronson, trying to steady himself at the Rock and Roll Heaven bar. Things had gone steadily downhill for Mick since I had drifted into his orbit, fuelled by a nose full of generously proffered Frankie Venom backstage blow. Frankie and I had been quite content to quietly destroy our septums in the employee's dressing room until someone floated through with the information that a very good jam was starting up. Leaving Frankie to fend for himself I made for the stage at the far end of the club where new sensation Bryan Adams had just finished his set and was now joined by the aforementioned Ronson, and Toronto's Holly Woods for a bit of standard bad White Guy blues.

Figuring that the front line could use a little improvement looks-wise, I stepped on stage, uninvited, where a beefy arm was momentarily thrust in my direction until Adams recognized me, and shrugged off the security. Taking a guitar from lead guitarist Keith Scott I launched into a beautiful series of licks, playing blissfully away in the key of E while my new friends on stage struggled on in the key of A. The audience, who wouldn't know a G-major from a D-molished, ate it up and soon all the happy jammers were back at the schmooze bar enjoying owner Gareth Brown's generous hospitality. Drink in hand, I set out to make new friends and acquaintances and soon was congratulating Adams on a wonderful set and inviting him over some time to write a song or three. Keep in mind that I hadn't really seen his set, as I'd been powdering my nose with Venom in the "ladies" and had no idea what he did. I was just trying to be nice.

"I met you in Vancouver at Gary Taylor's last year, man, and you didn't want to know then," he began and I could see where this was heading.

"So let's start again, shall we," I blurfed. "You expect things to change now because you're headlining here? Piss off!"

Which he did.

Making my way to the bar where Ronson was holding court, I soon became painfully aware that the dear boy was lambasting my Home and Native Land and its constituents!

"...a load of wankers who can't fucking drink, as well," he blorped and to that I took exception.

"I can drink any fucking Limey under the table anytime," I snarbled and the gauntlet had been thrown.

Now good old Gareth, safe on the working side of his bar but knowing the makings of a good story when he sees one, fetched our weapons of choice, two forty-ounce bottles of Bacardi White Rum, which he now placed in front of the combatants. Over much verbal abuse and the hurling of great nastiness, we launched into the duel like men possessed. Drink after drink was consumed, some with ice, some with mix, some straight up, but under no circumstances directly out of the bottle, as we were both nothing if not perfect gentlemen.

After one particular vicious assault, concerning his status as an ex-rock star, this fool on the other side of the bar leaped in to Mick's defence, a clear breech of etiquette intended to destroy the carefully mapped out series of subtle innuendos and put downs that was my master plan.

"You know Godovitz," the fool began, "you really are a fucking assho...," which was all he managed to get out as my right hand snaked out, caught his windpipe, and thus rendering him quite silent, save for a little choking sound that was escaping his once overactive lips. Dragging him over the bar and up the stairs I kicked open the club door and threw him into the bright, fresh morning before locking him out and rejoining the festivities in the bar below.

As the level on the bottles decreased, so too did our rapier wit and soon the insults were more in the order of, "You're a cunt!"

"You're the fucking cunt mate!"

"You are."

"Prick Canadian!"

"The Queen's a...a...stupid!" and so on until the battle was over.

As we were both still standing, sort of, the drinking contest was declared a draw!

Taking our leave of Gareth's fine hospitality we loaded ourselves into a cab and made for that most obvious of destinations, my Mother's place! Pulling into the driveway, the cabby, who had been wary of picking us up in that condition in the first place, was now looking over his shoulder in absolute horror as the blonde rock god deposited a rather large amount of vomit on his back seat.

"But he is being sick in my car!" the East Indian noted and I nodded sagely and offered that it was okay, as I was almost positive that a good tip would be forthcoming from the rock star.

My Mom, usually happy to see me at strange hours, opened the side door where her obviously impaired third born was leaning against an equally drunk pal covered in vomit.

"Hi Mom, this is Mick from The Spiders from Mars!" I bloofed but was denied immediate access.

"I don't care what planet he's from, put him in the backyard," was my Mom's advice and soon we were the recipients of lavish plates of eggs and bacon whereupon Mick felt that he had had enough fun and promptly dropped face first into his plate. Pulling the unconscious guitarist's face off of the eggs by his hair I pushed him back into a semi comfy position on his chair and continued happily with my own breakfast.

...later back at my apartment Mick fished out his room key and tried to focus on the floor numbers, thinking he was back at his hotel. Leaving him on the couch I crashed out and was later informed by LB that he had seen the confused guitarist, obviously lost in darkest Scarberia trying in vain to catch a cab out in front of our building. A few years later, after joining Ian Hunter on stage at the same Rock and Roll Heaven, we were introduced and while trying to place my name suddenly said, "Oh yes, I've heard ALL about you from Mick Ronson."

Okay, the book is winding down so perhaps we should have a little recap at this point.
1. I borrowed Danny Cooper's wagon to transport my first bass and amp to rehearsal.
2. I drank too much, did a shitload of drugs, and screwed a LOT of women.
3. I was a complete asshole.

...sounds right...onwards...

TORONTO SUN–FRIDAY, JUNE 11/82
FASHION CRITICISM
Funny pants can be injurious to your health, as guitarist Gino Scarpelli has discovered. Scarpelli, of the local rock trio Goddo, was beaten up by a biker after a gig at the Roxy Theatre in Barrie. A hospital visit was required to patch cuts and bruises. The reason for the beating? The biker didn't like Gino's pants.

Personally, I always liked those brown leathers.

A Rare Eastern Swing
Fredericton – Moncton – Dartmouth

We never played the eastern provinces much with the Goddos so a fifteen-hundred-mile journey made perfect sense and as it was summer at least the weather would co-operate. Piling into the van we anaesthetized ourselves into a haze and counted miles as we headed east. Catching up to the roadies, we were surprised to see not one but two flat tires impeding their progress and stopped to make merry with them until order could be restored.

Travelling in the van, we had loads of comfort but the crew saw fit to travel four to a cab meant for three and all the discomfort that that entailed. There was much speculation that the junior roadie taking up the extra space was something of a boy toy for our light man but being liberal-minded individuals, we simply wished them well as our sound man's naked ass flashed by us on the highway.

The weather, of course, did not co-operate and the rain pounded us mercilessly as we remained relatively comatose in the van. Having seen enough horrific accidents to last a lifetime while travelling the length and breadth of this fine country, it was better to reduce your mind to mush, buckle up, and hope for the best.

After a brief stopover in Fredericton, New Brunswick, where we emerged from our foul smelling capsule for a light-hearted feast of lobsters and buckets of French wine, we pulled into Moncton, twenty-two hours after departing Toronto, none the worse for wear, but bereft of humour as we began searching out our lodgings. This would take an additional two hours.

"We passed the fucking place a mile back, you asshole!"

"Forget the contract accommodations and just get us a room LB, we're fucking tired man!"

"Let me out of here now or I'm going to fucking hit someone, man!" And so on.

Our first gig was in Moncton where we played a huge wooden dance hall called The Metro, which had about one hundred people, hiding at the back. We ended up getting a standing ovation at the end of the night but were not too sure if it was because they liked us, or because we were finished.

The highlight of our stay was the fact that our motel was right across the street from the world famous Magnetic Hill. This amazingly tacky optical illusion is one of the world's greatest tourist traps and people come here from all over the planet to experience the goofy sensation of your car rolling backwards up the hill. It doesn't really happen but everyone in your vehicle will swear that it does and the gift shop features not only Elvis and Pope stuff but bottles of Magnetic Hill water and Lobstermen with googly eyes made out of actual lobster bits.

My Lobsterman stands proudly beside my Tennessee Turd Bird.

Our next three nights were in Dartmouth where nobody had a clue who or what we were, with the exception of the opening act that insisted on playing 'Sweet Thing' every night, better than our original version. It was obvious that we were not the band for down east and, loaded up with crates of fresh lobster we flew the hell out of there.

On Tuesday, July 6, Canada lost another musical treasure when the beautiful and talented Jane Vassey lost her battle with Leukaemia. The Downchild Blues Band keyboardist was always quick to flash her gorgeous smile, never turned down a drink, and could play piano like there was no tomorrow. Along with my old Fludd partner Brian Pilling, this horrible disease had taken another shining star far too early. I just wanted to mention Jane because I saw her picture taped into my diary and it made me cry.

America vs. Goddo
— The Rematch July 15 to August 4

Detroit – Chicago – Memphis – Baton Rouge – Shreveport Austin – Houston – Leesville – Dallas – San Antonio

After a great gig at the old Coronet in Kitchener, where Irvine brought along a full horn section we piled into the van for the trip to the border. For once, with no lost roadies, our paperwork in order, and with few questions asked we were waved through into the U.S.A. to do rock and roll battle with the locals. The first two gigs in Detroit and Chicago were memorable only for the fact that we played so bloody loud that half of our audience was gone by mid set to avoid permanent ear damage.

The trouble started the next morning when Inglis informed me over breakfast that the crew was heading home unless they were paid that day. The band had just been given a paltry raise and someone had leaked this info to the roadies, who were now lining up, demanding similar attention. My immediate reaction was to tell them to piss off and cancel the tour, but after a call to Blue at the office, it was decided to send them the money and continue on. The roadies, in a rare collective memory loss, had of course completely forgotten about the equipment falling off the back of the truck incident, which the group had to write off. With order restored and the mutineers back in the rigging, we set our course sou'west and set sail for Memphis.

"You boys all want your cocks sucked?"

It seemed like an unusual thing to hear while filling up at a gas pump but the question did have merit and as it had come from a honey-dripped female voice and not the good old boy doing the actual filling, I decided to investigate. At first I couldn't spot the source of the enquiry but soon noticed a very white and very large set of smiling teeth pointed in my general direction from the back seat of the Caddie parked at the next pump. Knowing a local garden variety prostitute from the village when I see one, I leaned into one of the blackest faces I'd ever seen and said, "So what's on the menu sweet thang?"

Feeling in an expansive mood, I negotiated the "blow job for two" appetizer and then told good old Red, who was our driver on this tour, that I had a little treat for him. Arriving back at the hotel our date insisted that she take my arm through the lobby so as to appear more than casual acquaintances and not draw the ire of hotel security. Realizing how ridiculous this whole thing looked but always ready for a good bit of fun, all five-feet-seven of me and all seven-feet-five of her sashayed through the packed lobby like old high school chums.

She left not long afterwards, alone.

No, it was not a guy.

With no sleep, fairly drunk, and somewhat freshly drained of energy, Red and I piled into the van and headed over to Elvis's place. At four a.m., the gates were shut tight and the only traffic on the street was, us. Standing in front of the famed musical gates, we studied the beautiful mansion at the top of the drive, now open to the public.

"I wouldn't be standing too close to those gates if I were you boys."

It was the security guard.

"If one of Elvis' hillbilly cousins come back they're just as likely to run y'all over as look at cha."

Stepping away from the gates we decided to race back to the hotel, shower, and return to be first in line for Graceland Tour tickets. Figuring our three hour wait in line would have us on the first bus up the hill we were somewhat dismayed to discover that pre-arranged tour groups were in fact ahead of us and it would be Bus 16 that we would be on. With no sleep and having been up for over twenty-four hours, things began to get very strange very quickly. Elvis fans, possibly the fattest and ugliest people on the planet, love to share photos and stories of The King with total strangers and therefore, much of our wait was spent listening to these idiots natter on about how Elvis had improved their lives. They really like to pass around the old cheap photos as well.

"An' this here's the shrub bush out back of Graceland that Elvis passed every time he went out!" The guy saying this looked inbred.

"This here one is real interestin' as its tire marks on the road where Elvis tore out of the front gates one night, it's a personal favourite of mine so try not to bend it."

With a vacant smile on my lips I studied the proffered trophies and wondered how many of these people had actually slept with close relatives. After hours of waiting, we were loaded onto Bus 16 and were soon standing in front of the main doors to Elvis' place. Here we were warned by a sweet young southern belle tour guide about not touching things, not to wander off, and above all, NO PICTURES!

"Blah blah blah blah Elvis blah blah blah blah Elvis blah blah blah and of course when Lisa Marie reaches the age of twenty five she will inherit the entire estate. Any questions? Yes, that man over there!" Before I could finish my question, which concerned the fact that having recently returned from Egypt where the pigments were still pretty fresh after five thousand years, why couldn't we shoot pictures inside and...

"Excuse me sir, are we gonna have a problem here with you concernin' our very simple rule regardin' no picha takin'?" The hairy knuckled hand on my shoulder did not belong to any of the Memphis Mafia but you instantly knew that this line of questioning was not to be pursued so I quickly accepted the true coward's stance and backed down.

"Now if y'all will follow me...," and soon we were being whisked through this room and that and truth be told, it was not as tacky as one might imagine. The Jungle Room was sort of tacky and the Billiard Room looked like a giant can of Budweiser so I take it back, the place was wonderfully tacky. Standing in amongst the faithful I waited for my moment.

"...and of course blah blah blah....Lisa blah blah...inherit the entire estate. Any questions? Yes, that man over there." Choosing my words carefully, and making sure that the hairy knuckled guy wasn't still around I said, "How soon after Lisa Marie moves in do you think the interior decorators will be called in?"

A gentle ripple of nervous laughter, then dead silence.

"Ah believe that Lisa Marie will adhere to her late Father's wishes, and maintain Graceland as it is in memory of The King of Rock and Roll, Elvis Presley. Now, if y'all will follow me."

So, this was how it was going to be then, was it?

I would have to double my efforts if I was to chink the armour of this miss smarty-pants tour guide.

"And this outfit here was the last stage costume worn by Elvis at the final concert that he gave and blah blah.... Lisa Marie blah blah...blah blah questions? Blah blah over there."

"Yeah, that suit seems a bit small, the photographs I saw of the funeral clearly showed a number of big lads straining under the weight of The King's remains. Exactly how large was The King at the time of his demise?" Not even a snigger.

Eyeing me through two slits that said, "Mr. I would just love to scratch your heart out," the tour guide gritted her teeth and said in an ominous voice, "Contrary to popular opinion Elvis was not overweight at the time of his death."

Sure, and Yoko's going into modelling.

Like lambs to slaughter we followed her to the trophy room, where I asked to see the Narc badge that Nixon had bestowed on the very gone King and soon after we were ushered out of the house. For five bucks a very entertaining afternoon indeed.

Visiting the Graceland Centre souvenir emporium, I carefully studied the vast array of items to be had before purchasing a frosted Elvis wine glass, a guitar shaped Elvis brush, a pair of orange Elvis socks, and a plastic dinner plate with a photo of a seriously greasy Elvis smiling back at you. Not long afterwards I would place this very same plate on a stove element, which was then accidentally turned on high. The ensuing melted plastic and subsequent clean up made for an interesting afternoon and the introduction of swear words hitherto unknown to the English language. In the heartland of blues, country, and all things Elvis, we died the death at the gig.

Visiting Sun Studios the following day and, with nobody else around, I convinced the teenager on duty to give me an acoustic tile from one of the walls. After removing it myself, I danced up Union Avenue with this wonderful treasure that Elvis, Jerry Lee Lewis, Johnny Cash, Carl Perkins and countless others had bounced their immortal music off.

One further bit of business was required before we split for Baton Rouge and that was the purchase of two cases of Always Elvis and Forever Elvis wine at the local liquor store. Twenty-four bottles of dry Italian wine with a totally cheesy poem on the back, courtesy of The Colonel were now acting as a footstool in the back of the van. I never did get to sample either wine as we left them in the van during the day and figured that the intense southern heat wave would have reduced an already questionable vintage to pure vinegar. Instead, I gave every bottle away as gifts upon our return.

What I loved best was a quote from a company spokesman for the wine company, who, when it was pointed out that Elvis did not drink wine, simply said, "Yes, but we feel if Elvis had liked wine, this is the one he would have chosen." You can't argue with logic like that.

With a night off, we took a slow and scenic cruise under a scorching summer sun and unbelievable humidity, to Baton Rouge. Small clusters of shotgun shacks, with huge families of blacks, dotted the Mississippi River banks, once again driving home the abject poverty of the region. The photographs would have been amazing, had we taken any, but, for once, we agreed that these folks should be left with at least their dignity, as we headed further south. Stopping in Canton, Miss., we were given the once over by two redneck sheriffs, toting really big guns, who looked curious but let us eat and quickly leave town. Clearing The Tallahachee Bridge we viewed the majestic Mississippi river as the sun set and arrived in Baton Rouge after ten. The boys booked in to the hotel and Red and I split for Bourbon Street in New Orleans.

Loaded up with drinks, we gorged ourselves on the spicy local fare before leaving the relative safety of the main tourist area to explore The French Quarter. Spotting a red light over a doorway down a very dark alley, we decided that the outcome may be worth the risk and knocked on the heavy wooden door. Behind a set of bars, a small window slid open and the doorman checked us out before letting us in. The bar was packed, and with drinks in hand, I casually asked the lady bartender what was going on upstairs.

"Why don't y'all go up and have a look fer yerselves," she cooed and up the stairs we went.

The sound in the room was deafening as the whole place was engulfed in a swirl of smoke, flashing lights and very hip dance grooves. The crowd was packed in like sardines and the dance floor was awash in bumping and grinding pleasure seekers. Adjusting my eyes to this surreal scene, I pulled Red over and yelled into his ear, "Hey Redman, you notice anything unusual about this place?"

Shaking his head negative, I leaned in closer and said, "It's all guys in here, it's a gay leather bar."

The Redman, no slouch at sizing things up himself, said, "What'll we do?"

"LET'S DANCE!" I yelled as we pushed our way onto the dance floor to cut the funk before heading out. The gig the next night was great. En route to Shreveport, Louisiana we passed a working cotton plantation with a perfect picture postcard southern antebellum mansion. Slaves were now replaced by combines and it was a good thing too as the heat was oppressive and the air conditioning in the van was useless, even at full blast. The gig was a disaster, as our excessive volume had people rushing for the exits and the club owner was fit to be tied.

Fetching a cassette from the van that had been left on the dashboard all day I was surprised to see that it had melted. The weather wasn't the only thing getting hotter, as there were dark murmurs that LB was leaving at the end of the tour. Things had been strained between us since he had vacated our apartment, when Renata came into the picture, and the fact that he was watching a total maniac self-destruct on a daily basis was now manifesting itself in mutiny. At sound check the next day, where we placed Gino's cabinets in the dressing room to cut the stage volume down, LB told me that the thought of leaving had crossed his mind but that I had nothing to worry about so that was that. With a dozen or more "Kamikazes" ingested, I went blubbering after the gig to Gino and Doug's room, in just a t-shirt, and demanded the truth as to their loyalty.

Pathetic, really pathetic. They assured me that it was one for all, etc., and talked me out of going to LB's room to get the gig money. Imagine my surprise the next morning when Renata called to tell me that LB was back in Toronto.

"You mean the same LB Show, my road manager, who is occupying the room next to mine?" I asked and raced next door to find an envelope with my name on it containing two hundred dollars, some gig sheets, a couple of contracts, and a Dear Greg letter. I had been had.

Returning to the phone I counted to ten, composed myself as best I could and then screamed down the line at Renata, "YOU TELL THAT MOTHERFUCKER HE'S A DEAD MAN WHEN I GET HOME!"

Seven guys with two hundred dollars in expense money, a couple of thousand miles from home. Not good.

After a quick strategy meeting, we decided to continue on and head off for Texas. At the Texas border we spotted a twister on the horizon and drove into the worst thunderstorm I had ever seen. The storm brewing in my mind was much worse.

Cardi's in Austin was part of a chain of huge nightclubs and the joint was packed, hot, and ready to rock when we hit the stage. The Texans ate up our "boogie," as they called it there, and everything was going great until after the set, when I saw a drunk stumbling across the stage perilously close to our guitars.

"Hey man, get off the fucking stage," I yelled up.

"FUCK YOU," he yelled back.

"FUCK ME?! OUTSIDE NOW, ASSHOLE!" and with that, I soon found myself out in the parking lot with my latest dancing partner.

The problem with wearing glasses is that they have a tendency to fly off when someone's fist connects with your map and finding them after the battle can be quite a chore. With this in mind, I removed my eyesight and handed my spectacles to our soundman Ettore, the Rod Stewart look-alike I've mentioned before. Ettore had graciously followed me outside to act as my gentleman's second, and also to make sure that I didn't get killed.

Trying to focus on the blur in front of me, I was somewhat surprised to hear Ettore announce, "Hey man, no fair!" at my nemesis.

"What's not fair, Ettore?" I asked.

"He's pulled out a big knife boss," he said, very matter-of-factly.

"A BIG KNIFE?!"

That wasn't very nice.

"KILL HIM!" I screamed and Ettore quickly disarmed the brute as the club's huge black bouncer came out and threw the guy to the ground, then stomped on him a bit. I actually felt kind of sorry for the guy but he crawled off, only a bit the worse for wear, and threatened to come back with a gun to kill me the next night.

Things weren't going very well on this tour.

Back at the hotel there were two chubby groupies and two skinny guys waiting for me. The chubby chicks turned out to be nutritionists and I guess I looked too unhealthy to eat so they split, leaving me with the two skinny guys who turn out to be a mental institution outpatient and a just paroled from penitentiary after serving twenty five years for manslaughter ex-con.

You really gotta love America.

After a couple of beers down by the pool with the lads, where we bonded over sordid tales of male rape and making booze out of toilet water, hotel security took exception to my visitors and soon fists were flying and handcuffs were required fashion accessories as my new fans were carted off by the police.

Just another day in hell.

The bouncers were on alert the next night for the possible return of my gun-toting enemy but he never showed and we left for Houston the next day.

The only thing that springs to mind regarding Houston was that it was one hundred and seven degrees Fahrenheit and we went over great. Oh yeah, we narrowly avoided getting killed as we entered the city limits when the cable between one truck pulling another truck snapped on the freeway, right in front of us, sending both vehicles spinning out of control. Red was at the wheel and, doing his best Indy 500 impression, managed to avoid the trucks as traffic piled up behind us.

Leesville, Louisiana was a perfect double for Mayberry, of Andy Griffiths fame, but instead of Barneys and Floyds and Gomers walking around, the place was crawling with off-duty soldiers in AC/DC t-shirts and nothing but Vietnamese women they had brought back with them.

A "place with a secret," as our lighting guy Tracy pointed out.

Fort Polk was the local army base and it was here that these music-loving types were taught the fine art of killing people while driving tanks. By eight o'clock the main street was more like Bourbon Street at Mardis Gras, with music blasting out from a dozen live entertainment venues and hordes of people packing the clubs. The soldiers all favoured these strange baseball caps that had feathers sticking out of them, giving the impression of their having long hair. Civilians and vicious-looking outlaw bikers on ultra loud Harleys drank openly in the street. We shared dressing room space with two hundred bottles of fine Bourbon and by the third song my clothes were sticking to my body, completely drenched in sweat as we rocked loudly. The strangest thing was meeting some soldiers who had all of our records and joining them in an abandoned building to smoke a joint. Gino was almost busted by the ever-present military police that prowled the streets in jeeps.

With the next night off, we split for Dallas and, discovering our old friend Pat Travers playing in town with The Nuge, the boys go to the concert and later to a local club where they were ejected after Tracy knocked out Ted's road manager. While all of this was going down, Gino, still in no mood for The Nuge, after his less than thrilling encounter with him at the outdoor festival the year before, joined me for dinner, where we cannot get a drink, as it's Sunday and cannot get a cab back to the hotel, as not one company will send one for us.

Goddo at Graceland: The "Arthur" as Elvis with the Hogtown Mafia.

Left to right: Doug Inglis, Gino Scarpelli, Greg Godovitz

The gig was cancelled in Dallas due to a schedule snafu but we got some money from the club owner and, after a side trip to Dealey Plaza, where I drove through the infamous Kennedy assassination parade route naked, while waving out of the full-windowed side door, we head for San Antonio and The Rock Saloon.

You just know that your reputation precedes you when you are told to turn down before you actually sound check but that's the word we got upon arriving at the huge San Antonio club.

Realizing another childhood fantasy, we visited The Alamo, which was situated in the very heart of the city, and later, limped our way through our set back at the club, to a handful of people.

After a great last gig in The Lone Star state we flew to Dallas for a connection to Toronto and spent the journey home drunkenly arguing about money.

The bloom was definitely off the rose.

diary – thursday, august 5 – toronto
...got wound up enough to go see LB Show (he had moved into an apartment in the same building after Renata and her growing belly had moved in with me).
Knock knock.
No answer.
Knock knock.
The girlfriend: "Hi, how'd it go?"
Me: "Where's LB?"
The girlfriend: "He's not here, he's at Tony's."
Me: "East?"
The girlfriend: "Yes, oh, did you get new moccies?"
Me: "What?"
The girlfriend: "Moccasins."
Me: "Tell him I'm on my way to see him."

LB managed to avoid me for the better part of a year after that. By the time I saw him again the group was finished and it wasn't worth the hassle to drag up the past. We're still friends today.

The truth of the matter was that we just weren't having any fun anymore. Playing six nights a week and not taking home a reasonable amount of money was just plain frustrating. I now had a very pregnant girlfriend to support, I wasn't getting any better as far as curbing my alcohol and drug intake, and Gino and Doug and I were constantly at each other's throats. At one point, Gino's old lady poured her drink on my head and slapped me, effectively ending a proposed trip up north to play. I couldn't stand her and Gino and she both knew it. It was like we had gone as far as we could go and the engine was out of steam. Even a week in the studio produced mixed results as this friend of Blue's came in to co-produce the sessions, to my great annoyance. The roadies were constantly threatening to quit and were always seeking raises in salary. At one point the three principal parties in Goddo Music Inc., Doug, Gino, and myself, along with Blue, met at our bank to discuss business with our bank manager and, in particular, a line of credit. The meeting went something like this:

Bank Manager: "Mr. Godovitz, you're the president of Goddo Music Inc., what are your assets?"
Me: "I have about twenty different guitars."
Bank Manager: "I'm sorry but you have nothing that this establishment would consider as collateral. Mr. Scarpelli, you're the vice president of Goddo Music Inc., what are your assets if any?"
Gino: "I have some guitars and a couple..."
Bank Manager: "I'm sorry Mr. Scarpelli but you also have nothing that we would consider equitable collateral. Mr. Inglis, you are just a shareholder in the company, what, if any, are your assets?"
Doug: (clearing his throat) "Well, um, er...in Ottawa I own a bus company, a strip mall, a couple of different properties..."
Me: "You have what?"
Doug: "...an apartment blah blah blah..."
Me: "YOU'VE GOT WHAT!?"

It seems old Dougy Wug had come into some money.

I was all of a sudden aware that my head was turning around like Linda Blair in The Exorcist as the usually frugal drummer listed all of the high priced stuff that he owned. Doug, normally reticent to flash any money at all in public, unlike Gino and myself, was in fact rich.

At least land wise.

The bank manager was now quite interested. Doug was not interested in the slightest and was very worried that he would end up co-signing for the line of credit, using his assets as the all-important collateral.

Me: "WE'RE STARVING TO DEATH AND YOU HAVE WHAT?!"

I knew that we were finished as a group the minute we left that meeting.

"GREG! COME QUICKLY, THERE'S SOMETHING WRONG!!!"

It was Renata, who, having just returned from a garlic friendly meal of veal-scaloppini courtesy of my brother-in-law Clay, had just broken her water and was about to go into panic as our Firstborn was about to make his entrance. Quickly remembering all those pre-natal classes, I began packing a goody bag for my time at the hospital.

"Where have you put the gun, Ssir?" I asked while stuffing potato chips into a plastic bag. I called her "sir" instead of the usual "honey" or "poopsie" or any other saccharine terms of endearment.

"GUN??!! WE DON'T HAVE A GUN!! WHAT ARE YOU DOING?!" she now cried.

By nine-thirty the next morning, November 8, 1982, my son, first named Nigel but soon changed to the more suitable Nile, in honour of his Egyptian conception, came plopping out and my world was changed forever.

At almost thirty-two years of age and in a continuing state of arrested development, I was little more than a child myself, and now I was expected to behave in a responsible adult fashion. Holding my son in my trembling arms, it suddenly dawned on me, my bank balance was zero, our oft-forecast world dominance as a rock group was by now pretty much out of the question, and I had no option other than to realize that I was in serious trouble.

Adjusting to being a new father wasn't as hard for me as one might imagine, and the assorted chores inherent in the new job were challenging and rewarding. Keeping the band alive, however, was quite another thing. Ever since the bank meeting, where Inglis's wealth was suddenly discovered, I had lost interest in trying to bail out this leaky boat and I was convinced that it was only a matter of time before we threw in the towel. Relations with Gino, never great to begin with, were strained to the bursting point when he messed up his hand, punching a wall during a fight with good old Gypsy. In order to keep working, The Dough Dough birds were hastily reassembled and we played a number of confusing dates while Gino's hand mended. The mutiny by the LB Show was constantly on my mind but it had much more to do with losing a good friend than the money or ethics involved in leaving a tour. The gigs were, by now, mere rituals of going through the motions to less than packed houses, performing sloppily to fans who were even drunker and more drugged up than the three on stage.

> *diary – thursday, november 25 – toronto*
> *Had a really small crowd at Spats tonight. Quite vocal though. Looks good on the prick that runs this place. He had to lay out $2,000.00, so he lost money. That's nice.*

This was a very bad attitude.

> *diary – friday, december 3 – toronto*
> *Gino phones me up at 9:30 p.m. to demand a raise. He had a few ounces of bottle courage and the witch was probably prodding him. I told him that he was already walking a fine line so don't bug me and hung up on him. He called back later and told Renata that he didn't mean to upset anyone but I'd already called Blue to vent my wrath. Blue cautioned me to be careful as Gino was quite crazy and just might be stupid enough to quit before I could find a replacement and fire him. At the gig Gino half-heartedly apologised. He still played like shit.*

Logical thinking from all concerned parties.

Queen Street east in The Beaches area is pretty amazing real estate, even on a bad day. The consumer-based yuppie mentality manifests itself in a wealth of fine restaurants, deli's, and interesting clothing and antique boutiques, and the sense of friendly community harkens back to the finer qualities of the hippie era'd Yorkville. With three days to Christmas and Toronto caught in one of those snow falls where the flakes are big and fat and the weather perfect for last minute shopping, I found myself with a pocket full of still arriving royalty money, zigging and zagging through the shoppers in search of the right gifts for my first Christmas with my own family

"Hello, Greg, over here!" It was guitarist David Wilcox standing on the opposite side of the street.

Making my way over, we decided to take a shopping break and, after a drink or two we made our way back to his place to really get into the old festive spirits. Tequila gave way to brandy, which soon became vintage wines, and then champagne, and all with a healthy supply of blow, until the beast in me was released, whereupon I tried to start a fist fight with famed drummer Whitey Glann, insulted Wilcox's girlfriend, and fell down his stairs, breaking all of the antique bric a brac that I had purchased that very afternoon. Delivered home by a slightly hesitant cabby, who figured that I would probably die in his car, I was in such a sad state that my Mom was summoned to attend to me, such was the severity of the situation. Renata, pissed off beyond belief, called Wilcox and demanded to know what he had done to me. It wasn't his fault, and it really wasn't my fault. We simply lived as people expected us to. Everyone that is, except our wives.

We played New Years Eve at the Knobby and, as disappointing as it was that another year had come and gone, with us no closer to making it, I had to look back and marvel at the things I'd seen and done, the places that I'd visited and the birth of my son in that short twelve months.

Maybe next year.

Goddo 1983

diary – thursday, january 6 – simcoe
...My priorities are in a constant state of turmoil. I much prefer life at home to any of this fleeting glory. If you could add up all of the spectacular moments in this career it would probably be a pitifully small fraction.

yin

diary – friday, january 7 – guelph
This was more like it. Arrive expecting little and find out that the place is sardine'd. The owner tells me that the kids lined up at 6 p.m. We play a good long set. I get a cigarette burn on my neck from an over zealous fan. We go into percentage tonight so everyone is happy.

yang

diary – thursday, january 13 – toronto
...Gino got so out of it tonight that he dropped his beloved guitar and put his former injured right hand through a wall once more. He didn't notice the blood gushing out of his wrist.
and moe

The four inch blue arc caught me square on the lips and sent me crashing backwards into Doug's drums as surely as a well placed punch. Rising slowly to my feet the guitar roared ear- shattering feedback as I stumbled off stage, Uncle Mike lifting the instrument from my still shocked body as I was escorted to the dressing room, where I immediately passed out. Faulty wiring was blamed for the near lethal belt of electricity I had just sustained and I was assured that it would not happen again.

With grave doubts I wondered if anyone could fix the faulty wiring that was Goddo.

I was feeling exactly the same as when I was about to leave Fludd. The mixed emotions were keeping me up at night. Could we sit down and work out our differences, record a new album, and make another run at the States? There was so much unfinished business but the more I thought about it the more it became evident that the group was history.

With an eye to the future, I began solo recordings, with Segarini producing, that included appearances by Fludd drummer John Andersen, Gary Craig, Paul DeLong, Lisa Dal Bello, BB Gabor, Paul Irvine, Drew Winters, GP Partland, and best of all, Domenic Troiano.

Donny, fresh from a Steely Dan session in New York and in top form as he ripped off a flawless solo on the unreleased 'It's Only Ego (If You Can't Back It Up).' Watching the guitar great at work brought back memories of a more innocent time, of standing in awe in a sweaty small town arena dressing room to watch his roadie light his guitar on fire. His job done, Troiano left as fast as he'd arrived, dripping cool as he did so.

diary – thursday, february 3 – toronto
Over half of our audience leaves before we're finished. It was packed when we started. Things are going from bad to worse. The strain is too much. I'd sooner go out strong than the way we're going about it.

diary – saturday, february 5 – niagara falls
...We play absolutely terrible. Uncle Mike does the sound out front tonite and later informs me that at points he turned Gino off (in the mix). The end is nigh.

diary – tuesday, february 8 – toronto
The big meeting went down today. Gino was, or at least appeared to be, oblivious to the nature of the meeting and didn't know what to make of it all. A lot of moot points were brought up and a few pressing issues. I knew that Gino would give me the old song and dance about, "How could you do this after eight years?" and sure enough he didn't let me down. I did it easily is how. Back to square one for all of us. Gino wants his amp, which the company owns. Doug is concerned over the fact that

we have our names attached to some serious money paper. Gino wasn't pleased about me recording a solo LP and especially if I attach 'Goddo' to it. Doug was cool about the whole thing. He can afford to be. Gino and Blue had a bit of a shout and I left to join Segarini (at that point The Iceman on Q107) on air to dispel rumours of a break up.

diary – saturday, february 19 – jubilee pavilion – oshawa
...A definite tenseness tonite. Everyone, including my Mom and Dad show up to witness our swan song. Gino looks sad. Gypsy is like ice. Doug shows up clean-shaven and sober. Too much to even think that it's in honour of the occasion, it seems Bryan Adams will show up to watch and audition Doug for his touring group. Sly bastard our Doug. Cathy (Doug's girlfriend) confides that she's not keen on Doug getting the gig. Neither am I. Adams will break this year and Doug doesn't deserve it. No hard feelings. Good sized crowd and we play well. Marty Pelz and company pie us all one last time on stage well before the set is over. This puts me in a very foul mood. I'm also a bit drunk which doesn't help. Gino and Tracy (light man) are crying. I have no feeling. Home to watch myself think.

And that, as they say, was that.

Photo: Pat Harbron

Lying on the cold pavement, I was suddenly aware that the rain was now completely covering my glasses, making my somewhat limited visibility even more limited, a small but important point that somehow seemed to overshadow the fact that Renata had just run me over with the family car.

Lifting my head from the pavement, I noticed that my left foot was now even with the concrete, totally devoid of activity, and screaming with red-hot pain. Rolling down the driver's side window, Renata yelled out to me to "Get up off the ground you asshole!" and after being dutifully informed that she had indeed crushed the life out of my left dancing apparatus, she then proceeded to park the car in its original spot, thus running over the foot a second time in the process.

All I could think of was that it was raining on my glasses.

With newfound vigour, my screams alerted not only the neighbours but also the local constabulary, who with the aid of an ambulance quickly whisked me to the local hospital, where fresh tortures awaited me. The attending physician quickly surmised that an over-the-top amount of wine had been previously consumed, and regardless of any hideous pain that I might be feeling upon arrival, it was deemed logical that no drugs be administered, lest I OD on his watch.

Pity.

Alone in my agony, I was somewhat comforted when a rather large black man entered my room. "You have to keep quiet Mon, you are disrupting the ward," he offered and having spent some time in Jamaica myself I instantly recognized his accent and proceeded to lighten up.

"You're Jamaican man, I've got lots of friends there and ...," but was rudely interrupted as he grabbed my pulverized foot and gave it a hearty twist. "YOU MOTHERFUCKING PRICK, I'M GOING TO FUCKING KILL YOU!" at which point a night duty nurse strolled in.

"What's going on in here?" she asked none too pleased.

"THIS FUCKING GUY JUST TORTURED ME!" I screamed.

"He's crazy Mon, drunk," said Sam the male nurse as he retreated from the room.

Wheeled into a new ward I was separated by curtains from my two roomies. A loud fart emanated from my right, quickly followed by three more in quick succession, then a low decibel moan.

Gas. The old lady on my right had a hideous gas malady!

The guy on my left was busy moaning "Oh Jesus, help me Jesus, oh God...HELP ME!"

A religious freak?

Faaaaarrt!

Stifling my laughter, a good fart being what it was, I sought to question my religious friend next door.

"Hey man, what's up with you?"

"Oh God," he began, "I was cutting my lawn and I bent over to pick up a stone and...OH JESUS HELP ME...OH GOD...my hand got caught in the blades!" At this point the guitarist in me took over and my own hands found safety in between my thighs as the lady on the left dropped a doozy of a fart.

"Hey man, it wasn't one of those new lawnmowers that mulch, was it?" I innocently inquired, always searching for that silver lining.

"THAT'S NOT FUNNY!!" he screamed as the old lady dropped another rose.

The next day, Dr. John Houston, not the famed movie director, but one of Canada's most celebrated orthopaedic surgeons, studied the x-ray of the pitiful remains of my foot and gave me his conclusion.

"The bones in your foot look like corn flakes."

Untold years of medical schooling to figure out "corn flakes"?

"Mr. Godovitz, it is highly unlikely that you will walk again on this foot, considering the extent of bone damage sustained as a result of your injuries."

Hello?

With a complex series of pins, gaffer's tape, and good old-fashioned Frankenstein know-how, the good doctor put together the jigsaw puzzle that was my left foot and sent me home to die.

So there I, with my foot crushed to death, my bank account totally depleted, my dream group finished, and a family to support. A lesser man would have been fucked, but being a natural survivor, I simply viewed the whole affair as a mild setback. Ronnie Hawkins says that, from what he's witnessed during our short time getting to know one another, I could be dropped into a remote jungle and have a thriving business going within a year.

Designer coconuts anyone?

Of course I paid no attention to the doctor's doom and gloom concerning my foot and, although it was two years of slipping, sliding, and falling down, I did indeed learn how to walk again. Renata never apologized once for running me over, claiming that, had she been trying to run me over, she would have aimed for my head.

The reason we were arguing?

At a dinner party that unfortunate evening, the other guests were smoking non-stop throughout a great meal of roast beef, so I, a non smoker, lit a cigarette, stood up, pulled my pants down and stuck the cigarette in my ass, filter tip first, of course. The other guests laughed, took the hint and butted out, so to speak. Renata was, of course, furious and dropped me off at our apartment before fleeing to my folks for the night. Rounding the driver side to stop her, I pounded on the window, just as she slammed the car in reverse, and proceeded to crush my poor little foot into a pancake. Another blow for women everywhere!

Adrift without a proper group to launch my solo career I took an under-rehearsed bunch of semi-pros on the road as 'GODO', dropping a "D" in a moment of divine inspiration. Having to sit in a chair with my foot propped up on pillows was not what the audience expected nor wanted from a former whirling dervish best known for scaling PA stacks and leaping on beer soaked tables while flailing wildly on the guitar. The reviews were unanimous, we stunk.

At one point, Gino even came back, grudgingly acceding to my desire to play lead guitar, but the old animosities reared their ugly heads on more than one occasion until we called it a day once more. Don't get me wrong, I like Gino, but by that point the rot had set into our friendship, from too many years of constantly being in each other's back pockets. With the exception of his current girlfriend, the ones that I had to deal with were mostly large breasted, stripper-type air heads who didn't seem to mind meddling in band affairs. The only time in all the years that I've known him where I was invited to his house ended up with his old lady spilling a drink on me and then whacking me one. It's those little things that can get a guy down.

Crushed foot anyone?

While Doug was off with a

Rolling Stones clone band, Gino was struggling in a succession of nowhere groups with the most defeatist of names like No Choice and Full Circle. Flexing his musical muscles, he began to feature his own compositions, primarily groove-oriented riff rock with insipid lyrics, to a largely uncaring public still pining for the good old days. From a distance I was digging the fact that he was at last getting up the motivation to write, rehearse, and record these songs instead of simply watching cartoons, smoking dope, and reading comic books. None of us were setting the world on fire so it was only a matter of time before reunion rumours started, none of which we ourselves took seriously, as we were in complete divorce mode.

Desperate to support my family I did the unthinkable and took a real-world job, selling a new line of guitar amplifiers. The job could have been very short lived as on the eve of my first trade show, I was high-jacked by some fans while setting up the display and, after a drunken night in the hotel, showed up for work in rumpled clothes, unshaven, and hung over. The American suits, up from California, were not impressed and avoided any contact with me until a guy walked into the sound booth for a demonstration. Emerging from that meeting the boss asked how it had gone and once I told him that the guy ordered ten thousand dollars worth of gear I was told to keep doing things my way, thus negating the bothersome need for a suit and tie.

Travelling first class to Chicago, Atlanta, Anaheim, and Frankfurt with these cowboys was amazing stuff and meeting people like Leo Fender, James Burton, Def Leppard, John Entwhistle and so many more made me realize how much I missed playing. With a warehouse full of guitar and bass amps at my disposal, the idea of a full-fledged Goddo reunion was making more and more sense. Casting aside our differences, Gino, Doug, and myself finally agreed to a trial run and the old magic was there from the first rehearsal.

On August 14, 1987 Renata gave birth to our daughter Jazzmin.

In 1989 we returned to the stage, sometimes in the company of original drummer Marty Morin, who played percussion and sang harmony. Older, fatter, a bit balder in my case, we were also a little wiser, having managed to exorcise our individual demons during the time off. Not to say we still weren't capable of the excesses that rocked our little world in the glory days, but the all night parties, the drug and alcohol abuse, and hanging over hotel balconies were definitely a thing of the past. With our twenty-fifth anniversary fast approaching I marvel at how quickly time does fly when you're having fun.

Reaching for my wine glass just now I see that it's still half full. The other half was delicious.

greg godovitz
11/14/2000

Photo: Janis Reese

Encore

"I wish I'd brought another shirt to change into, it's bloody freezing out here," I said, as Ed Pilling helped me load the PA into the back of my car. I was still soaked with sweat from our pub gig at The Black Dog and I knew that a cold would be coming. It seemed ironic that Ed and I were playing together again these many years on. We called our beat group No Flies On Frank.

"It's like England," he said, "damp," as we finally pushed my amp and bass into the back of the wagon. With the fog rolling in from the lake, I instantly felt a wonderful rush of long ago.

It was like England.

Momentarily lost in thought, my mind's eye conjured up our long lost brother Brian, joining us outside of the club.

"You need some air Godo," Ed said looking in the direction of my front left. My tire was near flat, probably from the full load in the back. I had said time and again that I would not hump any gear with this group, but it was already loaded so there was no point in making a fuss.

Brian vanished to memory once more as I hugged Ed good night and drove off. A thought suddenly occurred to me. I was now the old guy in the group with the station wagon.

I had come full circle.

Here I was, thirty-six years later, playing the same music as when I'd first started out. I even had a rented amp. I laughed out loud at the irony.

The 400 watt Yorkville amp and the 3/4 scale Fender Squire bass were now firmly in place on the wagon.

As I adjusted the rear view mirror I was not surprised in the slightest to see the face of Danny Cooper smiling back at me.

...nogaw a dah repooC ynnaD

Acknowledgements

I really want to thank the following people for helping me fill in the gaps...

BRUCE DUNCAN - Soundman (FLUDD/GODDO)

KATHY MINIDIS - Detroit fan (PRETTY ONES/FLUDD)

BARRY HARVEY - Roadie/now manager for Gordon Lightfoot (FLUDD)

WILLIAM 'SKINNY' TENN- Manager/now manages Hayden (FLUDD)

JOHN AND ROBIN BJARNASON - Musician/underwater chiropractor/lifelong friends (THE BACKDOOR/THE PYGGS/SHERMAN & PEABODY)

RAY DANNIELS - Squatmate/sometime roadie but too proud to admit it/now manages Rush and Van Halen (SHERMAN & PEABODY)

ANYA WILSON - Tour manager/publicist/lovely skin for an alcoholic (GODDO)

KERRY CRAWFORD - Guitarist/producer of Bruce Cockburn and Bob & Doug McKenzie (THE MUSHROOM CASTLE)

EDDIE SCHWARTZ - Songwriter supreme (THE MUSHROOM CASTLE)

MARTIN MELHUISH - Writer/visionary/manager (GODDO)

SKIP PROKOP - Drummer (THE PAUPERS/LIGHTHOUSE)

DAVID (BLUE) BLUESTEIN (GODDO)

The Players

The Wanderers
Brian Fraser-Piano/Vocals – Jim Stockley-Drums
Donny Janke-Guitar – Greg Godovitz-Bass/Vocals

The Pretty Ones
Brian Pilling-Rhythm Guitar/Vocals – Ed Pilling-Drums/Vocals
Don Harbor-Lead Guitar/Vocals – Greg Godovitz-Bass/Vocals
*George Kelly replaced Don Harbor on Lead Guitar

The Backdoor Blues Band
John 'BJ' Bjarnason-Harmonica/Guitar – Dave Wood-Lead Guitar
Wayne Wilson-Drums – Dieter Billinger-Organ
Greg Godovitz-Bass/Vocals

The Pyggs
John 'BJ' Bjarnason-Harmonica – Dave Wood-Lead Guitar
Wayne Wilson-Drums – Greg Godovitz-Bass/Vocals

The Mushroom Castle
Eddie Schwartz-Rhythm Guitar/Vocals – Kerry Crawford-Lead Guitar – Lyndon Henthorne-Drums – Peter Flaherty-Keyboards
Greg Godovitz-Bass
*Dave Wood replaced Kerry Crawford on Lead Guitar
*Wayne Wilson replaced Lyndon Henthorne on Drums

Sherman And Peabody
Douglas (Buzz) Shearman-Vocals – John Bjarnason-Harmonica
Dave Wood-Lead Guitar – Wayne Wilson-Drums
Peter Flaherty-Keyboards – Greg Godovitz-Bass/Vocals

Fludd
Ed Pilling-Vocals/Percussion – Brian Pilling-Lead Guitar/Vocals
Mick Walsh-Lead Guitar – John (Jorn) Andersen-Drums/Vibes
Greg Godovitz-Bass/Vocals
*Mick Hopkins replaced Mick Walsh on Lead Guitar
*Peter Csanky replaced Mick Hopkins on Mellotron/Piano
*Peter Rochon replaced Peter Csanky on Keyboards
*Pat Little replaced John (Jorn) Andersen on Drums
*Gord Waszek joined as 2nd Lead Guitar to assist an ailing Brian Pilling

Goddo
>Gino Scarpelli-Guitar/Bass – Doug Inglis-Drums/Vocals
>Greg Godovitz-Bass/Guitar/Piano/Vocals
>*Marty Morin-Drums/Vocals was the original drummer for 1975

The Roadies

'The band may work from nine til one, but the roadie's work is never done!'

John Flaherty, Bruce Duncan, Peter Rowland, John Malawaney, Pat Ryan, John Glover, Barry Harvey, Alan (C.A.) Henry, Lorne Wheaton, Stephen (Tex) Paquette, Tracey Hurst, Peter Friesen, Pat Arnott, Marshall Paul, John Hedgy, Bill (Billy Love) St. Amour, Brian Hall, Mike (Mazolla) Malonich, Marty Pelz, Rick (Red) Hoeg, Shawn Cottnam, Dan Nullmeyer, Dave Bailey, (Uncle) Mike Morin, Larry (L.B. Show) Berringer, Trevor (Lamar) Johnston, Steve (Killer) Hill, Bob Gray, Dave Phelps, Paul Crarey, Clark Graff, Al Black, Peter Lahti

Tour Managers

Pat Ryan (Fludd/Goddo), Larry Berringer (Goddo), Anya Wilson (Goddo), Dan Nullmeyer (Goddo)

Management

Jim Sawyer (The Pretty Ones), Henry Taylor (The Pyggs), G&G Productions (Mushroom Castle/Sherman and Peabody), William 'Skinny' Tenn (Fludd), Ritchie Yorke – Wil Webster Barry Cobus Vince Alexander – Martin Melhuish – Allan Katz Jan and Steve Bruce – Kim Kelly – David Bluestein (Goddo)

Other Notable Musicians

John Bjarnason, Harmonica – Paul Irvine, Saxophone
Drew Winters, Keyboards – Dwayne Ford, Fender Rhodes
Chris Yost, Guitar

Special Thanks

David and Diane Dietrich, Jim Hoeck, Bob Abbott, Pat Coffey, Susan Peacock, Penny Morrow, Guy Beresford, Rob Morin and Al Mackay (Two For The Show), Wayne and Steve Duncan, Frank and Joyce Soda, Paul LaChappelle (Quest Studio), Brian Eckler, Sam Boyd, Simon Wilson, Jaimie and Sharon Vernon, Dave Bidini, Mark and Chris Booth, John and Robin Bjarnason, Ronnie and Wanda Hawkins, George Webb, David Farrell, George Holjak (who was there from the very beginning), Bill and Joan Pilling, Ed Pilling, Bob Segarini and 'B', Joel and Danielle Rabinowitz, Andy and Harmonica Curran, Peter Burnside, Ray Paul Klimek, Dan Nullmeyer, Dave Bailey, Larry Berringer, John and Shirley Gibb, Bob Gray, Scream Freedom, Tim Mech's Peep Show, Margaret and Gene and Tanya Scarpelli, Stella Abesdris, Chris Yost, Matt and James O'Leary, Tim and Melissa West at Envoy Business Services, Madelyn Reynolds, Evert Wilbrink, Wim Reijnen, Harold Wood, Drew Winters, Johnny Bodnar, Virginia Wagner, Peter and Jenifer Miniaci, Nicki Nassas, Caroline Brown and John Morgan (The Harp And Crown), Ken Rueter (The Black Dog), David MacMillan (EMI), Warren Stewart (EMI), Phil Tinianov, Dave Cubitt, Virginia and Wally Larsen, Brad Lovatt and Rosemary Galloway, Ron and Julie Christian, Mike Pellarin, Jerome Godboo, Al Joynes (Q107), Cory Ferguson, Karen Petherick, Howard Mandshein and Gordo Fry (CITI FM), Joe Woods, Barrie Lapins (Hard Rock CafÈ), Bill Belfontaine, Gareth Brown, Frank and Linda Davies, Peter and Diane Jermyn, Nick Thiel, Ralph Alfonso, Tony and Chris Nolasco, Bob (Not-Reid) and Gina Reid, NutLik, debbieamericanburtonwoman, Luxton, and last but by all means not least Zontar (anti-luxton@egroups.com) ...oh yeah, and THE BEATLES, because without their influence I wouldn't have had a career or this story to tell.

Special love to my family

TedVeraTedGarySusanBrianLucasGaredJesseLeslieClayStephenKim TracyScotRandyColtonMadisonSandy SophieChelseaSpencer for their constant support year after year. Special love to my son Nile and my daughter Jazzmin.

If I've left anyone out please forgive me.
The ravages of time you understand.

Visit Simon Wilson's Australian Goddo Website @
http://www.goddo.net
or sign up to Denis Joliceur's
canadianclassicrock@egroups.com
through www.egroups.com

Recommended reading:
ON A COLD ROAD by Dave Bidini,
published by McClelland & Stewart Inc. 1998

Listen to 'Jersey To Mersey' with Johnny Bodnar
Sundays from 2-4 p.m. by clicking on www.wnti.org
(WNTI Hacketstown, N.J.)

When in Toronto visit The Beatlemania Shoppe
www.beatlemaniashoppe.com (416) 977-2782

As of this writing I currently play
on a regular basis with the following musical acts:

Goddo
(Gino Scarpelli, Doug Inglis, Marty Morin, Greg Godovitz)

The Anger Brothers
(Bob Segarini, Drew Winters, Brad (Mr. Anger) Lovatt,
Ron Christian, Greg Godovitz)

No Flies On Frank
(Ed Pilling, Dave McCluskey, Steve Walker,
Michael Hansen, Greg Godovitz)

Ronnie Hawkins And The Hawks
(Ronnie Hawkins, Robin Hawkins, Brent Bailey, Jerome
Godboo, Buzz Thompson, Doug Inglis, Greg Godovitz)

The Toronto Blues All-Stars
(Peter Jermyn, Jerome Godboo, Mike Pellarin,
Tony Nolasco, Greg Godovitz)

For booking info on the above acts contact
Ralph James or Nico Quintel at The Agency
(416) 368-5599
email: rjames@idirect.ca

A special thanks to Doug Inglis
for the initial grammar and spell check.

Goddo CD's available from:
BULLSEYE RECORDS OF CANADA
@ http://www.bullseyecanada.com
email: president@bullseyecanada.com

Thank you all.

P.S....for those that read it before it was published and didn't get it...
FUCK YOU!

Discography

1971 FLUDD - FLUDD
Warner Bros. (BS 2578) LP out of print

Turned 21	Birmingham
Sailing On	Mama's Boy
David Copperfield	Easy Being No One
The Egg	Make It Better
Come Back Home	You See Me
A Man Like You	Tuesday Blue

1972 ...ON! - FLUDD
Daffodil/Capitol Records (SBA 16020) LP

C'mon C'mon	Home Made Lady
Yes!	Ticket To Nowhere
Always Be Thinking Of You	Can You Be Easy?
Down! Down! Down!	All Sing Together
Cousin Mary	Gratitude

RE-ISSUED on CD as "Cock On"
1998 by Unidisc Records (AGEK-2157)

1977 '71 To '77: From The Attic - FLUDD
Attic Records (LAT 1027) LP out of print

*Turned 21	I Held Out
*Get Up, Get Out And Move On	Brother And Me
*Always Be Thinkin' Of You	Dance Gypsy Dance
*Yes!	What An Animal
*C'Mon, C'mon	I'm On My Way
*Cousin Mary	Help Me Back With You

* features Greg Godovitz

1994 Greatest Expectations - FLUDD
Pacemaker Entertainment (PACE-003) CD out of print

*Turned 21	*Homemade Lady
*Get Up. Get Out, And Move On	Brother And Me
*Cousin Mary	What An Animal
*Yes!	Billy Draft
*Down! Down! Down!	Missing You
*C'mon C'mon	

* features Greg Godovitz

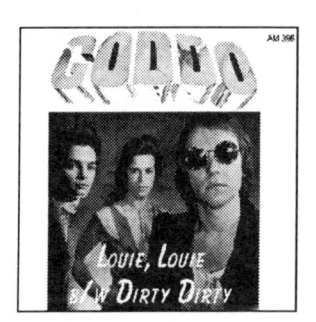

1975 Louie, Louie b/w Starstruck - GODDO
A & M (AM 398) 7" out of print

1977 Goddo - GODDO Fatcat/Polydor (2424 901) LP

The Bus Driver Blues	Let It Slide
Drive Me Crazy	Twelve Days
Let That Lizard Loose	Under My Hat
I'm Losing You	Hard Years

RE-ISSUED on CD
2000 by Bullseye Records (BLP-CD 2500)
www.bullseyecanada.com

1978 Who Cares? - GODDO Polydor (2424 902) LP

Tough Times	There Goes My Baby
Cock On	Oh Carole (Kiss My Whip)
You Can Never Go	Once Again
Back Anymore	Too Much Carousing
Drop Dead (That's Who)	Sweet Thing

RE-ISSUED on CD with 11 bonus tracks
2000 by Bullseye Records (BLP-CD 2501)
www.bullseyecanada.com

1979 An Act Of Goddo - GODDO
Polydor/Polygram (2424 189) LP

Anacanapanacana	Sign On The Line
So Walk On	Rosie (Just Hang On)
Chantal	Take Care
You're So Cruel	Work It Out
The Verdict's In	Anacanapanacana

RE-ISSUED on CD
2000 by Bullseye Records (BLP-CD 2502)
www.bullseyecanada.com

1980 Fortune In Men's Eyes/ Homemade Lady - GODDO
El Mocambo (ESMO 511) 7" out of print

1981 Goddo Lighve: Best Seat In The House - GODDO
Attic Records (2 LAT 1107) 2LPs

Anacanapanacana	Vampire Eyes
So Walk On	*Pimpmobile
Work It Out	*The Verdict's In
Sweet Thing	The Hard Years
*Sign On The Line	Oh Carole (Kiss My Whip)
Forget About Forgetting	You're So Cruel
Under My Hat	Cock On
Drop Dead (That's Who)	Drive Me Crazy
Let That Lizard Loose	Too Much Carousing

RE-ISSUED on CD
1996 by Attic Records (ACBD 1107) with the exception of *

1981 Pretty Bad Boys - GODDO
Attic Records (LAT 1120) LP

Ngorongoro	Pretty Bad Boy
Am I Crazy, Crazy?!?	Forget About Forgetting
If Tomorrow Never Comes	Vampire Eyes
Feelin' Strange Today	Let's Talk It Over
Shooting Stars	Orognorogn

RE-ISSUED on CD
1994 by Attic Records (ACBD 1120)

1990 12 Gauge Goddo: Blasts From The Past - GODDO
Justin/MCA (JED 21) CD out of print

Was It Somethin' I Said?	So Walk On
Drop Dead (That's Who)	Chantal
Sweet Thing	Sign On The Line
Oh Carole (Kiss My Whip)	There Goes My Baby
Too Much Carousing	Tough Times
Under My Hat	Cock On
The Bus Driver Blues	Quicksand
Anacanapanacana	

1992 King Of Broken Hearts - GODDO
Justin/BEI/MCA (JED 21) CD

Mirror Mirror	The Quest
Say You Will	Quicksand
Just Don't Know	Lost Without Your Love
King Of Broken Hearts	You Can't Do That
Was It Somethin' I Said?	Egypt
Dreams Of New York City	You Must Fight Back
It's Good To Be Alive	Please Baby Please

RE-ISSUED on CD with bonus tracks
2000 by Bullseye Records (BLP-CD 2503)
www.bullseyecanada.com

1994 Frog Curry - CARPET FROGS
featuring Greg Godovitz • Nile Records (NRCD 1004) CD

Baby Goes South	Long Lonely Nights
Cousin Mary	Shakin' All Over
Lisa's New Dress	Dear Prudence
Loving You Ain't Easy	Frog Curry
Fortune In Men's Eyes	*Christmas, All Over The World
Work Out Fine	

Also issued on CD in theU.S.
1994 by Permanent Press Recordings (70267-52700-2) with the exception of *

1994 Christmas, All Over The World - Carpet Frogs
featuring Greg Godovitz
Nile Records (NRCD 1003) CD out of print

Christmas All Over The World
The Frogs Christmas Message
Christmas All Over The World (Edit)
Christmas All Over The World (Sing-A-Long Version)

Coming in 2001 ...

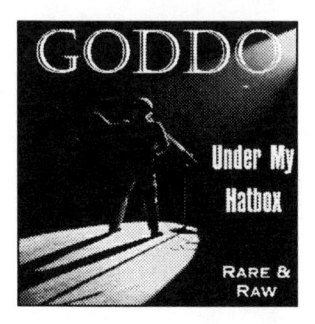

On **BULLSEYE RECORDS**
www.bullseyecanada.com

NEW YEAR
GODDO
FRANK SODA
AND
STAGE
ACCESS ALL AREAS
HUMBLE PIE
THURS., JULY 12/73
7:30 P.M.
VARSITY STADIUM
Goddo In Concert
FEBRUARY 26, 1982
Saturday July 08,
1115 Fennell Ave. Hamilton
ADVANCE $10 AT THE DOOR
A 19 Years and Over Event
"GODDO"
AND
"THE GUESSING"
GODDO
MAX WEBSTER
TICKET NO. 174
GODDO
Summer
Warm-up
Friday, May 8, 1981
APPEARING
GODDO
AND SPECIAL GUESTS
THE DIODES
AT BINGEMAN PARK
DOORS OPEN AT 7:30
GODDO
TEAZE
PLUMMER PLUS TAX
STUDENTS COUNCIL
DDO
"VIGILANTS"
18, 1980 — 8:00 P.M.
7:00 p.m.
Campus
$4.00 EACH
IBITION
BACKSTAGE
ACCESS
YHOUSE
ODDO
27
LEFT
MAIN FLOOR
1
28
MASSEY HALL
Golden Earring
$5.50
MAY 28
BALCONY
Priority
GODDO
2-1/2 HOURS
OF ROCK AND ROLL
DDO"
BENEFIT CONCERT